Research Methods in Linguistic Anthropology

OTHER TITLES IN THE RESEARCH METHODS IN LINGUISTICS SERIES

Data Collection Research Methods in Applied Linguistics, Heath Rose, Jim McKinley and Jessica Briggs Baffoe-Djan

Experimental Research Methods in Language Learning, Aek Phakiti

Experimental Research Methods in Sociolinguistics, Katie Drager

Quantitative Research in Linguistics, Sebastian Rasinger

Research Methods in Applied Linguistics, edited by Brian Paltridge and Aek Phakiti

Research Methods in Interpreting, Sandra Hale and Jemina Napier

Research Methods in Linguistics, edited by Lia Litosseliti

Research Methods in Linguistic Anthropology

Edited by
Sabina M. Perrino and Sonya E. Pritzker

BLOOMSBURY ACADEMIC
LONDON · NEW YORK · OXFORD · NEW DELHI · SYDNEY

BLOOMSBURY ACADEMIC
Bloomsbury Publishing Plc
50 Bedford Square, London, WC1B 3DP, UK
1385 Broadway, New York, NY 10018, USA
29 Earlsfort Terrace, Dublin 2, Ireland

BLOOMSBURY, BLOOMSBURY ACADEMIC and the Diana logo
are trademarks of Bloomsbury Publishing Plc

First published in Great Britain 2022

Copyright © Sabina M. Perrino, Sonya E. Pritzker and Contributors, 2022

Sabina M. Perrino and Sonya E. Pritzker have asserted their right under
the Copyright, Designs and Patents Act, 1988, to be identified as Editors of this work.

For legal purposes the Acknowledgments on p. xx constitute
an extension of this copyright page.

Cover image: Shutterstock

All rights reserved. No part of this publication may be reproduced or
transmitted in any form or by any means, electronic or mechanical,
including photocopying, recording, or any information storage or
retrieval system, without prior permission in writing from the publishers.

Bloomsbury Publishing Plc does not have any control over, or responsibility for,
any third-party websites referred to or in this book. All internet addresses given
in this book were correct at the time of going to press. The author and
publisher regret any inconvenience caused if addresses have changed or
sites have ceased to exist, but can accept no responsibility for any such changes.

A catalogue record for this book is available from the British Library.

Library of Congress Cataloging-in-Publication Data.
Names: Perrino, Sabina, editor. | Pritzker, Sonya E., editor.
Title: Research methods in linguistic anthropology / edited
by Sabina M. Perrino and Sonya E. Pritzker.
Description: London ; New York : Bloomsbury Academic, 2022. |
Series:Research methods in linguistics | Includes bibliographical references and index.
Identifiers: LCCN 2021029862 (print) | LCCN 2021029863 (ebook) |
ISBN 9781350117457 (paperback) | ISBN 9781350117495 (hardback) |
ISBN 9781350117471 (pdf) | ISBN 9781350117464 (ebook)
Subjects: LCSH: Anthropological linguistics–Research–Methodology.
Classification: LCC P35 .R43 2022 (print) | LCC P35 (ebook) | DDC 306.44–dc23
LC record available at https://lccn.loc.gov/2021029862
LC ebook record available at https://lccn.loc.gov/2021029863

ISBN:	HB:	978-1-3501-1749-5
	PB:	978-1-3501-1745-7
	ePDF:	978-1-3501-1747-1
	eBook:	978-1-3501-1746-4

Series: Research Methods in Linguistics

Typeset by Integra Software Services Pvt. Ltd.
Printed and bound in Great Britain

To find out more about our authors and books visit www.bloomsbury.com
and sign up for our newsletters.

Table of Contents

List of Figures xi
List of Tables xiii
List of Contributors xiv
Acknowledgments xx

Introduction: Research Methods in Linguistic Anthropology *Sabina M. Perrino and Sonya E. Pritzker* 1

I.1 Why Research Methods in Linguistic Anthropology? 1
I.2 Book Structure: Overview of the Twelve Chapters 3
I.3 Final Thoughts (For Now) 10
I.4 References Cited 11

1 Navigating Topics and Creating Research Questions in Linguistic Anthropology *Farzad Karimzad and Lydia Catedral* 13

1.1 Introduction 13
1.2 Navigating and Situating Research Topics 15
1.3 Ethical Considerations 33
1.4 Case Study: From Observation to Publication: Creating Flexible Research Questions around Discourse, Technology, and Migration 36
1.5 Conclusion 39
1.6 Ethnographic Activities 41
1.7 Questions to Consider 43
1.8 Note 43
1.9 References Cited 44
1.10 Further Reading 47

2 Reviewing the Literature in Linguistic Anthropology *Justin B. Richland* 49

2.1 Introduction 49

2.2 The Peril and Promise of Literature Reviews for Linguistic Anthropological Scholarship Grounded in Ethnographic Fieldwork 53

2.3 The Ethics of Literature Review 55

2.4 Tales of Promise and Peril in My Experiences with Reviewing Literature 56

2.5 Conclusion 66

2.6 Ethnographic Activities 67

2.7 Questions to Consider 68

2.8 Notes 68

2.9 References Cited 69

2.10 Further Reading 70

3 Planning Research in Linguistic Anthropology
Deborah A. Jones and Ilana Gershon 73

3.1 Introduction 73

3.2 Who, Where, and How 75

3.3 Pre-field Practicalities and Preventative Measures 84

3.4 Ethics: Compensating Interlocutors 86

3.5 When *Who*, *Where*, and *How* Intersect: Explaining Your Presence and Getting Access 89

3.6 Conclusion 93

3.7 Ethnographic Activities 94

3.8 Questions to Consider 94

3.9 References Cited 95

3.10 Further Reading 96

4 Care as a Methodological Stance: Research Ethics in Linguistic Anthropology
Steven P. Black and Robin Conley Riner 97

4.1 Introduction 97

4.2 Controversies and Concerns 102

4.3 Data Collection and Its Entailments 104

4.4 Case Study 113

4.5 Concluding Remarks 117

4.6 Ethnographic Activities 118

4.7 Questions to Consider 118

Table of Contents   vii

4.8   Notes 119
4.9   References Cited 119
4.10 Further Reading 123

5   Participant Observation and Fieldnotes in Linguistic Anthropology *Sonya E. Pritzker and Sabina M. Perrino* 125

5.1   Introduction 125
5.2   Participant Observation in Linguistic Anthropology 127
5.3   Fieldnotes in Linguistic Anthropology 138
5.4   Ethical Considerations in Participant Observation 146
5.5   Case Studies 148
5.6   Conclusion 150
5.7   Ethnographic Activities 151
5.8   Discussion Questions 151
5.9   References Cited 152
5.10 Further Reading 157

6   Interviews in Linguistic Anthropology *Sabina M. Perrino* 159

6.1   Introduction 159
6.2   Ethnographic Interviews in Linguistic Anthropology 162
6.3   Ethical Issues in Research Interview Practices 169
6.4   Intimacy in Interviews 171
6.5   Concluding Remarks 186
6.6   Ethnographic Activities 188
6.7   Questions to Consider 189
6.8   Notes 190
6.9   References Cited 191
6.10 Further Reading 195

7   Audio-Video Technology for and in the Field: A Primer *Gregory Kohler and Keith M. Murphy* 197

7.1   Introduction 197
7.2   Audio and Video Data: Some Bugs and Features 198

viii **Table of Contents**

7.3 Working with Audio in the Field 202
7.4 Working with Video in the Field 206
7.5 Final Words 218
7.6 Ethnographic Activities 219
7.7 Questions to Consider 219
7.8 References Cited 220
7.9 Further Reading 222

8 Video Ethnography: A Guide
Teruko Vida Mitsuhara and Jan David Hauck 223

8.1 Introduction 223
8.2 Before the Field 225
8.3 In the Field 241
8.4 Beyond the Field 250
8.5 Ethnographic Activities 252
8.6 Questions to Consider 254
8.7 Acknowledgments 255
8.8 Notes 255
8.9 References Cited 257
8.10 Further Reading 259

9 Transcription and Analysis in Linguistic Anthropology: Creating, Testing, and Presenting Theory on the Page *Merav Shohet and Heather Loyd* 261

9.1 Introduction 261
9.2 Taking Stock of What We Have and What More We Need: Logging 263
9.3 Decisions, Decisions: What and Why to Transcribe 266
9.4 Coding: How We Continually Build and Refine Theory 269
9.5 The Insights and Ethics of Representation: What Is Illuminated in Different Transcript Designs 276
9.6 Conclusion 287
9.7 Ethnographic Activities 288
9.8 Questions to Consider 289
9.9 Notes 289
9.10 References Cited 291
9.11 Further Reading 295

Table of Contents   ix

10 Online Research and New Media
Archie Crowley and Elaine Chun 297

10.1 Introduction 297
10.2 Areas of Inquiry 299
10.3 Rethinking Concepts 303
10.4 Data Collection and Data Analysis 310
10.5 Ethics 314
10.6 Case Study 316
10.7 Conclusion 322
10.8 Ethnographic Activities 322
10.9 Questions to Consider 322
10.10 Note 323
10.11 References Cited 324
10.12 Further Reading 329

11 Mixed Methods and Interdisciplinary Research in Linguistic Anthropology
Sonya E. Pritzker 331

11.1 Introduction 331
11.2 Mixed Methods in Linguistic Anthropology: Issues and Considerations 340
11.3 Ethical Concerns in Mixed Methods Research 351
11.4 Case Study: Combining Linguistic and Biocultural Anthropology with Communication Studies 352
11.5 Conclusion 356
11.6 Ethnographic Activities 357
11.7 Questions to Consider 358
11.8 Notes 358
11.9 References Cited 358
11.10 Further Reading 365

12 Grant Writing for Projects in Linguistic Anthropology *Sonia N. Das* 367

12.1 Introduction 367
12.2 Writing the Grant 369
12.3 Addressing Ethics 380
12.4 Conclusion 384
12.5 Ethnographic Activities 385

x   **Table of Contents**

12.6   Questions to Consider 385
12.7   Notes 386
12.8   References Cited 387
12.9   Further Reading 388

Index 389

Figures

1.1 Fractal patterns 17

8.1 Girl wearing GoPro with chest harness in conversation with her friend 230

8.2 Full spherical video still image from footage of a dinner table conversation filmed with a 360-degree camera. Courtesy Didem İkizoğlu 232

8.3 A zoomed-in section of the same still. Courtesy Didem İkizoğlu 233

8.4 Screenshot of folder structure on computer hard drive. Each folder contains a video file, an extracted audio file, an ELAN transcription file, a file for ELAN settings, and a subtitles file 239

8.5 Screenshot of a section of an Excel spreadsheet formatted as data table with multiple columns for different categories of metadata. Each entry (row) refers to one "session," i.e., a video file with its respective transcription and subtitle files 241

9.1 A funnel–spiral illustrates the recursive nature of collecting, selecting, transcribing, and analyzing data 263

9.2 Excerpt from the CELF study's activity logs 265

9.3 Excerpt from the CELF study's code definitions of activity logs 266

9.4 A funerary inscription coded for its placement (indoor or outdoor); material (paper or cloth); color (black and white or colorful); medium (printed or embroidered); script (Traditional Chinese, Romanized Vietnamese, or Sino-Romanized script); and audience (close family and friends or broader public) 275

9.5 Example of how images can supplement a written transcript 286

Tables

10.1 Types and examples of new media characterized by participation structure 306

11.1 Selected Methods 333

11.2 Designs for mixed methods studies (adapted from Fetters et al. 2013, 2136–7) 346

11.3 Strategies for triangulating data in mixed methods studies (adapted from Fetters et al. 2013, 2139–41) 348

11.4 Approaches for reporting data in mixed methods studies (adapted from Fetters et al. 2013, 2142–3) 350

Contributors

Steven P. Black is Associate Professor of Anthropology at Georgia State University. He has conducted research on global health discourses since 2008 with a focus on ethics, speech play, and performance. He is the author of *Speech and Song at the Margins of Global Health: Zulu Tradition, HIV Stigma, and AIDS Activism in South Africa* (Rutgers, 2019), is coeditor of a special issue of *Medical Anthropology* titled, "Communicating Care," and has also published articles in numerous edited volumes and in journals including *American Anthropologist, Annual Review of Anthropology, Ethos, Journal of Linguistic Anthropology, Language in Society*, and *Medical Anthropology*. His current research project, funded by National Geographic, is a collaborative multimedia ethnography based on fieldwork in Boruca Indigenous Territory, Costa Rica, and on indigenous knowledge, planetary health, and cultural sustainability.

Lydia Catedral is Assistant Professor in the Department of Linguistics and Translation at City University of Hong Kong. She is a sociolinguist whose research focuses on the intersections between language, identity, and morality across time and space, and the implications for marginalized groups including transnational migrants, domestic workers, and LGBTQ Christians. She has published in *Language and Communication, Language Policy*, and *Discourse and Society*. Her recent coauthored book, *Chronotopes and Migration: Language, Social Imagination, and Behavior*, published by Routledge, presents a chronotopic and scalar approach to sociolinguistic behavior in general and to the issues of migration and marginality more specifically.

Elaine Chun is Associate Professor of English and Linguistics at the University of South Carolina. Her linguistic anthropological research examines ideologies of language, race, and racism in the United States and transnational social media spaces. Drawing on methods of interactional analysis and ethnography, she has investigated language parody among multiethnic youth, representations of Asian speakers in popular media, and linguistic hybridity in transnational youth spaces. Her work has appeared in *Language in Society*, *Journal of Linguistic Anthropology*, *Pragmatics*, *Language & Communication*, *American Speech*, and *Discourse & Society*.

Robin Conley Riner is Associate Professor of Anthropology at Marshall University. Her book, *Confronting the Death Penalty: How Language Influences Jurors in Capital Cases* (Oxford, 2015), investigates how language shapes jurors' experiences during capital trials and impacts their life and death decisions. She also has a coedited book, *Language and Social Justice in Practice* (Routledge, 2018), which addresses the relationship between communicative practices and the creation of more just societies. Her most recent research project uses video ethnography to explore yoga and embodied communication as therapy for moral injury among military veterans. She teaches courses in cultural, linguistic, and legal anthropology.

Archie Crowley is a Linguistics doctoral student at the University of South Carolina. Their research focuses on language practices, ideologies, and activism within online and offline trans communities. Crowley is involved in various projects and organizations that facilitate greater affirmation of trans, nonbinary, and queer communities, including UofSC's LBGTQ+ Grad Student Affinity Group, the Harriet Hancock Center's Nonbinary Peer Support Group, and the Committee for LGBTQ+ [Z] Issues in Linguistics (COZIL) for the Linguistic Society of America.

Sonia Neela Das is Associate Professor of Linguistic Anthropology at New York University. Combining ethnographic, linguistic, bibliographical, and archival methods, she investigates how linguistic forms and ideologies interface with communicative practices to contribute to social inequality in Canada, the United States, and South Asia. Her current research analyzes the institutional, interactional, and ideological factors producing escalation, violence, and unfair legal outcomes ensuing from racially charged police-civilian interactions in the US South. She also investigates technocratic ideologies about unsociability among commercial seafarers. Her first monograph, *Linguistic Rivalries: Tamil Migrants and Anglo-Franco Conflicts*, won Honorable Mention for the Sapir Book Prize by the Society for Linguistic Anthropology. She is the recipient of grants from the National Science Foundation, Association for Canadian Studies in the United States, and Wenner-Gren Foundation. She is coeditor-in-chief of the flagship *Journal of Linguistic Anthropology* and a Junior Fellow in the Mellon Society of Fellows in Critical Bibliography.

Ilana Gershon is Ruth N. Halls Professor of Anthropology at Indiana University and studies how people use new media to accomplish complicated social tasks such as breaking up with lovers and hiring new employees. She has published books such as *The Breakup 2.0, Down and Out in the New Economy* and edited *A World of Work: Imagined Manuals for Real Jobs*, and *Living with Animals*. She has been a fellow at Stanford's Center for Advanced Study in the Behavioral Sciences, Notre Dame's Institute for Advanced Study, and is presently a visiting professor at the University of Helsinki. She is currently studying how working in person during a pandemic sheds light on the ways workplaces function as private governments.

Jan David Hauck is British Academy Newton International Fellow in the Department of Anthropology at the London School of Economics and Political Science. He has used video extensively in his research, recording verbal art, narratives, and cultural practices in a project to document the indigenous Aché language in Paraguay, as well as in a video-based socialization study of Aché children, recording interactions in children's peer groups, with caregivers, and with a variety of nonhumans in a village and on forest hunting treks. His theoretical interests are on the perception of language and linguistic difference, the ontological underpinnings of conceptions of language, language ideologies, ethics and morality, cooperation, child development, the perception of the environment, and human-nonhuman interactions.

Deborah A. Jones is Postdoctoral Fellow at the Max Planck Institute for Social Anthropology in Halle (Saale), Germany, where she specializes in the study of language, ethics, and political economy. She is currently preparing a monograph on language and violence in Ukraine, where linguistic differences are often cited as a factor in the war in the country's east, but suppositions about the sort of speech that incites, prevents, or facilitates healing from conflict have proven much more varied. Another project, pursued as part of the Max Planck—Cambridge Centre for Ethics, Economy, and Social Change, focuses on ghostwriting and the relinquishment of authorship in the digital age.

Farzad Karimzad is Assistant Professor in the Department of English at Salisbury University. His research focuses on theorizing context and semiosis in relation to issues of normativity, mobility, and marginality, and the implications of these theories for sociolinguistic and anthropological studies of discourse and behavior. His recent work has been published in the *Journal* of *Sociolinguistics*, *Language and Communication*, and *Applied Linguistics*. His recent coauthored book, *Chronotopes and Migration: Language, Social Imagination, and Behavior*, published by Routledge presents a chronotopic and scalar approach to sociolinguistic behavior in general and to the issues of migration and marginality more specifically.

Gregory Kohler is an AAAS American Science & Technology Policy Fellow with USAID. His PhD dissertation, "Accounting for Modernity: Calculative Infrastructures of Sardinian Dairy Production," is based on twenty-four months of ethnographic fieldwork in Sardinia, Italy, and was supported by the National Science Foundation and the Fulbright IIE. His research is rooted in a critical dialogue between linguistic anthropology, ethics, and critical food studies and explores the growth of audit cultures in governing global food chains.

Heather Loyd Heather Loyd consults as a business anthropologist and user experience researcher and is a lecturer in the Department of Anthropology at the University of California, Los Angeles (UCLA). Her work lies at the intersection of linguistic anthropology and cultural studies of urban youth, gender, morality, and the family in Italy and the U.S. As a consultant, she helps businesses understand and connect with customers. At UCLA, she teaches students anthropological field methods, as well as how to apply anthropological concepts, research methods, and analytical skills to a wide range of careers. As a business anthropologist, she conducts ethnographic research that helps businesses understand and connect with people, improving both customers' experiences and clients' businesses.

Teruko Vida Mitsuhara recently completed her dissertation, "Moving toward Utopia: Language, Empathy, and Chastity among Mobile Mothers and Children in Mayapur, West Bengal" at the University of California, Los Angeles. Her research interests include utopian and world-building movements in India and the United States. She is a linguistic anthropologist who has used video ethnography to document women and children in a religious utopian community in Mayapur, West Bengal, in northern India. She also works as a freelance entertainment market researcher carrying out remote, video-based ethnography.

Keith M. Murphy is Associate Professor of Anthropology at the University of California, Irvine. His research explores design and designing from the

xviii   **Contributors**

perspective of face-to-face interaction. He is the author of *Swedish Design: An Ethnography* (Cornell) and coeditor of *Toward an Anthropology of the Will* (Stanford), and *Designs and Anthropologies: Frictions and Affinities* (SAR Press).

Sabina M. Perrino is Associate Professor of Anthropology and Linguistics at Binghamton University. She has conducted research in Senegal, Northern Italy, and the United States. Her research examines racialized language in discursive practices, offline and online narratives, intimacy in interaction, language and migration, language revitalization, transnationalism, language use in ethnomedical encounters and in political discourse, and research methods in linguistic anthropology. She is author of *Narrating Migration: Intimacies of Exclusion in Northern Italy* (Routledge) and *Storytelling in the Digital World* (with Anna De Fina; John Benjamins). She has numerous publications on a wide range of linguistic anthropological topics. She has coedited eight special issues for journals including *Language in Society*, *Language & Communication*, *Narrative Inquiry*, *Multilingua*, and *Applied Linguistics*. She is the coeditor of the series *Bloomsbury Studies in Linguistic Anthropology*.

Sonya E. Pritzker is Associate Professor in the Department of Anthropology at the University of Alabama, where she teaches theory and method in linguistic anthropology and directs the UA Open Laboratory on Embodiment, Communication, and Health (ECHO). Her research focuses on the intersection of language and embodied experience in relation to culturally situated notions of health, social justice, intimacy, and well-being in the United States and China. As a linguistic and medical anthropologist as well as licensed practitioner of Chinese medicine and former clinical researcher in the UCLA David Geffen School of Medicine, she is committed to multidisciplinary, collaborative research. She is the author of *Living Translation: Language and the Search for Resonance in U.S. Chinese Medicine* (Berghahn Books, 2014) and the coeditor (with Janina Fenigsen and James Wilce) of *The Handbook of Language and Emotion* (Routledge, 2020). She has also published widely in journals across psychological anthropology, linguistic anthropology, and integrative medicine.

Justin Richland is Associate Professor in the Department of Anthropology at the University of California, Irvine. His research focuses on Native American law and politics in the contemporary moment, particularly the interface between tribal nations in the United States and the US federal and state governments.

Merav Shohet is Assistant Professor of Anthropology at Boston University. She is the author of *Silence and Sacrifice: Family Stories of Care and the Limits of Love in Vietnam* (University of California Press, 2021). Her work integrates linguistic, psychological, medical, and sociocultural anthropology to examine care, affect, ethics, gender, and the end of life in North America, Vietnam, and most recently, Israel/Palestine. She has published articles on morality and language socialization; care, social change, and the semiotics of funerary ritual; narrative and eating disorders; love, family, and gender politics; and hierarchy and forms of address/self-reference in *American Anthropologist, American Ethnologist, Ethos*, and the *Journal of the Royal Anthropological Institute*, among others. Two of her current projects include an SSRC-funded study of stigma syndemics and end-stage kidney disease in disenfranchised urban communities fighting COVID-19 and a longitudinal study of practices of elder care and inequality in Israel's transforming kibbutzim.

Acknowledgments

This book began to take shape during a vibrant conversation with Andrew Wardell at the 2018 American Association for Applied Linguistics (AAAL) meetings, in Chicago. We would like to thank him and Becky Holland of Bloomsbury Academic for their support and guidance throughout the development of our book. Likewise, we are very thankful to the reviewers of the book proposal and of the book manuscript for their advice and support. Special thanks go to the contributors of this volume who accepted our invitation to be part of this collection. We would like to acknowledge the enthusiasm and great care each of them took in writing and revising their chapters. Without their dedication and unique expertise in linguistic anthropology, this volume would have never materialized. We both thank our students and colleagues in the Departments of Anthropology at Binghamton University and the University of Alabama for their continuous intellectual and social support throughout the course of this book's preparation. Taking place within conversations about research methodology over coffee, in the hallways, and via Zoom, their contributions to this volume are immeasurable. Finally, we would both like to offer our immense gratitude to our advisors, mentors, and colleagues in linguistic anthropology who have supported us in our studies and careers: the reality that there are too many of you to name individually is a reminder to us of just how lucky we have been. We hope that this volume contributes, in whatever small way, to furthering the enormous legacy of innovative methodologies that you have developed, refined, and shared with so many students over the years.

Sabina M. Perrino and Sonya E. Pritzker

Introduction: Research Methods in Linguistic Anthropology

Sabina M. Perrino and Sonya E. Pritzker

I.1 Why Research Methods in Linguistic Anthropology?

Since linguistic anthropology was officially designated as one of the four anthropological subfields in 1964 (Duranti 2009; Hymes 1964), linguistic anthropologists have developed a range of distinctive methodologies for collecting and analyzing data. Though they overlap considerably with anthropological methods in other subfields, the methods of linguistic anthropology uniquely privilege the study of social interaction. Inclusive of language but also gesture, gaze, intonation, and movement, linguistic anthropologists emphasize the emergence of culture, experience, and ideology in social interactions that are always mediated by broader historical and political processes. The unique methodological repertoire of linguistic anthropologists thus also includes techniques and strategies derived from neighboring disciplines such as sociolinguistics, applied linguistics, and ethnomethodology. Although existing methods textbooks in anthropology often include one or more chapters discussing linguistic anthropology (e.g., Bernard 2018)—and conversely, overviews of linguistic anthropology often include one or more chapters discussing methods (e.g., Ahearn 2017; Duranti 2009; Wilce 2017)—*Research Methods in Linguistic Anthropology* is the first comprehensive volume to focus solely on methods in linguistic anthropology.

Based on our experience as graduate students and later as more experienced researchers and instructors, which has invariably involved the piecemeal gathering of material covering methodological articles, chapters, and books, we thus concurred that the time had come for a text devoted to methods in linguistic anthropology. Initially proposed to us as an edited volume, we quickly came to realize that, although it is somewhat unusual, a core instructional text in this format offers several key benefits to students, instructors, and other interested readers. A multiauthored approach introduces readers to the coherence of the methods drawn upon by linguistic anthropologists while also offering a perspective on the diverse ways in which those methods are conceptualized and applied across diverse sociocultural and historical settings. Each chapter of this volume here provides an inside view of the methods developed within multiple projects in a wide range of sociopolitical, cultural, historical, and economic fields of practice. Novice and experienced researchers interested in similar fields will benefit from having access to detailed methods that they may adapt and expand upon in their own studies. Even if one's field is very different from the particular sites discussed by our authors, however, the range presented here aptly illustrates the ways in which *methodological flexibility*, grounded in a consideration of particular communicative, social, and historical details, is critical at every stage of research in linguistic anthropology. The present volume, finally, attends closely to the nuanced details of the various aspects of research in linguistic anthropology, including both conceptual and practical steps that researchers take before, during, and after fieldwork. In doing so, each chapter provides readers with insight into the meaning and practical implications of a range of key concepts that are often considered, outside of the subfield, to be abstract and unwieldly.

Throughout the volume, authors adopt a variety of viewpoints to further address a set of central questions, including (1) what is distinctive about research methods in linguistic anthropology with respect to how sociocultural anthropologists and scholars in neighboring disciplines conduct research? (2) Why is it important to understand these methodologies, even if one is not planning on conducting a research study in linguistic anthropology? And, finally, (3) how might researchers in other subfields and/or disciplines draw upon these methods in their own projects? The twelve chapters of this volume address these questions in a range of interconnected discussions. Each of the chapters further demonstrates linguistic anthropology's overarching philosophical, theoretical, and ethical commitment to studying culture as it emerges in and through interaction. In this sense, research methods in linguistic anthropology are intimately connected to this core commitment, which often mandates a nuanced processual approach that attends to interactional and discursive fluidity (see Chapter 1 by Karimzad and Catedral). This volume is thus intended to be a resource for students as well as senior researchers in linguistic anthropology and related fields, who until now have had to seek advice from their mentors, colleagues, and so forth. With the COVID-19 pandemic, moreover, researchers have come to realize that there is a need to understand and study online interaction and digital data following a rigorous methodology. In this respect, linguistic anthropological methods can be easily adapted to the digital world and can be used across various disciplines, as Crowley and Chun demonstrate in Chapter 10.

Instructors will find this edited volume particularly useful. While the twelve chapters are connected by common, key topics and themes that run through them, they can also be used separately if students need to study one or two methodologies in more depth. Ethical issues, for example, are addressed in each chapter, showing how students and researchers need to carefully think about the ethical implications of their research at each turn. The chapter dedicated to ethical issues in linguistic anthropology, by Black and Conley Riner (Chapter 4), however, summarizes the central ethical principles that researchers undertaking a project in linguistic anthropology should follow while embarking in their research projects. Transcription which is also mentioned in several chapters, likewise has a dedicated chapter that covers transcription practices and the analysis of transcripts in great detail (see Shohet and Loyd, Chapter 9). To make these methodological practices more connected to realistic fieldwork situations, moreover, the twelve chapters in our volume offer targeted ethnographic activities, discussion questions, and further reading materials on every topic that is discussed. In this way, students and researchers have several possibilities to prepare for their various field research projects with more rigor and pragmatism.

I.2 Book Structure: Overview of the Twelve Chapters

The book contains twelve chapters, each offering detailed descriptions of methods in linguistic anthropology, including the process of creating research questions (Chapter 1); conducting a literature review

(Chapter 2); planning research (Chapter 3); ethical considerations (Chapter 4); conducting participant observation and recording fieldnotes (Chapter 5); interviewing (Chapter 6); using video recording and other technologies for capturing data (Chapters 7 and 8); transcribing and analyzing data (Chapter 9); conducting online research (Chapter 10); doing mixed methods research (Chapter 11); and grant writing (Chapter 12). All of these chapters are in conversation with each other and include various useful perspectives on the above topics. At the end of each chapter, contributors offer various ethnographic activities, discussion questions, and suggestions for further readings as creative ways to apply the methodologies and related concepts learned in one or more chapters. As we mentioned earlier, graduate students, novel and more seasoned researchers and instructors more generally will find a great utility in these pedagogical tools.

In Chapter 1, "Navigating Topics and Creating Research Questions in Linguistic Anthropology," Farzad Karimzad and Lydia Catedral describe the challenging process that researchers face in the beginning of their projects: finding an original topic worthy of being researched and creating one or more viable research questions. The authors describe this process as the *attribution of topical salience* within a complex system of interconnected objects, phenomena, and relations. Researchers, they demonstrate using an optical metaphor, can "zoom in" or "zoom out" in order to see the possible connections in the phenomena or system they wish to study. This is how, Karimzad and Catedral argue, research questions become *flexible*, developing and changing over time in a continuous dialogue with interrelated questions and subquestions. Drawing upon several cross-cultural case studies, the authors thus show how research questions in linguistic anthropology can be constantly refined, changed, and made more contingent to the realities that are under study.

Chapter 2, "Reviewing the Literature in Linguistic Anthropology," by Justin B. Richland, similarly discusses how the open-ended character of fieldwork in linguistic anthropology allows for and even requires some flexibility in the literature review process. Richland thus argues that reviewing the literature for a particular project entails *intertextual chains* that connect one's research question, fieldsite, and topic to ongoing conversations in linguistic anthropology and other disciplines. This interconnection or intertextuality, he demonstrates, is key in developing a sense of what the future collection of data might yield or contribute. Literature reviews are thus key in helping researchers create feasible research hypotheses before embarking on their field research. Richland further highlights how this is an ongoing, incremental communicative process through which linguistic anthropologists acquire knowledge and engage in academic conversations during every phase of the research. This process, he argues, also allows researchers to continuously update their research agenda and to attend to emerging ethical concerns (see Chapter 4). To explain the challenges that researchers face in reviewing the literature, Richland offers meaningful and detailed examples from his own experiences as a graduate student and as a more seasoned scholar.

In Chapter 3, entitled "Planning Research in Linguistic Anthropology," Deborah A. Jones and Ilana Gershon describe the difficult process of planning research, highlighting especially the ways in which such plans are often sidetracked by unexpected turns of events before or while researchers are in their fieldsite(s). While certain situations cannot be predicted and ethnographers need to acquire experience and knowledge of the people and locations that they study, they also need to prepare for possible, and at times very probable, changes to their overarching plan. As the authors argue, first-time ethnographers need to strategize ahead of time to be able to find research consultants who can help them answer their research questions; to manage their time productively; to take care of their personal safety, and to follow key ethical commitments. As Gershon and Jones write, their chapter "guides researchers in articulating the *who, where,* and *how,* of their projects." Crucially, through various significant examples drawn from their respective research expertise and experiences, the authors demonstrate that linguistic anthropologists should carefully prepare for their research but should also be ready to change their plans, hypotheses, ideas, and expectations once they are in their fieldsite(s) to conduct their research.

While ethical issues are addressed in each of the volume's chapters, Chapter 4, entitled "Care as a Methodological Stance: Research Ethics in Linguistic Anthropology," presents a comprehensive discussion of ethical orientations to conducting research in this subfield. Steven P. Black and Robin Conley Riner describe how ethics is foundational at every phase of a project, including its design. Like other aspects of research in linguistic anthropology, Black and Conley Riner discuss how ethical issues often emerge contextually and thus require continuous attention and flexibility throughout the research project. More specifically, after an overview of the main theories of ethics, the authors discuss key ethical issues such as sexual harassment, discrimination, and the multiple implications of collaboration between research participants and researcher(s). Through several examples pertaining to their fieldsite experiences in South Africa (Black) and in the United States (Conley Riner), they also examine issues of confidentiality and anonymity in interview settings; in everyday activities that are audio- and/ or video-recorded; during other methods of data collection; and in online interactions.

Focusing on how linguistic anthropologists use classic ethnographic methodologies such as participant observation and the crafting of fieldnotes, Chapter 5, entitled "Participant Observation and Fieldnotes in Linguistic Anthropology," describes how these practices are uniquely incorporated in linguistic anthropological fieldwork. Sonya E. Pritzker and Sabina M. Perrino examine the various ways in which participant observation and the collection of fieldnotes become integrated with other ways to collect data, such as audio and/or video recordings of naturally occurring conversations and interviews. The authors show how participant observation and the attentive, rigorous, and quotidian writing of fieldnotes are key research tools not only to enhance the value of the collection of audio- and video-recorded data, but, most importantly, to be able to understand certain nuances that would otherwise remain veiled. These are thus essential methodologies in this subfield. To illustrate how linguistic anthropologists make use of these practices, Pritzker and Perrino use several examples drawn from their respective fieldsites: China and the United States (Pritzker) and Senegal and Northern Italy (Perrino).

In Chapter 6, "Interviews in Linguistic Anthropology," Sabina M. Perrino examines interviews as they are developed, conducted, and analyzed in this subfield. While interviews are widely used across various disciplines such as anthropology, education, social history, social psychology, and sociolinguistics, Perrino underscores the ways in which linguistic anthropologists, in contrast to emphasizing content, prioritize the interactional dynamics that emerge in interviews. Perrino thus describes how linguistic anthropologists consider interviews, given their intrinsic interactional nature, as *situated speech events*. More specifically, she examines the discursive and interactional character of these speech events, showing how researchers prepare, conduct, and analyze interviews. She also shows how researchers need to be sensitive to the various sociocultural contexts in which they conduct their research and thus how they need to "learn how to ask" (Briggs 1986) their questions to their research consultants. In this respect, as Perrino argues, interviews are dynamic events in which the interactional dimension needs to come to the fore instead of looking at their content only (their *denotational text*). She offers various examples from her two fieldsites, Senegal and Northern Italy, to foreground the *situatedness* of interviews as unique interactional events.

Chapters 7 and 8 focus on key technological issues that linguistic anthropologists must consider. Readers will find some overlapping materials in these two chapters, both of which are useful to examine the different ways in which researchers can make use of new and old technology while collecting their data. Looking more at the technological aspect of research methodology, Gregory Kohler and Keith M. Murphy focus on audio- and video-technological tools for anthropological research. In Chapter 7, entitled "Audio-Video Technology for and in the Field: A Primer," the authors explain the complexities of audio- and video-recording practices for linguistic anthropologists, offering also a historical overview. The authors first introduce the main rationales for using digital audio and video in data collection. They then critically discuss the outcomes of using audio- and video-recording devices in fieldwork settings with an attentive eye to ethical issues that can emerge while using these research tools (Black 2017). Kohler and Murphy further offer key advice regarding (non)-digital audio and video recorders. They also describe situations in which researchers need to adapt and make sudden changes while audio and/or video recording during their research. In this respect, they highlight, these methodological and analytical tools cannot be taken for granted in all field settings, and researchers need to have backup plans in case the planned technology to collect their data is not possible. Kohler and Murphy use many examples from their fieldsites, Sardinia, Italy (Kohler), and Sweden (Murphy), but mention case studies from across the world as well.

Analogously, Teruko Vida Mitsuhara and Jan David Hauck continue to discuss video technology in Chapter 8, entitled "Video Ethnography: A Guide." Here, the authors focus more on the role played by video ethnographic practices during fieldwork. Importantly, the authors discuss ethical, technological, and practical issues related to this research method. What are the steps that researchers take before being able to collect video-recorded data? This chapter usefully describes the practicalities such as how to obtain consent and assent from research consultants, how to decide what equipment to purchase, how to create a database, and how to safely back up one's data. Notably, the authors explain the strategic use of these technological tools by incorporating several examples drawn from their respective fieldsites: West Bengal, India (Mitsuhara), and Eastern Paraguay (Hauck). In their examples, the authors describe situations that usually occur before, during, and after fieldwork and the various types of technology that can be utilized.

In Chapter 9, "Transcription and Analysis in Linguistic Anthropology: Creating, Testing, and Presenting Theory on the Page," Merav Shohet and Heather Loyd offer a unique perspective on the process of transcribing and analyzing audio- and video-recorded data once they are collected. They suggest that transcription and analysis should be considered *recursive processes* requiring continuous analysis and (re)interpretation. Transcription is a complex practice that helps linguistic anthropologists analyze and (re) interpret their collected data. Transcription is thus foundational, they argue, and constitutes the first step of analysis. Their chapter thus describes recent advances in technology, which researchers can use to create compelling transcripts for analysis and publication. These advancements in technology, argue the authors, are especially important to studying "the semiotically rich, multimodal nature of social life across domains—from interaction to interviews and other activities." Careful transcription thus allows researchers to connect micro-discursive practices to larger sociocultural, political, and economic processes. Shohet and Loyd also describe possible ethical issues that could emerge from transcription practices, emphasizing how the processes of coding, logging, transcribing, and translating are all naturally influenced by the analyst. To demonstrate the value and wide range of transcription practices, the authors use examples from their field experiences in Vietnam (Shohet) and Italy (Loyd) as well as several examples from other well-known scholars in the subfield.

Chapter 10, "Online Research and New Media," turns to how linguistic anthropologists conduct ethnographic research in a wide range of online or digital environments. Archie Crowley and Elaine Chun describe how online research has emerged, how novel ethical and methodological concerns have been addressed, how online communities of practice have coalesced, and how several concepts in linguistic anthropology have been revisited as a result of conducting online research. Drawing on their data and expertise, the authors also examine online discursive practices as they are created by transgender communities. Showing how digital spaces have offered unprecedented visibility to marginalized individuals and communities, they demonstrate how, ironically, such exposure has often reinstated their marginalization. Crowley and Chun thus emphasize that research conducted in the digital realm needs digital methods that are different from the ones used in more traditional ethnographic settings. They use examples from their own research on YouTube while citing research from other scholars specializing on other digital platforms such as Instagram, Facebook, Twitter, and TikTok. Especially in the context of the recent COVID-19 pandemic, digital methods and other research resources acquired new meanings and primary roles for many linguistic anthropologists, as the authors describe.

In Chapter 11, entitled "Mixed Methods and Interdisciplinary Research in Linguistic Anthropology," Sonya E. Pritzker examines how linguistic anthropologists might integrate methods from other disciplines in their research projects. By their very nature, Pritzker argues, many projects in linguistic anthropology benefit from a mixed methods approach. Increasing numbers of linguistic anthropologists are also becoming involved in large, collaborative projects that require cooperation across multiple disciplines. The chapter thus describes the process of designing, implementing, and reporting data from mixed methods studies in or inclusive of linguistic anthropology. Crucially, the author also shows how mixed methods need to be understood as one of the methods that linguistic anthropologists utilize and not just as a mixture of methods that are thrown together. Pritzker offers various examples from her research in China and in the United States to show the value of using interdisciplinary methods. Like in all the other chapters, ethical issues in mixed methods and interdisciplinary research are thoroughly discussed.

The final chapter of the collection, Chapter 12, "Grant Writing for Projects in Linguistic Anthropology," authored by Sonia N. Das, emphasizes the process and value of grant writing in this subfield. Das argues that rigor in describing the ways in which one will collect and analyze data is key in developing strong and compelling grant proposals. Das thus examines the challenges that researchers face when writing grant proposals, including how to elaborate a valuable research question, how to show that the project has an intellectual merit, and how the project connects research questions and/or hypotheses with strategies for collecting and analyzing data. This final chapter thus includes all the topics of our volume, offered from the perspective of a researcher who has successfully garnered funding from multiple major organizations. Das also highlights the professional benefits that grants entail for researchers' career advancement. She uses examples from her recent projects, which have received key professional grants and recognition from agencies such as the Wenner-Gren Foundation and the National Science Foundation. She also offers an overview of the most important grant agencies for linguistic anthropological projects, something that graduate students and researchers will benefit from having available before starting a new project. Importantly—as in all chapters—Das also examines ethical concerns in writing grants.

I.3 Final Thoughts (For Now)

As all the chapters of this volume highlight, research methods in linguistic anthropology develop and change at a very fast pace in relation to broad theoretical and technological advancements as well as local contextual shifts within particular projects. Contributors to this volume are thus consistent in arguing that researchers need to be flexible and amenable to adapting their methodologies and plans, sometimes multiple times, during the process of conducting their research. Authors underscore that it is critical to do so ethically and while continuously interacting with the surrounding context and people that are part of one's study. All the chapters in this volume have thus illustrated that linguistic anthropological research projects, and the methodologies used, are always fluctuating and in interaction with the diverse realities that researchers find in their fieldsites. At the same time, contributors highlight how a set of traditional tenets of anthropological research, such as participant observation and the writing of fieldnotes, the preparation of research questions, and the various planning activities before leaving for the field, still represent a key part of linguistic anthropological research methodologies.

While we have attempted to thoroughly cover the basic topics related to research methods in linguistic anthropology, there are other topics and methodological approaches that should be further explored. The integration of quantitative methods in qualitative research is a developing area, for example, that is only briefly examined by Pritzker in Chapter 11. The need to develop methods pertaining to a more applied linguistic anthropological perspective—for example, in social justice activities and sustainable communities studies—likewise deserves further examination (see Avineri et al. 2019). We would have also liked to include more details covering emerging methods in *sociophonetics* (Mendoza-Denton 2008, 2011, 2016). These are all important research venues requiring particular research methodologies that have been emerging in recent times, always, however, alongside of more traditional methods. By focusing on these more "traditional" methods in linguistic anthropology, this book aims to provide a basic guide for students, novice and seasoned researchers, and anyone interested in knowing how to conduct research in linguistic anthropology.

Our initial question then, "Why research methods in linguistic anthropology?", is answered by scrolling through the topics that the chapters in this volume have addressed. As our contributors have shown, and as we have emphasized in this Introduction, while some of the methods are shared with other anthropological subfields and with other disciplines, linguistic anthropological methods and analytical tools stand out for their distinctiveness. The attention, rigor, and care that linguistic anthropologists apply in their methodologies and analyses, which are always discursively mediated, are significant in showing how culture emerges in and through everyday interaction and vice versa. A textbook featuring this uniqueness has been overdue and opens up future explorations in research methodology not only in linguistic anthropology but in neighboring disciplines and cross-culturally as well. This is, at least, our hope.

I.4 References Cited

Ahearn, Laura M. 2017. *Living Language: An Introduction to Linguistic Anthropology*. Oxford, UK: Wiley-Blackwell.

Avineri, Netta, Laura R. Graham, Eric J. Johnson, Robin Conley Riner, and Jonathan Rosa. 2019. *Language and Social Justice in Practice*. New York: Routledge.

Bernard, H. Russell. 2018. *Research Methods in Anthropology: Qualitative and Quantitative Approaches, Fourth Edition*. 5th ed. Lanham, MD: AltaMira Press.

Black, Steven P. 2017. "Anthropological Ethics and the Communicative Affordances of Audio-Video Recorders in Ethnographic Fieldwork: Transduction as Theory." *American Anthropologist* 119 (1): 46–57.

Briggs, Charles L. 1986. *Learning How to Ask: A Sociolinguistic Appraisal of the Role of the Interview in Social Science Research*. New York: Cambridge University Press.

Duranti, Alessandro. 2009. "Linguistic Anthropology: History, Ideas, and Issues." In Alessandro Duranti, ed., *Linguistic Anthropology: A Reader*, 2nd ed. 1–39. Malden, MA: Wiley-Blackwell.

Hymes, Dell H. 1964. *Language in Culture and Society: A Reader in Linguistics and Anthropology*. New York: Harper & Row.

Mendoza-Denton, Norma. 2008. *Homegirls: Language and Cultural Practice among Latina Youth Gangs*. Malden, MA: Blackwell Publishers.

Mendoza-Denton, Norma. 2011. "The Semiotic Hitchhiker's Guide to Creaky Voice: Circulation and Gendered Hardcore in a Chicana/o Gang Persona." *Journal of Linguistic Anthropology* 21 (2): 261–80.

Mendoza-Denton, Norma. 2016. "Norteño and Sureño Gangs, Hip Hop, and Ethnicity on Youtube: Localism in California through Spanish Accent Variation." In H. Samy Alim, John R. Rickford and Arnetha F. Ball eds.,

Raciolinguistics: How Language Shapes Our Ideas about Race, 135–50. New York: Oxford University Press.

Wilce, James MacLynn. 2017. *Culture and Communication: An Introduction.* Cambridge: Cambridge University Press.

1

Navigating Topics and Creating Research Questions in Linguistic Anthropology

Farzad Karimzad and Lydia Catedral

1.1 Introduction

Research in linguistic anthropology—like research in any field—is not so much defined by particular questions, but rather by a specific way of approaching, addressing, and organizing these questions. At any given time, the same phenomenon is under discussion across multiple disciplines and subdisciplines, each of which has labeling practices that give salience to particular topics related to this phenomenon. Take for instance the topic of migration, which is studied not only in "migration studies," but also in political science, sociology, economics, and anthropology. Each of these fields not only prioritizes particular methodologies, but also foregrounds certain issues in relation to migration, such as political, sociological, economic, or sociocultural issues. Participation in these fields comes with an expectation that scholarship will not only theorize a topic of interest such as migration, but also contribute to the theorization of *intersecting* issues within that field.

The fact that the same phenomenon can be discussed simultaneously across multiple fields points to the porous nature of disciplinary boundaries. That is, disciplines do not operate as discrete entities that investigate separate or separable issues, but rather, they use different tools to investigate similar objects and phenomena that have considerable overlap (see Mannheim 2018). As such, disciplines are better understood as different ways of organizing data and analysis around particular topical concerns, rather than as bounded areas of study. The differentiating factor between disciplines and subdisciplines, then, is in the *attribution of topical salience* (cf., Agha 2007a; Karimzad 2020) or the decision about what to foreground or make central in scholarship within the field. The attribution of topical salience defines not only academic study, but also how non-discrete information is divided up more generally, (re)creating categories for identities, objects, and relations (see Irvine and Gal 2000). While any given category may appear to be stable, it is in fact the result of dynamic *categorization processes* (cf., De Fina 2011), which are precisely defined by the organization of data in relation to what receives topical salience. Such categorization is simultaneously an unavoidable fact of social life and a "double-edged sword": Categories enable an understanding of the world because of how they facilitate an organization of the varied and diverse pieces of information people encounter, but they also restrict understanding because they predispose people to recognizing familiar configurations of information and limit attention to what is considered to be "relevant" to the topic at hand (see Mayes and Tao 2019). The limitations imposed by categories can be countered, not by getting rid of them (see Gal 2018), but by developing a reflexive and "meta" understanding of how they are constructed and utilized in scholarship and in the social world more broadly (see Silverstein 1981; Urban 2018). Such a reflexive or meta-approach allows one to see the process of creating categories as not only unavoidable but also valuable in defining focus within and across interactions, reflections, and argumentations.

Coming up with a research focus involves similar meta-processes of categorization and in many ways resembles the processes through which an academic discipline is defined, albeit at a relatively smaller scale. Just as academic disciplines are defined through the repeated attribution of prominence to a particular set of issues, so a research question defines the scope of a research project by proposing to give prominence to some subset of issues in one's investigation. By organizing information around what has been determined to be topically salient, a research question allows the analyst to engage in categorization processes, which can both limit and expand their potential for understanding the issues at hand. In order to make the best use of research questions then, it is necessary to engage them in flexible, dynamic, and reflexive ways. In this chapter, we lay out a system within which such engagement can be situated: In this system one can *zoom in* on a particular topic to investigate and describe its details and *zoom out* to highlight and explain its connections to a broader range of phenomena, much in the way that one can zoom in and out on a high-resolution image to focus on one particular aspect or to see the picture as a whole (cf., Karimzad 2021; Karimzad and Catedral 2021; see also Pritzker and Perrino 2020). This approach also makes it possible to put one's research question in dialogue with other interrelated questions, categorizations, and conversations in ways that allow for the research focus to be expanded, restricted, modified, and changed.

Returning to the discussion of disciplinary boundaries, we also want to stress that from this perspective, there are no "off-limit" topics about which one can pose research questions. This is particularly true for linguistic anthropologists and sociolinguists, who study language use in the social world—a phenomenon that is involved in every aspect of human life (see Blommaert 2018; Silverstein 1981). Another way of putting this is that because discourse is the means through which categorization happens, any study of categories—whether aimed at challenging or utilizing them—is a study of discourse in its interactional, historical, political, and sociocultural contexts (see Foucault 1972; Jørgensen and Phillips 2002). The fact that *any* phenomenon can be the object of focus and the topic around which data are organized does not mean that the process of coming up with a research question is perfunctory or that it does not matter. Conversely, one makes their research *matter* precisely by choosing, articulating, and justifying this focus. Making research matter is admittedly a complex issue that is defined in relation to a wide range of personal, institutional, moral, and scientific values and value systems. Nonetheless, it is a process in which all researchers are engaged inasmuch as they confer importance to a topic by focusing their investigation on it and justify its importance through a demonstration of how it is in dialogue with the work of others.

1.2 Navigating and Situating Research Topics

1.2.1 A Fractal System of Knowledge Production

We find it useful to discuss knowledge production in terms of "presupposition" and "entailment" (Silverstein 1992): the construction of meaning involves *presupposing* some existing knowledge and categories, which allow for the *entailment*—or the *creation*—of new meanings and categories. Although this is a more general process at work in the social world, it also applies specifically to the production of academic knowledge. Scholars enter a research process with certain assumptions based on existing knowledge, which then allow them to categorize and understand their data, and their research projects as a whole, in particular ways, leading to the production of new knowledge.

In linguistic anthropology in particular, knowledge production is situated on the *pragmatics-metapragmatics nexus* as it plays out in the social world (Silverstein 1993). That is, the empirical, analytical, and theoretical focus of linguistic anthropological research is on social actors' language practices—a matter of *pragmatics*—and their interaction with the ideologies that mediate these practices—that is, *metapragmatics*. Importantly, "language" here is understood in terms of *semiosis*, which is the construction and construal of meaning through both linguistic and nonlinguistic signs. To be precise, semiosis or meaning-making is made possible through *indexical processes* in which (non)linguistic signs *point to*, or *index*, their presupposed or potential contexts of use and call upon histories of their meaningful usage. It is metapragmatics that mediates the indexical linkages of linguistic signs and their contexts of use, providing those involved in social interaction with some idea for producing and interpreting semiotic practices in relation to particular contexts (Agha 2007b; Silverstein 1993; see also Blommaert 2018; Moore 2020). Those scholars interested in semiosis at the pragmatic-metapragmatic nexus understand that the interaction between pragmatics and metapragmatics is an everyday process through which speakers, including researchers, negotiate and evaluate meaning. However, when linguistic anthropologists theorize the metapragmatics of (meta)semiosis, they are working as *meta-interpreters* who operate at a higher-order position above the contexts *from* and *about* which these acts are situated. Thus, the production of knowledge in linguistic anthropology is a matter of *meta-metapragmatics*: Scholars use ethnographic data to investigate and theorize language use as well as ideological–normative reflections on this language use, and they then draw on and/or create *meta*-categories and *meta*-discourses, which organize these data and analyses in relation to research questions and topical concerns.

Situating oneself in a meta-position allows for an imagination of research topics and questions within a *fractal system*, where objects, phenomena, and relations are linked across various interconnected scale levels (cf., Blommaert and De Fina 2017; Gal 2016; Irvine and Gal 2000; Karimzad

2021). The four images in Figure 1.1 are illustrations of fractality: the first is an image of fractal triangles, the second a branch of a tree, and the third and fourth a Romanesco cauliflower (also called Romanesco broccoli) from a zoomed-out and zoomed-in point of view, respectively.

While these images differ from one another in a number of ways, they are connected through their fractal patterns, that is, the recurrence of shapes or configurations at various scale levels, ranging from the microscopic to the macroscopic. Take the Romanesco cauliflower for instance: it is made up of pyramid-esque nodes, and each of these nodes is composed of smaller, similarly shaped nodes. The more zoomed-out image of the cauliflower makes it difficult to see all these fractal details and a viewer may miss the fact that each of the nodes is made up of smaller ones. The more zoomed-in image illuminates these details but may not give the whole picture of the cauliflower. If we look at the other images, we see that they differ in appearance from the cauliflower. Nonetheless, across these photos there is a similar way that recursive processes create patterns in which zooming in or out reveals repetitive fractal details and the interconnectedness of the structures as a whole. These structures are not merely the sum of individual

Figure 1.1 Fractal patterns[1]

parts or even of particular patterns, but rather more comprehensive and collective wholes. At the same time, the structures in these images are only approximations of fractals in the sense that their recursions end at some point, whereas within a fractal system such as the one we are imagining, one could zoom in or out infinitely and the fractal recursions would continue in any direction.

What we are discussing here applies specifically to knowledge production in that knowledge emerges from and in relation to a fractal system of interconnected and recursively organized information on which scholars can zoom in or out in their research processes. Such a system allows for reflection on research from multiple *scalar* positions (see Blommaert 2015, 2020; Canagarajah and De Costa 2016; Carr and Lempert 2016; Catedral 2018; Gal 2016). This, in turn, enables the possibility of *moving away from*, without *doing away with*, the categories that are used to define disciplinary- or project-specific focuses. This is because one can attend to a scalar level at which certain categories become relevant, or zoom in to consider a level at which these categories no longer matter as much as the microscopic social-semiotic details and nuances, or zoom out and consider a level at which the discrete nature of these categories is less relevant than the interconnectedness between them (see Karimzad 2021). To illustrate this further, let us return to the above images, but this time from the perspective of categories and categorization. While one might categorize and label what appears in the images as "triangles," "foliage," and "cauliflowers," limiting the possibility of observing connections between these images, a more zoomed-out perspective makes these particular categories less relevant and could instead emphasize the interconnectedness of "cauliflower" and "foliage" through a broader category such as "plants" or, as we have done, emphasize the nature of fractality in order to illuminate connections between all four images.

Moving across these multiple levels not only facilitates a flexible engagement with categories but also allows researchers to imagine their research topics and questions as multi-scalar, interconnected, epistemological objects. This does not mean, however, that a researcher needs to, or can, engage the entire fractal system. The important point is that although everything is interconnected within the system as a whole, scholars can enter the discussion at any particular scale level. Using questions and topics in ways that enable rather than restrict research, then, requires a navigation of this system, and a commitment to situating a focus at particular scale levels—and on the categories associated with those scales—within the larger interconnected system, in order to determine where new knowledge is being contributed to the ongoing discussions.

This ability to understand and navigate the fractal system is useful in relation to multiple practical concerns at various stages in the research process and in relation to different projects across one's research trajectory. As one example, take the fact that a young scholar who is starting their very first research project is likely to receive feedback in which they are told that their focus is too broad and that they need to make their research questions more specific. Alternatively, a scholar who is seeking funding for a research project may be asked to expand their view of their research focus and to explain why the issue matters at a broader level. These contrasting examples demonstrate that researchers need the ability to scale up and down within a fractal system, attributing salience to various possible research-related issues at different moments. In other words, while devising a research question or a research focus requires limiting oneself to an examination of a particular process or phenomenon, it also requires an understanding of how this process or phenomenon is situated, and the fractal system enables both. Let us now turn to how posing *flexible research questions* and navigating implications of research can be understood within this system.

1.2.2 Posing Flexible Questions

1.2.2.1 Attributing Salience in Empirical Data

The system of knowledge production outlined above illuminates the limitations of coming up with *only* one research question. In fact, in any given piece of data, one can observe many different semiotic patterns, phenomena, and processes, any of which could be given greater analytical attention. If a researcher rigidly restricts themselves to one and only one unchanging question throughout the research process, they miss out on the possibility of more flexible, dialogic engagements with research questions that are available within a fractal system. On the other hand, if one does not narrow down their focus, or does not organize their data, analysis, and discussion around particular questions and answers, their research becomes a representation of undifferentiated semiotic data that may lack coherence, argumentation, or theoretical significance. Thus, a researcher approaching a new project will typically need to start with clear research questions that shape their research process, but should also be prepared to modify and change them, attributing topical salience to various other issues, in response to their encounters with data. Coming up with the final version of one's research question(s), therefore, requires flexible, situated engagement with multiple topics that ends with the attribution of topical salience to particular, primary and secondary issues.

This discussion of how research questions evolve over time is somewhat abstract, because it is the specificity of the data and the way in which they are in dialogue with particular theoretical notions and tools that refines these questions. In order to explain these processes in a more tangible way, in what follows, we will focus on a particular piece of data and its relation to various theoretical ideas. This piece of data is chosen because it is used in two different articles—one by Perrino and Kohler (2020) and one by Pritzker and Perrino (2020)—in relation to interrelated, but distinct, research questions. Its appearance in these two articles allows for a demonstration of the dynamic relationship between the attribution of topical salience and the organization of data. However, we do not only focus on the end product— that is, how the data were utilized and theorized by the authors of these articles in their final forms—but also imagine ways in which other issues that appear in the data could be put in dialogue with different theoretical notions to give topical salience to alternative concerns. The excerpt in question is described by Perrino and Kohler in their article on "brand identities" as coming from a specific conversation with a northern Italian businessman who was explaining the history of his well-known fashion company (2020, 97–8).

Original Italian Version

1 **Moreno:** [...] il papa Carl-Carlalberto e lo zio maggiore Claudio **ripartirono**
2 praticamente **ricominciarono** da zero con trentasei dipendenti
3 e **fondarono** quella che è la M.Moda S.p.A.
4 quindi in realtà se guardiamo le- le- la storia senza nessun tipo d'interruzione
5 diciamo la storia data dal '58 ad oggi quindi 54 anni- anni
6 però se prendiamo invece anche la parte precedente
7 quindi diciamo il DNA le origini del nonno
8 allora ne fa molti di più con circa intorno a cento anni
9 perché è iniziata all'inizio degli anni degli anni venti- ven- col nonno [...]

English Translation

1 **Moreno:** [...] our dad Carl-Carlalberto and our older uncle Claudio **started again**
2 basically [they] **started again** from scratch with thirty-six workers
3 and [they] **founded** what is M.Moda S.p.A. [i.e., public company]
4 so in reality if [we] look at the- the- the history without any kind of interruption
5 let's say the history starting from 1958 until today so 54 years- years
6 but if [we] also take the previous part instead
7 so let's say the DNA, our grandfather's origins
8 then there are many more [years of history] about one hundred years
9 because [it] started at the beginning of the 1920s twent- with [our] grandfather [...]

Before we discuss what the authors have given prominence to in their analysis, let us imagine some of the possible topics that might come to mind in a first reading of the excerpt. The point of this is to demonstrate how different, yet intersecting, issues could be given topical salience. The following are some of the topics and research questions that came to mind for us (the authors of this chapter, Farzad and Lydia):

- **Success**: We first noticed how Moreno talks about success as he charts the trajectory of the company from its humble beginnings to its current status (lines 2 and 3). This made us think about discourses of success and how these discourses intersect with dominant ideologies and could lead us to the question:
  - *What are the discourses of success among the Italian executives interviewed and how do these discourses intersect with neoliberal ideologies?*
- **History**: The references to particular years (lines 5 and 9) and the passing of time (line 8) as well as the use of the words "history" (lines 4 and 5) and "origins" (line 7) drew our attention as well. This made us wonder how history is being represented in the moment of the interview and might lead us to the following question:
  - *How is language used to represent history in the narratives about these Italian companies, and what are the interactional and/or social purposes of these historical representations?*
- **Essentialization**: The third thing that drew our attention was the reference to DNA, as well as the related invocation of biological

relatives, such as "grandfather" (lines 7 and 9), "dad" (line 1), and "uncle" (line 1), which seems to imply some inherent connection between the family's biology and its engagement in the business. This could lead us to ask:

○ *How is the link between the family and the business discursively represented and what can this tell us about the processes of essentialization and ideologies of family that are present in the narratives?*

Of course, these three topics do not represent all possible topics—choices are always informed and constrained by previous knowledge. For example, since we were not present at the interview, have little knowledge of Italian business culture, and do not understand the Italian language, there are many semiotic details in this piece of data that escape our notice. On the other hand, because we have written and read about neoliberalism, success, and essentialization, these are topics that we more quickly recognize the significance of in the data. One thing to note about these research questions is that even though they are preliminary, they already allow for the attribution of topical salience to multiple, interrelated issues. Notice that each of the three questions first draws attention to patterns of discourse and then shifts the attention to accounting for why these patterns exist or what they mean. The questions allow for the exploration of patterns in the data and seek explanations of why these patterns are there and why they matter.

While we came up with these various questions after a relatively short period of reflection on one piece of data, if we were the ones actually conducting the study, it would be necessary for us to take these questions as a starting point for investigating patterns across the whole range of collected data and might even prompt us to collect more data related to these interests. Furthermore, we would need to read the related work of others in order to refine our theoretical approach and to ensure precise and nuanced ways of accounting for *why* certain patterns appear in the data. During this process, our research questions would likely shift and would need to be refined, and we might also discover that the three questions intersect with one another in our analysis or that they need to be allocated to different projects.

Now let us turn from our hypothetical choice of topic based on the excerpt to see how it was actually used by Perrino and Kohler (2020): how they recognized patterns and accounted for them after their engagements with both empirical data (i.e., primary sources) and the literature (i.e., secondary sources). In order to understand the argument and focus that Perrino and Kohler put forward, it is necessary to have some understanding of the Bakhtinian notion of *chronotopes* (Bakhtin 1981), which can be understood as semiotized images of times and places, populated by particular types of people, which organize social information and relations (Agha 2007a; Silverstein 2005). Scholars of linguistic anthropology have used this notion as a unit for understanding the semiotic processes through which the social world is imagined, experienced, discussed, and changed (Blommaert 2015; Dick 2010; Koven 2013; Wirtz 2014; Woolard 2013). Perrino and Kohler use the notion in their characterization of the above piece of data in the following way:

> By going back and forth through these historical facts, Moreno starts to construct his family's identity together with his company's identity. He does so by chronotopically linking the two histories and by traveling fluidly across spatiotemporal scales.
>
> (Perrino and Kohler 2020, 98)

In order to support this argument, they point to the blurring of boundaries between the chronotopes of "family histories" and those of "business histories" that is discursively accomplished through historical retellings and references to DNA. They give topical salience to some of the same issues we noted in our preliminary analysis; however, they have organized these observations in relation to other sets of data and in relation to their theoretical arguments, their broader reading of others' theorizations, and more specifically, the notion of chronotope. Thus, research is never just about describing what is happening in the data, but crucially, it is about organizing those descriptions in ways that allow engagement in knowledge production at various scale levels. This means that analysis of data is organized in relation to particular questions and that these questions, in turn, must be organized in relation to ongoing theoretical and analytical arguments in the field. While we do not know exactly what types of questions the authors foregrounded at the beginning of their research process, we have attempted to reverse-engineer their primary arguments, as laid out in their introduction, in the form of the following five research questions:

1 How are discursive representations of time and space used to construct brand identities in narratives?
2 How do brand identities emerge in executives' narrative practices through their enacted discourse strategies and what are the ideologies that are relevant to these strategies?

3 How are such ideologies reinforced and circulated across Italian executive culture and Italian culture more generally?

4 How can one account for these discursive practices, identities, and circulated ideologies through the theoretical notion of chronotope?

5 How does the notion of chronotope as used in this chapter contribute to ongoing theoretical discussions about the connection between discursive practice and identity?

We now turn to observe how this same piece of data is used in the Pritzker and Perrino (2020) article in relation to a broader set of data and other theoretically overlapping, but distinct, research questions. By giving greater topical salience to questions about intimacy and scale, as opposed to foregrounding brand identities, in this article, Pritzker and Perrino are able to use an expanded version of this piece of data to make slightly different arguments. They show how the above-discussed chronotopic links between "family history" and "business history" produce affective, embodied, and moral "intimacies" across the scales of self, family, and nation. Thus, the latter article has a different "center" around which this piece of data is organized, along with new sets of data—notably data coming from Pritzker's work on psychospiritual development programs (e.g., Pritzker 2016). This new "center" is essentially the attribution of topical salience to a different aspect of chronotopic theory—that of the *scalar* aspect of chronotopic relations—and its implications for the notion of "intimacy," which the authors understand as interactionally negotiated feelings of closeness, combined with vulnerability, trust, and sharedness (Pritzker and Perrino 2020). What the comparison between the two articles illustrates is that both empirical data and the theories of others can be read in relation to multiple topics. It is this second issue—the multiple possibilities of attributing topical salience in the work of others—to which we now turn our attention.

1.2.2.2 Attributing Salience in the Work of Others

The same processes of noticing interesting phenomena, recognizing patterns of semiosis, and attributing topical salience to these issues in the form of research questions are at work in scholarly engagement with the literature (see Richland, this volume). In the same way, researchers bring their existing knowledge and constraints on this knowledge to their interpretation of these texts, leading different readers (or the same reader at different times) to confer importance to differing aspects of the text. To illustrate this, we have reproduced a portion of the introduction of Jan Blommaert's (2010) *Sociolinguistics of Globalization* and have indicated the two different ways in which it was highlighted by Farzad at different points along his academic trajectory. On the left is the text with the highlights that were made in 2015 upon his first reading of the book, while on the right are the highlights that he made in 2018. In the excerpt, Blommaert is writing about the horizontal and vertical organization of space or *sociolinguistic scales*.

If the act of "highlighting" is understood as a visual means of attributing topical salience to particular aspects of a text, then one can read Farzad's

Read and highlighted in 2015 (paperback)	Reread and highlighted in 2018 (e-book)
Such distinctions are *indexical* distinctions, which project minute linguistic differences onto stratified patterns of social, cultural and political value-attribution. They convert linguistic and semiotic differences into social inequalities and thus represent the 'normative' dimensions of situated language use (Silverstein 2006a; Agha 2007; Blommaert 2005). The stratified and ordered nature of such indexical processes I have called, by analogy with Foucault's 'order of discourse', *orders of indexicality* (Blommaert 2005: 69), and every (horizontal) space is filled with such orders of indexicality – with stratified normative complexes that organize distinctions between, on the one hand, 'good', 'normal', 'appropriate', and 'acceptable' language use and, on the other, 'deviant', 'abnormal' etc. language use. Orders of indexicality define the dominant lines for senses of belonging, for identities and roles in society, and thus underlie what Goffman called the 'interaction order' – which is an *indexical* order(Silverstein 2003a; Agha 2007). I return to this in the next chapter.	Such distinctions are *indexical* distinctions, which project minute linguistic differences onto stratified patterns of social, cultural and political value-attribution. They convert linguistic and semiotic differences into social inequalities and thus represent the 'normative' dimensions of situated language use (Silverstein 2006a; Agha 2007; Blommaert 2005). The stratified and ordered nature of such indexical processes I have called, by analogy with Foucault's 'order of discourse', *orders of indexicality* (Blommaert 2005: 69), and every (horizontal) space is filled with such orders of indexicality – with stratified normative complexes that organize distinctions between, on the one hand, 'good', 'normal', 'appropriate', and 'acceptable' language use and, on the other, 'deviant', 'abnormal' etc. language use. Orders of indexicality define the dominant lines for senses of belonging, for identities and roles in society, and thus underlie what Goffman called the 'interaction order' – which is an *indexical* order (Silverstein 2003a; Agha 2007). I return to this in the next chapter.

(Blommaert 2010, 5–6)

highlights in 2015 as an indication that he was organizing his understandings of this excerpt in relation to the ideas of inequality and indexical value. This was in part because at the time, he thought that the theories about the unequal distribution of linguistic/semiotic resources could help him understand the experiences of particular minoritized communities he was working with. In 2018, the highlights confer greater importance to issues of normativity as they relate to the notion of "indexical order" in line with the new theoretical interests he had developed.

While every piece of scholarly writing will attribute topical salience in ways that shape the reader's understanding of the issue at hand, it is not only the writer's concerns, but also the reader's own concerns and focuses that influence what they take away from what they read. Thus, the research questions one may have in mind—however vaguely or specifically formed—can have an impact on what one attributes topical salience to in the work of others. At the same time, this is a dialogic and iterative process, such that what one attributes topical salience to also informs one's research questions and lines of argumentation. The process of knowledge production is happening at the same time as the process of knowledge building. New material is understood in relation to what one is already familiar with, and the reader notices those things that they are equipped to notice in the readings. At the same time, this ability to notice is always evolving as one constructs and organizes new knowledge through, and in relation to, the work of others, their own data and observations, their own writing, and so forth.

In short, research questions cannot be developed in a vacuum, but only through dialogue with both empirical data and the literature. At the same time, reviewing empirical data or reading the work of others does not reveal in any straightforward way what should be focused on, but rather opens up a number of different theoretical, analytical, and empirical possibilities from which one can choose interrelated topics to focus on. This choice of a topic necessarily includes a certain type of narrowing, in the sense that a researcher can only attribute topical salience to a question by giving greater attention to it and giving less attention to other issues. The ways in which one chooses to narrow their research questions and topics should be goal-oriented and as such will depend upon the particular types of writing with which they are engaged, for example, whether they are writing an academic article, a book, or a grant proposal (see Das, this volume). Scholars may even write popular articles for a more general audience, requiring them to give more attention to what is temporally salient in the news, and give less detail about dense theoretical ideas (compare Alim and Smitherman 2012a, 2012b,

2020). These differences exist because each type of writing involves different audience and communicative goals, and each goal requires particular types of topical narrowing.

This narrowing does not mean erasing either the complexity of the data or of the work of others, but simply giving it less elaboration at a particular moment in time if it is not central to the main questions and arguments. That is, one must consider which aspects of data to zoom in on in order to give an account of the semiotic and ethnographic details and which aspects of the data to zoom out on in order to show their connection to broader ideas. That is, a scholar might zoom in to explain all of the details of a particular theory if it is topically salient, or they might mention it in passing in order to relate it to other theoretical notions from a zoomed-out perspective, if it is less topically prominent. Furthermore, as seen in the example of the "Moreno excerpt," aspects of complexity, which remain unelaborated in one project, could form the basis for future research and be attributed greater salience in another project. The *flexibility* in good research questions thus derives in part from the fact that these questions are constantly in flux as they are in dialogic relation with existing and new knowledge, but also from the fact that research questions for one project can evolve into related, but fundamentally different questions for another project.

1.2.3 The Implications of Research Questions

1.2.3.1 Navigating and Evaluating Possible Significance

"So what?" is a question encountered by both novice and experienced scholars of linguistic anthropology at various stages in conceiving, carrying out, and writing up their research projects. This question may be asked by advisors, peers, reviewers of a journal, a committee, or it may be a question the researcher asks themselves about the value, contributions, and/or significance of their work. The "so what?" question is impossible to answer in a vacuum and, as a result, can send a scholar into an existential spiral if they do not have a reference with respect to which they can establish common understandings of "significance," "value," and "contribution." While we will discuss some of the different ideologies at work in the more fundamental processes of establishing value for research in the next section, here we are primarily concerned with demonstrating how one can understand the contribution of any research in relation to multiple scales and differing levels of detail. That is, we aim to show how situating research within the fractal system we have proposed allows one to determine and articulate the scales at which they are theorizing and adding nuance to existing knowledge within and across multiple projects.

When linguistic anthropologists situate their contributions within one particular part of the large and complex fractal system of knowledge production, it is easier to see both the significance and limitations of each piece of their work. Take for instance a class project for which a student is asked to complete a standalone literature review. Such a project might seem to contribute nothing to the field, since the student is only summarizing and/or paraphrasing what others have discussed. However, such a project is still unique and valuable because *this specific student* is the one who, in synthesizing the materials, attributes topical salience to certain themes, arguments, or types of data based on their own research interests and existing knowledge. In saying such a project is valuable, we mean that through the process of defining topical salience within a particular body of literature, the student is outlining a unique view of the field that could be beneficial to others *and* that they are coming to a better understanding of how their interests intersect with ongoing discussions in the field.

Of course, in order to attribute topical salience to certain concerns over others, the writing of a literature review must be guided by research questions that require zooming in on the particular details of what might be quite a broad topic within the field of linguistic anthropology. For instance, writing about "language and migration" will not result in a particularly beneficial literature review as the issue is too broad to result in a synthesis that makes a specific and coherent contribution. An alternative question might ask, "How have scholars in linguistic anthropology characterized the impact of language ideologies on migrants' education?" In the literature review then, one would still need to zoom out in order to give some broader context about how the field has approached migration. The fact that the writing is driven by this more specific question, however, would allow the writer to do so in a more pointed way (see Richland, this volume).

Writing such a literature review paves the way for subsequent projects in which researchers collect their own primary data. Another way of asking a research question in engagements with secondary data sources could be to focus on the theoretical and analytical tools utilized in the relevant scholarship. For instance, a question like "What theoretical tools have linguistic anthropologists used to discuss migrants' discursive and linguistic connection to the homeland?" would allow one to observe and evaluate the utility of various tools and to choose one in particular, which they might decide to apply to their own empirical data. When one is relatively new to research, they are likely to choose frameworks that are straightforward and easy to understand and apply based on their previous knowledge. Applying an already established theoretical tool to a new set of data can be a type of contribution in and of itself and can also work its way into a research question. Take for instance the "tactics of intersubjectivity" outlined by Bucholtz and Hall (2004, 2005), which is a theoretically robust *and* accessible framework that many new scholars interested in discourse and identity find to be a useful starting point for analysis of their data. This analytical toolkit could be applied to the researcher's data through the question: "How do the migrants in my data use these tactics of intersubjectivity when discussing their relationship to those in the homeland?" While the theory is not new, its application could again be situated within the larger fractal system in such a way as to show the broader applicability of the theory across contexts and also to reveal some new insights about the empirical data.

What does it look like to make a contribution at what is considered a higher scale in academic work? While the field of linguistic anthropology attributes a high value to zoomed-in accounts of ethnographic detail, perhaps more so than most disciplines, all scholars eventually come to a point in which they are also expected to make contributions that can be seen most clearly from a zoomed-out perspective because of their broader applicability across multiple ethnographic contexts and multiple literatures. Such contributions are typically referred to as theoretical contributions, which require an understanding of relevant, ongoing discussions of theory in and across disciplines. One becomes acquainted with such theoretical debates through their training, attendance at conferences, and engagements with the literature over time and may also specifically find texts such as annual reviews in linguistic anthropology to be helpful guides in navigating theoretically prominent issues in the field.

To understand how theoretical issues can be given more or less topical salience—let us return to the research questions we reverse-engineered from Perrino and Kohler's paper earlier—it can be seen that the list includes questions that are operating at various levels (i.e., questions that ask the researchers to both zoom in and out). For instance, the question "How are discursive representations of time and space used to construct brand identities in the Italian executive's narratives?" asks the researchers to zoom in on the linguistic and semiotic details of the interviews they conducted and look for clues in those details about the slightly zoomed-out question of "brand identities." On the other hand, the question "How does the notion of chronotope as used in this paper contribute to ongoing theoretical discussions about the connection between discursive practice and identity?" operates at a slightly higher level, which takes the empirical data as its starting point but aims to make a contribution that extends beyond this particular case and that engages with ongoing dialogue about how best to approach research on language and identity. Given that there are potentially five different research focuses informing Perrino and Kohler's article, at some point, they have had to decide which of these various questions they wanted to give greater topical salience to across their article.

In general, when greater topical salience is given to some research questions, the remaining questions are then organized around these more central ones. In other words, the decision to zoom in on a particular question means that it is considered more salient and deserving of greater attention than the others. Most research papers will deal with multiple questions, but they differ from one another in terms of style, depending upon whether they give greater attention to theoretical issues or ethnographic ones. Take for instance, Agha's (2003) *The Social Life of Cultural Value*, which is an example of a piece that, while drawing on substantial empirical data, has made theoretical issues the most topically salient and organized all other questions and concerns around these theoretical ones. The organization of his article gives it a substantially different feel when compared to a typical IMRD (Introduction—Methods—Results—Discussion) paper in linguistic anthropology. He offers up interesting empirical data on Received Pronunciation (RP)—a standard register of spoken British English, which is known colloquially as the "Queen's English"—in its historical context and in relation to the various levels of semiosis associated with it. However, these ethnographic and semiotic details are used in the service of making broader claims about how social values associated with certain forms of semiosis are constructed and recognized or *enregistered*. The attribution of importance to theoretical issues can be seen not only in the article itself, but also in the way that it is taken up, as most linguistic anthropologists would reference this piece to put their own work in dialogue with the notion of *enregisterment*, rather than to give their readers a better understanding of RP.

Researchers, thus, have choices about which of the above examples are more similar to what they want to do with their projects. Of course, this will also change across one's research trajectory, as at certain points it may become more important to give detailed, ethnographic accounts and one may write their research questions accordingly, while at other moments, one might want to frame questions more in terms of theoretical implications and/or give more prominence to those questions that are more theoretically oriented. The value of working with theoretically robust ideas is that this can allow for the development of broader theoretical systems in which different topics can be linked together through reference to more broadly applicable theoretical notions. While this is ideal, scholars will not always find themselves building upon their own past research through these relatively smaller shifts in topical salience to build a coherent system, particularly if their past theoretical orientations do not offer them productive ways of engaging with multiple topics and questions. In these cases, one should be open to "unthink" and "rethink" the assumptions and the broader theoretical understandings they have used to enter the field (Blommaert 2010, 2018). This is because the new knowledge that is produced through research— whatever rigorous testing processes it may go through in the interim—is still fundamentally shaped by its initial assumptions and questions.

For instance, a study asking about the differences between "how men talk" versus "how women talk" may use a variety of methods to answer the question and produce new knowledge about variation in patterns of semiosis across these categories. However, the starting question does not allow for critical thinking about what gender is and, furthermore, reinforces the idea that "men" and "women" are real, separable, and relevant categories for investigating language use in its various social contexts. Thus, regardless of whether the study finds similarities or differences between the two categories, the starting assumption is the basis for the analysis by the researcher as *meta-interpreter*, and the interpretation erases heterogeneity within members assigned to the category of either "men" or "women," people with non-binary genders who cannot be assigned to either category, variation in the culture-specific meanings of gender across localities, and the notion of gender as performativity rather than category to begin with (cf., Bucholtz 1999; Butler 1988; Eckert 1989). This brings us to a second way in which research questions determine significance.

1.2.3.2 Interaction of Research Questions and Research Design

Thus far, we have been primarily concerned with how research questions might allow a researcher to contribute to ongoing scholarly conversations within an interconnected system of knowledge production. In other words, we have been discussing how research questions can shape one's work in such a way as to make it significant for the audience that they want to engage.

We now move to consider how research questions are significant in relation to the project itself, in determining the planning of the project, the literature review, the methods, and the way it is written.

Significance in this sense is not only about the topic around which one organizes information, but also about how the choice to attribute topical salience at particular scale levels within a fractal system shapes the way one gathers, and reflects on, this information. In other words, the questions a researcher is operating with construct and constrain their research process, such that their questions influence which literature they will need to review (see Richland, this volume); how they can feasibly plan their research (see Gershon and Jones, this volume); what kind of data they can/should collect and how (see Perrino; Pritzker and Perrino; Mitsuhara and Hauck; Kohler and Murphy; Chun and Crowley; this volume); how they can most productively analyze these data (see Shohet and Loyd; this volume); and where and how they choose to make their work public. Take for instance the case of quantitative versus qualitative versus mixed methods: the choice of one of these methods should not be solely dependent upon disciplinary tradition, personal preference, or academic branding, but rather should be chosen in a way that shapes and is shaped by the questions an analyst is trying to answer.

Analysis of both quantitative and qualitative data contributes to knowledge within the fractal system. *Quantification* is a process that operates in a zoomed-out way, in the sense that details are less clear, but the larger connections and trends become more visible. Data analyzed through such processes provide a *lower resolution* (Karimzad 2021; Karimzad and Catedral 2021) or *flattened* (Kockelman 2006) image of "what is going on" at lower scales, but because it operates at a higher scale, it enables a clarity about broader patterns and creates possibilities for being in conversation with other disciplines (see Pritzker, this volume). On the other hand, if one wants to answer questions about the fractal details of how or why people experience and make sense of certain larger-scale phenomena, it may be necessary for them to use other methods to zoom in and give a higher resolution image of these issues at a lower scale, often involving qualitative approaches. Qualitative studies that aim to unpack "the total linguistic fact" (Silverstein 1985; see also Blommaert 2018; Karimzad 2021; Nakassis 2016) can also allow for creation of links across disciplines and sciences (see Kockelman 2017), when they utilize higher-order theoretical/analytical tools—those that could be recursively applied across scalar levels within the fractal system (Gal 2016; Irvine and Gal 2000). Let us now turn to the significance of topical salience as it relates to ideological and ethical concerns.

1.3 Ethical Considerations

In research, like in any other process in social life, while there are dominant identities, roles, power relations, and ideologies, there is also a multiplicity that creates different centers to which one might orient. The way in which a scholar navigates this type of academic *polycentricity* (Blommaert 2010, 2018) depends on their trajectory and identity as a researcher, but also on the moral and social identities they bring along with themselves from their past experiences, social positionalities, and their belief systems more generally. Here we present some of what we find to be relevant ethical considerations given our own experiences and values as they intersect with values that have been articulated by the field of linguistic anthropology.

One of the ethical considerations relevant to all academic work is the issue of acknowledging and citing the work of others. These individual acts of "giving credit" can be situated within the understanding of the fractal system described in this chapter, which highlights the fact that all knowledge production is dialogical and interconnected (cf., Nakassis 2012). One can say that collective learning is at the heart of knowledge production since scholars are contributing varying levels of fractal details to this system at different scales and in relation to different topics, and because all of these contributions are interconnected and interdiscursive. The fact that all knowledge is connected might lead to the belief that one should cite everything or cite as much as possible. As this is an impossible task, it might be more beneficial to think about citation practices instead as (1) carefully chosen evidence of the researcher's academic biography and trajectory in relation to their investigation of the topic at hand; (2) choices about which scholars and discussions they find useful to put their questions and arguments into conversation with, including those that have been previously overlooked or excluded; and (3) reflections on which materials from others would clarify their topic for the particular audience they have in mind.

Taking these three factors into consideration, let us turn to a particular ethical and ideological issue that may come up in making decisions about citations. While citations are generally understood as "giving credit to sources," what those sources are is a complex issue. Priority tends to be given to "original sources" despite the fact that all text is *re-entextualized* (Bauman and Briggs 1990; Silverstein and Urban 1996). Yet, at times, a scholar's understanding of concepts might come through their engagement with sources that have applied earlier ideas in other contexts or that have synthesized these ideas in relation to other topics. In such situations, while following the interconnections back to earlier sources is valuable, acknowledging the subsequent interpretations and re-applications one has encountered in their own trajectory is also beneficial to one's work and to the field. At the same time, because "expertise" and scholarly importance are constructs embedded in the intersection of gendered, raced, classed, and other marginalizing social practices, scholars should not only consider citing those through whom they have come to an understanding of a relevant topic but may also need to seek out and cite the relevant work of those who have been excluded from or marginalized in academic conversations within the field (see also Bhatt 2005; Kubota 2020). That is, seeking out, incorporating, and citing knowledge that has been undervalued and/or that comes from groups of people that have been systematically marginalized within a scholarly conversation because of race, country of origin, institutional affiliation, gender, ability, and so forth is both an ethically sound practice and one that can lead to particular types of new knowledge through the inclusion of relevant, but overlooked voices. Finally, the attribution of importance through citations may in part differ across disciplines and subdisciplines. Because linguistic anthropology is in many ways an interdisciplinary field, this results in negotiations over which citations are more important or relevant. These negotiations can be seen as a valuable process through which scholars entering linguistic anthropological discussions from other related fields (e.g., linguistics, history, gender studies, media studies, and education) can highlight their own trajectories, use scholarly work that is given prominence in other disciplines, and put all of this into dialogue with ongoing discussions in linguistic anthropology.

While not always interdisciplinary, collaboration in the form of coauthorship can also introduce new types of polycentricity into one's work, meaning that the relevant centers taken into account in navigating a research question multiply when more authors are involved. Many of the examples put forward in this chapter are coauthored works, and while these papers in their final form reflect a coherent narrative, it is likely that along the way each individual author has attributed topical salience to particular issues that differ from those of the topical concerns of the other. Although anthropology and other fields in the social sciences still primarily encourage and reward single-authored work, it is worth acknowledging the extra labor that can go into coauthored scholarship because of the negotiation of additional and at times conflicting views about where to attribute salience. Each author will orient to different aspects of the data and literature when considering the issue at hand, and the dialogic negotiation between the authors over these differing aspects and their intersections can lead to much more refined research questions, which result in more detailed, comprehensive, and higher resolution, theorizations of the relevant topic.

While the practices discussed earlier concern giving salience to the ideas encountered in engagements with the literature and other scholars, there are also ethical considerations in relation to engagements with what one chooses to make topically salient in their empirical data. In the attribution of topical salience, a researcher must necessarily construct margins and peripheries within their research. However, we want to note that making a particular topic central does not always mean that one is valorizing it. For instance, at certain moments a scholar may make dominant discourses of the nation-state topically salient in their work in order to critique these discourses (e.g., Lorente and Tupas 2013). On the other hand, these same scholars or others may choose to focus on groups of people that are impacted by these discourses and who are often overlooked in order to give attention to the concerns and experiences of those who are marginalized along lines of race, gender, and class (e.g., Lorente 2018). Whether one chooses to make a topic central to their work in order to critique it or to valorize it, and how they choose to go about doing this, is also a moral concern that depends in part on their theory of change, as well as their identities as researchers and social actors more generally. It is beyond the scope of this chapter to detail how researchers should go about engaging in this work; however, having a meta-level awareness of *what* one is making central in their work and *why*, and reflecting on how one might want this focus to shift across their trajectory, can allow for engagement with individual and collective moral concerns as researchers choose their research questions. Similarly, while it was noted above that there are no "off limit" topics from the perspective of disciplinary boundaries, this does not mean that linguistic anthropologists should investigate any and all research topics. The *how* and *why* of the investigation, whose interests are being prioritized and whose interests are being overlooked, how concepts are operationalized, and the impact of the research on the real-world situation of marginalized groups are all considerations that might not make a topic outside the bounds of linguistic anthropology but could make it unethical to pursue.

1.4 Case Study: From Observation to Publication: Creating Flexible Research Questions around Discourse, Technology, and Migration

In the earlier sections we have outlined some of the ways in which research questions can emerge; how one can flexibly navigate a fractal system to expand or narrow these questions, how these questions guide, and are guided by, the rest of a research procedure; and some of the ethical considerations that come up in this process. Here, we aim to cover the same issues, but with a focus on one of our own projects (Karimzad and Catedral 2018a) in order to demonstrate how our actual research questions and topics shifted and changed throughout our work on this project. This project started in 2016 and was eventually published in 2018. In order to retrace our experience of working on it, we consulted the abstracts and PowerPoint slides for conference presentations, our notes and multiple drafts, our responses to reviewers, and our own memories of the process. To give a bit more context, when we started this project, we were both graduate students in the same department and were doing fieldwork in different communities of migrants living in the United States for our respective dissertation research. In what follows, we recount the different steps involved in the process of coming up with and refining our research questions.

Step 1: Recognizing a Pattern
Research questions may emerge in part from engagement with the literature and collected data, as noted above, as well as embodied experiences from one's personal life and participant observation (see Pritzker and Perrino, this volume). We were both enrolled in a class on language and superdiversity, in which we read various articles putting forward theories of globalization and transnationalism. Particularly salient, in the early readings for the class, was the role that technology was claimed to have in facilitating transnational connections and identities (cf. Appadurai 1996; Vertovec 2001). Around this time, Farzad, as a migrant himself, had the experience of interacting with his family in Iran over video chat, and while he was talking to his brother, he had noticed his father in the background absorbed in his smart device. Farzad was struck by the image of his father using technology in this independent way with a great deal of familiarity and sustained interest, as the image was

drastically different from the one he remembered when he lived in Iran. That is, when Farzad had left home six years before, his father had had little to no familiarity with new technology whatsoever, making this observation a striking one that gave Farzad a strange feeling of disconnection, which he could not immediately explain. Lydia, on the other hand, was visiting the home of one of her participants living in the Midwest, where a number of women from Uzbekistan had gathered. At some point during the socializing, these women turned to YouTube to play videos of music concerts and various celebrities from Uzbekistan. While those present seemed to enjoy the videos and music, they also used these technologically mediated images as opportunities to critique certain aspects of life in Uzbekistan "these days." For both Farzad and Lydia, these experiences in dialogue with the literature they were engaging led them to feel that explanations of technology as facilitating connection to the homeland were somewhat insufficient. When Farzad approached Lydia about writing a paper together, the experiences that they had had were reformulated into an initial research question along the lines of:

- How exactly is technology "connecting" people and why does it not always make them feel really closely connected to people in the homeland?

Step 2: Consideration of Data in the Formulation of a Question

After reflecting on the preliminary question, there was a consideration of framing it, alternatively, as "Does social media make migrants feel disconnected?" The idea was to explore this question by using large-scale data mined from social media to tease out and quantify instances in which expressions of disconnection were articulated by migrants. However, after further reflection and revisiting the types of data that we had already collected, we decided that it made more sense to explore these questions of disconnection through a discourse analytic investigation of how social media were invoked and talked about in migrants' discourses. This led us to reformulate the question yet again as:

- How do migrants invoke social media in their discursive construction of their identities and in their adequation and differentiation with those in the homeland?

Using this question to guide us, we revisited old data and also continued to collect new data, paying particular attention to the invocation of social media and new technologies in our participants' discourses.

Step 3: Consideration of Theoretical and Analytical Tools

In our formulation of the above research question we were already drawing on some of our theoretical knowledge regarding language and identity in order to make the question more specific. However, we were also continuing to read the latest theories of identity and semiosis and were working on other projects that influenced our approach. Specifically, we were coauthoring another paper in which we had utilized the notion of chronotope to discuss migrants' language ideologies and practices (Karimzad and Catedral 2018b). We found the notion of chronotope to be useful across multiple contexts and decided to try and apply it to our data for this project in order to give a more detailed and comprehensive account of *how* exactly migrants were experiencing these technologically mediated feelings of disconnection from the homeland. In working to apply this theory, we decided to propose the notion of *rechronotopization* or the dynamic process of transforming chronotopic images. Our idea was that migrants updated their chronotopic images of the homeland (i.e., rechronotopized them) in response to the new information they received via new technology and that this process often led to feelings of disconnection for them. Thus, at this stage, we began to operate in relation to multiple research questions that were oriented to both empirical and theoretical issues:

- How do Iranian and Uzbek migrants in our data invoke new technologies in their discursive (dis)alignment with those in the homeland?
- How do migrants rechronotopize, or update their chronotopic images of, the homeland in relation to information they receive via new technology?

These research questions guided us through to the first full draft of our manuscript, and at this point we submitted it to a journal for publication.

Step 4: Incorporating Reviewer Comments and Further Refinement

The main concerns raised by the reviewers were that the paper felt a bit fragmented and that other scholars of migration had already made claims about migrants feeling disconnected, even when being in touch with those in the homeland via new technologies. In order to differentiate our work from the work of those they referred us to, we considered the details of our theory and data to see where specifically we were adding nuance to knowledge about technology and migration. Additionally, in order to make our work more coherent, we decided to make the notion of rechronotopization—which was initially discussed in relation to only some parts of our argument—more central to all aspects of the manuscript. While the rewriting required an incorporation of new literature and some additional explanation, this was mostly about organizing new information around the same topically salient issues. That is to say, our research questions did not shift drastically, but rather we shifted them in relation to one another, such that they were all organized around the central theme of rechronotopization.

- How do migrants update their chronotopic images of the homeland in relation to information they receive via new technology?
- How do these new images impact their (dis)alignment patterns with those in the homeland?
- What does a theory of rechronotopization add to our understanding of identity, space, and time?

At this point we continued to clarify some details of the paper, but the research questions remained fairly intact the way they are presented here until its final publication (Karimzad and Catedral 2018a).

Step 5: Extending Central Questions

While this project concluded in 2018, we have continued to make the notion of rechronotopization central in our subsequent individual and collaborative projects. That is, the notion of rechronotopization has continued to feature in our research questions, but the data and theories in which we situate these questions differ, as does the attribution of topical salience. For us, this has led to a broader understanding of the multiple contexts in which the notion of rechronotopization can apply, but also to a more fully theorized and expanded understanding of (re)chronotopization, as a primary socialization and social learning process (Karimzad 2020, 2021; Karimzad and Catedral 2021). In fact, the ideas we have presented in this chapter stem from such theorization and discussion. All of this is to say that coming up with certain research questions can lead to other related research questions (with shifts in data, situatedness, and topical salience) beyond one particular project, helping to construct a larger, coherent research agenda.

1.5 Conclusion

In this chapter, we have applied linguistic anthropological theories of semiosis and metasemiosis to processes of knowledge production and, more specifically, to the process of crafting compelling research questions. In so doing, we have turned linguistic anthropological tools on linguistic anthropology itself in order to improve our research methods (cf., Briggs 1986). Our goal in using these tools reflexively is to make the processes involved in our work as researchers more explicit, less mystified and, as such, more empowering.

The fractal system not only allows us to situate our work within a broader system of knowledge production, it furthermore gives us an explanatory tool for understanding the process of developing and refining a research question before, throughout, and after collecting data. It also supports researchers in maintaining awareness of their own positions and identities as they move along this trajectory. We have tried to present meta reflections on the system within which particular projects can be imagined and to show how these projects are also organized in relation to central themes and arguments within the field. Understanding both the internal system of projects and the ways in which they can be situated in relation to a larger system brings clarity to the process of navigating and considering the limitations and possibilities of one's academic work. The way in which researchers traverse this system has implications for their trajectories as scholars in that they will present themselves in part, as people who focus on some particular topics in relation to specific ongoing conversations. In this sense, the research questions that one works with are not only defining what one gives salience to, but also over time, and in shifting ways, are defining some aspects of one's identity as a researcher.

While all scholars have some degree of choice over what they give prominence to in their work, not all researchers and not all projects have the same degree of flexibility, depending on the particularities of the research arrangements in which people are engaged. The material conditions in which researchers in different positions are working will also have a significant impact on the flexibility they have in terms of giving time and space to engage in the iterative process of research. Access to resources may also differ in terms of having the financial and institutional support necessary to survive inside and outside academic settings. Additionally, the various and intersecting social positionalities of researchers may result in their work being evaluated through the lens of their perceived (lack of) prestige or competence, rather than its own merits (cf., the notion of *indexical inversion*, Inoue 2003; Rosa and Flores 2017). Given the unequal, real-world conditions involved in knowledge production, how then might we think about the system we have laid out here as an empowering one for researchers?

We do not intend to argue that by navigating topical possibilities and creating good research questions a scholar can determine how their work is read, whether or not it will be taken up in the field, or how it will impact their ultimate trajectories as academics. Rather, in invoking empowerment, we find it useful to draw on Kockelman's idea of a multiplicity of agencies. We would refer to what we have put forward here as providing scholars of language in society with a type of "representational agency," which relates to managing knowledge and power (Foucault 1980) in terms of utilizing choices about "what we argue about" and "how we argue" (Kockelman 2007, 384). In being more explicit and specific about what is involved in creating research questions, we hope to have demystified some of the processes at work in the academic system of knowledge production in order to enable a more conscious ability to agentively navigate choices—at least at the level of topics.

1.6 Ethnographic Activities

1 Below we have provided some brief excerpts from the case study discussed in the chapter. The data come from a participant we refer to as Erfan, an Iranian Azerbaijani educational migrant living in the United States, as he is discussing his experience of migration. The original text is on the left, while the translation into English is on the right. Note that the original text is in multiple languages: Azeri, Farsi, and English in regular, italicized, and bolded fonts, respectively. Read through the data and see what issues draw your attention. Use this reflection to try and come up with three research questions that allow you to zoom in on particular aspects of the data, following the process laid out for you in Section 1.2.2.

1. **E:** Burda rahatsan, chox rahatsan. Müshkülün yoxdi. væli bir elemanlari var, xa:tiræ zatdar, millætin, oki mæsælæn danɪshmɪllar sænin diliyæn ((water running)). Mæsælæn bæyram mænæ mæsælæn hæmishæ böyüh **example** di.	1. **E:** Here, You're comfortable. You're very comfortable. You don't have any problems. But there are some elements, memories and stuff, your people, the fact that, for instance they don't speak your language ((water running)). For instance, Nowruz for me, for instance, is always a big **example**.

2. **F:** uhum	2. **F:** uhum
3. **E:** Mæsælæn Esfand, sæn næ ha:li olurdun Iranda? ((water running)) burda o yoxdi. Do:reye Christmas-dæ dæ, **you don't have the same feeling.** Væ budi ki mæn choxtær ehsa:s-e **disconnection** eli:ræm. Yani buki hæmishæ, biliræm ki **immigrant**-am. **I don't belong here.** (…)	3. **E:** For example, Esfand (the last month of the Iranian calendar), How would you feel in Iran? ((water running)). It doesn't exist here. During Christmas time, **you don't have the same feeling.** This is why I feel more **disconnected**. It means that always, I know that I am an **immigrant. I don't belong here.** (…)
10. **E:** Vaqeæn **obviously** hæm Iraniæm (0.3) bi: jænbeha'i æz Amrika'i varımdi, væli næ **full** Iraniæm, næ **full** Amrika'i. Bir shey væsætdeyæm. Sizlærinæn bizlær mæsælæn ba:hæm, yani bizlær ba:hæm ertebatımız, yani biz özümüzi behtær düshünürıx. Væli chox **minority**-dayıx. Væ **obviously** özünæ göræ bir **culture** di (0.2) væli xob **recognized** döli æslæn be hich onvan. Yani æslæn hæmishæ ehsas eli:sæn ki dær va:qe væsætdæsæn (0.2) yani demillær ki sænin **culture**-in var. Diyillær *sæn æz inja rande æz unja mandæ*-sæn.	10. **E:** Actually I am **obviously** both Iranian (0.3) and I also have some American characteristics, but I am neither **fully** Iranian nor **fully** American. I am something in the middle. You guys and us together, I mean our connection with each other, I mean, we understand ourselves better. But we are so much in **minority**. And **obviously** it is a **culture** in and of itself, (0.2) but, well, it is not **recognized** whatsoever. I mean you always feel that you are in fact somewhere in the middle (0.2) I mean they don't say that you have a **culture**, they say you *have fallen between the cracks*.
11. **F:** hmm	11. **F:** hmm
12. **E:** Sikimxia:ri bæhsdi (0.2) ((sighs)) æsfordæ-konændæ bæhsdi.	12. **E:** It is a fucked-up topic (0.2) ((sighs)) It is a depressing topic.

2 Think about how the research questions you came up with for Activity 1 could be related to each other and about the additional ethnographic information you would need in order to answer these questions.

3 Look at an academic text you have recently read. What did you highlight or make notes on? Use this to reflect on what you are giving *topical salience* to in this reading. If possible, compare with a peer to see similarities and differences. What does this activity reveal about possible individual or collaborative research interests and ideas?

1.7 Questions to Consider

1 We have described differences between disciplines according to the attribution of topical salience. How could you use this idea to think about getting involved in developing a research question for a study in linguistic anthropology? What about in interdisciplinary research?

2 We say that no topics are "off limits" for linguistic anthropologists. Think of a topic that seems unrelated to the field and discuss how you might study it as a linguistic anthropologist. What kind of situation might make a topic not necessarily "off-limits" but unethical?

3 Although linguistic anthropology promotes flexibility in developing research questions, at what point do you think one should stop refining a research question and solidify it?

4 We have noted that the "so what?" question in response to someone's research can be difficult to answer because it is vague. How could you frame this question in a more situated and specific way to ask about the significance/value of a particular research topic?

5 In our conclusion, we argue that this chapter has been about using linguistic anthropological tools to understand how to come up with research questions and topics. Are there other ideas from linguistic anthropology that you find useful for thinking about topics and research questions?

1.8 Note

1 Image attribution by row:
(1) "Sierpinsky triangle" by Dmitry Djouce is licensed under CC BY 2.0 https://www.flickr.com/photos/46721940@N00/272393590
(2) "Foliage in fractal pattern" by dizznan is licensed under CC BY-SA 2.0 https://www.flickr.com/photos/32122437@N00/126275632
(3) "最美的蔬菜–Romanesco Cauliflower" by IsaacMao is licensed under CC BY 2.0 https://www.flickr.com/photos/isaacmao/74151462
(4) "Romanesco—fractal cauliflower" by dailyfood is licensed under CC BY 2.0 https://www.flickr.com/photos/28970677@N04/4655214681

1.9 References Cited

Agha, A. 2003. "The Social Life of Cultural Value." *Language & Communication* 23 (3–4): 231–73.

Agha, A. 2007a. "Recombinant Selves in Mass Mediated Spacetime." *Language & Communication* 27 (3): 320–35.

Agha, A. 2007b. *Language and Social Relations.* New York: Cambridge University Press.

Alim, H. S., and G. Smitherman. 2012a. *Articulate while Black: Barack Obama, Language, and Race in the U.S.* New York: Oxford University Press.

Alim, H. S., and G. Smitherman. 2012b. "Obama's English," *The New York Times*, 8 September.

Alim, H. S., and G. Smitherman. 2020. "Of Course Kamala Harris Is Articulate," *The New York Times*, 8 September.

Appadurai, A. 1996. *Modernity at Large: Cultural Dimensions of Globalization.* Minneapolis, MN: University of Minnesota Press.

Bakhtin, M. 1981. *The Dialogical Imagination.* Austin: University of Texas Press.

Bauman, R., and C. L. Briggs. 1990. "Poetics and Performances as Critical Perspectives on Language and Social Life." *Annual Review of Anthropology* 19 (1): 59–88.

Bhatt, R. M. 2005. "Expert Discourses, Local Practices, and Hybridity: The Case of Indian Englishes." In S. Canagarajah ed., *Reclaiming the Local in Language Policy and Practice*, 25–54. New York: Routledge.

Blommaert, J. 2010. *The Sociolinguistics of Globalization.* New York: Cambridge University Press.

Blommaert, J. 2015. "Chronotopes, Scales, and Complexity in the Study of Language in Society." *Annual Review of Anthropology* 44: 105–16.

Blommaert, J. 2018. *Durkheim and the Internet: Sociolinguistics and the Sociological Imagination.* London: Bloomsbury.

Blommaert, J. 2020. "Sociolinguistic Scales in Retrospect." *Applied Linguistics Review.* https://doi.org/10.1515/applirev-2019-0132.

Blommaert, J., and A. De Fina. 2017. "Chronotopic Identities: On the Timespace Organization of Who We Are." In A. De Fina and J. Wegner eds., *Diversity and Super-diversity*, 1–14. Washington, DC: Georgetown University Press.

Briggs, C. L. 1986. *Learning How to Ask: A Sociolinguistic Appraisal of the Role of the Interview in Social Science Research.* Cambridge: Cambridge University Press.

Bucholtz, M. 1999. "'Why Be Normal?': Language and Identity Practices in a Community of Nerd Girls." *Language in Society* 28 (2): 203–23.

Bucholtz, M., and K. Hall. 2004. "Language and Identity." In A. Duranti ed., *A Companion to Linguistic Anthropology*, 369–94. Malden, MA: Blackwell Publishing.

Bucholtz, M., and K. Hall. 2005. "Identity and Interaction: A Sociocultural Linguistic Approach." *Discourse Studies* 7 (4–5): 585–614.

Butler, J. 1988. "Performative Acts and Gender Constitution: An Essay in Phenomenology and Feminist Theory." *Theatre Journal* 40 (4): 519–31.

Canagarajah, S., and P. I. De Costa. 2016. "Introduction: Scales Analysis, and Its Uses and Prospects in Educational Linguistics." *Linguistics and Education* 34: 1–10.

Carr, E. S., and M. Lempert. 2016. "Introduction: Pragmatics of Scale." In E. S. Carr and M. Lempert eds., *Scale: Discourse and Dimensions of Social Life*, 1–21. Oakland: University of California Press.

Catedral, L. 2018. "Discursive Scaling: Moral Stability and Neoliberal Dominance in the Narratives of Transnational Migrant Women." *Discourse & Society* 29 (1): 23–42.

De Fina, A. 2011. "Discourse and Identity." In T. A. Van Dijk ed., *Discourse Studies: A Multidisciplinary Introduction*, 263–82. London: Sage Publications.

Dick, H. 2010. "Imagined Lives and Modernist Chronotopes in Mexican Nonmigrant Discourse." *American Ethnologist* 37: 275–90.

Eckert, P. 1989. *Jocks and Burnouts: Social Categories and Identity in the High School*. New York: Teachers College Press.

Foucault, M. 1972. *The Archaeology of Knowledge*. London: Tavistock Publications.

Foucault, M. 1980. *Power/Knowledge: Selected Interviews and Other Writings 1972–1977*. New York: Pantheon Books.

Gal, S. 2016. "Scale-making: Comparison and Perspective as Ideological Projects." In E. S. Carr and M. Lempert eds., *Scale: Discourse and Dimensions of Social Life*, 91–111. Oakland: University of California Press.

Gal, S. 2018. "Discursive Struggles about Migration: A Commentary." *Language & Communication* 59: 66–9.

Inoue, M. 2003. "Speech without a Speaking Body: 'Japanese Women's Language' in Translation." *Language & Communication* 23 (3–4): 315–30.

Irvine, J., and S. Gal. 2000. "Language Ideology and Linguistic Differentiation." In P. Kroskrity ed., *Regimes of Language: Ideologies, Polities and Identities*, 35–83. Santa Fe, NM: School of American Research Press.

Jørgensen, M. W., and L. J. Phillips. 2002. *Discourse Analysis as Theory and Method*. London, UK: Sage Publications.

Karimzad, F. 2020. "Metapragmatics of Normalcy: Mobility, Context, and Language Choice." *Language & Communication* 70: 107–18.

Karimzad, F. 2021. "Multilingualism, Chronotopes, and Resolutions: Toward an Analysis of the Total Sociolinguistic Fact." *Applied Linguistics, amaa053*, https://doi.org/10.1093/applin/amaa053.

Karimzad, F., and L. Catedral. 2018a. "Mobile (Dis)Connection: New Technology and Rechronotopized Images of the Homeland." *Journal of Linguistic Anthropology* 28 (3): 293–312.

Karimzad, F., and L. Catedral. 2018b. "'No, We Don't Mix Languages': Ideological Power and the Chronotopic Organization of Ethnolinguistic Identities." *Language in Society* 47 (1): 89–113.

Karimzad, F., and L. Catedral. 2021. *Chronotopes and Migration: Language, Imagination, and Social Behavior*. New York: Routledge.

Kockelman, P. 2006. "A Semiotic Ontology of the Commodity." *Journal of Linguistic Anthropology* 16 (1): 76–102.

Kockelman, P. 2007. "Agency: The Relation between Meaning, Power, and Knowledge." *Current Anthropology* 48 (3): 375–87.

Kockelman, P. 2017. *The Art of Interpretation in the Age of Computation*. New York: Oxford University Press.

Koven, M. 2013. "Antiracist, Modern Selves and Racist, Unmodern Others: Chronotopes of Modernity in Luso-descendants' Race Talk." *Language and Communication* 33: 544–58.

Kubota, R. 2020. "Confronting Epistemological Racism, Decolonizing Scholarly Knowledge: Race and Gender in Applied Linguistics." *Applied Linguistics* 41 (5): 712–32.

Lorente, B. P. 2018. *Scripts of Servitude: Language, Labor Migration and Transnational Domestic Work*. Bristol, UK: Multilingual Matters.

Lorente, B. P., and R. F. Tupas. 2013. "(Un)emancipatory Hybridity: Selling English in an Unequal World." In R. Rubdy and L. Alsagoff eds., *The Global-local Interface and Hybridity: Exploring Language and Identity*, 66–82. Bristol/Buffalo/Toronto: Multilingual Matters.

Mannheim, B. 2018. "Preliminary Disciplines." *Signs and Society* 6 (1): 111–19.

Mayes, P., and H. Tao. 2019. "Referring Expressions in Categorizing Activities: Rethinking the Nature of Linguistic Units for the Study of Interaction." *Studies in Language* 43 (2): 329–63.

Moore, R. 2020. "Registers, Styles, Indexicality." In A. De Fina and A. Georgakopoulou eds., *The Cambridge Handbook of Discourse Studies*, 9–31. Cambridge: Cambridge University Press.

Nakassis, C. V. 2012. "Brand, Citationality, Performativity." *American Anthropologist* 114 (4): 624–38.

Nakassis, C. V. 2016. "Linguistic Anthropology in 2015: Not the Study of Language." *American Anthropologist* 118 (2): 330–45.

Perrino, S., and G. Kohler. 2020. "Chronotopic Identities: Narrating Made in Italy across Spatiotemporal Scales." *Language & Communication* 70: 94–106.

Pritzker, S. E. 2016. "New Age with Chinese Characteristics? Translating Inner Child Emotion Pedagogies in Contemporary China." *Ethos* 44 (2): 150–70.

Pritzker, S. E., and S. Perrino. 2020. "Culture Inside: Scale, Intimacy, and Chronotopic Stance in Situated Narratives." *Language in Society*. Online First: doi: 101981.

Rosa, J., and N. Flores. 2017. "Unsettling Race and Language: Toward a Raciolinguistic Perspective." *Language in Society* 46 (5): 621–47.

Silverstein, M. 1981. "Metaforces of Power in Traditional Oratory." Ms. Read to PERL Lecture Series, *The Rhetoric of Politics*, University of Chicago, January.

Silverstein, Michael (1985a). Language and the culture of gender: At the intersection of structure, usage, and ideology. In Mertz, Elizabeth & Parmentier, Richard J. (eds.), *Semiotic mediation: Sociocultural and psychological perspectives*, 219–59. Orlando, FL: Academic Press.

Silverstein, M. 1992. "The Indeterminacy of Contextualization: When Is Enough Enough?" In P. Auer and A. Di Luzio eds., *The Contextualization of Language*, 55–76. Amsterdam: John Benjamins Publishing.

Silverstein M. 1993. "Metapragmatic Discourse and Meta-pragmatic Function." In J. Lucy ed., *Reflexive Language*, 32–58. New York: Cambridge University Press.

Silverstein, M. 2005. "Axes of Evals: Token vs. Type Interdiscursivity." *Journal of Linguistic Anthropology* 15 (1): 6–22.

Silverstein, M., and G. Urban, eds. 1996. *Natural Histories of Discourse*. Chicago, IL: University of Chicago Press.

Urban, G. 2018. "The Role of Metaforces in Cultural Motion." *Signs and Society* 6 (1): 256–80.

Vertovec, S. 2001. "Transnationalism and Identity." *Journal of Ethnic and Migration Studies* 27 (4): 573–82.

Wirtz, K. 2014. *Performing Afro-Cuba: Image, Voice, Spectacle in the Making of Race and History*. Chicago, IL: University of Chicago Press.

Woolard, K. 2013. "Is the Personal Political? Chronotopes and Changing Stances toward Catalan Language and Identity." *International Journal of Bilingual Education and Bilingualism* 16 (2): 210–24.

1.10 Further Reading

Agee, J. 2009. "Developing Qualitative Research Questions: A Reflective Process." *International Journal of Qualitative Studies in Education* 22 (4): 431–47.

Heller, M., Pietikäinen, S., and J. Pujolar. 2017. *Critical Sociolinguistic Research Methods: Studying Language Issues That Matter*. New York: Routledge.

2

Reviewing the Literature in Linguistic Anthropology

Justin B. Richland

2.1 Introduction

There are many different ways to consider the question of how to undertake a review of literature for a project in linguistic anthropology. The most straightforward approach is to recount what I have found works best for me. I start my efforts by perusing established venues that publish annotated bibliographies and literature reviews about certain key topics; the *Annual Review of Anthropology*,[1] the *Oxford Bibliographies of Anthropology*,[2] and the Year in Review section of the *American Anthropologist*[3] are three resources that I have come to rely on when I need to take my first dive into the extant anthropological literatures. I then cross-check the import of texts that seem most relevant to me, or most important in the reviews I have read, by doing additional database searches for how those texts are being cited in even more recent scholarship. I regularly find that practices, which were central to doing library-based research in the pre-digital era, are still relevant and useful today. This includes going to the physical stacks of books or journals in the topic areas where some key texts are shelved and simply perusing what else appears there that might also speak to your project but which wouldn't have been captured by your natural language digital database searches and thus otherwise overlooked.

I regularly use all of these approaches, being careful to keep track of the terms of my database searches and the titles and author names of relevant texts, until certain texts would start to repeatedly emerge across my searches. To me, the reemergence signals that these texts were either the articles, books, and other textual materials that were continuously being cited by other authors or central to the themes being captured by my choice of search terms. And this is how I ensure that I had hit upon the key works in the extant literature, both in terms of import to the relevant fields of scholarship and because they so overlapped with how I described the main themes of my own project.

After speaking with colleagues in linguistic anthropology and other fields, I have heard them describe practices similar to my own. Nonetheless, this way of describing the literature review process leaves too much underdetermined. Indeed, when I first started out developing my own research agendas in graduate school, I quickly discovered that what I had initially thought were the relevant concepts and theoretical commitments of my ethnographic project turned out to not entirely match up with the way those concepts and theories were being described in the relevant literatures I was encountering. As a result, I either missed entire bodies of scholarship with which my project should have been in conversation simply because I was using a particular search terminology, or I would abandon a potentially fruitful way of thinking about my topic because I assumed that I was conceptualizing it in a way that was fundamentally wrong. Neither was necessarily true, of course. But only time and experience allowed me to eventually realize that with literature reviews there is always the risk of getting tricked by the path dependencies of our preliminary search queries into thinking that what is initially turned up is all there is to know about a given subject.

In light of this risk, I think it is important to reflect more broadly on what a review of the literature in fact entails and how to go about the accomplishment of the literature review as part and parcel of the particular way in which a linguistic anthropologist does her work. Insofar as texts, and people's engagement with them, constitute one of the key objects of linguistic anthropological inquiry, reflecting on what we are up to when we review the literatures relevant to our projects provides us a unique opportunity to consider the pragmatics and metapragmatics of the work of academic scholarship more generally. At the same time, in saying this I don't intend to fetishize what I call "literature" or its "review." For me, this would push against the very gains that so much linguistic anthropological investigation of reading and textuality (Boyarin 1992; Collins and Blot 2003; Finnegan 1988; Heath 1983) have made in overthrowing earlier social scientific scholarship (Goody and Watt 1963; Ong 1982), which argued that "literacy" constitutes a cognitive and social phenomenon different in kind than orality.

Instead my approach in this chapter to the doing of a literature review is informed by what I have learned from the linguistic anthropological scholarship on entextualization, intertextuality, and citationality (Agha 2005; Bauman and Briggs 1990; Goodman et al. 2014; Nakassis 2013; Silverstein and Urban 1996). This scholarship, like much of linguistic anthropology generally, takes its inspiration from some combination of Mikhail Bakhtin's (1981, 1984) theories of dialogism, J. L. Austin's (1962) performativity, and Roman Jakobson's (1960) communicative functions model of language use. As such, much of the work on intertextuality and citationality orients to the ways in which the engagement with texts (whether written or spoken) always involves a communicative act that re-presents a prior token of text or discourse in a current context of social action and does so in ways that, to varying degrees, foregrounds and elides how the re-presented text is constituted through a performative admixture of preservation and innovation in the forms and meanings attributed to it in the present. Theories of intertextuality and citationality show that speech acts re-presenting prior talk and texts do so to effectuate some social act that, in the specific contexts of their accomplishment, has consequences (intended and unintended) in the unfolding arcs of the social present. Linguistic anthropologists, analyzing texts for their intertextual and citational elements, thus interpret those forms and contents in light of the social activities to which they contribute.

Thus, for example, my citing of Bakhtin's scholarship in the previous paragraph with the paraphrastic reference to his "theories of dialogism," coupled with the in-line citation, "(Bakhtin 1981, 1984)," only alludes to the actual formal content of Bakhtin's re-presented texts. There are no direct quotations here. The intertextual format I chose for the previous citation elides the differences between those aspects of his original text that could be considered preserved, and those that are my own innovations, behind a veneer scholars sometimes call "summarizing," "paraphrasing," or "glossing."

I could have employed a different form of citation to the text in question, perhaps re-presenting as a direct quote Bakhtin's famous line, "I live in a world of other's words" (1984, 143). Had I done that the reader would have been pointed more explicitly to those parts of Bakhtin's theory I was specifically referencing, and thereby getting the sense that I was specifically invoking his ideas of heteroglossia in the course of suggesting how linguistic anthropologists ought to think about literature reviews. But it would have also revealed that the text to which I was citing, the 1984 edition of his

Problems with Dostoyevsky's Poetics, was in fact Caryl Emerson's translation of a book originally published in Russian in 1963 and which itself was a second edition of an even earlier book published in 1929 (Bakhtin 1984, xxix).

Arguably, this alternative mode of intertextual citation would have more explicitly maintained the distinction between the form and content from Bakhtin's original text (or really, Emerson's intertextual transduced gloss of Bakhtin's 1963 text) and those accretions of form and content to which I might seek to add to it by my re-presenting it here. But it still would also pull the original line of text ("I live in a world of others' words") out of the co-textual surround in which it was originally entextualized (again, by Emerson), thereby leaving a lot of Bakhtin's original meaning perhaps still elided and underdetermined. Even more, by doing this, I would have risked foregrounding for the reader a whole different set of co-textual concerns, directing their attention to matters of textual provenance and the accuracy of translations that are far afield from my reasons for citing to Bakhtin's work in the first place, namely a discussion of literature reviews in linguistic anthropological projects.

What this example reveals is that, as Bauman, Briggs, Nakassis, and others have persuasively argued, attending to *how* we mark our communicative acts as embedded in intertextual chains that re-present and re-purpose prior texts and discourses is just as consequential for our claims as deciding *what* texts and discourses we re-present. It thus behooves us, as linguistic anthropologists, to understand how our own scholarship reviews extant literature and how these necessarily intertextual aspects of our work shape the meanings of the prior texts they re-present, while also informing how we come to understand the novel insights we hope to impart through our own ethnographic analyses.

In what follows, I discuss some of the challenges and opportunities that the intertextual effects of literature reviews offer to the specific ways in which linguistic anthropological research proceeds for those scholars who remain committed to the intentionally open-ended quality of ethnographic research. But these are not just methodological or analytical issues; they are ethical ones as well. I thus consider some of the ethics entailed in the work of preparing an effective literature review and how sometimes it is precisely where the ethical representation of others' work emerges as an issue that the real contributions our own scholarship can make are revealed. Then, I will describe two cases from my own experience that highlighted these issues for me and that have helped me refine my own practices of "re-viewing" literatures. I call them "tales" in Section 2.4. Finally, I end the chapter with several discussion questions and an exercise that can be used to help test whether or not a literature review is successful in striking the balance between ensuring that one's work is properly marked, intertextually and citationally, as embedded in relevant scholarly texts and discourses that have come before it, while at the same time remaining open to the lessons and insights gained from the novel experiences of one's ethnographic field research.

2.2 The Peril and Promise of Literature Reviews for Linguistic Anthropological Scholarship Grounded in Ethnographic Fieldwork

As linguistic anthropologists, we are both predisposed and trained to think about language less as a discrete object and more as a social practice, a toolkit whose content and form are thoroughly shaped by, and likewise shape, the social activities accomplished through them. For some of us, we agree with our colleagues' in sociocultural anthropology (albeit with our own distinct methodological and technological flourishes) in thinking that the best way to study language is through ethnographic inquiry or what the eminent legal and sociocultural anthropologist, Dame Marilyn Strathern, once described as "the deliberate attempt to generate more data than the investigator is aware of at the time of collection" (Strathern 2004, 5). That is, linguistic anthropological work grounded in ethnographic field research is singularly unique in the humanistic and social sciences that study language in that we don't decide in advance what methods and data will be necessarily relevant for understanding the role that language plays in the sites of social engagement we are investigating.

Strathern continues her characterization of the ethnographic method, describing it as "a participatory exercise which yields materials for which analytic protocols are often devised after the fact" (Strathern 2004, 5–6). If we agree with this characterization, we arguably see a tension between the pursuit of our particular kind of open-ended inquiry and the need of things like "literature reviews" to situate our work in the context of the scholarship that has come before it. Ethnographic inquiry demands, to the extent possible, that we don't decide ahead of time what will and will not count as relevant data before collecting it. This is what makes ethnographic fieldwork so rewarding, but also intensive, immersive, and challenging. I certainly have had the feeling, both during and after fieldwork, of being utterly convinced in the relevance of almost every aspect of the sociocultural and interactional contexts I had set out to ethnographically account for, and thus overwhelmed, almost to the point of panic, at the prospect of ever making sense of any of it. In those moments, some channeling of my attention was helpful in getting me through the shock of trying to account for it all and a turn to the extant scholarship was always helpful in this. At the same time, it is also absolutely true, at least in my experience, that my most important analytic insights and perspectives came from my parts of my fieldnotes that I can remember thinking at the time were largely about uninteresting or unimportant details. And sometimes I wondered how much I might have missed because my hewing so closely to the extant scholarship trained my attention away from the novelty of my particular moment of ethnographic fieldwork.

Reckoning with this tension and helping others in identifying and working through it seem a paramount concern when talking about literature reviews in linguistic anthropology. At least for me, an effective literature review demands something more than an exhaustive survey of the extant scholarship in one, two, or even multiple areas of ostensibly relevant scholarship.

Instead, an effective review of the literature is one that captures both the analytic question motivating an anthropologist's decision to pursue a particular inquiry (and, I would argue, ideally emerging from the site of one's inquiry itself) and also how that question emerges from and responds to insights and limitations of the scholarship that has come before. Failure to adequately attend to the former leads to doubts about what one hopes to learn from a new project, while failure to attend to the latter just leaves readers wondering why they should care about the inquiry in the first place.

What kinds of techniques and tools might put us in the best position to review the literature relevant to our specific linguistic anthropological inquiries? How each of us answers this question, I would suggest, is not just an issue of our particular scholarly contribution; it is also one of professional ethics (see also Black and Conley Riner, this volume).

2.3 The Ethics of Literature Review

The most obvious ethical issue with regard to reviewing any literature is, of course, the question of proper attribution and citation to authorities and relevant works on which your own arguments are based. Different scholarly disciplines have different citational conventions. In the publishing conventions of legal scholarship, for example, proper attribution of extant scholarship is a much more elaborated affair than it is in anthropological writing. Even a quick perusal of a leading law review journal will show that, in any given article, virtually every assertion comes with a footnote citation to the point that often the footnotes take up more space on the printed page than the main text.

Publications that appear in anthropological outlets don't ever go that far, but it is of course wise to give credit where credit is due.

At the same time, the issue is typically more complicated than simply citing more often than not. This is true for a couple of reasons. First there is the idea, sometimes attributed (apocryphally, I think) to Alfred Einstein, that "the secret to creativity is knowing how to hide your sources." In linguistic anthropological scholarship, Marjorie Goodwin and Asta Cekaite make a related claim, arguing, "Creativity can be viewed as the achieved product of selectively recombining and reworking the walk or actions of another ... to transform talk" (Goodwin and Cekaite 2018, 195). And while we might cynically read this as saying that there is nothing ever new under the sun, I am inclined to interpret the insight differently. That is, that in some ways, citing too much, or otherwise claiming that one is merely bringing forward the insights and arguments of others can be a rather convenient way to avoid taking responsibility for one's own claims. Thinking of the hyper-citationality of legal scholarship in this light reveals how novelty and creativity might be something that one would rather not claim for their work, if by doing so they open themselves up to criticism.

This leads to a second ethical complication around matters of literature review. And that is the question of whether it is even possible to ascertain where the influence of someone else's work on your own ends and where your novel contribution begins. As Richard Bauman's and Charles Briggs's important work on entextualization long ago showed (Bauman and Briggs 1990; Briggs and Bauman 1992), the management of intertextual gaps between a present text and those that came before it is an ongoing accomplishment, in which the expansion or contraction of those gaps signals different kinds of commitments, political, ethical, and otherwise, that authors have to the audiences of their work. As they taught us, there is no quick and dirty rule (beyond some baseline perhaps, that if you are using a direct quote, cite it) for how intertextuality should be handled by an author, and so I cannot offer one here. Rather, I would suggest that the ethics of citation and of reviewing literature more generally demand that we be aware of and consciously reflect on how our work relates to that which comes before—drawing on, adding to, or diverging from it—and that in the process we acknowledge, generally, how our scholarship is always, invariably, in conversation with that which has come before.

I would even suggest that the question of the nature of this conversation, and how it is captured in literature reviews, not only involves matters of scholarly ethics, it actually comes to inform the process of our thinking and argumentation as well. Consider these issues in the following two stories from my own experiences over the course of my career. Both reveal, I think, the promise and peril that reviewing literature holds for linguistic anthropological inquiry in particular.

2.4 Tales of Promise and Peril in My Experiences with Reviewing Literature

2.4.1 A Tale of Promise: Answering the "Hasn't everything been said about that already?" question

I remember quite clearly the first time I described my dissertation research to an eminent anthropologist from outside my immediate circle of graduate advisors and other professors with whom I worked on the way to completing my PhD. We were actually introduced through family connections and she had graciously offered to meet with me over tea at her house when I happened to be passing through her area. I was particularly keen to discuss my project with her because she is one of the world's leading legal anthropologists.

My research at the time emerged from work I had been doing in the legal system of the Hopi Tribal Nation, first as a law student and then, after graduating from law school, as a researcher and clerk for the Justices of the Hopi Appellate Court, the Hopi Nation's highest court. Specifically, the Justices were facing a slew of cases that had come before them in which at their heart concerned matters of what Hopi litigants and the tribe's law called "Hopi custom and tradition."

The Justices wanted someone to explore the circumstances and consequences of Hopi tribal members who decide to file complaints in a court that relied on Anglo-American legal norms of adversarial due process, where both sides have to prove their cases in open court before a Hopi judge. But upon getting to the court, Hopi litigants would often attempt to argue their claims based on Hopi *navoti* (which they translate as "tradition"), which was grounded in Hopi norms that turned on the exclusive and secretly held knowledge and authority of ceremonial leaders and which couldn't be told in public hearings. The opposing demands made on Hopi litigants and judges between the norms for keeping esoteric Hopi traditions secret and what the norms of due process demand in the Anglo-style procedures of the Hopi court proved a confounding issue of Hopi legal process and one that Hopi judges were hard-pressed to resolve. I was thus both honored and more than a bit nervous that the Chief Justice of the Court at the time, the Hopi linguistic, lawyer, and anthropologist Emory Sekaquaptewa, invited me to take on the project under his guidance. Nonetheless it was an invitation I readily accepted.

When I first started the project it was 1997, and theories of indigenous cultural revitalization were still gaining traction, at least in the scholarship on US Native American law and Native Nation legal systems. Ideas of what came to be called "cultural sovereignty" (Coffey and Tsosie 2001) and later "indigenization" of tribal governance structures that were originally premised on settler colonial models were still in their nascency (see Pommersheim 1997). So too, for that matter, were arguments about the need of tribal governments to "return to tradition," culture, and custom when making policy and law decisions that would enact the ongoing trajectories of tribal self-governance.

But in anthropology—particularly in sociocultural anthropology concerned with the law and politics of indigenous peoples—notions of "custom," "tradition," and "culture" had been all but abandoned. At best they spoke to a politics of indigenous identity and authenticity that anthropologists had no business weighing in on. At worst they were relics of the disciplines' colonialist foundations. This was in full evidence in the so-called "invented tradition" debates of the mid-1980s, when anthropologists studying indigenous cultural revitalization movements sought to extend to them the critiques that historians Eric Hobsbawm and Terence Ranger (1983) originally applied to the supposedly timeless symbols and ceremony of European nation-states like the Scottish Tartans or the elaborate Royal processions of the English Crown. Some anthropologists argued that the "ancient" ceremonial practices and traditions indigenous political actors and leaders were reintroducing in their contemporary governance were not *really* ancient and, in some cases, not all that traditional. Others went even further, arguing that notions of culture, tradition, and custom should be discarded lest our scholarship continue to be used in the dispossession and abjection of indigenous and other peoples tarred by them. Against this backdrop, even by the late 1990s, claiming to want to study matters of Hopi tradition raised the specter of an outmoded anthropology that many in the discipline believed had rightfully been discarded.

In retrospect, the response to my research that I received from the eminent legal anthropologist in whose kitchen I was sitting on that gray autumn day in 2000 was perhaps not so surprising. After telling her about my project her response, I recall, was something like "Tradition? Hasn't everything been said about that already?"

To say I was disappointed by her reaction is an understatement. I was already three years into my PhD program and was in the midst of drawing up my reading lists for my qualifying exams, one of which centered around the anthropological study of "tradition" and its critique. And yet here was the first time I had spoken about my work to someone who didn't already know my history and background or who had worked closely with me to develop the project from the ground up. To hear her vocalize a critique that asked the "What's new about this?" question that I had privately asked myself already a thousand times was terrifying. But to say I was completely crushed by her comment would be to overstate matters. In truth, I *had* been aware of this issue—my reviews of the literature had in fact prepared me for this. I had noticed that the themes emerging in the current socio-legal and indigenous law scholarship of the late 1990s and early 2000s required that I trace their arguments through the indigenous social movements of the 1970s and 1980s, movements that had been the object of anthropological inquiry during the same period. It was from these movements that much of the "invented tradition" debates originally exploded, both as the objects of their critique by anthropologists, but also the powerful response that indigenous activists made rejecting those critiques and in some cases rejecting the anthropologists that made them as no longer welcome in their communities (Clifford 2013).

So the question was: how to reconcile the fact that there was something of a conceptual time lag operating in the topic I was planning to undertake for my dissertation research? That is, the notions that had come under anthropological critique a decade or two before were still being deployed in the context of indigenous law and politics, including most importantly in the ways in which Hopi tribal legal actors were engaging in the ongoing work of contemporary Native governance. I needed to develop an answer to responding to my host's critique, one that I hoped to get from other corners of the anthropological discipline. After what I am sure was an extended amount of hemming and hawing, I alighted on an answer that I would later realize was one grounded in some of the classic themes of linguistic anthropology. That is, I explained that whatever else "tradition" might be as an analytic category of anthropological inquiry, it is, for my purposes, first and foremost a discursive and textual practice of contemporary Hopi law, one that can and should be investigated for the kinds of social acts that get accomplished in and through it.

Of course, I don't think I stated it that clearly at the time. More likely I mumbled something over the lip of my mug, hoping that I could sip my chamomile tea in a way that would get me through the moment without sounding too foolish. But I do recall coming to the realization that I had figured out both the broad contours of the literatures with which my work would have to engage, but also, with the way in which a specifically linguistic anthropological approach could make a novel intervention in bridging what might otherwise have stood as an unresolved, and perhaps even widening, split of purposes between anthropology, indigenous legal studies, and most importantly, what was going on in Hopi courts.

Another way to say this is that I came to appreciate the value of intertextually positioning my own research as the nexus that tied different extant bodies of literature together, in a way that was inspired by the lessons I had already learned from my preliminary work in the field with the Hopi legal system. By taking seriously the insight from my ethnographic fieldwork that tradition was a relevant notion organizing Hopi law, and then analyzing that fact in light of extant linguistic anthropological literatures, I could make a particular intervention into both the ongoing scholarly conversations about issues of intentionality, ideology, and metapragmatics and in the work of those Hopi Justices who had first encouraged me to undertake the project.

Research Methods in Linguistic Anthropology

This perspective would certainly come to clarify my own orientation to linguistic anthropology and its goals more generally. Indeed, elsewhere (Richland 2012), I have considered my approach in relation to the "three paradigms" of US-based linguistic anthropology that Duranti (2003) once attributed in his programmatic review of the twentieth-century historic development of the field. I found that my work hewed most closely to his third paradigm, where "language [is] no longer the primary object of inquiry ... but an instrument for gaining access to complex social processes" (Duranti 2003, 332). As such, as I went through my own processes of exploring questions of "tradition" as ones that turn to and rely upon the study of language as a collaborative, social, meaning-making activity, I had come to let my ethnographic and advocacy experiences working with the Hopi court drive my intellectual engagement with the extant literatures. Then, and what in retrospect I think was an awareness, even then, of the ways such intertextual and citational practices not only canalize how I'd analyze my ethnographic data but also point to how I was inevitably re-presenting extant texts in ways that gave them novel meaning, my engagement with those literatures refined how my own work could contribute to them and that strikes me as appropriate in light of the openness of anthropological modes of inquiry.

2.4.2 A Tale of Peril: Avoiding the "Everything that has come before is wrong" claim

If the answer I eventually lit upon in my kitchen-table meeting in the previous example could be described as my "I DO have something new to say" moment, then this second tale is perhaps best understood as the fallout from my time spent under the delusion of "I'm the only one who gets it" grandeur. Both have their ground in the work that literature reviews accomplish for linguistic anthropological research, and both are highlighted when approached with an analytic eye toward their intertextual and citational dimensions and affects.

This second example relates an experience I had toward the end of my graduate career. It was the summer of 2002, and I had been back from my extended fieldwork stay for about a year and a half. I had already gotten some distance on drafting two of the three chapters of my dissertation thesis that would form the "core" of the write-up, focusing as they did on three different analyses of audio-recorded interactional data from the Hopi courtroom (see Richland 2008 for the versions that would form the published manuscript).

I remember feeling pretty confident about the progress I was making toward completing the thesis and thus felt it was a good moment to start thinking about life after the PhD, and specifically how I was going to fare on the job market. Though I still had another year or two of writing ahead of me, I decided to try my hand at submitting versions of the chapters for publication as stand-alone journal articles. I took the summer months to retool the first of two chapters, keeping much of the core data analysis as it currently stood, but then building up around it an introduction to the central argument of the manuscript that drew on a combination of linguistic anthropological, legal anthropological, and Native American/Indigenous studies literatures on theories of sovereignty, self-determination, and the role of indigenous cultural revitalization in those theories. Much of what I was using for my literature review was taken from materials I had originally drafted as part of my qualifying exams for advancement to candidacy. And because I had had the good fortune of working with the Hopi courts before entering graduate school, and during which time my future dissertation project had been developed in consultation and at the direction of the court, my "quals," as we called them, were nicely tailored to the analyses I would ultimately do on the data I collected for my dissertation. By the end of the summer I had what I thought was a solid draft of a manuscript offering well-reasoned, stand-alone analysis of some of the pragmatic and interactional details of Hopi courtroom discourses of custom and tradition, and I sent it off to what at the time was, and I think still is, the top journal for linguistic anthropology, sociolinguistic and discourse analytic scholarship.

One day, a couple of weeks later, I got a ping in my email inbox with the subject line that said something like, "Decision on your submission," from the editor of the journal to which I had sent the manuscript. In retrospect, I perhaps should have been prepared for what was coming, especially given that it had been less than a month since I had first submitted the article—an impossibly quick turnaround for any journal to which I have ever submitted manuscripts. But I was feeling bullish, and I actually knew the editor, and assumed she liked my work based on a prior discussion we had a few years earlier. I thus remember thinking something fool-hearty like, "Clearly she sees how fantastic and important the paper is," and so immediately sent out the manuscript out for review, demanding a one-week turnaround from reviewers, who all likewise saw its immediate brilliance and timeliness and sent their rave reviews sent back to her immediately, and now she was conveying her acceptance of the manuscript to me. Yep, I was sure feeling my oats.

The email was short, merely directing me to the document that was digitally attached to it. When I opened the document, I saw that it was a letter, printed on journal letterhead. I don't have the original, but this is my reconstruction of its tone and content, and, for reasons that I hope are obvious, I'd venture to say the memory of it has been seared on my psyche:

Dear Mr. Richland:

Thank you for submitting your manuscript to XXXXXX. I regret to inform you that I will not accept it for publication in this journal. In fact, I have not sent it out for review. While the data you provide are potentially very rich, your treatment of the relevant literature is poorly conceived and overly simplistic. Indeed, it reads more like a term paper for a graduate-level course than a manuscript ready for publication in a peer-review journal.

As a bit of professional advice; you need to rethink the strident tone of your criticisms of the legal language scholarship, and the self-congratulation with which you describe how you cure their errors. You would also do well to recall that the scholars whose work you are trashing are the very ones I would be approaching for reviews. They are also going to be some of the first scholars to find value, if any, in the linguistic dimensions of your work. I wish you the best of luck in your future endeavors.

Yeah, it was bad. Needless to say it took some time for me to get over the shock that I felt at discovering that the letter wasn't the heralding of my soon-to-be brilliant professional career that I assumed it would be. And then there was the gut-punch of the critique itself. Was my work on the manuscript really nothing more than just a dressed-up term paper? And if so, given that the part that was receiving the most heated criticism came from the literature reviews from my qualifying exams, had I completely messed those up too? And if that was true, had the whole project been ill-conceived from the beginning? Forget revising the manuscript or even working on anything else related to the dissertation for that matter. I was ready to pack the whole thing in.

Eventually I got myself off the floor and out of the fetal crouch that the letter had put me in. Then I did what I suspect many graduate students have done before and since: I went to my advisor and promptly melted down in his office. But it was while I was there, and with his help, that I first started to think about what was wrong with my literature review and how, in a sense, the editor had done me a service. A tremendous service, really. For when I went back through the manuscript, and looked back at the offending parts of the literature review, I saw that I had indeed engaged in overly broad, actually rather lazy, scorched-earth style critique of the legal language scholarship that had come before. I had done what I have heard called the "graduate student slash-and-burn." In my effort to justify the value of my research, I had carved (and with a rather dull blade I might add) what I claimed was a gap in the literature that had come before.

But it wasn't persuasive. And this is true for several reasons. For one thing, in order to find what I claimed were errors and oversights in the extant legal language scholarship, something that my work would for the first time correct, I had to attribute to that prior research purposes and goals that frankly weren't there. It wasn't that I perpetrated a ham-fisted mischaracterization of their work—something so obvious as, for example, claiming that it failed to account for racialized power disparities, while not mentioning the fact that it largely focused on the proceedings of a single case in which all the legal actors were Euro-American. No, my criticism was accomplished through a variety of intertextual metadiscourses that were subtler than that. For example, I argued that because the scholarship that had come before didn't account for the different sociolinguistic variations that legal speech acquires in different regions across the country, it failed to contemplate how social authority—even legal authority—is always crosscut with other modes of legitimizing presentations of social capital.

I still believe that the critique I was making was not wrong, per se. The scholarship to which I was citing in fact didn't account for these variations in their analyses of legal language. Rather, the problem was that these omissions were never part of the original purpose of those manuscripts. It was an unfair critique to lay on that literature, holding its authors accountable for something their work never set out to do. This is a classic problem, one that many graduate students who are newly entering a field of expertise, as well as a mode of critical thinking, often fall victim. I think this was what the editor was after when she described my manuscript as having more in common with a graduate school term paper. And she was right to do so.

But there was a second problem with my literature review, one that in some ways was subtler still. In my headlong rush to prove the worth of my work by intertextually distinguishing it from the work that came before, I neglected to see all that it owed to that extant literature to even be legible in the first place. I think this point is subtler because it sometimes gets taught to young scholars in a shorthand form that can sound too much like a facile admonition to "respect your elders." But that's not it. This isn't about professional politesse or even just being a decent colleague (though that never hurts). It is about the fact that the contributions that most of us will ever make to our fields of inquiry are necessarily the incremental kinds that require a precise understanding of both the kinds of claims it can be said to be making, and what kinds of claims are beyond its ambit, and that only comes from knowing how it articulates, in a precise way, with the extant scholarship with which it is in dialogue. This goes back to the ethics of intertextuality that I described in the previous section. Scholarship is always dialogic and thus demands a cooperative orientation to the unfolding meaning that we are collaboratively producing, even when our dialogue is made up of heated debates. If the two sides to a debate do not understand the premises they share, they risk talking right past each other.

The problem, then, with the critical way in which I had framed the extant literature in my manuscript was not just that I had failed to appreciate how my work stood on the shoulders of the scholars who had come before. Even worse, for my own purposes, in mischaracterizing the extant literature, the claims I was making for my own work misunderstood their actual contributions. I had engaged in sloppy reasoning, sloppy argumentation, and made a less persuasive case for my own work precisely because I overstated its divergence with what had come before and ultimately failed to see the sharper insights that it actually offered in furthering (rather than redefining) the study of legal language.

A few days later, after getting over the initial sting of the rejection, I went back to the manuscript and rethought how I should restate the relationship between my analyses and arguments of my ethnographic data and the linguistic anthropological scholarship that had come before. A lot of this involved retooling the intertextual discourses and metadiscourses I had used to characterize that literature. Instead of describing other legal language scholarship as "failing" to attend to the discursive and interactional details I would now provide, I now described my work as "building on" and "extending" the important arguments first made by this prior work on the value of analyses of legal language more generally. And this really was the case. My work was not possible without theirs. The insights I relied on to get to the novel contributions my analyses of Hopi courtroom speech made were ones that I derived directly from that work. And even where my work disagreed with some of their findings, they were less direct contradictions than further refinements of arguments and insights that in many ways remained valid. In short, my work stood on the shoulders of their giant interventions, and it was much more ethically and intellectually valid to describe its relationship to the extant literature in that way than to frame my first manuscript as some sort of scholarly David taking on the Goliaths that had come before.

Beyond the mechanics of knowing where to look, and how, for the good reviews and bibliographies, these two tales from my own experiences suggest to me that a good literature review involves a kind of intertextual "tacking and jibing" between the prior scholarship and one's own data—such that both are being refined and clarified in the process. In the first tale, I showed how by staying true to my own work and the aims and goals of Hopi legal actors with whom I had long been engaged, I learned that what made the prior literatures on "tradition" relevant to me was how they were or were not speaking to my experiences working in the Hopi court. And this in turn motivated and made relevant the particular orientation I ended up taking to the literatures in linguistic anthropological and legal language scholarship with which my work was engaged and on which it drew. By allowing my work to remain open to the particularities of the site where I was conducting my fieldwork, I stayed true first and foremost to the ways in which my anthropological inquiry was grounded in the engagements I encountered in the field.

In the second tale, about my first foray into publishing some of my scholarship and the scathing rejection I received, I explained how much of the problems of the manuscript I submitted turned on the way in which I described my work in relation to the extant legal language scholarship. In short, I failed to account for the ethics and pragmatics presumed and produced by the fact that our work is necessarily in dialogue with, and thus builds upon, the work that comes before. Indeed, even when our analyses and arguments differ, or even disagree, with the extant literature, it does so not in spite of, but *because* that prior scholarship has given us the intellectual framework with which could have the debate in the first place. This intertextuality needs to be honored, and in the act of doing so, and getting clarity on what the extant literature both says and (equally important) doesn't say, we come much closer to understanding the stakes for the ethnographic site where we are working, but not just this. We also gain clarity on how we have come to those stakes intellectually and what our analyses and arguments do and (again, importantly) do not contribute to the scholarly dialogues with which they are necessarily, just one turn in an ongoing and unfolding conversation.

So how might we train ourselves (and others) in the important, but oftentimes nuanced and somewhat unruly issues of intertextuality and citationality of reviewing the literature? That is, how do we work toward striking just the right balance between ensuring our work is properly in dialogue with the scholarship that has come before and at the same time guarding against closing ourselves off prematurely to the lessons from our fieldwork experiences that, as anthropologists, sit at the heart of our work? Moreover, I think too often the "scorched earth" mode of critique in which we sometimes attack the scholarship we read, however appropriate to trying out new ideas and ways of thinking, unfortunately leads to a misunderstanding about the works under consideration, but also about what our scholarly contributions are supposed to look like. I wonder if we could begin to remedy that problem by consciously undertaking what my colleague Tom Boellstorff calls "generous engagement" (Boellstorff 2016, 404) by attending not just to the deficiencies of scholarship we read, but to its constraints—that is, the way in which an author has delimited her inquiry in a given bit of writing and whether or not our critiques in fact honor those limits or talk past them. We might then think about what more would need to be done in the way of data collection in order for our critique to even be relevantly compassed by the work before them. And then perhaps we might discover that doing just that is the start of how our own work could make its contribution to the scholarly debates and paths of knowledge production of which it is (intertextually, citationally, and otherwise) always a part.

2.5 Conclusion

In the course of this chapter I have tried to describe and then exemplify the sometimes-overlooked challenges that literature reviews pose for anthropologists. After laying out some of the basic mechanics of undertaking reviews of literature generally, I suggested that the issues are in fact much more complicated than simply ones of what terms to use in our online database searches. More specifically, I described the tension between reviews of literature and the particular kind of open-ended inquiry that characterizes anthropological investigation, particularly through ethnography. On the one hand, a review of literature is an effort to situate one's own research in work that has come before. And this is obviously important because without such situation we cannot even begin to motivate why we, or anyone else, should engage our work. On the other hand, with the idea that anthropological data collection often involves collecting "more data than the investigator is aware of at the time of collection" (Strathern 2004, 5), situating one's work in the extant literature can seem to work against the grain of productive open-ended anthropological inquiry—the reason we go to the field in the first place. And this is true even after we have come home and are looking at what we have in our notes and recordings and trying to figure out what we can ever say about it.

Appreciating these larger stakes that are involved in devising an effective review of the literature, including both the ethical and intellectual implications that back practices of literature review, is what I have dedicated this chapter. And I have tried to show how, in two experiences I had with my own work, the very conceptualization of one's own work, and its successful dissemination, often starts with a proper appreciation of the role that an effective review of literature plays in anthropological scholarship.

2.6 Ethnographic Activities

1   Choose a concept or a topic from one of your projects, and for which you will need to become familiar with the relevant extant literature. As you undertake your review, keep track of the digital databases you've searched, and within each database the specific search queries you've used, and what each uncovered. Try and be deliberate in the different search queries you use, modifying only one term at a time, keeping all the others constant. As you do this, while keeping track of the different results under each term, you will produce an intellectual roadmap or decision tree of your literature review that will give you a sense of intertextual engagements that will later form the basis of the literature review that appears in writing.

2   Repeat the same process, but this time do it using your institutions' library catalogue and in physical stacks at the library. After a search of one or two queries, go to the relevant sections of your library's holdings and explore the books that appear on the shelves adjacent to the ones your queries actually retrieved. Do you find other relevant holdings?

3   After doing activities 1 and 2, take the resources you have retrieved and check their bibliographies. Note which authors and resources in one bibliography are cited in others and retrieve those if you have not already done so.

Undertaking these activities will give the researcher a metapragmatic awareness of the paths she took to the insights and theories gained from the extant scholarship, while keeping track of any lacunae that the researcher might consider addressing in their own library research. It will also allow the researcher to keep track of the broader social and conceptual context within which the literatures reviewed originally emerged.

2.7 Questions to Consider

1 In beginning to undertake a literature review, what search methods are the ones you use most regularly? Are there some you never use? Why?
2 How do you think the search methods you use shape the intertextual paths that ultimately inform your literature reviews?
3 How do you ensure that you have compassed all the literature relevant to a given project?
4 Have you ever had experiences like those described in the two tales above, where you had to reflect on the contributions that your scholarship can make to a field of inquiry because someone questioned its value or the way you described its relationship to the extant scholarship? Please explain.
5 Are there methods of literature review that you use that are different than those described above? What are they?
6 What lessons would you impart from your own experiences in undertaking literature reviews that you think other linguistic anthropologists might find helpful?

2.8 Notes

1 Donald Brenneis, and Karen E. Streir, eds. *Annual Review of Anthropology.* Available online: https://www.annualreviews.org./journal/anthro (accessed October 24, 2019).
2 John L. Jackson, ed. *Oxford Bibliographies in Anthropology.* Available online: https://www.oxfordbibliographies.com/page/158 (accessed October 24, 2019).
3 Deborah Thomas, ed. *American Anthropologist.* Available online: https://anthrosource.onlinelibrary.wiley.com/journal/15481433 (accessed October 24, 2019).

2.9 References Cited

Agha, Asif, ed. 2005. "Special Issue: Discourse across Speech Events: Intertextuality and Interdiscursivity in Social Life." *Journal of Linguistic Anthropology* 15 (1): 1–150.

Austin, John L. 1962. *How to Do Things with Words*. Oxford, UK: Clarendon Press.

Bakhtin, Mikhail M. 1981. *The Dialogic Imagination*. Michael Holquist, ed. Austin, TX: The University of Texas Press.

Bakhtin, Mikhail M. 1984. *Problems of Dostoyevsky's Poetics*. Caryl Emerson, ed. Minneapolis, MN: University of Minnesota Press.

Bauman, Richard, and Charles L. Briggs. 1990. "Poetics and Performance as Critical Perspectives on Language and Social Life." *Annual Review of Anthropology* 19: 59–88.

Boellstorff, Tom. 2016. "Reply to Comments on for Whom the Ontology Turns: Theorizing the Digital Real." *Current Anthropology* 57 (4): 387–407.

Boyarin, Jonathan, ed. 1992. *The Ethnography of Reading*. Berkeley and Los Angeles, CA: University of California Press.

Briggs, Charles L., and Richard Bauman. 1992. "Genre, Intertextuality, and Social Power." *Journal of Linguistic Anthropology* 2: 131–72.

Clifford, James. 2013. *Returns. Becoming Indigenous in the 21st Century*. Cambridge, MA: Harvard University Press.

Clifford, James, and George E. Marcus, eds. 1986. *Writing Culture. The Poetics and Politics of Ethnography*. Los Angeles: University of California Press.

Coffey, Wallace, and Rebecca Tsosie. 2001. "Rethinking the Tribal Sovereignty Doctrine: Cultural Sovereignty and the Collective Future of Indian Nations." *Stanford Law and Policy Review* 12: 191–222.

Collins, James, and Richard Blot. 2003. *Literacy and Literacies. Text, Power, and Identity*. Cambridge, UK: Cambridge University Press.

Duranti, Alessandro. 2003. "Language as Culture in U.S. Anthropology. Three Paradigms." *Current Anthropology* 44 (3): 323–47

Finnegan, Ruth. 1988. *Literacy and Orality*. Oxford, UK: Basil Blackwell Press.

Goodman, Jane E., Matt Tomlinson, and Justin B. Richland. 2014. "Citationality: Knowledge, Personhood, and Subjectivity." *Annual Review of Anthropology* 43: 449–63

Goodwin, Marjorie H., and Asta Cekaite. 2018. *Embodied Family Choreography: Practices of Control, Care and Mundane Creativity*. New York: Routledge.

Goody, Jack, and Ian Watt 1963. "The Consequences of Literacy." *Comparative Studies in Society and History* 5 (3): 304–45.

Heath, Shirley Brice. 1983. *Ways with Words: Language, Life and Work in Communities and Classrooms*. Cambridge, UK: Cambridge University Press.

Hobsbawm, Eric, and Terence Ranger, eds. 1983. *The Invention of Tradition*. Cambridge, UK: Cambridge University Press.

Jakobson, Roman. 1960. "Closing Statement: Linguistics and Poetics." In Sebeok, Thomas A., ed., *Style in Language*. 350–77. New York: MIT Press.

Lee, Benjamin. 1997. *Talking Heads. Language, Metalanguage, and the Semiotics of Subjectivity*. Durham, NC: Duke University Press.

Murray, Stephen O. 1998. *American Sociolinguistics. Theorists and Theory Groups*. Amsterdam: John Benjamins Publishing Company.

Nakassis, Constantine V. 2013. "Citation and Citationality." *Signs and Society* 1 (1): 51–78.

Ong, Walter J. 1982. *Orality and Literacy: The Technologizing of the Word*. London, UK: Metheun & Co. Ltd. Publishers.

Pommersheim, Frank. 1997. *Braid of Feathers. American Indian Law and Contemporary Tribal Life*. Los Angeles: University of California Press.

Reed, Adam. 2018. "Literature and Reading." *Annual Review of Anthropology* 47: 33–45.

Richland, Justin B. 2008. *Arguing with Tradition. The Language of Law in Hopi Tribal Court*. Chicago: University of Chicago Press.

Richland, Justin B. 2012. "Discourse Analysis and Linguistic Anthropology." In James Paul Gee and Michael Hanford eds., *The Routledge Handbook of Discourse Analysis*. 160–73. London: Routledge Press.

Silverstein, Michael, and Greg Urban, eds. 1996. *Natural Histories of Discourse*. Chicago, IL: University of Chicago Press.

Starn, Orin, ed. 2015. *Writing Culture and the Life of Anthropology*. Durham, NC: Duke University Press.

Strathern, Marilyn. 2004. *Commons and Borderlands: Working Papers on Interdisciplinarity, Accountability and the Flow of Knowledge*. London: Sean Kingston Publishers.

2.10 Further Reading

There are a number of very good resources for conducting literature reviews in the social sciences of the sort described above. Here are a few of the best I have found:

1 "How to Write a Literature Review." *San Jose State University King Library Resources Guide for Anthropology Students*. Available online: libguides.sjsu.edu/c.php?g=230076&p=4424462 (accessed March 2, 2020).

2 "Literature Review." *University Libraries, The University of Toledo Library Guides.* Available online: libguides.utoledo/litreview/home (accessed March 2, 2020).

3 Bruce, Christine S. 1994. "Research Students' Early Experiences of the Dissertation Literature Review." *Studies in Higher Education* 19 (2): 217–29.

4 Machi, Lawrence A., and McEvoy, Brenda T. 2016. *The Literature Review: Six Steps to Success.* Thousand Oaks, CA: Corwin Publishing.

3

Planning Research in Linguistic Anthropology

Deborah A. Jones and Ilana Gershon

3.1 Introduction

Clifford Geertz (1998) famously described participant observation as "deep hanging out." When anthropologists spend time in informal settings with their interlocutors, he argued, they gain access to information and insights that a survey-and-interview type of researcher never will. Many ethnographers will attest to the truth of this, often citing kitchen-table conversations, long bus rides, or helping with chores as the moments in which they found their best material.

The effectiveness of "deep hanging out" as a research methodology presupposes, however, that one knows and has access to the very people one would need to hang out with. It presumes the researcher has a good sense of *who* they need to speak with, *where* to find these interlocutors, and *how* to actually collect data from them. As a methodology, "deep hanging out" also assumes one's intended interlocutors would even want to spend time with a researcher. Of course, Geertz (1973) himself acknowledged that this is nothing to be taken for granted, memorably describing that he and his wife were initially ignored by the Balinese people with whom they assumed they would quickly build rapport. But this is a point worth revisiting at the start of any research project. Ethnographers often become so excited about their own interests that they forget they are studying people who have lives and commitments and are not necessarily interested in anthropological research questions or might even be a bit uncomfortable with a fieldworker around. This goes double when said fieldworker pulls out a recording device, something linguistic anthropologists often wish to do.

Let's flip the script. Imagine that someone from Brazil wanted to study informal conversation among anthropologists in your country. Preferably gossip-type interactions, just to step things up a notch. What skills and resources would that person need to carry out the project? Language capacity, for sure, and probably also recording equipment. But how would they gain access to anthropologists? Would they study a department? If so, which one and why? What sorts of anthropologists should they study? What sorts of conversations would they hope to record? What might be the stakes in speaking to graduate students, contingent faculty, or pre-tenure professors? What sorts of events might our researcher attend—and how would they access them? Would they need a letter of introduction? A visa? Where would they live? How long would they stay? Would they conduct interviews or just set up recorders in likely classrooms and coffee shops? Would they just lurk on Facebook or Twitter? Just as importantly, when studying gossip-type interactions, how would they avoid seeming like a total creep?

Thinking about our imaginary researcher reminds us just how much there is to account for in planning a project. It can be easy—tempting even—to get lost in the details. So where to begin? And where to return to when the details become overwhelming or one's initial plan no longer seems feasible?

We suggest fieldworkers organize their planning around three primary questions: *who?*, *where?*, and *how?*. In the next section, we discuss how these questions can be approached both prior to and during the data-collection process, so that one plans not once, but rather understands planning as an iterative process. We draw on examples from our own and our colleagues' research experiences to show how identifying *who*, *where*, and *how* can be translated into constructive thinking about sampling, access, and resource management. We then delve deeper into questions of access and the researcher's position in the field through some notes on the ethics on gifts for informants and case studies on recruiting (and recording) research participants. We conclude with ethnographic activities and specific questions to help readers sketch preliminary research plans, outline potential methods to use, and even anticipate what might go wrong.

3.2 Who, Where, and How

Consider these sample research questions:

How do theater costume designers decide what characters should wear, and how does this reflect implicit assumptions about class, generation, gender, and race?

Why have Japanese started performing funerals for robot dogs?

If civil society conversations are essential for democracy to take place, what actual conversations take place in civil society contexts and how do they support that country's democracy?

How do time banks affect the ways their users understand the relationship between time, work, and money?

Why has Latin-American migration to Europe surged in recent years? How do Spanish-speaking migrant communities in Europe differ from those in North America?

Pursuing any of these projects requires first thinking about *who*. Who is it I should be speaking with? What is the population of people from which I can acquire data? Why should it be these particular people and not some other ones?

What initially seems like an easy-to-answer question can quickly become slippery. Who should be included in or excluded from the category of costume designers? Should the study be limited to people with professional costume-designing credentials, or do students and amateurs count? Who comprises civil society, and what are the stakes in studying people of certain professional or class backgrounds and not others? A research project on Latin American migration to Europe could quickly become complicated by the tremendous diversity of people moving back and forth across the Atlantic. Is Spanish-speaking truly the right analytic to be starting from? Is it the one that is actually meaningful to the people being studied?

Getting a sense of who exactly one should be speaking to requires questioning the extent to which one is studying a clearly definable group at all. In this sense, the question of *who* (and also *where*, which we'll discuss shortly) is directly implicated in debates in linguistic anthropology about "speech communities" (see Irvine, ed. 1996). Is it reasonable to talk about "Japanese," "robot dog owners," or "time-bank users" as if they were homogenous, consistently coherent, and easily locatable populations? As researchers, our wariness of treating groups of people as bounded or stable bumps up against our need to set the parameters of our studies. How to overcome this?

3.2.1 Naming "Who?"

To begin with, the research question must be carefully honed (see Hall, this volume). Recall our imaginary Brazilian gossip-in-anthropology researcher. Gossip is a fairly vague thing to set out to study, even though linguistic anthropologists have long and successfully argued for just how powerful such supposedly unimportant conversation can be (see Besnier 2009). What sort of gossip our researcher would retrieve for analysis would likely depend on whom they were studying. If our researcher were interested in how hierarchy is built and maintained through everyday interaction in anthropology departments, they might study a university where graduate programs were offered and research emphasized. If they were interested in, for example, student and instructor responses to required courses on race and ethnicity, they might wish to study a department with a large undergraduate program.

Initial formulations of research questions often yield multiple possible answers to the question *who?*. A researcher's next step is to explain why the *who* they choose is the right one for answering their particular question. This is important not only for impressing a grant-making committee or passing departmental review (see Das, this volume). Deciding who you are talking to is the first step to deciding which methods of data collection will be appropriate. Further, if you are going to ask for someone's time—or make it past a gatekeeper who controls that time—you need to be able to explain why that person should be talking to you and demonstrate you are prepared to engage with them in a meaningful and ethical way (see Black and Conley-Riner, this volume).

What should ground answers to the question of *who?* Extant literature? Prior experience? Conversations with a mentor? Intuition? While there are certainly moments in ethnographic research to go with your gut, our intuitions, especially if they are based on limited experience, are rarely portable. Likewise, methodologies that worked well for one researcher in one particular context may not translate well to another, which may make it difficult to rely on secondary literature or even a mentor's guidance. Thus, planning a project requires knowing the history of your proposed fieldsite as well as keeping tabs on current events (see Richland, this volume). It also means being open to the possibility that the *who* might change as a project develops.

Let's look at how the population of study can expand or contract by taking a closer look at an actual study. When Deborah Jones was planning her dissertation project in Ukraine, she was inspired by two topics that were in vogue at the time: anthropological approaches to bureaucratic documents and the global land grab (Jones 2017; see also Hull 2012a and b; and Edelman et al. 2015). It seemed that these literatures would be easily applicable to post-Soviet Ukraine, where the government was preparing to end a long-standing moratorium on agricultural land sales, sending 32 million hectares of recently privatized but formerly state-owned or collectivized land onto the world market.

Jones had spent a couple summers in rural Ukraine and knew that lifting the moratorium was very controversial. Many of her interlocutors feared the country, famous for both its fertile soil and its corrupt government, would be unable to fend off foreign and domestic land grabbers. However, many of these same people also saw opening a farmland market as an important step toward European integration or quietly looked forward to the cash they might receive by selling the few hectares they had received during de-collectivization to a private farmer or agribusiness. Because the pending land reform, and any subsequent land sales, would require small landowners to assemble many new documents and navigate numerous business and legal interactions, Jones saw this as an opportunity for a study of how political economy turns on talk, text, and talk about text. She organized her research plans around the date the farmland market was to open: January 1, 2013. Before then, for phase one of the project, she planned to spend time with small landowners to try to understand how they valued their plots (as productive farmland, as family or cultural heritage, as a financialized asset, etc.). Her mentors advised her to "walk the land" with her interlocutors, whom they all assumed would be the people who owned, worked, or at least felt attached to the parcels that would be for sale.

However, when Jones arrived in her fieldsite, she quickly learned that most of the landowning villagers did not in fact know where the plots they had been allocated a mere ten years earlier were actually located. They attended daily to their kitchen gardens and the animals they raised in their backyards, but when Jones asked them where their agricultural land shares were—possessions they claimed were among their most valuable—the most typical response was "somewhere in that big field over there." Further, it turned out that Jones's interlocutors were not in fact handling their land rights themselves but rather had signed power-of-attorney agreements that redistributed legal authority between genders, generations, and community members. To top things off, the opening of the farmland market was postponed for three years almost immediately after Jones started her fieldwork (as this chapter is being written, the market *still* has not opened).

Research Methods in Linguistic Anthropology

Did Jones plan poorly? Not necessarily. She arrived in her fieldsite with enough language skills and cultural and historical knowledge to be able to cultivate relationships with one group of people she knew she needed to be speaking with: former state and collective farm workers who had received a few hectares of land as compensation during the post-Soviet era but were prevented by the moratorium from selling them. When Jones realized she needed access to a broader spectrum of people (such as village council members, notaries, farmers, relatives beyond the village, legal aid teams), the small landowners she had been talking to were quite happy to make these introductions. Jones's time gardening and tea-drinking with elderly people who did not know where their land was also yielded an important insight. She learned that power-of-attorney agreements were often demanded by village councils negotiating with farmers and were key to how large agricultural businesses had already taken over huge tracts of land across Ukraine despite the moratorium on land sales. Additionally, when Jones spent time with these elderly landowners and learned to understand nonstandard dialects, milk cows, make sausage, and pick beetle larvae off of garden plants, she was also earning a tremendous amount of credibility that would facilitate her access to other interlocutors and fieldsites down the line. Jones's knowledge and reputation would become even more important once the armed conflict in Ukraine developed a year later, dramatically reshaping both her research agenda and her relationships with her interlocutors.

Although we hope that your research period will be less tumultuous, Jones's experiences remind us just how unpredictable anthropological research can be. This doesn't mean that research planning doesn't matter or that there is no sense in taking advice from people who have worked on similar projects but in different places. Rather, it means that good planning begins with doing the background research and skill development necessary to formulate solid preliminary answers to the questions of *who*, *where*, and *how*, but also to be able to make informed adjustments to these plans as circumstances change.

3.2.2 Locating: "Where?"

Let us turn to our second question, *where?*. Like *who*, *where* can seem obvious at first glance, especially if one takes *where* to be primarily about location (e.g., Balinese village; rural Ukraine; US anthropology department). We think *where* is less about geography and more about the situations and environments in which the people you need to be speaking with spend their time. For linguistic anthropologists, *where* often means "where can I observe the sort of conversations that interest me?"

Although semi-structured interviews (see Perrino, this volume) are perhaps the bread and butter of the humanistic social sciences, people studying language often find themselves on the search for spontaneous speech. Yet capturing the perfect instance of spontaneous speech requires being in the places where such speech is spoken (and audible, and ideally able to be recorded). Thus, *where* and *who* are always connected. As the *who* of Jones's project expanded, so did the *where*. Although she initially imagined spending the bulk of her fieldwork in a pair of sleepy villages, she eventually found herself attending seminars for notaries in regional capitals and bumping around the countryside with a roving team of lawyers offering legal consultations (which she was not permitted to record, but at least got to observe).

Our Brazilian gossip researcher might face a similar enlargement of *where* in studying how hierarchy is produced and maintained in anthropology departments. Perhaps our researcher would start off by going to classes and parties, hanging around the graduate student lounge, and attending graduate student association meetings. However, if they became interested in job market rumors (a rather salacious topic at times), they might find it necessary to expand the *where* of their study to online fora where search information is shared. Other good sites for collecting news and speculation about the job market might be coffee queues, alumni gatherings, and book release parties at the American Anthropological Association conference. Even in cases in which the *who* stays relatively consistent, the *where* often expands dramatically as one develops a better sense of the places and environments from which material can be retrieved.

That said, researching the *where* before starting a project is essential. In some cases, focusing on the *where* can dramatically reshape a project even before it begins. When Ilana Gershon set out to study hiring in corporate America (Gershon 2017), she thought she wanted to study how new media affected hiring and firing practices—the entries into and exits from workplaces. The more she talked to people in the business world to learn how feasible her project would be, the more it became clear that companies would not want her to observe either one for fear of lawsuits. Observing hiring might allow Gershon to be an expert witness in discrimination lawsuits; observing firing might allow her to be an expert in unlawful dismissal suits. She had to find a way to study hiring without watching anyone hire someone else. Gershon decided to study instead the advice that circulated around hiring and attended over fifty workshops on how to create a resume, a brand, a LinkedIn profile, and so on. She also interviewed people about their experiences implementing the advice that they were being told and interviewed hiring managers, recruiters, and HR people about how they understood the hiring process. In the end, Gershon's research focused far more on the genres people have to produce to prove that they are employable and the advice that circulates about how to find work than she had initially anticipated.

What happens if, in brainstorming *where*, you realize that you are unlikely to be able to access the spaces and environments where your proposed interlocutors spend time? We all face limitations in the sort of data we can collect, and it is up to each individual researcher to determine whether substituting one point of data collection for another still allows them to answer their research question. In asking *where else?* Gershon found a fieldsite that made her project not only more feasible, but also more coherent and relatable. Asking *who else?* can also lead one to different *wheres*, some of which might be more accessible. Although some settings are better than others for data collection (e.g., a quiet, indoor space is better for collecting audio than a windy hilltop or crowded restaurant), there are very few research questions that can only be pursued in one place. As you develop your project, ask (yourself, mentors, colleagues, potential informants) *who else?* and *where else?* By doing this, the decisions you do make will be more informed, and you will head off for data collection with a backup plan ready.

3.2.3 Describing "How?"

Thinking through *where* quickly leads to pondering *how*. There are things one's funding, professional obligations, and personal commitments just don't permit. The question *how?* is certainly about deciding which specific methodologies to use for the study, and we will turn to one related topic, recruitment techniques, later in the chapter. Here, however, we also encourage researchers to think about *how?* in a more pragmatic sense. In project planning, *how* means "what resources can I draw on to make this happen?" And "how can I use these resources to set myself up for success?"

There is no one way of defining resources. One way to think about resources is as things you have or don't have but could fairly easily borrow or procure with the help of a small grant—for example, basic recording equipment, books about your fieldsite, and small gifts for your hosts. Another way to think about resources is in terms of competencies, relationships, and assets (including research funding) you might be able to develop or acquire within a particular period of time, such as foreign language capabilities, training in a particular research methodology, locally valued skills, or social connections that help you gain access to your research subjects. A third sort of resource might also be thought of as privilege, those advantages you have by virtue of being you: your citizenship may enable or hinder your ability to do research in a certain country; your age, gender, skin color, religion, sexuality, marital status, health needs, and so on may ease access to or exclude you from a particular interactional setting. Finally, there are the biggest, and often scarcest, resources of all: money and time.

Certainly, there can be slippage between these four categories: people at elite institutions tend to have access to more money, research leave, and equipment; they also are more likely to come from affluent families in wealthy countries with powerful passports. There are certainly some parallels between what we have outlined here and Pierre Bourdieu's discussions of economic, social, and cultural capital (Bourdieu 1986). But the funny thing about fieldwork is that many of the advantages you enjoy in your home environment evaporate the moment you step into a research setting—or can even work against you. Researchers who conduct fieldwork in their home countries, but outside of their regular social circles, report needing to adjust their speech lest their interlocutors find them nerdy or posh. They often notice that they are held to different standards than foreign researchers are, or aren't told certain things because some information is presumed to be common knowledge. Letters of introduction that impress the intelligentsia might be scoffed at by people who pride themselves on practical skills. One of Jones's most humbling moments as a researcher came when she presented her business cards to an important interlocutor, who looked at the big, yellow University of Michigan "M" and declared, "This looks like McDonalds!" (After this happened a second and third time, Jones downloaded a copy of the university seal and had new cards made locally with the seal as the insignia. Although the seal looked a bit grainy and almost none of her post-Soviet interlocutors had heard of Michigan, it was better than being associated with a brand that screamed American capitalism.)

Every project is different and every researcher faces different challenges. Some face more than others. Accounting for what resources you do or don't have should be part of every researcher's planning process. However, we cannot account for all contingencies here, so we close this section with discussion of two *how* questions we think everyone needs to ask in the project planning stages: "how should I plan my time?" and "how can I keep my project focused and manageable?" Two more *how* questions, "how am I going to get people to talk to me?" and "how do I keep their data safe?" are briefly introduced here but taken up more fully in the case study section, which focuses on sampling methods and positionality in the field.

Time management is about more than discipline; it is about breaking up a research project into smaller tasks and figuring out what order to do them in. Ideally, your project can be divided into phases, each of which has a specific set of tasks and goals. Sometimes, these phases are shaped by the rhythms of our interlocutors (e.g., our Brazilian gossip researcher might need to plan for AAA and its proximity to US Thanksgiving); sometimes they are shaped by our own obligations and commitments (Jones would like to go to Ukraine next month, but being maid of honor at her friend's wedding is more important). As one begins to plan research, natural breaks often emerge. However, the phasing of a project is often dependent upon resources. It can take time to acquire funds and develop skills. Further, anthropologists often find certain research tasks are better done once the fieldworker has spent some time in their fieldsite and built rapport.

For example, Joshua Shapero wanted to study how environmental experience impacts spatial language and cognition among speakers of Central (Ancash) Quechua. He determined that this would require extended contact with Ancash speakers, whom he would recruit to participate in a controlled experiment involving describing the location of a set of cards in relation to each other (a modification of Levinson's "chips" experiment [Levinson 2003]). It would also require extended contact with local herders, as one of Shapero's hypotheses was that people engaged in pastoralism would be more likely to use absolute frames of reference rather than relative ones. (For the results of this study, see Shapero [2017a, 2017b].)

Shapero spoke excellent Spanish and intermediate-level Southern Quechua, which he had been able to study at his home institution. He also had spent a good amount of time in Peru and had many contacts there through his advisor, colleagues, and friends. Shapero did not, however, have strong knowledge of Ancash or highland pastoralism and he didn't have time to study more on his own while working as a teaching assistant and preparing for his candidacy exams. Therefore, Shapero decided to divide his project into phases. He would use the skills and contacts he already had to find an appropriate fieldsite before leaving for Peru, but upon arrival he would spend several months developing fluency in Ancash and uncovering ways to build rapport. Only after conducting sustained ethnographic fieldwork would he start the experimental portion of his study. His diligence paid off: because he established his trustworthiness and dedication to learning Ancash and herding practices before beginning his experiment, he had fewer problems with recruitment than he might have had he attempted this sort of data collection from the start.

In Shapero's case, time management meant slowing down his project. In fact, he delayed the experimental portion of his research until his last few months of fieldwork (personal communication with Jones, February 5, 2020). Shapero was able to do this in part because he was in a PhD program that expected its students to do at least one, possibly two and sometimes even three cumulative years of fieldwork. However, most scholars are not going to have that amount of time for research. Outside of the doctoral years (and within them, should you have other time commitments in your life, such as a partner and/or children), researchers rarely have more than several weeks to a few months to collect data. Moreover, the same researchers who have short data collection periods are also often the ones that are juggling numerous other responsibilities. In such cases, it is extra important to bring a project down to manageable scale.

Another example comes from Ilana Gershon's work on how people use new media to break up with each other (Gershon 2010). One of the reasons Gershon chose to do this project was that her university was giving her a semester of leave, but she'd had no time the year prior to write grants to get funding for the project she had originally imagined doing. That project would have taken her to New Zealand, which Gershon knew from her previous research project (Gershon 2012) was a fairly expensive place both to get to and to do fieldwork. Given these time and financial constraints, Gershon decided to do a project locally on how people used technology designed to connect people in a way it wasn't designed for—breaking up. The project was inspired by Gershon's own undergraduates, who in semesters prior had told her sometimes funny, sometimes harrowing stories about dating in the age of social media. Gershon already had *who* and a *where*, and she required no funding applications, no travel, no visas, and no language learning to get started. However, the project did come with one big complication: talking to students about personal matters. We delve further into Gershon's experience in the case study section, which goes further into the questions of recruitment and sampling that are of special relevance to linguistic anthropologists.

3.3 Pre-field Practicalities and Preventative Measures

Naming the *who*, locating the *where*, and describing the *how* of your study often take a few tries. Above, we provided examples of researchers who scaled back their studies, slowed down their timelines, or changed projects entirely to better reflect the resources they had and the demands they faced. In this subsection, we offer some tips for researchers who have identified the *who*, *where*, and *how* of their projects, have set feasible and reasonable goals, and are now focused on practicalities. This section will be of particular use to researchers planning a first trip abroad but also acts as a checklist for anyone preparing to embark on data collection.

Research projects have many moving parts. We have imagined how our Brazilian gossip researcher might identify the *who*, *where*, and *how* of their project, but we have not yet dealt with any of the logistical struggles they might face. How would they acquire a visa? Or housing? Do they need to figure out the housing and the plane ticket before or after applying for the visa? How much is all of this going to cost? Will there be any money left over for recording equipment, or will our researcher just need to use their phone? (See Kohler and Murphy; Mitsuhara and Hauck, this volume on the merits and drawbacks of using mobile technology in the field.)

To answer these questions, we recommend reaching out to people working on similar topics and/or in the same region. People who have recently completed research or fieldwork are full of useful logistical information (e.g., is that expensive coding software worth buying? how long will it take to get a visa? how much is an apartment? what medications can I buy on-site versus what do I need to bring from home?) that can help researchers both novice and seasoned with budgets and scheduling. Reaching out to them is a great way to discuss the feasibility of a project; get leads on housing, transportation options, or even research assistants; and cultivate collegial relationships that will last beyond the project.

Mentors, colleagues, and peers can also help researchers think through how to manage mental and physical health during data collection. The academy is often a place where working oneself to the bone is taken as evidence of great passion rather than great pressure. Anthropology often takes this a step further with its mystification of fieldwork, especially when done in difficult environments that may take a toll upon the body. However, the days when anthropological fieldwork required immersing oneself in a remote, malaria-ridden fieldsite, occasionally sending letters home via an imperial postal service, are long gone. In recent decades, anthropologists have done wonderful work in large international cities, with online communities, and in their home communities. The discipline is better for this diversity, and it has made room for people who cannot—or choose not to—sacrifice their social relationships and personal well-being for a research project.

That said, we would be remiss to assume that a comfortable fieldsite automatically brings both work-life balance and research success. Whether working locally, online, in a global city, or in a tiny village, setting oneself up for a satisfying research experience requires forethought. Think about it this way: before going abroad it is advisable to update your vaccinations. You inoculate yourself against known risks. This keeps you safe and gives you peace of mind as you go about your travels. Here are some other preventative measures you can take to smooth your research experience:

Technical: Set aside time to learn to use any new equipment. Figure out where you are going to store data and how you are going to keep it safe. Make certain you have a way to retrieve data if your equipment is stolen. Have a plan for backing everything up; especially if you will be somewhere it is difficult to access anything online.

Medical: Schedule appointments with the doctor, dentist, optometrist, psychologist, and so on well before your research start date. If going abroad, fill your prescriptions for the duration of your research period. If this is not possible, plan for how you will refill your prescriptions before they run out. Do not assume you can send medications through the post.

Postal: If you are planning on sending electronics, medical supplies, prescription drugs, metal keys, foodstuffs, or even just a box of books to your fieldsite, confirm that what you plan to send can in fact be transported. You should also find out what it would take to *receive* your package. If you are conducting research abroad, carefully check the address registration, customs, and VAT regulations for the country you are working in; be sure to find out what qualifies as a gift versus what is subject to taxes. Ask diaspora members how they send packages home; they may be able to suggest a courier service. Consider taking on extra suitcase on your flight—this is often less expensive and time-consuming than navigating the postal system and customs.

Financial: Contact your funding sources and find out when exactly you can expect to receive money. (Or, if you have a grant that works on a reimbursement basis, set up a meeting to confirm exactly how this works.) If going abroad, contact your bank and your credit card providers and let them know if you will be out of the country. Find out how you can access your money while doing research. Will you be able to go to a cash machine? If so, will you be charged for transactions? How can you access your money in an emergency?

Professional: Take steps to protect your time: plan to wind down other responsibilities before starting your project; if possible, set up auto-replies on your email accounts to let senders know that you are less available. But don't isolate yourself: set up regular appointments with a peer (every 2–4 weeks, perhaps) to check in, brainstorm, commiserate, and hopefully celebrate during your research period.

Personal: Keep in mind that research takes a toll on people other than the researcher. Talk to your loved ones about your plans and discuss ways you can support each other. If you are going to be far away, discuss how and how often you will keep in touch. Pull out your calendars to discuss when and how you will spend quality time together, whether before, during, or following your research period.

This brings us to a final suggestion for planning research: give yourself a break. We mean this in two senses. First, relaxation time with friends, family, or even by yourself will help you phase your work and keep up your energy. (If you're living with a host family, it can also be nice to give them a little break from you!) If you are going away for a year, plan to take one or two weeks off after about six months so you can have time away from your fieldsite to regroup and think about what you have been learning. Second, give yourself a break when writing your research goals. Setting yourself up for research success means setting goals that can be achieved with a limited set of resources and within a particular time frame. That doesn't mean you can't pursue big questions, but that good researchers break their questions into bite-sized pieces. We hope cycling through *who*, *where*, and *how* will help researchers and their mentors tighten plans, develop pre-project task lists, and embark on a productive and not too stressful research experiences.

3.4 Ethics: Compensating Interlocutors

In the preceding section, we asked fieldworkers to think about who their research questions require them to be in contact with and where and how they might reach these interlocutors. In this section and in the case study to follow, we delve into complications that can arise as a researcher tries to gain access to their intended informants.

Answering the question *how?* means attending to methodology, data collection, data security, and other requirements of the Institutional Review Board (IRB). For linguistic anthropologists, thinking about ethics often means giving people choice in terms of recording (e.g. audio only versus audio and visual) and taking extra steps to maintain confidentiality, for example through face blurring, using oral consent scripts (versus written and signed ones), or erasing video after transcription (see Black and Conley, this volume). However, ethics also means thinking carefully about how and when to compensate people we encounter in the field.

The American Anthropological Association tells us that "[t]here should be no exploitation of individual informants for personal gain. Fair return should be given them for all services." But what do "services" or "fair return" mean, and how can this be factored into research planning? Should fieldworkers be applying for funding with which to compensate informants? Should they be stuffing their suitcases with gifts? If you are going to offer something to a research participant, when should you do this—when they first agree to participate or after your interview or experiment? Is paying for research even ethical?

The answer to all of these questions is—it depends. This is not only because research projects differ, but because accessing interlocutors is often less a matter of compensation than it is of cultural competence. Think back to our imaginary researcher studying gossip-type interactions in US anthropology departments. It would be quite strange if they paid to come to a graduate student party, but they would probably be welcome to help set up, clean up, or contribute food or drink. Or consider one of the example projects from the previous section: studying Japanese robot dog funerals. In Japan, it is customary to give the family of the deceased (human) money to help pay for the event, so a researcher would need to determine if this was appropriate to do in cases involving pets and other nonhumans.

This does not mean that researchers should not plan on giving gifts (or in some cases, money) to their interlocutors. Anthropologists have long demonstrated that gift-giving, and reciprocity more generally, can be an important part of cultivating and maintaining social relationships. However, just because one's fieldsite has a gift-giving tradition does not mean that one will be able to participate in it in the same way as one's interlocutors. Likewise, a researcher cannot expect to use the same approach with everyone they meet. In some instances, a researcher may be regarded as a researcher.

Research Methods in Linguistic Anthropology

In others they may be considered a guest, student, journalist, intern, aid worker, spy, English teacher, prospective business partner, honorary child, babysitter, foreign person with access to lots of money, foreign person who might get someone into trouble for accepting a bribe—the list goes on. These multiple and shifting roles require us to think carefully about when and how to offer gifts. Fieldworkers should also think broadly about what gifts might look like. In many cases, they may find that other forms of reciprocity, such as labor exchange, go a lot further in building social relations.

For example, when Nick Emlen started studying indigenous language contact in the Peruvian Amazon, he needed a place to live. Nineteen men in the community he was studying helped him build a house over a two-day period. As a result, Emlen owed each of these men two days of his own labor. Working for the men and their families proved to be a great way for Emlen to pursue his research, and he continued to labor alongside them even after he had paid off his housing debt. Emlen writes (personal communication with Jones, September 17, 2019; also discussed in Emlen 2020):

> One of the most effective things I did was exchange my own agricultural labor for their linguistic labor. To the extent they'd ever met academics or government functionaries, those people generally don't sweat and swing a machete in the coffee fields with them. Seeing me working my butt off for hours on end established a degree of trust and camaraderie that is difficult to achieve otherwise.

Swinging a machete may not be an option for every researcher, but there are many other ways to engage in reciprocal labor. Jones spent hours working in Ukrainian gardens, but because she was not as fast or skilled at weeding, hoeing, or chopping wood as most of her villager interlocutors, she was often asked to look after children while their parents did chores. Jones also taught English courses at village schools. Sometimes it was frustrating to spend so much time with the kids instead of the adults, but Jones earned the appreciation of the parents. After the work was done, they graciously answered her questions and often sent her home with fresh produce—small gifts that kept the cycle of reciprocity going.

The point is that there are many ways to think about "services" and "fair return." Depending on one's research design, gift-giving, financial reward, labor exchange, or even a simple thank-you note may be most appropriate. Those doing internet-based projects may find thank-you notes are the only option they have. Researchers studying up the ladder or interviewing people in bureaucratic positions also need to tread carefully, lest their gift be interpreted as an attempt at a bribe.

As you plan your research, keep returning to *who*, *where*, and *how*. Doing so will allow you to anticipate what sorts of environments you might find yourself in (perhaps at a student party, a robot dog funeral, a religious gathering, a garden, a shop, an office) and subsequently how and when to offer compensation (bring pizza, possibly offer cash, pay for a blessing, help weed and hoe, buy something small from the business, bring chocolates for the staff, send a thank-you note). Researchers should also consult literature about their fieldsite's history and traditions, especially in the realms of hospitality and business. Language teachers, fellow researchers, diaspora members, and other people familiar with the fieldsite can also offer insight. Finally, researchers should not forget to consult mentors, internal review board, or other people responsible for overseeing the project (funders, for example), to make certain whatever compensation methods they decide on are also institutionally permissible.

One last tip: prepare yourself for how to handle gifts that are offered to (or even feel forced upon!) you. Knowing when and how to refuse a gift is just as important as knowing when and how to accept one, and another way to demonstrate cultural competence.

3.5 When *Who*, *Where*, and *How* Intersect: Explaining Your Presence and Getting Access

Once you figure out whom you need to be in touch with and where to find them, how are you going to gain access to them? Can you cold-call them and set up an appointment, or do you need someone to introduce you? Would snowball sampling be appropriate, or do you need to locate a certain number of people from particular demographics? How are you going to explain who you are and why people should be invested in what you are doing?

In the preceding section, we discussed the role reciprocity and mastery of social norms can play in creating and keeping contacts. Later chapters of this book go deep into specific methods researchers can use to collect data. However, before one can give gifts, conduct interviews, or participate and observe, one needs to get in touch. This means that a key aspect of project planning is brainstorming access. In a sense, access is where the *who*, *where*, and *how* of a project intersect.

As discussed at the very start of this chapter, anthropologists tend to assume that their research will automatically be interesting to the people they are studying. The truth is that it often takes several tries to both recruit research subjects and get them invested in what we are doing (see Black and Conley, this volume, for a discussion of ethically involving community members in research design). It also isn't unusual for interlocutors to be curious about the researcher, puzzled as to why they have even shown up or suspicious as to why they are hanging around for so long. Jones encountered such suspicions regularly in her research in rural Ukraine, especially after the war in the country's east began and she began to study a landmine-affected community near the Russian border (DeAngelo and Jones 2019). On the one hand, people were accustomed to the idea of journalists and aid workers coming by to ask questions, and they often described Jones as a foreign journalist and/or associated with the humanitarian de-mining organization that had negotiated permission for her to stay in the border zone. On the other hand, villagers could not understand why Jones was sticking around a place other people were fleeing from. Was she actually a spy for an agroholding that would snap up all the land once it had been de-mined? Why else would she be staying with a woman who was close to the former state farm director? What should they make of the fact that Jones was American? Was she more of a threat or an avenue to resources desperately needed?

In this final section, we consider how recruitment and sampling can pose quandaries for the researcher. By sampling, we mean the practice of collecting data from which one can extrapolate about a larger population or trend. There are a variety of ways to sample, such as interviews, surveys, experiments, or collecting and analyzing audiovisual materials. What most of these sampling methods have in common is that, at some point, the researcher needs to make contacts and explain to them why they should participate in a study. Often, we also rely on the contacts we do make who help us find other contacts, a process known as "chain referral" or sometimes "snowball sampling" (Bernard 2011).

Identifying contacts is often fairly easy (although, as we saw earlier, sometimes you identify only a small slice of the people you should speak to). Convincing people to participate in your project *and* help you find your next informant can be much harder. Prospective interlocutors may have limited time or interest. They may also be wary of being associated with an interloping researcher. Another challenge linguistic anthropologists encounter is that much of what we study often comes across as a bit abstract.

Additionally, sometimes, by telling people we are interested in how they communicate, we immediately put our interlocutors—the people we are communicating with—on edge.

Cheryl Yin ran into this problem when she came to Cambodia for her doctoral research on honorific language and how it had changed under the Khmer Rouge (Yin 2021). Like many linguistic anthropologists, she was extremely concerned about collecting audio recordings that she could bring back for analysis. However, people kept declining her requests to record. It wasn't just that Cambodia has a very difficult history—the Khmer Rouge were a genocidal regime that killed nearly a quarter of the Cambodian population between 1975 and 1979. Yin realized that in introducing herself as "a PhD student interested in language," she may have been making people self-conscious about their own speech.

> In hindsight, my informants may have said no to recording because they felt like the people in the setting I was in (Buddhist pagodas/temples, for example) did not use the "correct" or "ideal" honorific register. They assumed I wanted the model/exemplar examples, which was not the case. Some of the monks even suggested I go on YouTube to find examples of individuals fluent in the monk register!
>
> (personal communication with Jones, June 4, 2019)

Yin was left wondering if she would have had better luck obtaining recordings if she had described her research as being on religion or Buddhism. Or perhaps, she reasoned, she could have been more insistent that she was interested in *all* varieties of speech—but maybe that would have made the situation even worse?

Yin's research was still successful and valuable even though she did not come back from the field with as many recordings as she had hoped. What her reflections remind us, however, is that part of research planning is thinking through how you are going to introduce yourself and explain your work to other people. You might not use the same tactic every time; as with gift-giving, you will likely have multiple social relations to navigate.

That said, it is important to be aware that who you are and how you present your research will shape your data sample and also affect who you do or don't talk next. When Gershon was seeking people to interview for her project on mediated breakups, she asked everyone she met if they had a story about using new media to end a relationship. She also emailed large majors on campus asking for volunteers and gave surveys in large classes. Why a survey? For Gershon, the most important question on the survey was the last question—it was the moment she asked for the email addresses of people willing to tell their stories to her in an interview. This survey and follow-up interview became Gershon's primary method of recruitment, and she turned to it after her first plan, chain referral, didn't work out.

Although people of all ages begin and end romantic relationship, in a university town, the people who are breaking up fast and furiously are most likely going to be undergraduates. Gershon talked to a few people over the age of twenty-five, but most of her eventual interlocutors were in their late teens and early twenties. Gershon had to think carefully about what it meant to be a professor interviewing students. The *who* of her study quickly affected the *where* and *how* of her project, including recruitment methods. For example, Gershon would sometimes meet study participants in coffee shops, but people were also very willing to meet her in her office—a perk of being a faculty member is having an office that allows for private conversations. However, Gershon's position as professor and access to private spaces also shaped what sort of data she retrieved. Sometimes, conversations that began as interviews began to uncannily resemble therapy sessions. After all, many undergraduates were comfortable talking to an older stranger about intimate issues if that person were a counselor. However, Gershon was not a therapist, but a professor, and sometimes her interlocutors had been her students in previous classes. Her interviewees often told her things about their relationships that they wouldn't tell their friends, but they also refused to tell her things that they would have been telling their friends in great detail. For example, she knew very little about the sex lives of the people she was interviewing (she also didn't want to know). And she very rarely got both sides of the story because no one she interviewed was comfortable passing along the contact information of their ex—she only talked to both members of a not-so-stable couple once out of seventy-three interviews when the girlfriend wanted to tell her side of the story months later.

The way Gershon found people to interview affected what she ended up discovering. After her first set of interviews, Gershon thought she would be able to "snowball" her way to other interlocutors. This had worked in her earlier fieldwork with Samoan migrants in New Zealand. But chain referral didn't work with people who dumped or had been dumped in Indiana. No one was willing at the end of an interview to tell her the name of someone else she might speak to. People felt very protective about their friends and didn't want to volunteer them to a professor that their friend didn't know.

As a result, Gershon would talk to people from different pockets of practice, which led to a significant insight: people figure out the norms surrounding new media by talking to their friends and families about what to do in a given situation—do I answer by email or should I media-switch? Or what should I text back when she says this kind of thing to me? But the norms had not yet become widespread, and Gershon wasn't interviewing people who had figured out together what to do. As a result, in every single interview, she heard about a media ideology or a practice that she had never heard before (e.g., giving your ex-boyfriend and your current boyfriend the same ringtone because it was the "boyfriend" ringtone). She had to learn not to blurt out: "wait, you do what?" in the middle of an interview. Gershon was learning how much variation there was in mediated breakups simply because "snowball sampling" didn't work as a way to recruit subjects. What had initially seemed to be an obstacle turned out to reveal meaningful insights into how norms surrounding new media become widespread.

Each of the researchers discussed here began their data collection with a recruitment and sampling plan in mind. Each of them also found that, at some point, they needed to adjust their methods to account for their position in the field and the interests and concerns of their interlocutors. For Jones, that meant demonstrating her investment in the people of the village—and not only the village's farmland—by attending every possible community function, visiting the elderly and caring for children, and, upon realizing her interlocutors had been cut off from coal deliveries and faced a severe shortage of firewood, using her network to find out about winterization grants the village council was eligible for. For Yin, the key to data collection was figuring out how to introduce herself and her project in a way that was both honest and didn't immediately put her interlocutors on edge. For Gershon, effective recruitment required thinking about how her new project and more senior role changed what sort of sampling techniques she could use.

3.6 Conclusion

Good research isn't random. Although so much of the anthropological canon seems to revolve around the "breakthrough into rapport" (Harr 2019), that one unexpected incident that blew the study wide open, we have argued in this chapter that the key to sparkling and surprising ethnography is in fact good planning. Being in the right place at the right time—and then, having the means to document what you observe—means thinking carefully about the *who*, *where*, and *how* of your project long before you set off for the field. It also means approaching research planning as a reflexive and iterative process requiring assessment even after data collection has begun.

No matter how often the actual practice of fieldwork will make you feel like the Accidental Fieldworker, cycling through the *who*, *where*, and *how* of your project will help YOU foresee obstacles, avoid pitfalls, and gain insight into what you are about to encounter. Below, we offer ethnographic activities and discussion questions to help fieldworkers novice and seasoned prepare for the deepness of "deep hanging out."

3.7 Ethnographic Activities

1. (a) Refer back to the sample projects on page 75. Using *who*, *where*, and *how*, bullet-point a brief research plan for one or more of them.

    (b) What assumptions did you have to make to complete your plan for 1(a)? (Did you assume you would have a certain amount of funding? That you had language competency? That people would let you record them?) To what extent were these assumptions reasonable ones to make? Why or why not? What steps can you take to confirm these assumptions are valid?

2. Practice introducing yourself and explaining your research to different people. If you have a sense of whom you might encounter, try this role-play exercise: choose a partner. Now, ask your partner to assume an identity (e.g., a village grandmother, an urban bureaucrat, a language teacher, a church minister). Introduce yourself and explain your research—or just what you're doing here!—to your partner. Then, switch roles. Do this until you can explain your presence as a researcher concisely—and in three different ways.

3.8 Questions to Consider

1 What contingencies might arise in your research and how might you plan in advance for these? For example, what health and safety concerns might you face during your research? Are there any preventative measures you can take? What is something you cannot control?

2 How are you planning to use or not use social media during your research period? What are the plusses or minuses to being online?

3 What is a research methodology that you are hesitant to use? (For example, a survey or video analysis of face-to-face interaction). Why? What would be gained or lost by planning (or not) on using this methodology? Can you defend your answer in terms of *who, where,* and *how?*

4 How are you planning on compensating your research participants? Why? Who else in your fieldsite might compensate someone in the same way or for similar tasks? Do you want to be associated with them or to distance yourself from them?

3.9 References Cited

Bernard, H. Russell. 2011. *Research Methods in Anthropology: Qualitative and Quantitative Approaches.* 5th ed. Lanham, MD: AltaMira Press.

Besnier, Niko. 2009. *Gossip and the Everyday Production of Politics.* Honolulu: University of Hawaii Press.

Bourdieu, Pierre. 1986[1983]. "The Forms of Capital." In Richardson, J. ed., *Handbook of Theory and Research for the Sociology of Education,* 241–58. Westport, CT: Greenwood.

DeAngelo, Darcie, and Deborah A. Jones. 2019. "Explosive Landscapes." *Anthropology News* website, November 15, 2019. https://doi.org/10.1111/AN.1312.

Edelman, Marc, Carlos Oya, and Saturnino M. Borras, Jr. 2015. *Global Land Grabs: History, Theory and Method.* London: Routledge.

Emlen, Nicholas Q. 2020. *Language, Coffee, and Migration on an Andean-Amazonian Frontier.* Tucson, AZ: University of Arizona Press.

Geertz, Clifford. 1972. "Deep Play: Notes on the Balinese Cockfight." *Daedalus* 101 (1): 1–37.

Geertz, Clifford. 1998. "Deep Hanging Out." *The New York Review of Books* 45 (16): 69.

Gershon, Ilana. 2010. *The Break-Up 2.0: Disconnecting over New Media.* Ithaca, NY: Cornell University Press.

Gershon, Ilana. 2012. *No Family Is an Island: Cultural Expertise among Samoans in Diaspora.* Ithaca, NY: Cornell University Press.

Gershon, Ilana. 2017. *Down and Out in the New Economy: How People Find (or Don't Find) Jobs These Days.* Chicago: University of Chicago Press.

Harr, Adam. 2019. "Sociolinguistic Scale and Ethnographic Rapport." In Zane Goebel ed., *Rapport and the Discursive Co-Construction of Social Relations* in *Fieldwork Encounters*, 97–110. Berlin, Boston: De Gruyter. https://doi.org/10.1515/9781501507830-007.

Hull, Matthew. 2012a. *Government of Paper: The Materiality of Bureaucracy in Urban Pakistan*. Berkeley: University of California Press.

Hull, Matthew. 2012b. "Documents and Bureaucracy." *Annual Review of Anthropology* 41: 251–67.

Irvine, Judith, ed. 1996. "Language and Community." Special issue of *Journal of Linguistic Anthropology* 6 (2): 123–222.

Jones, Deborah A. 2017. Afterlives and Other Lives: Semiosis and History in 21st Century Ukraine. PhD diss., University of Michigan.

Levinson, S. C. 2003. *Space in Language and Cognition: Explorations in Cognitive Diversity*. Cambridge, UK: Cambridge University Press.

Shapero, Joshua. 2017a. "Does Environmental Experience Shape Spatial Cognition? Frames of Reference among Ancash Quechua Speakers (Peru)." *Cognitive Science* 41 (5): 1274–98.

Shapero, Joshua. 2017b. Speaking Places: Language, Mind, and Environment in the Ancash Highlands (Peru). PhD diss., University of Michigan.

Yin, Cheryl. 2021. Khmer Honorifics: Re-emergence & Change after the Khmer Rouge. PhD diss., University of Michigan.

3.10 Further Reading

Hillewaert, Sarah. 2016. "Tactics and Tactility: A Sensory Semiotics of Handshakes in Coastal Kenya." *Journal of Linguistic Anthropology* 118 (1): 49–66. https://doi.org/10.1111/aman.12517.

Souleles, Daniel. 2018. "How to Study People Who Do Not Want to Be Studied: Practical Reflections on Studying Up." *Political and Legal Anthropology Review* 41 (S1): 51–68. https://doi.org/10.1111/plar.12253.

Wulff, Helena. 2002. "Yo-Yo Fieldwork: Mobility and Time in a Multi-Local Study of Dance in Ireland." In "Shifting Grounds: Experiments in Doing Ethnography." *Anthropological Journal on European Cultures* 11: 117–36.

4

Care as a Methodological Stance: Research Ethics in Linguistic Anthropology

Steven P. Black and Robin Conley Riner

4.1 Introduction

Although this chapter appears toward the beginning of this volume, consideration of ethics is not limited to the initial planning of a project. Rather, ethics is the foundation on which all parts of a study should be built (Meskell and Pels 2005). This means attending to ethical issues *throughout* one's research, from research design to data collection, analysis, and presentation. When beginning research, it is important to keep in mind that ethical principles are distinct from political and legal considerations (AAA 2012). Sometimes, what is politically relevant or legally required is dissimilar from or even in conflict with what is ethical. Add to this the need to consider how human actions and choices are shaped by cultural differences, socioeconomic and sociohistorical inequities, and power differentials, and the topic of research ethics becomes quite complex.

While linguistic anthropological scholarship can take many forms, analysis of language and communication in the context of long-term ethnographic participant-observation is perhaps the default version of research in the subfield. Here, participant-observation means observing research

---

This chapter is the result of equal co-authorship.

participants and taking fieldnotes while participating to various degrees in social activities. For linguistic anthropologists, this is often complemented by audio and video recording of interviews and/or everyday speech. Before beginning to carry out these and other data-collection activities with human subjects, Institutional Review Boards (IRBs) must review all research plans. Universities, hospitals, and other institutions have their own IRBs comprised of experts whose job is to evaluate research according to established ethical principles. IRB rules and regulations, especially the "common rule" for the protection of research subjects and the medically derived maxim of "do no harm,"[1] are dictated by the United States Department of Health and Human Services. IRB approval of one's research documents should be considered a starting point to guide the initiation of fieldwork, not an ending to one's engagement with research ethics.

In this chapter, we draw from scholarship that describes how the concept of *care* may be used as a methodological standpoint for research ethics throughout the research process (e.g., Boellstorff et al. 2013, 129). Our discussion challenges the idea that ethics should be thought of in terms of researcher/research participant dichotomies, which assumes that the researcher is either occupying a position of power with respect to a marginalized community or is "studying up," which refers to conducting research with groups and institutions that wield power in society (Nader 1972). Rather, a care standpoint expands ethical consideration beyond researcher/participant dichotomies, emphasizing how complex webs of personal and institutional connections in fact constitute relationships in any research project. We argue that research from a care standpoint requires interrogating power structures in a given social context and analyzing the unequal relationships between institutions, interlocutors, and social groups.

Care has been defined in several overlapping ways in recent scholarship (see Buch 2015). Here, we adopt a definition in which care both contributes to the well-being of individuals (as psychological and physiological entities) and responds to existing social, political, and economic inequities in research and professional contexts. This also shifts anthropological conversations from "doing no harm" to considering the possibility of "doing some good" (see Briody and Pester 2015; Boellstorff et al. 2013, 146–7). The care standpoint also reorients conversations about the ethics of researcher-participant dynamics from discussions of connection (e.g., rapport/empathy) to discussions of action. This does not mean that rapport and empathy are not actions (especially in the sense that language is a social action) or are not important in the research process. However, it does suggest that rapport and empathy may not be sufficient, possible in some contexts, or always desirable. There are concerns that doing action-driven (or "engaged" anthropology) introduces bias into research, as it involves explicit and active participation of the researcher and thus involves her own desires and aims in the research product. However, focusing on action in fact responds to a pervasive existing structural bias in research paradigms wherein common research design practices tend to reproduce existing socioeconomic inequities.

4.1.1 Defining Terms

Ethics is a vital component of linguistic anthropology research. While many scholars implicitly separate research ethics from theories of ethics, this dichotomy is misguided. A theory of ethics that does not consider the circumstances in which that theory was produced is incomplete at best (see Black 2017). Anthropological theorizations of ethics, especially those focused on language and communication, indicate an overlap between *morality* (everyday, taken-for-granted perspectives and actions) and *ethics* (conscious, often linguistic, reflection on what one could or should do) (Keane 2016, 135; Zigon and Throop 2014). Applying this understanding to research ethics means both recognizing the ways that particular ethico-moral stances are taken for granted in traditional research methodology and also reflecting on these stances.

Researchers in anthropology and elsewhere have not always considered ethical concerns to be paramount in their work. Early scientific research often prioritized the acquisition of knowledge above concerns about the rightness or wrongness of the conditions under which such knowledge was obtained. The implementation of IRB review of human subjects research was intended to respond to unethical knowledge production. With some exceptions, IRB review has been relatively successful in enacting the narrow biomedical principle of "do no harm." While the American Anthropological Association's Principles of Ethics present a broader picture of research ethics, proposing seven principles that apply to the design, implementation, and dissemination of anthropological research, these principles also assert that doing no harm is one of a researcher's primary ethical obligations (AAA 2012). One question for scholars to think through is whether the mere absence of "harm" is the same as being ethical (we think not). A primary focus on the prevention of harm may yield an overly passive orientation toward research ethics. Recently, ethnographic encounters have been theorized as inherently interventionist in terms of the need to create social situations (e.g., interviews, recordings, participant-observation) in order to "reveal otherwise obscured aspects of the social worlds we study" (Murphy 2017, 111). Instead of merely preventing harm, a care standpoint suggests that researchers should actively search for ways to reduce existing harms.

Moreover, the concept of harm itself is not straightforward. Identifying different types of harm and how they might be precipitated by research is complicated. Riner's research with military veterans can illustrate such a conundrum. In her current work, Riner interviews military veterans about their combat experiences. She is aware that this could cause individual psychic harm as participants recollect trauma experienced during their service. At the same time, these interviews can provide insight into veterans' combat experiences and if we understand these experiences better, we may be able to reduce veterans' collective harm by implementing practices that can aid in their recovery from trauma. In this case, it is not clear if the obligation to "do no harm" is being met. Questions that arise when working through this dilemma echo those asked in other aspects of research practice: Who is being harmed? By whom? To whom are we responsible? This chapter serves as a guide to some of the ethical questions that should be addressed when conducting linguistic anthropological fieldwork. We do not, however, offer specific rules to follow, as ethics entails negotiating relationships and questions in situ. Each research context is different and will bring with it its own ethical considerations. Research oriented by care, as we propose, approaches ethics as a daily practice, rather than a set of abstract rules (Pantazidou and Nair 1999).

"Care" has become a popular term in cultural (especially medical) anthropology. Thinking critically about care has occupied scholars in diverse fields including philosophy, health care, and science and technology studies. Initially established by feminist scholars, "care ethics" was developed as an alternative to existing models of morality, and many academics and practitioners adopted it as a framework by which to orient their work (Gilligan 1982; Noddings 1984). Care emphasizes responsibility, concern, respect, and relationships. Care ethics stresses that ethical considerations should be based on interpersonal relations between people, rather than rules or maxims that govern behavior, the latter of which are historically and erroneously based on idealized relationships between supposed equals or between supposed "experts" and the purportedly unknowing and/or ineffectual research participant. In the context of anthropological research, care can be an especially useful orientation, because if there is any universal maxim for ethnography, it is to expect the unexpected. A care orientation affords the flexibility to act ethically in the context of differing relationships in different fieldwork situations. This is especially important given that any scientific inquiry involves negotiations of responsibility at every level of the research process (Meskell and Pels 2005).

Care is generally described as action that takes the needs and concerns of others as its starting point (Tronto 1994, 105). Often conceptualized as an affective state, to care for is to feel a sense of attachment and commitment to someone or something. But care also refers to a practice, or form of labor, in which one works to maintain and better the world (Tronto 1994, 103). Such labor is embedded in and shaped by particular socioeconomic configurations (Buch 2015; Glenn 2010). In numerous cultural contexts, marginalized persons often disproportionately shoulder care-work that is devalued by society at large (Folbre 2014). Taken in this sense, a care orientation in research begins with a critical appraisal of existing inequities so that one's research design can respond to and attempt to redress some of those inequities.

Care apparatuses, including medicine and anthropology, may entail problematic transformations of their subjects: by placing them at the center of their attention, they situate them as exceptional and incapable of self-care (Munyikwa 2019). Anthropologists now tend to problematize the hierarchical self/other relationship on which ethnography was initially built, in which knowledge of the "foreign other" is shaped by the anthropologist as authoritative arbiter of such knowledge (Abu-Lughod 1991; Fabian 1983; Jacobs-Huey 2002). Some worry that framing anthropology as care will reinscribe this problematic relationship (Munyikwa 2019). This critique makes it imperative that we reflect critically on how and why we position certain people as deserving and in need of our care (Munyikwa 2019).

Care may also suggest concern for those whose voices are traditionally undervalued. While this may seem noble at first, it arguably reinforces a power differential in which a distant other is seen as unable to speak and in need of voicing by the anthropological authority figure (Spivak 1988). In addition, one may ask whose cares are directing any research endeavor. In a research project focused on the lives of marginalized persons, especially, a relationship conceived as care-giver and care-receiver has the potential to recreate a problematic, paternalistic dynamic. Notwithstanding these limitations, a care standpoint urges the researcher to remain responsible and attentive to the ongoing development of relationships fundamental to the research process and to, whenever possible, address inequities that lie at the base of such relationships.

4.2 Controversies and Concerns

There are a number of controversies and concerns that shape linguistic anthropological research ethics, many of which we view as being about how scholars could or should engage in care practices in situations of inequity. Here we mention a few core concerns that are not unique to linguistic anthropology but that take on different configurations in the subdiscipline: sexual harassment and discrimination and collaboration and community partnerships.

4.2.1 Sexual Harassment and Discrimination

In recent years, professional dialogue has become increasingly explicit about the impact of sexual harassment on the field of linguistic anthropology. This includes discussions centered around the actions of pioneering sociolinguist Dell Hymes, who was credibly accused of sexually harassing many women while serving as a dean at the University of Pennsylvania in the 1970s and 1980s (see Elegant 2018; Heller and McElhinny 2017, 215; Philips 2010). Hymes may serve as a point of departure for conversations about harassment, conversations which should happen not only in classrooms, but also in mentorship relationships and research planning meetings. His actions and their consequences remind us that ethics should inform the basis of relationships not only with research participants but also with colleagues and teachers/students. We must also consider the impact of his actions on the legacy of his work. Should we always add a note about this when citing Hymes's work, for instance, or perhaps discontinue citation of his work given the revelation of his pattern of harassment?

Such conversations should also be expanded to include other forms of harassment and discrimination on the basis of race, religion, gender, sex, and sexual orientation. While harassment and discrimination can and do occur in a wide variety of settings, two facets of linguistic anthropology make the field potentially vulnerable to these behaviors. First, like other field-based disciplines, linguistic anthropology often includes long-term fieldwork in situations where access to research contexts may be controlled by a single scholar or community member and where connections to researchers' home social support networks are limited. This sort of setup is conducive to harassment and discrimination by people in positions of power (Clancy et al. 2014). Second, the small and sometimes-insular nature of the subfield of linguistic anthropology (the smallest of the four traditional subfields of anthropology) results in the potential for an individual scholar to have a large impact on another's career. Here, a care orientation focused on inequities means that scholars—especially those in positions of authority—need to be aware of these imbalances, to structure research projects so they limit the power of any single individual over others' ability to conduct fieldwork, and to support and to speak up on behalf of others when scholars become aware of harassment or discrimination.

4.2.2 Collaboration and Community Partnerships

Another concern related to care ethics is the arrangement and management of collaboration/community partnerships. There is a long and robust tradition of applied, activist, and engaged scholarship in linguistic anthropology (e.g., Brandt 1988; Labov 1972; Philips 1983; Zentella 1997). Still, more and more researchers are now speaking and writing openly about how to make sure that one's research not only does "no harm," but also does some good, as is evident in the activities of the Society for Linguistic Anthropology's Committee on Language and Social Justice (Avineri et al. 2018).[2] The care orientation originates in part from the "imbalance of benefit" (Boellstorff et al. 2013, 129) between researchers and participants, suggesting that researchers ensure that participants themselves gain something from the research. From this perspective, it is essential to begin the research design process in conversation with research participants and other relevant stakeholders and to maintain communication with them throughout the research process. Here, questions of whom to include and how to include them are largely context-dependent (see Jaffe 2012). However, a cross-cutting issue is the fact that terms like "reciprocity" and "partnership" may idealize socioeconomic relationships between researchers and participants as equal when they are in fact not equal (Dobrin and Schwartz 2016). We recommend assessing each research context to determine who requires care and who is already providing it and, in principle, orienting one's research both to address gaps in care and to support those who are providing care.

The impact of the researcher and their outcomes on each research context can range widely. In some cases, one's research outcomes (publications, reports) will be useful and will be desired by community members or stakeholders. For instance, in a context of language obsolescence, perhaps a scholar plans to create a dictionary, grammar, or activities designed to aid in community language revitalization efforts (e.g., Kroskrity et al. 2002). In other cases, it may be that the researcher can provide other services. For example, a researcher may leverage their academic skills to aid in translation of bureaucratic documents, to help write a grant application, or to help a population gain the communicative competence they need to initiate a legal or political battle. Traditional ethical guidelines, which have been crafted with an emphasis on biomedical and psychological studies that rely on controlled and time-limited experiments or surveys, may negatively evaluate these sorts of non-research services as being coercive with regard to research participation. However, in the context of long-term ethnographic fieldwork and the extensive care-work often provided by research participants for little or no compensation (e.g., as fieldwork "families" and friends), a researcher's care services are actually part of a fair exchange. Researchers have much to gain from fieldwork—degrees, jobs, and professional prestige—and it is only fair that we should provide something to research participants, communities, and stakeholders to begin to compensate them for their time and their sharing of knowledge and cultural patrimony. It is important when providing such services that researchers pay attention to what research participants actually need or desire, instead of simply assuming that a given service will benefit them.

4.3 Data Collection and Its Entailments

Data collection must begin with an informed consent process. Research participants must be informed about the study in which they are participating, including its benefits and any potential harms that may result from participation, and they must agree to be a part of the project. Many scholars associate the informed consent process with institutional review boards (IRBs). With regard to the main issues discussed below, taking a care orientation to research ethics means thinking of IRB rules and approval for informed consent as a starting point rather than a finish line, as previously mentioned (see also Fluehr-Lobban 1994).

For instance, while chairing the AAA Committee on Ethics, Black learned that informed consent documents may be official but they are not always legally binding. In one situation, which must remain confidential, a researcher was legally required to share photographic data that in effect revealed research participants' identities and other information that was supposedly protected by informed consent documents. This occurred through a Freedom of Information Act inquiry with a researcher working at a public university. The outcome of this conflict and its consequences for participants are unknown. Furthermore, while it is true that one must obtain informed consent from research participants according to IRB guidelines and in dialogue with relevant evaluation of the fieldwork context at the outset of a study, researchers should also continue to check in and monitor participants' understanding of and wishes regarding consent throughout the fieldwork period and beyond. With this understanding of consent and our key terms and core concerns in mind, we now turn to a discussion of four main issues regarding research ethics in linguistic anthropology: attending to confidentiality and anonymity, conducting interviews, audio-video recording everyday activities, and engagement with new media and online data.

4.3.1 Confidentiality and Anonymity

Ethnographic research does not often pose physical risks to participants but is more likely to involve "informational risk," which is the risk that one's private information could become public (Boellstorff et al. 2013, 133). Protecting the privacy of research participants is thus paramount in social science research, and it can involve two related and often confused processes: confidentiality and anonymity. Confidentiality relates to how we handle the information we collect as a result of our relationships with our research participants. Maintaining confidentiality includes considering when and how identifying information, such as names, locations, group affiliation, or medical information, is collected and how it is protected once it is collected. Unlike anonymity, confidentiality starts with the assumption that some identifying information has been shared between research participants and researcher. Anonymity, on the other hand, implies that no one (including the researcher) can identify the research participants. It is possible to include a combination of confidential and anonymous data collection in one project. For instance, if someone is conducting research on the language of doctor-patient interactions, they may video-record doctor visits and change the names and blur the faces of the participants to maintain their *confidentiality*. At the same time, the researcher could conduct an *anonymous* survey that asks patients about their visits to the doctor.

If a researcher has any concerns about anonymity—for instance, when working with undocumented migrants or other research participants who fear reprisal in response to providing information to the ethnographer—all identifying information should be destroyed *in the original data*. For linguistic anthropologists, who tend to utilize audio-video recording, this may mean going beyond the use of pseudonyms to refer to participants in any analysis or publication to blurring faces in video recordings, masking voices in audio recordings, and then erasing the original recordings. Doing this ensures that the researcher can honestly and legally comply with potential litigation while also protecting the information of marginalized or otherwise endangered research participants.

Given that linguistic anthropological research is typically based on developing longer-term relationships between research participants and researcher(s), it is unlikely that such research would be done anonymously, but it is likely that it would be done in a way to ensure confidentiality. How one handles confidentiality depends on the research project, but common considerations in linguistic anthropological work include editing audio and video data to conceal or delete identifying information and changing identifying information such as people and place names in transcripts and publication of data. An additional, often overlooked consideration regarding confidentiality is maintaining participants' confidentiality among other community members, not just one's academic audience. For instance, when considering where to conduct interviews or other research activities, it is often necessary to think about whether talking to research participants in a particular location will reveal subjects' participation in the research project. Participants may not want to disclose their participation to other community members, requiring special discretion when engaging with research subjects (Black 2017). On the other hand, there may be instances where some or all research participants wish to be publicly identified—for instance, when a participant is a musician, scientist, or other figure whose professional career might be enhanced by participating in research (e.g., Samuels 2004). This can lead to difficult dilemmas when the identification of one individual would threaten the confidentiality of the organization(s) or social group(s) with which they affiliate. These cases may involve careful negotiations in order to protect the confidentiality and needs of all those involved in a project.

As anthropologists increasingly conduct engaged and advocacy-based research, which involves collaborating with communities and persons, it has become more difficult and sometimes disadvantageous to conceal participants' identities. Working from a relationship of care, moreover, requires engaging participants as individuals rather than as mere data points within a research project. Fostering and maintaining ongoing relationships of care can complicate the confidentiality aspect of research, as the research process requires more than converting individuals' behavior into recordable and thus concealable formats.

4.3.2 Interviews

The interview is a powerful tool for gathering information that is used widely in anthropology, other social sciences, and fields outside of academia, such as psychotherapy and business (see Perrino, this volume). Despite its ubiquity, there are relatively few accounts of the nature of interviewing, the kinds of information it obtains, and the ethical and theoretical implications of the practice (Briggs 1986, 2; see also Bernard 2011). Early anthropological and linguistic research used interviews unproblematically as the primary means of gathering information about who research participants were, what they did, how they spoke, and how their languages worked. In his now famous critique, linguistic anthropologist Charles Briggs (1986) dissects interviewing as a communicative practice, arguing that relying on interviewing is an act of political power. He suggests that in many linguistic communities, interviews are not a well-known communicative practice and are certainly not how people typically learn about others. Relying on interviews in these contexts is thus an assertion of power of the researcher over the participants, in which the former requires the latter to conform to her communicative norms. Furthermore, Briggs argues that while we think interviews give us information about others and their ways of life, they often reveal more about the interview situation itself than any "truth" about our research participants. For these reasons, Briggs urges researchers to learn from research participants' other ways of sharing information.

Briggs's discussion unravels many of the ethical entanglements involved in interviewing. One of these, inspired by the care orientation, is to engage participants on their own terms, rather than imposing our own ways of doing things on them. While we may be tempted to conduct a traditional interview where we sit face to face in a quiet room with a video or audio recorder running and a script of questions to follow, it may be more beneficial to garner information through another communicative event that makes more sense in our research context. This helps level the power imbalance inherent in the interview process and fosters meaningful relationships with research participants that help break down the traditional researcher/participant divide. For example, when Aaron Fox (2004) set out to do his research on country musicians in Texas, he didn't invite participants to answer a set of questions in his office, away from the spaces of their everyday lives. Instead, he sat in honky-tonks, drank beer, and talked to people, as they would have with their fellow musicians. Like Briggs, we do not suggest doing away with interviewing altogether, but, rather, rethinking what it means to interview. As described in Perrino (this volume), there are many types of interviews, from open-ended, person-centered interviews, to scripted, replicable questionnaires for the purposes of quantifying responses. What type of interview you conduct and how exactly you go about it will be informed in part by your research goals but should also take these ethical considerations into account.

"Learning how to ask" (the title of Briggs's [1986] book) also entails learning not just how but also *what* to ask. Asking ethically, in other words, involves considering what topics to broach in the interview process. The choice of interview topics will depend on your research goals but should also be informed by cultural and communicative norms of your research participants. If one decides to ask about potentially sensitive topics, for instance, it is generally best to spend time with one's participants getting to know them and their ways of sharing sensitive information before asking. Ethnography usually entails being with people in their day-to-day lives and, when interviews are used, conducting many of them over a span of time. This is generally the best practice for maintaining an ethical relationship with research participants, as it allows dialogue to develop, rather than setting up the interview as a unidirectional flow of information from participant to researcher. Interviewing participants can also be an instance of providing care for them, as ethnographic interviews often allow participants to process ideas and issues they may not have had space or time to consider in other contexts.

Linguistic anthropological perspectives on communication can provide useful insight into other ethical issues involved in interviewing, especially those related to miscommunication and asymmetrical participant structures. For example, in contrast to the tendency to focus analyses of interviews on what is said by the interviewee, Briggs suggests analyzing the linguistic details of interaction among all participants in order to uncover when misunderstanding might have occurred between researcher and participant (1986, 4). This requires us to turn an analytic eye to what is said by the interviewer, thus demystifying them as the authority who is mediating information received through the interview. It also disavows us of the assumption that an interview is a universally unproblematic communicative event, in which information is transparently communicated from participant to researcher. It is important to remember that interviews are co-constructions of meaning (De Fina and Perrino 2011; Talmy 2011), in which the researcher and participant together create reflections on and analyses of the lives of the research participants. A care orientation urges us to consider an interview as just one of many speech events that constitute the relationships between members of a research project and to pay special attention to the potential hierarchies that are embedded in the interviewing process.

4.3.3 Audio-Video Recording

Linguistic anthropologists have been at the forefront of audio-video recording data collection (see Kohler and Murphy, this volume; Mistuhara and Huack, this volume), which has been a signature method of linguistic anthropology and sociolinguistics since at least the 1970s (Duranti 1999; Heath et al. 2010). Traditionally, the maxim that many students have learned from mentors is to record as often as possible in order to capture nuances of speech and interaction that would be missed or mis-recorded if captured only with pen and paper. However, even a video recording focuses on what its operator wishes to focus on and thus has a perspective embedded in it (Goodwin 1994). Video recording is thus an additional locus at which inequities regarding knowledge production in the research process can emerge. Furthermore, recordings in many cultural contexts are incomprehensible even to scholarly audiences without a significant amount of interpretive work that is provided by the ethnographer. Recording should therefore be thought of as a complement to participant-observation and not a substitute for it (Duranti 2006). Recorded speech data are not an end goal of linguistic anthropology but rather are one of a number of methods that can be used to document and theorize communicative practices in their situational, cultural, and socioeconomic context. Ethical research in linguistic anthropology, as this book argues overall, includes participating in and documenting communication in many forms from many different types of participants.

When understood in this way, an important question to ask is how research participants understand, orient toward, and evaluate the use of recording devices in each research context (Speer and Hutchby 2003). Especially in the age of social media and smartphones, researchers in almost any fieldwork context need to investigate culturally specific attitudes, ideologies, and models surrounding the appropriate use of recording devices and should respond to these in the design and implementation of data-collection activities. Similar to how "learning how to ask" questions in appropriate ways in a given cultural context is a necessary prerequisite to conducting interviews, *learning how to record* in culturally appropriate ways is a prerequisite for collecting audio and video data. For instance, while doing fieldwork in South Africa with people living with HIV/AIDS, Black had to understand not only typical South African uses and understandings of cell phones and video cameras, but also specific concerns and attitudes related to the use of such devices in the context of pervasive HIV stigma. The audio and video recorders became extensions of the ethnographer's social self, extensions through which he could display an ethico-moral stance on the protection of research participants' anonymity, dignity, and freedom. Sometimes, having the recorder but not using it served as a way to demonstrate that Black understood the (sensitive/shifting) dynamics of disclosure, especially in home/community contexts (Black 2017). This example reinforces the idea that what is possible, legal, or allowable within the confines of one's IRB consent documents or common linguistic anthropological practice for recording is not always the same as what is advisable or ethically sound in a particular cultural context or fieldwork situation.

Once recordings have been made, linguistic anthropologists engage in a range of transcription, translation, and playback activities in order to capture research participants' communicative practices on the written page and to analyze these practices (see Shohet and Lloyd, this volume). In some cases, it may be possible for a researcher to rely on their own expertise in interpreting recorded and transcribed data. However, such analysis is enhanced, and sometimes challenged, by playback interviews and annotated transcription activities (Bucholtz 2001, 179–80; Schiffrin 1996). Interviewees and transcription assistants should be fairly compensated for their time and expertise in these activities.

In playback and annotated transcription activities, ethical issues may arise with respect to the fact that the interviewee or assistant may be a third party, often from the same community as the speakers in the recorded discourse, who is given access to conversations and information to which they would not otherwise have access. In some contexts, research participants may feel comfortable allowing academics and students who are distant socially (and often, geographically) to hear and see recorded conversations but may not feel comfortable allowing community or family members to do so. One reason for this is that socially distant persons may not have a stake in familial, social, or political conflicts and issues that are significant to research participants. In South African fieldwork, Black could share audio and video data with American academic audiences, but sharing data with South Africans was predicated on a careful evaluation of their social ties, community membership, and background. Participants were not concerned about American academics learning about their HIV positive status because there was little chance of these audiences ever coming into contact with the research participants. During fieldwork, Black worked with a research participant to transcribe, translate, and annotate data in which she was a participant, and he also completed annotated transcription activities with a student at a nearby university who had no ties to participants' home communities.

Researchers should approach the question of if and how to engage in playback or annotated transcription activities from the perspective of care, asking questions such as these: Who could be harmed through these activities? Who is in need of care being taken to protect anonymity and confidentiality? What would the benefits of these activities be, and would the group of people who are benefiting overlap with the group of people in need of care? Black's recent fieldwork studying communication among global health professionals demonstrates how the answers to these questions can be complicated even when studying powerful institutions. Global health professionals occupy positions of relative power, sometimes controlling the flow of millions of dollars and the administering of life-saving medications. Still, their efforts are dependent on donations from wealthy philanthropists and pharmaceutical companies as well as government grants. If Black were to reveal negative information about a particular global health professional or organization, this might impact not only the individual's career or the organization's success, but also the health and well-being of aid recipients. In this context, care for marginalized aid recipients also entails a certain amount of care for powerful aid givers. The ethics of the ethnographic study of language, we suggest, always entails complex and multifaceted relationships that extend far beyond a narrow understanding of the researcher-research participant dichotomy.

4.3.4 Online/New Media Data Collection

While some scholars have been investigating communicative practices in online settings since the 1980s and 1990s (Wilson and Peterson 2002), more recently there has been a proliferation of scholarship on this topic in linguistic anthropology (e.g., Gershon 2010; Hillewaert 2015; Ross 2019; Thurlow and Mroczek 2011). Professional conventions for appropriate ethical practices in online contexts are still being discussed and constructed (Boellstorff et al. 2013; Collins and Durington 2013). However, based on our review of available literature, below we suggest that linguistic anthropologists should devote more space in publications to describe the ethical considerations that are inherent in data collection from online sources.

Researchers often begin by applying existing ethical principles on anonymity, confidentiality, and care to these distinct contexts. However, this approach is not necessarily valid, given the complex connections (or lack thereof) between virtual and actual world personas (Boellstorff et al. 2013, 130) and the ambiguously "public" nature of many online activities. Dynamics of confidentiality may vary dramatically from one platform to another. For instance, Facebook and Twitter handles are often but not always aligned with persons' offline names and lives, while Reddit and Tumblr provide more anonymous forums. With the prevalence of Facebook, WhatsApp, Twitter, and other media apps around the globe, one important consideration for all fieldworkers is how to manage their own digital profiles and their documentation (if any) of research participants' digital practices (Modan 2016). A researcher may want or need to keep their digital personal life separate from their fieldwork life and may create a separate professional or research profile in order to do so. While this might seem misleading or disingenuous, it mirrors the ways that people sometimes maintain a clear distinction between work life and home life, and in certain research contexts this separation between work and home may prove essential for the mental health of the researcher. On the other hand, online interactions may become a crucial resource for bridging the personal-professional divide in ways that make the researcher a more integral part of a fieldwork community. For instance, during fieldwork in South Africa, even though Black had become Facebook friends with numerous research participants and he had broad consent to document their communicative practices through his participant-observation, he decided not to collect any data from research participants' Facebook activities. Online communication was not the primary focus of Black's research and he felt that to collect this data would have required in-depth conversations with participants about what aspects of their online presence they considered private, what (if any) they considered public, and what sorts of information they would give consent for him to collect.

Some of the most confusing questions in the study of online communication are these: What counts as public discourse and what kind of consent is required for different media platforms and communities? When a scholar is studying discourse in a private online chat group, for instance, it is clear that they must communicate their status as a researcher, obtain informed consent to collect data, and maintain anonymity and confidentiality in accordance with consent agreements (e.g., Vernon 2014). When information is clearly situated as public, as is generally the case with blog posts, podcasts, or YouTube videos posted for public consumption, researchers can usually collect data without informed consent, subject to IRB approval (see Markham and Buchanan 2012; SACHRP 2013). However, some cases initially seem clearer than they actually are. For instance, is documenting what people write in the comments section of a Facebook post whose privacy setting is "public" more like documenting a comment at a community meeting open to reporters and the public? Or is it more like sitting in a crowded plaza and overhearing what some research participants and other community members are saying to one another in what they think is a relatively private conversation? Or, perhaps, does it entail novel communicative norms not comparable to face-to-face interaction? In addition to the need to fulfill informed consent requirements as stipulated by the IRB, we suggest that fieldworkers should once again approach these ethical questions from the standpoint of a care orientation. Who might be hurt through the documenting of these discourses, and who might benefit? How would this online data collection contribute to the overall care goals and respond to the overall care concerns that are embedded in other facets of the research? Finally, when in doubt about public-private distinctions in online research contexts, it is generally better to err on the side of caution and ask for permission.

4.4 Case Study

A case study is presented in this section that illustrates many ethical issues entailed in doing linguistic anthropological research, especially the ethical complexities that result from the entanglement of researcher and participants in institutional research contexts. We discuss Riner's work studying military veterans enrolled in a Veterans Administration (VA) yoga program. In 2019, Riner set out to conduct research in partnership with the VA and she is just beginning data collection at the time of writing this chapter. Collaborating with an institution such as the VA that is designed to care for others can entail particular ethical complexities, as there are layers to the care structure embedded in institutional research relationships. Structuring a research project around "care" for an institution such as the VA can purportedly help the institution enact care for its patients. Because care for veteran patients is the goal of both the research project and the VA, deciding whether and how to critically evaluate the institution is difficult, as damage to the institution via public or academic criticism could be deleterious to those hopefully benefiting from it (i.e., the veteran patients). However, a research project may reveal inequities or types of harm endemic to the institution and revealing these could arguably serve as a form of care for its beneficiaries. The ethical complexities of critiquing institutions of care are further complicated by anthropology's potential complicity in the institutions it seeks to critique (Munyikwa 2019).

Riner's research project investigates yoga as a form of therapy for veterans suffering from mental trauma, focusing on embodied posture, movement, and communication as mechanisms for recovery (Black 2019; Koch et al. 2012; Mattingly 1998; Van der Kolk 2014). She was therefore committed to video-recording VA yoga sessions so she could analyze the veterans' bodies as they talked and practiced yoga together. In order to protect the interests of the veterans and the VA, the VA had numerous requirements to allow her to conduct her research. Such requirements serve to protect military service members and veterans as a vulnerable population who have historically been submitted to manipulative, unconsented, and often dangerous research practices (Annas and Grodin 1999).

For one, Riner was required to obtain non-compensated work status at the VA. She was therefore institutionalized as a VA employee during her research, which subverted in part her status as an institutional outsider, a typical ethnographic positionality. Being subsumed under the VA has provided her with a new set of allegiances and responsibilities to which she would not have been attuned had she not been indoctrinated as an employee. This has proven crucial to maintaining an orientation of care toward her research participants. Riner's allegiance as a VA employee (at least as she understands it) is first and foremost to the well-being of the veterans, and second to her research goals.

While there is potential for the VA's institutional oversight of her research to shape its methods and outcomes, this is outweighed by the benefits of operating as an insider, which affords unparalleled access to the workings of the institution. It also solidifies her position as a collaborator with, rather than merely a voyeur of, VA practices. Because Riner is not a veteran herself, she would never have been able to achieve equal footing with the research participants, though her status as a VA employee has certainly crystalized an asymmetrical relationship with the veterans, the implications of which remain to be seen. As a VA employee, she has been positioned as a "care provider" vis-à-vis the veterans alongside the other VA providers. This may foster the potentially problematic asymmetrical, sometimes paternalistic care relationship discussed above—the sort of relationship that anthropologists have attempted to eschew by leveling inequities in knowledge production between researchers and their participants through collaborative project design, data-gathering practices, and dissemination of the research. Maintaining a care orientation in her research has thus required her to stay attuned to such power differentials and develop ways to level them. Riner therefore framed her project to the veterans participating in it as a way for them to promote and expand their yoga program. One of their chief complaints is that despite the immense benefits they have received from the program, it remains largely invisible to the VA administration and to many providers. She can thus position herself as an institutional insider who can help validate and advocate for the program.

The VA is fervently committed to protecting the identities and sensitive information of its veterans. Therefore, in addition to having her project reviewed by her university's IRB, Riner was required to go through a multi-step approval process internal to the VA. This included having the potential benefits of the project, methods for maintaining confidentiality, and potential harms to participants vetted at multiple institutional levels, including by the VA director. Because the majority of VA research follows the biomedical model, there are federally mandated provisions in place for how to obtain informed consent and how data should be managed, all of which follow the model of weighing harms versus benefits in the research process. While such a system is good at avoiding easily identifiable forms of harm, such as potential side effects of an experimental treatment plan, it does not facilitate the development of relationships very well, as it involves extensive bureaucratic practices that are often disruptive to building trust and rapport in an ethnographic setting and that in many cases do not parallel the types of research being conducted by linguistic anthropologists. The templates for the VA consent process, for instance, are all drawn from biomedical research, which is conducted extremely differently from ethnographic research (the project was in fact submitted under the biomedical IRB, through which all local VA studies are processed). They thus include language that often does not make sense to the participants involved in ethnographic research. Additionally, many veterans Riner has encountered see themselves as powerless cogs in the vast, inefficient, and, to some, corrupt machinery of the VA. Many of them indeed do not have the resources to seek medical care elsewhere, even if they wanted to. They are used to overwhelming paperwork, a majority of which they automatically sign because of their need for treatment and desire to quicken the process at any cost.

Riner's consent form could easily have been presented as just another paper for them to sign, and compliance in the project could have been perceived as just another step required to maintain their treatment. The VA consent form is seven pages long, written in bureaucratic language that was not easy for many of her participants (nor Riner herself) to follow. Since she was not permitted to engage with the veterans before they signed the consent form, this document marked the entry into their relationship. However, given her quasi-outsider status within the VA, she was able to use the consent process as a way for them to collectively explore, evaluate, and provide meta-commentary on the project and the research process itself. Riner is also committed, as maintained above, to keep the consent process an ongoing, developing conversation, rather than one that begins and ends with the signing of a document. These bureaucratic hurdles required to complete research are of course not unique to the VA; any informed consent process will have to contend with these issues.

Receiving permission to video-record proved to be a complex process, given the VA's commitment to protecting veterans' identities and confidential information.[3] First, Riner is required to use VA-provided recording equipment with no hard drive on which video is stored. The camera records onto an SD card and after each recording session she transfers the video file to an encrypted VA computer and erases the SD card's memory. She then uses editing software on the VA computer to blur the faces of the participants and erase any audible identifiers, after which she saves the edited file to the VA network and erases the original audio and video files. As discussed earlier, deleting non-edited, original data files can be an important step for many researchers, as their data are always potentially open to subpoena, which would override any IRB agreements in place.[4] Riner will transcribe the edited recordings on the VA computer and thus any and all data and data-based files she takes with her off the VA campus for the dissemination of her research will be de-identified.

Riner is also conducting interviews to understand the veterans' perspectives on the yoga program and their experiences during their yoga practice. For the interviews, her primary concern is to make sure the veterans feel secure, as many of them may share personal information about their past experiences that may have been traumatic and may continue to be traumatic to recall. For this reason, as well as the fact that most of them are comfortable with the setting of psychotherapeutic interview, she decided to conduct the interviews in a secure space in the VA mental health wing. Because Riner has been attending the yoga sessions and talking and spending time with the veterans in that context, the interviews have taken the format of continued conversations, rather than abruptly disparate communicative events.

While the interview setting Riner chose is familiar to veterans, and thus follows the "learn how to ask" recommendation, it nonetheless reinforces the hierarchical relationship of care provider/patient that she is subsumed under given her VA status. In an attempt to at least partially subvert this asymmetry, in her interviews she has chosen to put the research participant in an explicit position of objectifying their actions and the researcher-participant relationship. To accomplish this, Riner is using a version of the playback strategy, in which she will, in subsequent interviews, review video data of the yoga sessions with the veterans. While the researcher traditionally holds the position of objectifying and evaluating the actions of research participants, this strategy allows the participants to be the ones to observe, evaluate, and categorize their own behavior, the researcher's behavior, and their interactions depicted in the video, thus flipping the typical power differential embedded in research.

4.5 Concluding Remarks

As illustrated in the case study that we discussed in this chapter, the care orientation to research is just that: an orientation. It is a stance from which to consider research methods and practices given the inequities, power differentials, and needs of participants involved in any research project, rather than a fixed set of universally applicable ethical guidelines. The solutions available in any given research context may not be ideal, but the care orientation urges us to continually reevaluate our relationships with participants and their needs from a place of respect when conducting research. Such an orientation also encourages us to critically evaluate inequities and hierarchies in the broader institutional, community-wide, and social contexts in which our research is set. Crucially, this is neither an all-or-nothing approach nor a zero-sum game. Depending on the research context, care might mean aligning with certain institutional goals while critiquing other institutional priorities, supporting one group of research participants while keeping another group at arm's length, or disavowing an institution and aligning with a marginalized community. Across contexts, a care approach involves moving conversations about research ethics from an emphasis on connections with research participants (something that is important but not sufficient for research ethics) to an examination of actions that might be taken in response to existing care deficiencies and inequities—both known deficiencies and deficiencies that researchers may become aware of during fieldwork.

4.6 Ethnographic Activities

1 Choose a hypothetical context in which you could conduct linguistic anthropological research. Try to identify all the potential actors (including groups and institutions) linked to your research context. What are the different needs of each of these actors? How might you weigh these different needs against each other? Which needs would you prioritize and why?

2 Choose an example of existing ethnographic research on language and culture. Read through the study with an attention to research ethics, and answer the following questions: Does the study mention ethical approvals? Does it mention any other ethical issues, questions, or concerns? If so, what are they? If not, what are some possible issues, questions, or concerns that you think could have been productively addressed in the study's write-up, and why?

4.7 Questions to Consider

1 What is the difference between "doing no harm" and "doing some good"? Provide specific examples while you describe this difference.

2 What are some ways that you care for others in your everyday life? How might these relate to doing ethnographic fieldwork?

3 Describe the difference between confidentiality and anonymity. How do these principles figure into linguistic anthropological research?

4 What are some of the ways that the case study presented in this chapter complicates both (a) the common stereotype of an ethnographer studying a marginalized community and (b) the idea of "studying up" (where the ethnographer is studying a wealthy/powerful community)? And how can a care standpoint help the researcher to navigate these complexities?

4.8 Notes

1   https://www.hhs.gov/ohrp/regulations-and-policy/regulations/finalized-revisions-common-rule/index.html
2   http://linguisticanthropology.org/socialjustice/
3   Riner is indebted to many VA staff for helping her navigate this process.
4   It may be possible in research on sensitive topics to obtain confidentiality agreements that allow researchers to protect the private information of their participants, even if legal action is taken (Monette et al. 2010, 60).

4.9 References Cited

Abu-Lughod, Lila. 1991. "Writing against Culture." In R. G. Fox ed., *Recapturing Anthropology: Working in the Present*, 466–79. Santa Fe, NM: School of American Research.

American Anthropological Association (AAA). 2012. "Statement on Ethics." Available online: https://www.americananthro.org/LearnAndTeach/Content.aspx?ItemNumber=22869&navItemNumber=652

Annas, George J., and Michael Grodin 1999. "Medical Ethics and Human Rights: Legacies of Nuremberg." *Hofstra Law and Policy Symposium* 3: 111–24.

Avineri, Netta, Laura R. Graham, Eric J. Johnson, Robin Conley Riner, and Jonathan Rosa. 2018. *Language and Social Justice in Practice*. New York: Routledge.

Bernard, H. Russell. 2011. *Research Methods in Anthropology: Qualitative and Quantitative Methods*. New York: AltaMira Press.

Black, Steven P. 2017. "Anthropological Ethics and the Communicative Affordances of Audio-Video Recorders in Ethnographic Fieldwork: Transduction as Theory." *American Anthropologist* 119 (1): 46–57.

Black, Steven P. 2019. *Speech and Song at the Margins of Global Health: Zulu Tradition, HIV Stigma, and AIDS Activism in South Africa*. New Brunswick, NJ: Rutgers University Press.

Boellstorff, Tom, Bonnie Nardi, Celia Pearce, and T. L. Taylor. 2013. "Ethics." In T. Boellstorff, B. Nardi, C. Pearce, and T. Taylor eds., *Ethnography and Virtual Worlds: A Handbook of Method*, 129–50. Princeton, NJ: Princeton University Press.

Brandt, Elizabeth A. 1988. "Applied Linguistic Anthropology and American Indian Language Renewal." *Human Organization* 47 (4): 322–9.

Briggs, Charles. 1986. *Learning How to Ask: A Sociolinguistic Appraisal of the Role of the Interview in Social Science Research*. Cambridge: Cambridge University Press.

Briody, Elizabeth K., and Tracy Meerwarth Pester. 2015. "'Do Some Good' and Other Lessons from Practice for a New AAA Code of Ethics." Available online: http://ethics.americananthro.org/do-some-good-and-other-lessons-from-practice-for-a-new-aaa-code-of-ethics/

Buch, Elana D. 2015. "Anthropology of Aging and Care." *Annual Review of Anthropology* 44: 277–93.

Bucholtz, Mary. 2001. "Reflexivity and Critique in Discourse Analysis." *Critique of Anthropology* 21 (2): 165–83.

Clancy, Kathryn B. H., Robin G. Nelson, Julienne N. Rutherford, and Katie Hinde. 2014. "Survey of Academic Field Experiences (SAFE): Trainees Report Harassment and Assault." *PLOS ONE* 9 (7): e102172.

Collins, Samuel, and Matthew Durrington. 2013. "An Ethics of Multimedia Practice?." *AAA Ethics Blog: A Forum Sponsored by the AAA Committee on Ethics*. Available online: http://ethics.americananthro.org/an-ethics-of-multimedia-practice/

De Fina, Anna, and Sabina Perrino. 2011. "Introduction: Interviews vs. 'Natural' Contexts: A False Dilemma." *Language in Society* 40 (1): 1–11.

Dobrin, Lise M., and Saul Schwartz. 2016. "Collaboration or Participant Observation? Rethinking Models of 'Linguistic Social Work.'" *Language Documentation and Conservation* 10: 253–77.

Duranti, Alessandro. 1999. *Linguistic Anthropology*. New York: Cambridge University Press.

Duranti, Alessandro. 2006. "Transcripts, Like Shadows on a Wall." *Mind, Culture, and Activity* 13 (4): 301–10.

Elegant, Naomi. 2018. "Penn Removes Portrait of Former GSE Dean with Alleged History of Sexual Harassment." *The Daily Pennsylvanian*, April 11, 2018. Available online: https://www.thedp.com/article/2018/04/gse-getup-sexual-harassment-dell-hymes-portrait-removal-upenn-penn-philadelphia

Fabian, Johannes. 1983. *Time and the Other: How Anthropology Makes Its Object*. New York: Columbia University Press.

Fluehr-Lobban, Carolyn. 1994. "Informed Consent in Anthropological Research: We Are Not Exempt." *Human Organization* 53 (1): 1–10.

Folbre, Nancy. 2014. *Who Cares? A Feminist Critique of the Care Economy*. New York: Rosa Luxemburg Stiftung.

Fox, Aaron. 2004. *Real Country: Music and Language in Working-Class Culture*. Durham, NC: Duke University Press.

Gershon, Ilana. 2010. *The Breakup 2.0: Disconnecting over New Media*. Ithaca, NY: Cornell University Press.

Gilligan, Carol. 1982. *In a Different Voice*. Cambridge, MA: Harvard University Press.

Glenn, Evelyn Nakano. 2010. *Forced to Care: Coercion and Caregiving in America*. Cambridge, MA: Harvard University Press.

Goodwin, Charles. 1994. "Professional Vision." *American Anthropologist* 96 (3): 606–33.

Heath, Christian, Jon Hindmarsh, and Paul Luff. 2010. *Video in Qualitative Research*. Los Angeles: Sage Publications.

Heller, Monica, and Bonnie S. McElhinny. 2017. *Language, Capitalism, Colonialism: Toward a Critical History*. North York, ON, Canada: University of Toronto Press.

Hillewaert, Sarah. 2015. "Writing with an Accent: Orthographic Practice, Emblems, and Traces on Facebook." *Journal of Linguistic Anthropology* 25 (2): 195–214.

Jacobs-Huey, Lanita. 2002. "The Natives Are Gazing and Talking Back: Reviewing the Problematics of Positionality, Voice, and Accountability among 'Native' Anthropologists." *American Anthropologist* 104 (3): 791–804.

Jaffe, Alexandra. 2012. "Collaborative Practice, Linguistic Anthropological Enquiry and the Mediation between Researcher and Practitioner Discourses." In Sheena Gardner and Marilyn Martin-Jones eds., *Multilingualism, Discourse and Ethnography*, 334–52. New York: Routledge.

Keane, Webb. 2016. *Ethical Life: Its Natural and Social Histories*. Princeton, NJ: Princeton University Press.

Koch, Sabine, Thomas Fuchs, Michela Summa, and Cornelia Muller. 2012. *Body Memory, Metaphor and Movement*. Amsterdam: John Benjamins.

Kroskrity, Paul V., Rosalie Bethel, and Jennifer F. Reynolds. 2002. *Taitaduaan: Western Mono Ways of Speaking*. Norman: University of Oklahoma Press.

Labov, William. 1972. *Language in the Inner City: Studies in the Black English Vernacular*. Philadelphia: University of Pennsylvania Press.

Markham, Annette, and Elizabeth Buchanan. 2012. *Ethical Decision-Making and Internet Research: Version 2.0*, recommendations from the AoIR ethics working committee. Available online: https://aoir.org/reports/ethics2.pdf (accessed January 21, 2020).

Mattingly, Cheryl. 1998. *Healing Dramas and Clinical Plots: The Narrative Structure of Experience*. New York: Cambridge University Press.

Meskell, Lynn, and Peter Pels, eds. 2005. *Embedding Ethics*. London: Berg Publishers.

Modan, Gabriella. 2016. "Writing the Relationship: Ethnographer-Informant Interactions in the New Media Era." *Journal of Linguistic Anthropology* 26 (1): 98–107.

Monette, Duane, Thomas Sullivan, and Cornell DeJong. 2010. *Applied Social Research: A Tool for the Human Services*. Belmont, CA: Brooks/Cole.

Munyikwa, Michelle. 2019. "On Gratitude, Ethnography, and Care." *Synapsis*. Available online: https://medicalhealthhumanities.com/2019/10/27/on-gratitude-ethnography-care/

Murphy, Keith M. 2017. "Art, Design, and Ethical Forms of Ethnographic Intervention." In Gretchen Bakke and Marina Peterson eds., *Between Matter and Method: Encounters in Anthropology and Art*, 97–116. New York: Bloomsbury Academic.

Nader, Laura. 1972. "Up the Anthropologist: Perspectives Gained from 'Studying Up.'" In D. Hymes, ed., *Reinventing Anthropology*, 284–311. New York: Random House.

Noddings, Nel. 1984. *Caring: A Feminine Approach to Ethics and Moral Education*. Berkeley: University of California Press.

Pantazidou, Marina, and Indira Nair. 1999. "Ethic of Care: Guiding Principles for Engineering Teaching and Practice." *Journal of Engineering Education* 88 (2): 205–12.

Philips, Susan U. 1983. *The Invisible Culture: Communication in Classroom and Community on the Warm Springs Reservation*. New York: Longman, Inc.

Philips, Susan U. 2010. "The Feminization of Anthropology: Moving Private Discourses into the Public Sphere." *Michigan Discussions in Anthropology* 18: 283–323.

Ross, Scott. 2019. "Being Real on Fake Instagram: Likes, Images, and Media Ideologies of Value." *Journal of Linguistic Anthropology* 29 (3): 359–74.

Talmy, Steven. 2011. "The Interview as Collaborative Achievement: Interaction, Identity, and Ideology in a Speech Event." *Applied Linguistics* 32 (1): 25–42.

Samuels, David. 2004. *Putting a Song on Top of It: Expression and Identity on the San Carlos Apache Reservation*. Tucson: University of Arizona Press.

Schieffelin, Bambi. 1990. *The Give and Take of Everyday Life: Language Socialization of Kaluli Children*. New York: Cambridge University Press.

Schiffrin, Deborah. 1996. "Interactional Sociolinguistics." In Sandra Lee McKay and Nancy H. Hornberger eds., *Sociolinguistics and Language Teaching*, 307–28. New York: Cambridge University Press.

Secretary's Advisory Committee on Human Research Protections (SACHRP). 2013. Considerations and Recommendations Concerning Internet Research and Human Subjects Research Regulations. Available online: https://www.

hhs.gov/ohrp/sites/default/files/ohrp/sachrp/mtgings/2013%20March%20
Mtg/internet_research.pdf (accessed January 21, 2020).

Speer, Susan, and Ian Hutchby. 2003. "From Ethics to Analytics: Aspects of
Participants' Orientations to the Presence and Relevance of Recording
Devices." *Sociology* 37 (2): 315–37.

Spivak, Gayatri Chakravorty. 1988. "Can the Subaltern Speak?." In Carrie
Nelson and Lawrence Grossberg eds., *Marxism and the Interpretation of
Culture*, 271–316. Chicago: University of Illinois Press.

Thurlow, Crispin, and Kristine Mroczek eds. 2011. *Digital Discourse: Language
in the New Media*. New York: Oxford University Press.

Tronto, Joan. 1994. *Moral Boundaries: A Political Argument for an Ethic of
Care*. New York: Routledge.

Van der Kolk, Bessel. 2014. *The Body Keeps the Score: Brain, Mind, and Body in
the Healing of Trauma*. New York: Penguin Books.

Vernon, Muriel. 2014. "Transsexual Women's Strategies of Disclosure and
Social Geographies of Knowledge." In Mark Davis and Lenore Manderson
eds., *Disclosure in Health and Illness*, 120–37. New York: Routledge.

Wilson, Samuel M., and Leighton C. Peterson. 2002. "The Anthropology of
Online Communities." *Annual Review of Anthropology* 31: 449–67.

Zentella, Ana Celia. 1997. *Growing Up Bilingual: Puerto Rican Children in New
York*. Malden, MA: Blackwell Publishers.

Zigon, Jarrett, and C. Jason Throop. 2014. "Moral Experience: Introduction."
Ethos 42 (1): 1–15.

4.10 Further Reading

Black, Steven P. 2017. "Anthropological Ethics and the Communicative
Affordances of Audio-Video Recorders in Ethnographic Fieldwork:
Transduction as Theory." *American Anthropologist* 119 (1): 46–57.

Boellstorff, Tom, Bonnie Nardi, Celia Pearce, and T. L. Taylor 2013. "Ethics."
In T. Boellstorff, B. Nardi, C. Pearce, and T. Taylor eds., *Ethnography and
Virtual Worlds: A Handbook of Method*, 129–50. Princeton, NJ: Princeton
University Press.

Jaffe, Alexandra 2012. "Collaborative Practice, Linguistic Anthropological
Enquiry and the Mediation between Researcher and Practitioner
Discourses." In Sheena Gardner and Marilyn Martin-Jones eds.,
Multilingualism, Discourse and Ethnography, 334–52. New York: Routledge.

5

Participant Observation and Fieldnotes in Linguistic Anthropology

Sonya E. Pritzker and Sabina M. Perrino

5.1 Introduction

Participant observation, which usually involves extensive time spent in a particular community of practice or among a group of people engaged in a shared set of practices, constitutes one of the core methods in anthropology. Requiring researchers to pay careful attention to the mundane details of everyday life while simultaneously participating in activities and interactions, participant observation "is both a product and a process," writes Barbara Tedlock, which requires researchers to make an ongoing and constant set of *interactive choices* (1991, 72) while also crafting detailed and systematic fieldnotes that can be later analyzed as data. Through participant observation and long-term fieldwork, anthropologists, as Mathews and Izquierdo (2009, 9) argue, are able to understand "the complex cultural meanings that exist within a given society." For anthropologists in different subfields, however, the meaning of "cultural meaning" varies considerably. Researchers emphasizing a cognitive approach to culture, for example, often foreground the various forms of knowledge one needs in order to function in a given society, as well as the distribution of such knowledge across individuals (Goodenough 1957). Those emphasizing material culture, on the other hand, focus on the ways in which cultural meaning in both past and present societies might be derived from the shape, size, and appearance of objects (Tilley et al. 2006).

For linguistic anthropologists, generally speaking, understanding the meaning of meaning in a given context involves the close study of the way actors draw upon and refashion culturally salient forms of significance through words, gestures, eye gaze, and other forms of expression (e.g., Duranti 1997; Farnell and Graham 2015; Goodwin and Goodwin 2000; C. Goodwin 2018). Linguistic anthropologists thus foreground the ways in which culture emerges through discursive practices and within moment-to-moment interaction. This does not mean that linguistic anthropologists view culture as coming to life spontaneously or extemporaneously in particular conversations. As Charles Goodwin (2018, 3) keenly suggests, interaction—or what he calls "co-operative action"—constitutes a site where cultural meaning is "progressively shaped by a consequential past." Here, past interactions, structures of power, and ideologies permeate the present in ways that variably constrain the extent to which actors participating in a given conversation might be considered capable of challenging or transforming existing forms of cultural meaning (see Wortham and Reyes 2015). Within such constraints, however, C. Goodwin (2018, 3) argues that it is also important to consider cultural meanings as they are (re)produced and/or questioned in interaction as variably "contingent and open-ended" to the extent that their maintenance requires cooperative participation. Linguistic anthropologists thus examine not only the details of particular interactions, but also attend to the ways in which such encounters are always mediated by broader structural forces and systems of power. As Wortham and Reyes (2015) note, this can only be apprehended over time in studies that move beyond specific speech events.

The dual focus on the details of particular interactions as well as culture over time distinguishes linguistic anthropology from neighboring—and often complementary—approaches such as conversation analysis or sociolinguistics. Contrary to the belief that linguistic anthropologists rely on video or audio recording as primary methods of data collection, the centrality of understanding both broad cultural processes and particular interactions compels linguistic anthropologists to conduct rich ethnographic studies involving systematic participant observation and the writing up of fieldnotes. As we detail in this chapter, the process of participating in everyday activities and interactions over time, while also carefully recording fieldnotes, provides the perspective required to even begin make sense of the dynamic ways in which cultural meaning is reproduced, contested, or transformed within particular interactions over time.

In this chapter, we therefore provide an overview of the interconnected methods of participant observation and the development of fieldnotes in linguistic anthropological research. Throughout, our discussion focuses on both practical and ethical concerns. We especially foreground the dynamic relationship between participant observation, the recording of fieldnotes, and the collection of video and audio recordings in the field (see Kohler and Murphy, this volume). Overall, we examine phases of research involving active data collection, but we also discuss the ways in which the organization and storage of fieldnotes are implicated in the future analysis of such material for publication and presentation (see Shohet and Loyd, this volume).

5.2 Participant Observation in Linguistic Anthropology

As the chapters throughout this volume detail, studies in linguistic anthropology draw upon a wide and diverse range of approaches in terms of the research questions scholars aim to address, how studies might be organized in relation to a specific community or set of communities, and the literature researchers seek to contribute to. Depending on the specific research questions, for example, one's central fieldsite(s) may consist of a single physical or online location or multiple locations that may traverse both on- and offline communities (Bonilla and Rosa 2015; see also Crowley and Chun, this volume). Depending on the aim of the project and the literature it seeks to be in conversation with, a study may draw on a range of different perspectives on and approaches to understanding the very notion of "community." While early research often attempted to focus on collecting data within a distinct "speech community" (Gumperz 2001 [1968]), for example, in the past several decades linguistic anthropologists have increasingly come to question researcher-led attempts to define the location, boundaries, and makeup of speech communities (Ahearn 2017). Many researchers thus opt to focus on "communities of practice" (Lave and Wenger 1991), specifically upon groups that form around a particular activity (see Ahearn 2017).

Reframing the notion of community in terms of practice, as Ahearn (2017) describes, has allowed linguistic anthropologists to significantly expand the scope of their research in ways that afford recognition of the diversity inherent within human groups. Moving away from thinking of anthropological research as necessarily tied to a specific fieldsite, instead foregrounding particular kinds of *activities*, further offers linguistic anthropologists the opportunity to conduct participant observation in multiple and diverse settings. Research focusing on the organization of various forms of political protest and social activism (Barahona et al. 2012; Fine 2019; Lindgren 2013; Tufekci and Wilson 2012) or on gender identities (Bucholtz and Hall 2004, 2005), for example, has allowed linguistic anthropologists to conduct participant observation among groups of individuals engaged with one another across a range of contexts and web platforms as well as moving between on- and offline engagement (Bonilla and Rosa 2015; Calhoun 2019; Fine 2019; Smalls 2019).

No matter how one approaches the question of defining community, practice, or activity, participant observation—as its name implies—requires researchers to balance the demands of being an immersed *participant* while also being a "distanced" *observer*. Depending on the fieldsite, or field activity, one's study might involve more or less "passive" or "complete" forms of participation. This also depends on the appropriateness of the researcher's involvement and the setting in which the research is conducted (Duranti 1997, 99). Depending on funding, employment, and other opportunities/ constraints, moreover, one's fieldwork might be designed to consist of long-term immersion, short bursts of engagement, or some combination of the two. Regardless of these variations, participant observation offers immense value to the study of cultural meaning-making and human behavior. Participant observation, especially early on in a research project, Schensul and LeCompte (2013, 83–4) detail, also benefits anthropologists in the following ways:

- It is central to identifying and building relationships important to the future of the research endeavor.
- It gives the researcher an intuitive as well as an intellectual grasp of the way things are organized and prioritized, how people relate to one another, and the ways social and physical boundaries are defined.
- It demonstrates—and over time can confirm—patterns of etiquette, political organization and leadership, social competition and cooperation, socioeconomic status and hierarchies in practice, and other cultural patterns that are not easily addressed or about which discussions are forbidden.
- It legitimates the presence of the researcher in the community.

Participant Observation and Fieldnotes **129**

- It provides the researcher with cultural experiences that can be discussed with key informants or participants in the study site and treated as data.

(Schensul and LeCompte 2013, 83–4)

Spending time conducting initial phases of participant observation, we would add to this list, further offers researchers the opportunity to understand if their particular research questions—or even their particular fieldsite(s)—are valid and/or viable. Before fully embarking on a project requiring ethnographic fieldwork, for example, it would be valuable to have the chance to spend one or two summers of preliminary research in the selected fieldsite(s). This would offer researchers the invaluable opportunity to assess whether a particular fieldsite is a good match with the ethnographer's expectations and research agenda. Sometimes, moreover, sudden changes in the fieldsite location, such as social and political unrest, natural disasters (Perrino 2018), and/or a global pandemic (Briggs 2020; Kumar 2020), would force researchers to adapt to new situation(s) or to revisit their project in its entirety. In this respect, a great adaptability is expected in any kind of ethnographic fieldwork. These general points arguably pertain to *any* type of participant observation. When conducting research in linguistic anthropology, however, it is important to think deeply about what a researcher needs to pay particular attention to collecting as *data* that address one's specific research questions.

5.2.1 What Qualifies as "Data" in Participant Observation?

In participant observation, there is no single right answer to the questions of "what should I notice?," "what should I observe?." Even in linguistic anthropology, the answer is always contingent on one's research questions as well as particular fieldsite(s), the time spent conducting research, and many other emergent variables. As Duranti (1997) lists, ethnographers generally, and linguistic anthropologists in particular, might attend to tracking and documenting:

- what people do in their daily lives (e.g. the activities they engage in, how they are organized, by whom and for whom)
- what they make and use (artifacts)
- who controls access to goods (land products) and technologies

130   Research Methods in Linguistic Anthropology

- what people know, think, feel
- how they communicate with one another
- how they make decisions (e.g. what is right or wrong, what is permissible, what is strange, unusual, what is true)
- how they classify objects, animals, people, natural, and cultural phenomena
- how the division of labor is organized (across genders, ages, social classes, ranks, etc.)
- how the life of the family/household is organized, etc.

(Duranti 1997, 90)

No matter what the focus is, however, research in linguistic anthropology often further prioritizes the study of how culture emerges across speech and other communicative practices (Farnell and Graham 2015), as well as sounds (Eisenlohr 2018; Kunreuther 2018) and texts (Pritzker 2014), to name just a few. If one's focus is on the organization of daily activities, one might conduct an ethnographic study of a single location or multiple locations in which such activities take place. Researchers in the interdisciplinary Center for the Everyday Lives of Families (CELF) project, for example, centered their research within the homes of middle-class families with two children in multiple international locations (see, e.g., Kremer-Sadlik and Kim 2007; Ochs et al. 2006; Saxbe and Repetti 2010; see also Shohet and Loyd, this volume).

In an analysis of activities among families who participated in CELF in Sweden and the United States, M. Goodwin and Cekaite (2018), for example, offer detailed examples of and embodied forms of expression as children and their parents interact while they prepare for school and work, cook meals, negotiate "screen time," do their homework, and read books together at bedtime. While their study relied on video recording, researchers were also spending time with the families as participant observers, albeit this research often involved more passive than active forms of participation. If a study is focused on how people within a certain professional environment make decisions, on the other hand, participant observation might involve sitting in on staff meetings or other situations where decisions are negotiated. As part of her long-term ethnography of an addiction treatment facility in the United States, for example, Carr (2011, 158) sat in on many board meetings in which, she writes, "[t]he linguistic labor ... consisted of collectively deciding the language that would evoke desired behaviors, practice, and sentiments in clients, staff, and funders alike." Whatever one's fieldsite or research question is, it is important to highlight that regardless of whether one is focused on "activities," "decisions," or "classifications," there is often a great deal of overlap in these categories.

While collecting video recordings of interaction is therefore helpful in making sense of what is happening in any given conversation, participant observation is necessary to interpret such data in a way that connects seemingly disparate interactions together. While conducting participant observation in linguistic anthropology, Duranti (1997, 92) notes, it is important to learn how to identify what types of interactions or encounters belong to the same "kind"—greetings, requests, apologies, or snubs, for example. In-depth participant observation, Duranti continues, allows researchers to notice such categories as well as to "make predictions about what a given act (including words) produces and where or how it might have originated" (1997, 92). *Making predictions* here affords a deeper understanding of the underlying beliefs, norms, or values that inhere (or vary) among participants. Upon first moving to the Southern United States, for example, one might assume that the use of the address terms "sir" and "ma'am" always references politeness. Over time, however, it would become clear that such terms variably signify politeness, sarcasm, or an indirect confrontation, depending on the discursive context (Davies 1997). In studies involving participant observation, understanding what constitutes "data" that are locally meaningful thus requires that researchers become as familiar as possible with the everyday worlds that participants inhabit, something that cannot be done with video recordings alone. As we discuss more later, understanding what constitutes data is also something that requires researchers to acknowledge the ways in which their own positions and perspectives, including their political, moral, and cultural biases as well as how their perspective may have had to do with where they were sitting or standing at the time any particular data were collected (Duranti 1997, 92). Understanding what constitutes "data" also depends on the kinds of relationships one has cultivated with research participants (Goebel 2019, 2020).

5.2.2 Participant Observation as Relational Method

As opposed to data-collection strategies that demand distance on behalf of researchers, participant observation is a *relational* method (Phipps 2010).

Relationship-building, as Schensul and LeCompte (2013) note, forms a critical first step in conducting participant observation in a given setting. Relationship building and relationship maintenance are arguably actually processes that are ongoing throughout the entire research, sometimes lasting many years beyond the conclusion of a particular study. In the early stages of a project, however, it is especially important for researchers to build rapport with potential participants. Becoming part of a community—however one defines it—is thus often likened to a form of "hanging out," which, Bernard (2018, 293) highlights, "builds trust, or rapport, and trust results in ordinary conversation and ordinary behavior in your presence." This often takes considerable time and effort and—for all anthropologists, but perhaps especially for linguistic anthropologists—requires researchers to learn how to communicate with participants across various sociocultural settings. Even if you are a native speaker of the language that your participants speak, participant observation requires attending to the ways in which specific people use language *pragmatically* in order to successfully maintain connections, achieve goals, or enact activities. Just like in "real life" when one is learning how to fit in among a new group of friends, colleagues, or neighbors who have developed certain ways of communicating with one another over time, a researcher must often learn new phrases or grammatical formations that hold currency among participants.

When learning how to communicate within a new environment, or even when learning how to engage with a familiar environment as a participant-observer rather than simply a participant, Bernard (2018, 292) underscores the value that "being a newbie" offers. At the start of a new project, even experienced anthropologists thus often make a number of potentially embarrassing mistakes. Such blunders, Blommaert and Dong (2020) highlight, can provide invaluable insights into one's topic or fieldsite. Bernard argues that even once one has become familiar with the people and the fieldsite, however, working at maintaining the perspective of a newbie is often quite rewarding. "Try ... to develop your skill," he writes, "at being a novice—at being someone who genuinely wants to learn a new culture" (Bernard 2018, 292). Taking the position of a "learner" when interacting with research participants not only helps ensure you will not be operating on assumptions, but arguably also helps to develop and maintain rapport with people who see you as someone who genuinely wants to learn—and continue learning—from them. Bernard (2018, 292) does highlight, however, that researchers must learn how to navigate between maintaining a novice's sense of curiosity and eagerness to learn and the display of cultural competence in situations where it is appropriate. Here, Bernard offers the example of an anthropologist whose work focused on heroin addicts in an urban environment. "His informants made it plain that Agar's ignorance of their lives wasn't cute or interesting to them" (Bernard 2018, 292). Whether or not one's research involves drug addicts or other marginalized lifestyles, however, high-stakes situations often demand researchers to enact whatever cultural competence they do have in order to establish legitimacy among participants. Ethically, it is important to respect participants as much as possible (see Black and Conley-Riner, this volume). If acting like a novice can cause harm to them, for example, ethnographers should make sure to act differently. Through these various enactments, moreover, ethnographers and participants co-construct a long lasting and solid rapport across time and space (Goebel 2019; Perrino 2021).

5.2.3 Participant Observation as an Experiential Method

It is important to recognize the ways in which participant observation is also an *experiential method* (Rapport 2010; Skinner 2010). Interaction between researchers and participants in *any* kind of research that involves at least some form of communication might arguably be assessed as involving the kind of embodied co-presence that marks all forms of "co-operative action" (Goodwin 2018). In participant observation, however, rather than simply being considered as something that ideally has little to no effect on the data, such experiences often constitute the very core of the data. "Ethnographic research calls for engagement in direct learning through physical and social involvement in the field setting," write Schensul and LeCompte (2013, 27). In this sense, the authors continue, "*[k]nowing … is first and foremost experiencing*" (Schensul and LeCompte 2013, 27, emphasis in original). What exactly does it mean to say that participant observation is an experiential method, however? One key role that experience plays in participant observation, notes Duranti (1997, 89), is that researchers "try to come as close as ethically appropriate to their subjects' cultural experience." Participant observation thus involves developing an understanding of what it feels like to live in a certain environment, to consume certain foods, to move in certain ways, to perform certain rituals, to greet and take leave of one another following certain norms and so forth. Even in the case of internet and/or virtual world research, researchers' experience spending hours of one's day interacting in online environments (e.g., Boellstorf et al. 2012; Nardi 2015; Postill and Pink 2012) can be construed as a form of "immersive cohabitation" in which one develops various levels of embodied co-presence with participants (Bluteau 2019). Immersing oneself in the activities of daily life during participant observation, whatever such activities may be and to whatever extent that one can join in, thus involves "an actively embodied and kinesthetic sensibility" (Burrell 2016, 147) in which researchers themselves become tools for collecting data that can later be analyzed alongside data collected by other means, including video and/or audio recorders.

Participant observation, in this sense, implicates and *affects* researchers themselves, including, for example, the ways in which simply by becoming immersed in a community, an activity, or an environment, researchers "become 'enlanguaged' by those social worlds" (Phipps 2010, 98). As a result, Phipps (2010, 98) concludes, "their ways of being and dwelling change, often profoundly, though also imperceptibly, as a result." At the same time, however, a second key step in the process of conducting research using participant observation involves the honed ability to make observations as a researcher whose attention is guided by particular research question(s). As noted briefly above, participant observation thus frequently shifts— sometimes rapidly—between what Duranti (1997) describes as "passive" and "complete" types of participant observation.

When Pritzker was conducting research in China on self-growth workshops in which participants engaged in "inner child work" (Bradshaw 1990; Pritzker 2016), for example, her fieldwork often involved intense participation in particular exercises and conversations, including drawing pictures of her own inner child or enacting the role of a participant's mother as she was guided into the past in order to face long-buried emotions. These intimate encounters afforded her the opportunity to develop a great deal of rapport with participants, as did sharing meals and living together in the same hotel for a week. Although there was never a moment in which Pritzker completely "forgot" that she was there doing research, the opportunity to stand back and simply observe was rare. In contrast, when Pritzker was conducting research on Chinese medical psychology in a busy Beijing hospital, the other physicians positioned her as a hospital intern who was there to observe senior physicians interacting with patients. Though still fully immersed in the activity of the clinic, this positioning afforded more time spent in the role of observer who stayed mostly quiet and took notes as well as, when patients agreed, video recordings. Here, it was only when she had the opportunity to interview patients privately that she was able to establish personal rapport, but such interactions tended to be relatively short. On the other hand, over several years of returning to the hospital, she did establish significant rapport with physicians and interns in the clinic precisely because of their shared positionality as "experts" vis-à-vis the patients.

Similarly, during her fieldwork in Senegal (West Africa), Perrino found herself in many sociocultural activities and situations in which she shifted from a more detached way of observing these events to ways in which she was actively included in them. In these cases, she had to take the time to reflect upon these events during the following days or at night when she was by herself. This last scenario was very frequent during her fieldwork in the village of Koungheul, in inner Senegal, where she was living with an extended family. She became so much part of the family that it was difficult to find times in which she was by herself. She would thus make an effort to write her daily fieldnotes at night when everyone else was asleep.

How can ethnographers find the most productive balance between closeness and detachment vis-à-vis their research consultants? Is there a balance that all ethnographers should aim at? As Perrino describes in Chapter 6, interviewees often make ethnographers as part of their life in important ways such as by including them in their daily activities or by telling them their intimate family stories. It is thus crucial that ethnographers reflectively keep all this in mind when they analyze the data collected under these circumstances. The practice of "*recording* and *reflecting* upon [one's] observations and experiences" (Schensul and LeCompte 2013, 27) is thus central to the goal of participant observation. The multitiered process of experiencing, observing, and then reflecting upon both in one's fieldnotes constitutes the dialogic emergence not only of culture (Tedlock and Mannheim 1995), but also of ethnography as a distinct and very rigorous method.

5.2.4 Participant Observation as Dialogic Method and the "Problem" of Objectivity

As Rapport (2010, 78) argues, studies conducted with participant observation are never able to capture "culture" as such. Because of their relational and experiential nature, any results are, in this sense, always dialogically situated within an intersubjective network generated by "the constitutive discourses in which fieldworkers have partaken while engaging in the activity of research" (Rapport 2010, 78). Just as linguistic anthropologists regard culture as continually emergent in interactions that reproduce and maintain but also sometimes challenge and inform existing values, meanings, and expectations, Rapport underscores the ways in which ethnography itself emerges in the conversations that ethnographers have with research participants, colleagues, professors, students, and friends over time. The dialogical nature of participant observation as a scientific method, however, raises a series of questions regarding the notion that *objectivity* is and should be the quintessential goal of all scientific research. What is commonly known as "the Oberver's Paradox" in linguistic anthropology and sociolinguistics was coined by William Labov (1972) as a way to talk about the tension that exists between the need "to find out how people talk when they are not being systematically observed" and the irony that researchers "can only obtain this data by systematic observation" (1972, 209), becomes particularly relevant. Also discussed as "the Hawthorne effect" based on Landsberger's (1958) observation that people's behavior changes when they are aware that they are being observed, the idea of having access to, let alone recording, ordinary behavior points to debates surrounding whether participant observation, as a method deployed by social scientists, ultimately qualifies as a form of "science."

Imagined as free from the contamination of "subjective" interpretations and biases, objectivity is considered to be the hallmark of research about the "real" (in contrast to the "imagined") world. Researchers in linguistic anthropology and related fields have thus developed a range of specific methods in order to mediate the observer's effect on participants' behavior. As cited earlier, Bernard, for example, draws a direct causal line between the rapport and trust developed between researchers and participants and the likelihood that participants will engage in "ordinary conversation and ordinary behavior" even while one observes as a researcher who will be reporting findings in a (sometimes) completely separate scientific community. Labov, on the other hand, addressed the Observer's Paradox by developing a technique involving asking participants to describe emotionally intense experiences such that they are more likely to "forget" about being observed. As De Fina and Perrino (2011, 4) point out, however, such an approach contains many questionable assumptions, including the notion that the method through which data are gathered (e.g., through interviews, observations, etc.) is "seen more as a context to be erased than as … interactional event[s] whose specificity should be understood" and the idea that research participants should be understood as "producer[s] of talk" that is "analyzable independently of the interaction." Such assumptions

Participant Observation and Fieldnotes 137

have been scrutinized as deeply problematic in terms of the ways in which early anthropological accounts developed notions of "culture" based on observations of talk and behavior that were not only *decontextualized* in the sense that data were "extracted from the multiple practices, events, and sites associated with their production" (Briggs and Bauman 1999, 486) but were also *detextualized* by separating talk and behavior from particular persons (Briggs and Bauman 1999, 486). Even more egregious, Briggs and Bauman (1999, 486) suggest, were the ways such data were then *recontextualized* or "inserted into new discursive contexts and contrastive historical and political-economic locations." The production of texts, museum exhibits, and popular narratives about particular and discrete "cultures" based on this kind of extracted evidence is thus arguably *less* rather than *more* scientifically valid. As Perrino (this volume) describes, linguistic anthropologists are thus advised to approach ethnographic interviews as *situated* discursive practices (Mishler 1986). Participant observation, in this sense, is no different in that it requires individual researchers to keep track of the ways in which their experiences and observations are always situated.

On the other hand, as Duranti notes, it is also important not to overestimate one's effect on research participants. Unlike a researcher-initiated interview, he reminds us, in participant observation there are many things that occur, which do not, in fact, implicate the researcher. "While in the field," Duranti (1997, 92) thus writes, "there are all kinds of interactions and transactions around us, the majority of which are (fortunately) not just caused by our mere presence." Duranti further cautions anthropologists and researchers from other disciplines to carefully examine how the very concept of objectivity is itself embedded in a particular set of cultural meanings, practices, and structures of power. "The problems with the term 'objectivity,'" he writes, "arise from its identification with a form of positivistic writing that was meant to exclude the observer's subjective stance, including emotions, as well as political, moral, and theoretical attitudes" (Duranti 1997, 85). In conducting ethnographic research that involves participant observation, Duranti thus concludes, objectivity "is not only impossible to achieve" but "is also a questionable goal" (Duranti 1997, 85). Questioning objectivity here does not mean that "anything goes" in participant observation. Studies must be organized in relation to a specific research question that is grounded in reasonable evidence, often a preliminary study. Studies are also often hypothesis driven in the sense that based on existing literature, study of the field, and/or preliminary research, researchers make educated guesses regarding what they will find in a given study.

Questioning objectivity, similarly, does not mean that researchers conducting participant observation are encouraged to let their "subjective" biases affect the research in an unrestrained manner. No matter what, throughout the process of conducting participant observation, the cultivation of one's ability to systematically *self-reflect* is thus critical. The self-reflexivity of the participant observer might be understood, as Duranti (1997, 86) suggests, as "the attempt to control or put between brackets one's value judgement[s]." Even though "observations are always filtered through the researcher's interpretive frames" (Schensul and LeCompte 2013, 88), in other words, one is often unaware—at least initially—of the types of moral, political, emotional, or intellectual "judgments" that shape such interpretative frames until and when one engages in exercises that develop such awareness. These kinds of judgments furthermore often develop over time, especially as one engages in fieldwork. Schensul and LeCompte (2013, 25) thus argue that participant observation requires "constant self-conscious reflection" in which researchers repeatedly revisit the ways in which they are thinking about the people, behaviors, and other activities that generate their data. As we discuss further later, a key process in the production of fieldnotes while conducting participant observation thus involves becoming aware of one's own emotional, embodied, and social experience over the course of the research, noting, for example, where one is drawn to sit, how it feels, and so forth. In this sense, ethnographic products dialogically emerge out of a continuous process of participation, observation, and reflection in which the researcher never "assumes *one* perspective," but rather "establishes a dialogue between different viewpoints and voices, including those of the people studied, of the ethnographer, and of [their] disciplinary and theoretical preferences" (Duranti 1997, 87). In the next section, we turn to how linguistic anthropologists use fieldnotes during and after their participant observation.

5.3 Fieldnotes in Linguistic Anthropology

Writing, organizing, and analyzing fieldnotes are other core skills that anthropologists must develop in conducting any kind of participant observation. Although they take many different forms, "fieldnotes," explain Schensul and LeCompte (2013, 48), "is a general term for recorded observations of any kind made in the field." Taken as a whole, they argue, the goal of fieldnotes is tracking "as accurately as possible the surrounding context, the behaviors, conversations, processes, and institutional structures that unfold in the presence of or manifest themselves to the researcher" (2013, 48). "Recordings," as the authors explain, might refer to anything from written descriptions of events, interactions, settings, or behavior to illustrations, photographs, collected objects and/or texts, or "brief videos" (Schensul and LeCompte 2013, 48). They thus underscore the range of modalities through which ethnographers collect and keep fieldnotes over the course of a project. During Pritzker's various projects, for example, she has predominantly taken fieldnotes by writing things down in the (in)famous "ethnographer's notebook" but has also frequently drawn out quick sketches, taken photographs, or sent herself short emails and texts. Similarly, Perrino has used notebooks to take notes even during her audio- and video-recording activities; she has taken photographs and used voice memos as well. Fieldnotes, in this sense, are not technologically restricted, and participant observers are encouraged to make use of both old and new technology. The voice memos and notes feature on many phones, for example, are new ways to add quick reflections when ethnographers are in a rush or don't have the time to sit down and write their fieldnotes. With the availability of recording apps in phones and tablets, moreover, recording thoughts and ideas on these devices has become more common (see also Kohler and Murphy, this volume).

As our previous description of what to pay attention to while conducting participant observation details, the way ethnographers take fieldnotes depends on their research questions but also on their individual attention to what happens around them when they are in their fieldsite(s). Schensul and LeCompte (2013) provide a general list, however, of what "good fieldnotes" consist of, including

- detailed descriptions of behaviors, structures, rituals, activities, events, and event sequences
- [answers to] the classic questions, "who, when, where, what, what for, for whom, how long, what happened next?"
- spatial arrangements
- clothing styles
- food and food preparation
- steps in the conduct of community rituals or regular daily activities.

(Schensul and LeCompte 2013, 58)

Especially in the beginning of a project, the authors note, fieldnotes may contain *a lot* of detail that may or may not become important in one's future analysis. "Over time," they add, however, "the balance shifts to selection based on an emerging focus" (Schensul and LeCompte 2013, 58). Here, the work of self-reflection further plays a critical role in the sense that what

> ethnographers must learn is how to get outside of their own heads, or how to go beyond their own ethnocentric frameworks for valuing, noticing, and naming so that they begin to notice—and to write down information about—items, domains, events, objects, animals, plants, people, and behaviors that have been defined as noteworthy to other ... people and cultures.
>
> (Schensul and LeCompte 2013, 62–3)

Learning how to do this responsibly and ethically is a skill that researchers develop over a lifetime. Reinforcing self-reflection—and in Schensul and LeCompte's (2013, 62) terms "getting outside of one's own head"—requires enormous discipline, commitment, and experience to the rigor of participant observation.

5.3.1 Fieldnotes versus Audio and Video Recording in Linguistic Anthropology

For linguistic anthropologists, audio and video recordings of everyday interaction are often significantly more involved than the "brief videos" that Schensul and LeCompte (2013) suggest. Linguistic anthropologists furthermore often tout the advantages of video recordings due to the fact that they allow researchers to repeatedly return to the data in order to analyze nuanced layers of particular interactions that might not be captured in the moment (Clemente 2014; Farnell and Graham 2015). It is nevertheless critical to understand the range of other ways to make "recordings" in ethnographic research in linguistic anthropology, and why it is therefore never recommended to *rely* solely on audio or video to collect data. As Black (2017, 54, emphasis added) points out, "[v]ideo recordings are particularly prone to *problematic*, unreflexive acceptance as objective 'data.'" What makes the "unreflexive acceptance" of video data as problematic relates to the reality that "*any process of documentation is, by definition, partial, that is it assumes a point of view and it is selective*" (Duranti 1997, 114, emphasis in original). Each recording tool, whether audio or video recorder (see Kohler and Murphy, this volume), or notebook, has both benefits and drawbacks. "Once we know the specific limitations and advantages of each tool," writes Duranti (1997, 114), however, "we are in a better position to know how to integrate technology to provide richer descriptions and more comprehensive analyses of complex sociocultural phenomena." While it may seem redundant to make notes when one is going to be able to review a video, it is important to recognize the ways in which video data may only offer limited perspectives on situations. Keeping a record of interactions or events that occurred prior to or after recording, for example, allows researchers to better situate the events included in the recording. If one is using only a single camera, as most researchers do, it is likewise critical to maintain a record of anything that might be occurring in frames not currently being recorded. Fieldnotes are further important ways that researchers can "document information about the participants in an interaction, including their cultural background, their profession or social status, age, previous knowledge of one another, their relationship with us" (Duranti 1997, 115).

There will also inevitably be times when one cannot or should not record. As Black (2017) details, for example, it is sometimes critical *not* to record using either audio or video equipment, especially when participants are discussing sensitive personal information. Confirming that you will not record a certain conversation that you recognize as sensitive, Black (2017) points out, is not only ethical in a basic sense but also important for building and maintaining trust and showing empathy (see Black and Conley-Riner, this volume). To relate this to our previous discussion, this is a time when demonstrating cultural competence is key even though ethnographers might "lose the opportunity" to collect those particular data. Depending on the nature of the conversation and the willingness of the participants, however, one can write it up later using pseudonyms and disguising other confidential information that might be identifiable on video. At other times, even if it is entirely appropriate to collect video, researchers may find themselves with an uncharged battery or even—if an invitation to an event was spontaneous, for example—without a professional video recorder or with a discharged phone (which could be used as a video recorder, too [see Kohler and Murphy, this volume]).

Pritzker's students in her linguistic anthropology methods course, for example, were having trouble understanding how one could conduct "real" linguistic anthropology without video. As an exercise, they all brought their notebooks when they attended a protest march being held by the Black Students Association (BSA) on the campus of the University of Alabama. After meeting to discuss their observations, students were astounded to see how much they had noticed and jotted down about interaction at the event. Their notes included reflections on—to name a few—the prosody of formal speakers and interactants in the crowd and the ease with which those marching together seem to cross both age and racial boundaries in striking up conversations. The central point here is that fieldnotes often provide an immense amount of detail about interaction that can supplement—and even sometimes replace—video recording.

Relying on video does not evade the reality that ethnographic research is both relational and experiential, however. "Even if we could approximate such a total audio-visual documentation," Duranti (1997, 113) writes, "it would still never be the same as the experience of 'being there,' and ... there might be situations for which a written record might be more revealing than a visual one." Collecting video also involves "subjective" decisions such as when to start and stop the video recorder, where to stand, who to follow in case two interactants split off, and other emergent situations. In some cases, researchers have given video recorders to participants in order to gather data that reflect their experience and perspective. Such research still involves intensive participation by the researcher(s) in terms of whom they give the video recorders to, where and when they advise them to record, and what they make of the data that participants capture. Keeping fieldnotes is important, finally, because it is often impossible to know in advance what will become important over the course of a project. For this reason, it is important to collect as much information as possible about whatever seems potentially relevant. The fact that we will not be able to know *everything* is not a reason to know *nothing* (Duranti 1997, 115, emphasis in original). The following discussion thus details the multiple different types of fieldnotes that anthropologists across a range of subfields have elaborated.

5.3.2 Types of Fieldnotes

Though the process of writing fieldnotes is often messy to begin with, it is important for researchers to develop a system for keeping track of different types of notes. This not only helps them to better remember what occurs around them, but also helps them begin to develop potential lines of analysis and develop their hypotheses. However, the process of keeping up with the crafting and organizing of fieldnotes is fairly tedious, often requiring multiple hours of writing and file maintenance at the end of exhausting days in the field. Throughout the process, the following categories of notes, which have been elaborated by anthropologists in a range of subfields, are helpful in guiding researchers:

1 **Head Notes:** Sanjek (1990) coined the term "head notes" to refer to the things that researchers in the field notice but don't, for whatever reason, have time to write down. Head notes, explain Schensul and LeCompte (2013, 60), "can be thought of as memories or mental notes kept in the ethnographer's head or memory until such time as it is possible to actually 'write things down.'" While conducting her fieldwork among Senegalese healers in several villages in Senegal, for example, Perrino would not have the time to sit down and write everything she noted while she was video-recording healer-patient interactions. More specifically, while she was interviewing her research participants, she would note healers' family members intervening in the interview or in the video-recording activity. She had to keep in mind some of the remarks they were making, the time when they were making their appearance, the reasons for such unexpected activities, and so forth. Perrino had to thus keep in mind many details and make the relevant connections after the event that she was video recording and after the interviews that she often conducted soon after the recorded healing encounters.

2 **Jottings or Scratch Notes:** Jottings or what Sanjek (1990) refers to as "scratch notes" include anything a researcher jots down quickly during the course of conducting fieldwork. Here, one might use a notebook or even the back of a napkin. Jottings could also include sending oneself a text message or record a voice memo/note on one's phone. Regardless of the medium, experienced anthropologists recommend getting the overall idea of a head note down in some form so it can be revisited later. Quick notes are helpful, Duranti (1997, 116) points out, in "correcting our shaky recollections" of specific events or interactions. Often helping to fill in important descriptive details that one can flesh out once there is more time, these notes might also consist of information that the researcher should add to log notes, methodological notes, or analytic notes (see below). For example, while conducting her interviews in Senegal and Northern Italy, Perrino would jot down notes on pieces of paper when certain details of the surrounding context were becoming relevant and could not be captured in the recording. It is important to then put all these separate notes together as soon as ethnographers have the time to sit down and write their daily fieldnotes.

3 **Descriptive Notes:** Descriptive notes are more detailed fieldnotes that researchers should generate at some point on each day of conducting fieldwork. These types of notes, explains Bernard (2018, 316), often consist of material based on things ethnographers observe by watching or listening and should be aimed at providing as thorough an account of "what's going on" as possible. In the process of recording descriptive fieldnotes, it is often extremely helpful to have any jottings, messages, or other data (textual, audio, visual, etc.) generated or gathered throughout the day nearby. Though sometimes fieldwork and/or travel prevents researchers from creating descriptive notes on a daily basis, doing so "as soon as possible," Duranti (1997, 116) highlights, is "imperative."

4 **Logs:** "A log," explains Bernard (2018, 312), "is a running account of how you plan to spend your time, how you actually spend your time, and how much money you spent." Though keeping such a detailed account of one's activities may sound mundane in comparison to descriptive notes, logs are important, Bernard (2018, 313) clarifies, because "the process of building a log forces you to think hard about the questions you really want to answer in your research and the data you really need." Especially because of the ways in which participant observation and ethnographic fieldwork are iterative and dialogic (see above), a log helps researchers keep track of the specific day-to-day activities through which new research questions develop (see Shohet and Loyd, this volume).

5 **Diaries:** Keeping a personal diary is critical when conducting participant observation. This is the place where researchers engage in the important work of self-reflection (see above). Because it is personal, one is allowed to be honest in ways that perhaps would not be appropriate in other types of notes. A diary can also serve, Bernard (2018, 311) writes, as "a place where you can run and hide when things get touch … It will help you deal with loneliness, fear, and other emotions that make fieldwork difficult." One can also use the diary format in order to keep track of what Skinner (2010, 121) calls "bodynotes" and defines as "a muscle memory, such as a dance step or dance lead." Like head notes, bodynotes here usually point to the kinds of embodied memories that all researchers accumulate over the course of conducting research. Learning how to write about such experiences within a private diary can lead to many unexpected insights in formulating other types as notes and can further contribute to analysis later on.

6 **Methods Notes:** Methods notes are exactly what their name suggests: notes about the ways in which data are collected. A researcher might make note of when they began recording using a video camera, for example, and when they stopped. They might also make a note about why they chose, in a given instance, *not* to use the video camera or why they shut off the audio recorder at a particular moment. Methods notes, adds Bernard (2018, 315), "are also about your own growth as an instrument of data collection."

7 **Analytic Notes:** Over the course of a project, researchers often have at least preliminary ideas about the ways in which data collected (in whatever form) contribute to the future analysis of a project. These types of notes, explains Bernard (2018, 316), "are often the basis for published papers or for chapters in dissertations or books." This usually happens when researchers go back to their fieldsites after their preliminary research.

5.3.3 Organizing and Analyzing Fieldnotes

Individual researchers must often experiment, over time, with the best ways in which to keep their fieldnotes organized and, most importantly, to protect them and to save them electronically. This, of course, depends on both personal preferences as well as contingencies of the fieldsite, such as access to electricity or WIFI, the availability of external hard drives, cloud spaces, and so forth. Fieldnotes might be organized, explain Schensul and LeCompte (2013, 79), "by date or by topic or by the persons involved, or all three." Researchers might further choose to use a certain kind of software program that allows them to attach fieldnotes of various types to specific video or audio clips (see Mitsuhara and Hauck, this volume, for a description on creating databases).

Although the focus of this chapter is on the active phases of data collection, we would like to underscore that keeping fieldnotes organized over the course of a project (in whatever way makes sense) is critical for a number of reasons that will become clear in later phases of research when one's study, no matter whether it is long term or relatively short term, is complete. While we speak of "phases" here, the temporality of this term can be misleading, since at least rudimentary forms of analysis inevitably take place on a daily (sometimes even hourly) basis while one is conducting participant observation and recording fieldnotes. This is why keeping analytic notes throughout the project, as described above, can be considered part and parcel of active data collection. It is even helpful to begin thinking about and constructing one's *coding scheme*—or list of themes and topics that repeatedly come up throughout the research (e.g., rebuttals, requests, and so forth)—concurrent to the writing of fieldnotes. The process of beginning to notice such themes, Bernard (2018, 321) suggests, often begins with what he calls "the ocular scan method, or eyeballing." Basically, Bernard (2018, 321) continues, this involves reviewing your notes and other data, "[y]ou live with them, read them over and over again, and eventually get a feel for what's in them." Bernard (2018, 321) calls the second stage of generating a coding scheme "the interocular percussion test, in which patterns jump out and hit you between the eyes." Both of these stages are often easily done in various software programs such as NVivo, Atlas, Dedoose, or Transana, which are designed such that researchers can "tag" notes, videos, audio clips, or downloaded webpages with various codes (or "nodes" in NVivo) that can later be edited, rearranged, or merged (see also Shohet and Loyd, this volume). It is also sometimes useful, especially when dealing with a lot of handwritten notes or textual objects such as flyers, brochures, and books, to go "old-school" and create piles on the floor of things that one thinks belong together. Regardless of how one goes about this process, it is important to keep in mind that coding schemes are not necessarily stable lists of themes that one *must* maintain rigidly over the course of a project (Bernard 2018). The ways in which a coding scheme utilizes mnemonics, labels, or subcodes is also flexible and may change over time. A researcher's consistent engagement with variations of the coding scheme throughout the course of data collection may be tedious and may lead to what may feel like a lot of "dead ends." Doing this work, however, often helps researchers refine their research questions and hone their attention on practices and facts that they had not anticipated or perhaps would not have noticed without beginning to code.

5.4 Ethical Considerations in Participant Observation

Besides following some important general ethical principles, all linguistic anthropological research projects also involve the requirement to consider unique ethical dynamics. More specifically, ethical issues, as connected to participant observation, relate to the ways in which ethnographers might bond with their research participants. Sometimes, these bonds can blur the lines between researcher(s) and collaborator(s), who can become close friends, and this entails some ethical considerations. As Kohn (2010, 194) reminds us:

> The spaces between and beyond the controlled environment of a "field," often well out of reach (in space and time) of consent forms, are fertile sources of reflexive understanding, which we as sensitive informed researchers should be able to harvest, but current institutional guidelines on ethical research practice determine that we shouldn't do this.

Any possible rapport between ethnographer(s) and research collaborators thus emphasizes an important "pragmatic morality" as it is situated within particular relationships across time and space (Kohn 2010, 91). As we mentioned earlier, sometimes linguistic anthropologists might opt to practice just participant observation instead of audio and/or video recording to respect the privacy of their research participants. As Black (2017) has argued, doing so can actually build a better rapport and develop trust between researcher(s) and research collaborators. It is thus key to weigh each situation carefully and be ethically sensitive by not imposing any research methodologies when research participants do not seem comfortable with them. Even by just practicing participant observation, linguistic anthropologists can still attend to language by writing down all the linguistic and pragmatic points that emerge in conversations, in interviews, and in their fieldwork everyday life, more generally.

Ethical concerns are also related to power dynamics between researcher(s) and collaborators. As Duranti (1997, 95) keenly argues, "[b]eyond ethnographers' intentions, motivations, or awareness, there are political and global processes that enter into the relationships they establish in the field … At the same time, one should not overestimate the power of researchers over their subjects or informants." It is thus crucial that researchers spend some time in their fieldsite(s) to better understand and appreciate the sociocultural setting before embarking into the relationships that emerge from intense participant observation. Duranti (1997, 95) thus reminds us that participant observation might better be considered as an ethical interpersonal negotiation within which "[w]e must fit into their lives just like they need to fit into ours."

Ethics in participant observation, as in every other linguistic anthropological research methodology and beyond, as demonstrated by the chapters of this collection, also extends to how ethnographers represent their collected data. Besides treating their data as highly confidential, researchers also need to think about how they will represent the materials collected in their projects. It is indeed ethically immoral for ethnographers to think that they can access their collaborators' perspectives and ideas even after fully participating in their daily lives for a long stretch of time (Rapport 2010). Along these lines, it is also key to know when to set one's boundaries in order to follow the preestablished ethical values. As Duranti (1997, 120–1) writes, "[t]here is no way of escaping the responsibility we have as researchers to the people we study ... We need to develop a theoretical understanding of our position and positioning in engaging in ethnographic methods." This does not mean that researchers should always write in a way to please their participants. Researchers should, however, carefully decide what to say publicly and weigh the potential consequences of their claims. We now turn to some case studies from our respective fieldsites to contextualize participant-observation practices even more.

5.5 Case Studies

As detailed in Chapter 12, which focuses on *mixed methods*, Pritzker learned first-hand the value of fieldnotes in conducting a study on self-development at a mind-body-spirit center in Beijing. She went into the field expecting to record video while also using fieldnotes as a supplementary form of data collection. Once she arrived and was welcomed by the center staff, however, she was told that they had decided she could no longer record any audio or video but was welcome to participate in events and workshops as a researcher (pending, of course, the consent of participants). This unexpected shift forced Pritzker into more of a mixed-methods approach than originally planned. The need to "pivot" in terms of specific methodological approaches, as she discusses in Chapter 12, is something that occurs often during fieldwork. Here, however, it is important to note the ways in which the total immersion afforded Pritzker precisely *because* she was unimpeded by the need to manage cumbersome video equipment allowed her to collect an incredibly rich dataset that has led to multiple publications and presentations (Pritzker 2016; Pritzker and Duncan 2019).

These products can be, of course, limited in key ways that challenge audiences especially in linguistic anthropology. In presenting her findings as part of a linguistic anthropology panel at a major conference after returning from fieldwork, for example, the panel discussant distinctly commented on how Pritzker's paper was the only one that did not offer either video or transcripts. This absence, the discussant suggested, made it difficult to make sense of Pritzker's conclusions. During the panel discussion, however, the methodological limitations of the fieldwork were approached as an opportunity to think collaboratively about what lack of video also affords in terms of the ways in which findings emerged from nearly continuous forms of participant observation and engagement with participants. In later products, Pritzker has thus foregrounded the methodological questions emerging from relying solely on fieldnotes to conduct research in linguistic anthropology (e.g., Pritzker 2019). Describing the ways in which the video camera had become the lens through which she had become accustomed to viewing the world, for example, Pritzker questioned if and how it would be possible to *not* engage with one's data as if recording. In Pritzker (forthcoming), moreover, the lack of video has allowed her to conduct a detailed analysis of what she noted, over the course of the project, was left unspoken. Having a camera would have been no help, for example, in noting the ways in which certain *unsaid* things often conveyed significant meaning.

Analogously, Perrino found herself in situations in which the use of her camcorder was not welcome. While she was often allowed to audio-record healer-patient interactions while she was conducting her research in Senegal (Perrino 2002, 2006, 2007, 2011), for example, it was not always appropriate to use her video recorder during these interactional events. In these cases, she would then use her notebook and pen to write down as many details of the surrounding context as possible. These details included children coming in and out the healer's cabin, healers' apprentices carefully observing the ongoing healing practices, the relatives of the various patients who were, or were not, allowed in the cabin, the conversations before and after the healing encounters, and so forth. All this contextualized information and movement would have never been caught in the video frames that Perrino was set to record. Nor was it caught in the audio recording that she often was allowed to collect. Her detailed fieldnotes thus became her main source of information when she analyzed those particular interactions once she was back in the United States.

In several of the Senegalese villages where Perrino conducted her research, moreover, electricity was available only during certain times of the day and was mainly used to aliment fridges and other essential machineries in the household where she was living. Audio and video recording was hardly an option under those conditions. She would then write detailed fieldnotes

5.6 Conclusion

very often during the day when she was left by herself or during the night, as we mentioned earlier. Like Pritzker, this also meant that she didn't need to go around with heavy video-recording equipment and she could thus concentrate on observing the various sociocultural and discursive practices while being part of them. She would also write down linguistic particularities that she would hear in the healing practices that she was observing. To make sure that her linguistic notes were correct, she would then ask follow-up questions to healers and patients whenever it was possible and appropriate. As it was often the case, healers would happily offer extra time to go over their healing practices and herbal remedies with her.

5.6 Conclusion

Why should linguistic anthropologists value more general, classic anthropological research methodologies such as participant observation and the collection and interpretation of their fieldnotes? Can audio- and/ or video-recorded data replace fieldnotes? Would writing fieldnotes while collecting audio- and/or video-recorded data be redundant? In this chapter, we have answered these questions and have described the key role that these classic anthropological research methods have for linguistic anthropological research. Against the naive assumption that audio- and video-recording practices, which are extensively used by linguistic anthropologists, generate "objective" data that are inherently superior to "subjective" observations recorded in fieldnotes, we have demonstrated that data collected with these tools can have different, more complete meanings if enriched by the detailed and meticulous collection of fieldnotes and the attentive practice of participant observation. Audio- and/or video-recorded data alone are unable to unveil foundational, contextual human processes, for example. Throughout the chapter, we have thus emphasized the centrality of participant observation and the careful documentation of events and interactions through the scrupulous writing of daily fieldnotes across fieldsites, including virtual ones.

Using examples drawn from our research, we have also highlighted the relational and pragmatic nature of these methodological practices, which are always dialogically situated within the particular research context(s) where researcher(s) and participants act. The dialogue that emerges between these social actors, moreover, is never limited in time and space. Rather it is carried over time and across space—when, for example, ethnographers continue their conversations with research participants at a distance. In this respect, we have also discussed the important notion of objectivity in research practices related to participant observation and fieldnotes recording, echoing well-known efforts to show that there is always a tension existing between the need "to find out how people talk when they are not being systematically observed" and the irony that researchers "can only obtain this data by systematic observation" (Labov 1972, 209). In this vein, we have examined some of the most significant ethical issues that can emerge while conducting fieldwork and engaging in participant observation.

5.7 Ethnographic Activities

1 Organize yourself to spend an hour in a public location, such as a café, a restaurant, a bar, and so forth and start observing people. Bring a notebook or laptop and take notes on the interactions that you note, the language that you hear, the context in which you are, and so forth. Write down as many details as possible in one hour. Write a minimum of 500 words.

2 Write fieldnotes about your own daily life as if you were a participant-observer. Write a minimum of 700 words. You can also include photographs, drawings or other images in your notes. What interesting facts emerge as you create and reflect on your fieldnotes?

3 Pick one of your classes this semester (online or face to face). While you are in class, observe the interactional dynamics carefully. Once class is finished, write extensive fieldnotes on the dynamics that you observed and make some connections with possible theories that you have been studying in your linguistic anthropological course. Write a minimum of 700 words.

5.8 Discussion Questions

1 What do you think is the difference between data collected with participant observation and fieldnotes and data collected by other means such as video and/or audio recording? What value might each format offer toward analysis?

2 Review our discussion about objectivity in participant observation. (a) Discuss your ideas about how developing rapport with participants, being rigorous about self-reflection, etc., help to mediate what is often construed as total bias or total subjectivity within a study involving participant observation. (b) Discuss how the ideal of objectivity might be overestimated in other forms of social science such as psychology. What about "hard" sciences such as chemistry or astronomy? How is objectivity considered within these scientific realms?

3 What are the ethical issues that linguistic anthropologists might encounter while practicing participant observation? What are the steps that they should take before engaging in participant observation? You can also refer to the other chapters of this volume in your answer.

4 Why do linguistic anthropologists, and anthropologists more generally, write their fieldnotes while conducting their research? Why are fieldnotes key in their research? What can fieldnotes add to audio- and video-recorded data and to participant observation? Be detailed in your answer and use the examples described in this chapter.

5 What could linguistic anthropologists do if they find themselves in a fieldwork situation in which there is no electricity to charge their audio- and video-recording devices? What alternatives do they have? Are those alternative valuable? Why?

6 In your own words, describe participant observation as a research method used by linguistic anthropologists. What are the benefits of using participant observation in one's research? How much ahead of time should participant observation be planned in a linguistic anthropological research project?

5.9 References Cited

Ahearn, Laura M. 2017. *Living Language: An Introduction to Linguistic Anthropology, Blackwell Primers in Anthropology*. Chichester, Malden, MA: Wiley-Blackwell.

Bernard, H. Russell. 2018. *Research Methods in Anthropology: Qualitative and Quantitative Approaches, Fourth Edition*. 5th ed. Lanham, MD: AltaMira Press.

Black, Steven P. 2017. "Anthropological Ethics and the Communicative Affordances of Audio-Video Recorders in Ethnographic Fieldwork." *American Anthropologist* 119 (1): 46–57.

Blommaert, Jan, and Dong Jie. 2020. *Ethnographic Fieldwork: A Beginner's Guide*, 2nd ed. Bristol, UK: Multilingual Matters.

Bluteau, Justin. 2019. "Legitimising Digital Anthropology through Immersive Cohabitation: Becoming an Observing Participant in a Blended Digital Landscape." *Ethnography* 22 (2): 267–85.

Boellstorff, Tom, Bonnie Nardi, Celia Pearce, and T. L. Taylor. 2012. *Ethnography and Virtual Worlds: A Handbook of Method*. Princeton and Oxford: Princeton University Press.

Bonilla, Yaromar, and Jonathan Rosa. 2015. "Digital Protest, Hashtag Ethnography, and the Racial Politics of Social Media in the United States." *American Ethnologist* 42 (1): 4–17.

Bradshaw, John. 1990. *Homecoming: Reclaiming and Championing Your Inner Child*. New York: Bantam Books.

Briggs, Charles. 2020. "Beyond the Linguistic/Medical Anthropology Divide: Retooling Anthropology to Face COVID-19." *Medical Anthropology* 39 (7): 563–72.

Briggs, Charles, and Richard Bauman. 1999. "'The Foundation of All Future Researches': Franz Boas, George Hunt, Native American Texts, and the Construction of Modernity." *American Quarterly* 51 (3): 479–528.

Bucholtz, Mary, and Kira Hall. 2003. "Language and Identity." In Alessandro Duranti ed., *A Companion to Linguistic Anthropology*, 369–94. Oxford: Blackwell.

Bucholtz, Mary, and Kira Hall. 2004. "Language and Identity." In Alessandro Duranti ed., *A Companion to Linguistic Anthropology*, 369–94. Malden, MA: Wiley-Blackwell.

Bucholtz, Mary, and Kira Hall. 2005. "Identity and Interaction: A Sociocultural Linguistic Approach." *Discourse Studies* 7 (4/5): 585–614.

Burrell, Jenna. 2016. "'Through a Screen Darkly': On Remote, Collaborative Fieldwork in the Digital Age." In Roger T. Sanjek and Susan W. Tratner eds., *Efieldnotes: The Makings of Anthropology in the Digital World*, 132–52. Philadelphia: University of Pennsylvania Press.

Calhoun, Kendra. 2019. "Vine Racial Comedy as Anti-Hegemonic Humor: Linguistic Performance and Generic Innovation." *Journal of Linguistic Anthropology* 29 (1): 27–49.

Carr, E. Summerson. 2011. *Scripting Addiction: The Politics of Therapeutic Talk and American Sobriety*. Princeton: Princeton University Press.

Clemente, Ignasi. 2014. "Conversation Analysis and Anthropology." In Jack Sidnell and Tanya Stivers eds., *Handbook of Conversation Analysis*, 688–700. Oxford: Wiley-Blackwell.

Davies, Catherine E. 1997. "Social Meaning in Southern Speech from an Interactional Sociolinguistic Perspective: An Integrative Discourse Analysis of Terms of Address." In Cynthia Bernstein, Thomas Nunnally, and Robin

Sabino eds., *Language Variety in the South Revisited*, 225–41. Tuscaloosa: University of Alabama Press.

De Fina, Anna, and Sabina Perrino. 2011. "Interviews vs. 'Natural' Contexts: A False Dilemma [Special Issue]." *Language in Society* 40 (1): 1–11.

Duranti, Alessandro. 1997. *Linguistic Anthropology, Cambridge Textbooks in Linguistics*. New York: Cambridge University Press.

Eisenlohr, Patrck. 2018. *Sounding Islam: Voice, Media, and Sonic Atmospheres in an Indian Ocean World*. Berkeley: University of California Press.

Farnell, Brenda, and Laura Graham. 2015. "Discourse-Centered Methods." In H. Russell Bernard and Clarence C. Gravlee eds., *Handbook of Methods in Cultural Anthropology*, 391–438. London: Rowman & Littlefield.

Fine, Julia C. 2019. "#Magicresistance: Anti-Trump Witchcraft as Register Circulation." *Journal of Linguistic Anthropology*, accessed April 4, 2020. https://doi.org/10.1111/jola.12249.

Goebel, Zane. 2019. *Rapport and the Discursive Co-Construction of Social Relations in Fieldwork Encounters*. Boston: De Gruyter Mouton.

Goebel, Zane. 2020. *Reimagining Rapport*. New York: Oxford University Press.

Goodenough, Ward. 1957. "Cultural Anthropology and Linguistics." In Paul L. Garvin ed., *Report of the Seventh Annual Round Table Meeting on Linguistics and Language Study*, 167–73. Washington, DC: Georgetown University, Monograph Series on Language and Linguistics No. 9. P.

Goodwin, Charles. 2018. *Co-Operative Action*. Cambridge and New York: Cambridge University Press.

Goodwin, Marjorie Harness, and Charles Goodwin. 2000. "Emotion within Situated Activity." In Alessandro Duranti ed., *Linguistic Anthropology: A Reader*, 239–57. Malden, MA: Blackwell.

Goodwin, Marjorie Harness, and Asta Cekaite. 2018. *Embodied Family Choreography: Practices of Control, Care, and Mundane Creativity*. New York and London: Routledge.

Gumperz, John Joseph. 1968. The Speech Community. In *International Encyclopedia of the Social Sciences*. New York: Macmillan.

Izquierdo, Carolina, and Gordon Mathews. 2009. *Pursuits of Happiness: Well-Being in Anthropological Perspective*. New York: Berghahn Books.

Kohn, Tamara. 2010. "The Role of Serendipity and Memory in Experiencing Fields." In Peter Collins and Anselm Gallinat eds., *The Ethnographic Self as Resource: Writing Memory and Experience into Ethnography*, 185–99. Oxford and New York: Berghahn Books.

Kremer-Sadlik, T., and J. L. Kim. 2007. "Lessons from Sports: Children's Socialization to Values through Family Interaction during Sports Activities." *Discourse & Society* 18 (1): 35–52.

Kumar, Harini . "Ethnographic Disruption in the Time of COVID-19." *Anthropology News*, May 22, 2020. DOI:10.1111/AN.1406.

Kunreuther, Laura. 2018. "Sounds of Democracy: Performance, Protest, and Political Subjectivity." *Cultural Anthropology* 33 (1): 1–31.

Labov, William. 1972. *Language in the Inner City*. Philadelphia: University of Pennsylvania Press.

Landsberger, Harry A. 1958. *Hawthorne Revisited*. New York: Cornell University Press.

Lave, Jean, and Etienne Wenger. 1991. *Situated Learning: Legitimate Peripheral Participation*. Cambridge: Cambridge University Press.

Lindgren, Simon. 2013. "The Potential and Limitations of Twitter Activism: Mapping the 2011 Libyan Uprising." *tripleC* 11 (1): 207–20.

Mishler, Elliot George. 1986. *Research Interviewing: Context and Narrative*. Cambridge, MA: Harvard University Press.

Nardi, Bonnie. 2015. "Virtuality." *Annual Review of Anthropology* 44: 15–31.

Ochs, Elinor, Anthony P. Graesch, Angela Mittman, Thomas Bradbury, and Rena Repetti. 2006. "Video Ethnography and Ethnoarchaeological Tracking." In Marcie Pitt-Catsouphes and Ellen Ernst Kossek eds., *The Work and Family Handbook: Multidisciplinary Perspectives, Methods, and Approaches*, 387–409. New York and London: Routledge.

Perrino, Sabina M. 2002. "Intimate Hierarchies and Qur'Anic Saliva (Tëfli): Textuality in a Senegalese Ethnomedical Encounter." *Journal of Linguistic Anthropology* 12 (2): 225–59.

Perrino, Sabina M. 2006. "Senegalese Ethnomedicine: A Linguistic and Ethnographic Study of Medical Modernities between Senegal and Italy." Dissertations available from ProQuest. AAI3246220. https://repository.upenn.edu/dissertations/AAI3246220

Perrino, Sabina M. 2007. "Cross-Chronotope Alignment in Senegalese Oral Narrative." *Language and Communication* 27 (3): 227–44.

Perrino, Sabina M. 2011. "Chronotopes of Story and Storytelling Event in Interviews." *Language in Society* 40 (1): 91–103.

Perrino, Sabina M. 2018. "Narrative Aftershocks: Digital Retellings of an Earthquake in Emilia-Romagna, Northern Italy." *Discourse, Context & Media* 25: 88–97.

Perrino, Sabina. 2021. "Intimacy Through Time and Space in Fieldwork Interviews." In Zane Goebel ed., *Reimagining Rapport*, 73–95. New York: Oxford University Press.

Phipps, Alison. 2010. "Ethnographers as Language Learners: From Oblivion and Towards an Echo." In Peter Collins and Anselm Gallinat eds., *The Ethnographic Self as Resource: Writing Memory and Experience into Ethnography*, 97–110. New York and Oxford: Berghahn Books.

Postill, John, and Sarah Pink. 2012. "Social Media Ethnography: The Digital Researcher in a Messy Web." *Media International Australia* 145:123–34.

Pritzker, Sonya E. 2014. *Living Translation: Language and the Search for Resonance in U.S. Chinese Medicine*. Oxford and New York: Berghahn Books.

Pritzker, Sonya E. 2016. "New Age with Chinese Characteristics? Translating Inner Child Emotion Pedagogies in Contemporary China." *Ethos* 44 (2): 150–70.

Pritzker, Sonya E. In Prep. *Learning to Love: Intimacy and the Discourse of Development in China*. Ann Arbor: Michigan University Press.

Pritzker, Sonya E., and W. L. Duncan. 2019. "Technologies of the Social: Family Constellation Therapy and the Remodeling of Relational Selfhood in China and Mexico." *Culture, Medicine & Psychiatry* 43 (3): 468–95.

Rapport, Nigel. 2010. "The Ethics of Participant Observation: Personal Reflections on Fieldwork in England." In Peter Collins and Anselm Gallinat eds., *The Ethnographic Self as Resource: Writing Memory and Experience into Ethnography*, 78–94. New York and Oxford: Berghahn Books.

Sanjek, Roger. 1990. "A Vocabulary for Fieldnotes." In Roger Sanjek ed., *Fieldnotes: The Making of Anthropology*, 92–121. Ithaca and London: Cornell University Press.

Saxbe, Darby E., and Rena L. Repetti. 2010. "For Better or Worse? Coregulation of Couples' Cortisol Levels and Mood States." *Journal of Personality and Social Psychology* 98 (1): 92–103.

Schensul, Jean J., and Margaret D. LeCompte. 2013. *Essential Ethnographic Methods: A Mixed Methods Approach*. 2nd ed., Lanham, MD: AltaMira Press.

Skinner, Jonathan. 2010. "Leading Questions and Body Memories: A Case of Phenomenology and Physical Ethnography in the Dance Interview." In Peter Collins and Anselm Gallinat eds., *The Ethnographic Self as Resource: Writing Memory and Experience into Ethnography*, 111–28. Oxford and New York: Berghahn Books.

Smalls, Krystal A. 2019. "Languages of Liberation: Digital Discourses of Emphatic Blackness." In Netta Avineri, Laura Graham, Eric J. Johnson, Robin Conley Riner and Jonathan Rosa eds., *Language and Social Justice in Practice*, 52–60. London and New York: Routledge.

Tedlock, Barbara. 1991. "From Participant Observation to the Observation of Participation: The Emergence of Narrative Ethnography." *Journal of Anthropological Research* 47 (1): 69–94.

Tedlock, Dennis, and Bruce Mannheim. 1995. *The Dialogic Emergence of Culture*. Urbana: University of Illinois Press.

Tilley, Christopher, Webb Keane, Susanne Küchler, Michael Rowlands, and Patricia Spyer. 2006. *Handbook of Material Culture*. London: SAGE Publications Ltd.

Tufekci, Zeynep, and Wilson Christopher. 2012. "Social Media and the Decision to Participate in Political Protest: Observations from Tahrir Square." *Journal of Communication* 62 (2): 363–79.

Wortham, Stanton Emerson Fisher, and Angela Reyes. 2015. *Discourse Analysis beyond the Speech Event*. London and New York: Routledge.

5.10 Further Reading

Bernard, H. Russell. 2015. *Handbook of Methods in Cultural Anthropology*. 2nd ed. Lanham: Rowman & Littlefield.

Duranti, Alessandro. 1997. *Linguistic Anthropology, Cambridge Textbooks in Linguistics*. New York: Cambridge University Press.

Schensul, Jean J., and Margaret D. LeCompte. 2013. *Essential Ethnographic Methods: A Mixed Methods Approach*. 2nd ed., Lanham, MD: AltaMira Press.

6

Interviews in Linguistic Anthropology

Sabina M. Perrino

6.1 Introduction

Interviews are not just methodological tools to collect information and anthropological data. Rather, most importantly, they involve human encounters that can develop in long-term relationships, especially in anthropological fieldwork settings. As Mishler asks:

> What is the role of the interviewer in how a respondent's story is told, how it is constructed and developed, and what it means? … how do an interviewer's questions, assessments, silences, and responses enter into a story's production? … How can the presence and influence of an interviewer be taken into account in the analysis and interpretation of a respondent's story?
>
> (Mishler 1986, 96)

While scholars across various disciplines have addressed Mishler's important questions on the interactional dynamics emerging between interviewer(s) and interviewee(s) in narratives in interview settings with more or less success, ethnographic interviews have only recently been examined as *situated speech events*. As a "form of discourse" (Mishler 1986, vii), interviews became a central focus in linguistic anthropology and sociolinguistics in the late 1980s, thanks especially to Briggs's (1986) and Mishler's (1986) pioneering research on the discursive and interactional dimensions of interviews. These scholars' innovative look at interviews came at a moment when interviews were considered solely as surveys[1] or means to gather content-information from research consultants. The role of the interview as a research method and source of data has indeed been at the center of many discussions among researchers from various traditions. Rapley (2001), for example, argues that interview data could be considered as resources or as topics. In the interview-data-as-resource approach, "the interview data collected are seen as (more or less) reflecting the interviewees' reality outside the interview," while in interview-data-as-topic, "the interview data collected are seen as (more or less) reflecting a reality jointly constructed by the interviewee and interviewer" (Rapley 2001, 304). Furthermore, there are scholars who have tried to erase the interactional context of the interview, considering it as a distracting point of the interview. On the other end, there are researchers who see interviews as "artificial" contexts. In both extremes, the interview ends up being a problem to overcome (De Fina and Perrino 2011, 1).

In his well-known book entitled *Learning How to Ask*, Briggs (1986) keenly unveiled the discursive and interactional nature of interviews as key moments for anthropologists who need to learn "how to ask" their questions to research consultants in diverse sociocultural settings. In his perspective, ethnographic interviews are thus not just surveys; rather, they have an important discursive dimension: they are contextualized speech events. This is also clearly stated by Mishler (1986, ix) in the four propositions that he elaborated at the very outset of his book, *Research Interviewing: Context and Narrative*:

> The contrast between this view [i.e., the interview as a form of discourse] and the assumptions of mainstream survey interviewing is used to develop a framework for systematic exposition of the alternative. Four propositions are specified as its essential components: (1) interviews are speech events; (2) the discourse of interviews is constructed jointly by interviewers and respondents; (3) analysis and interpretation are based on a theory of discourse and meaning; (4) the meanings of questions and answers are contextually grounded.

Linguistic anthropologists have used interviews for various functions. They have appreciated their referential function, such as the collected information, for their linguistic analysis, as in the classic interviews elaborated by Labov (1972) and his research teams. But they have also valued interviews as key sites in which "situated speech" (Fuller 2000) can be explored for its interactional, discursive nature, or the emerging dynamics between researcher(s) and interviewee(s) during the course of this type of speech event (Fontana and Frei 2004; De Fina and Perrino 2011; Wortham et al. 2011). In this vein, interviews are actual speech events that are (co)created, and developed, by researcher(s) and interviewee(s), and thus need to be studied as such because of their interactional dynamic nature. As Mishler (1986, 53, my emphasis) puts it, the interview is a "joint construction of meaning," since "[one] way an interview develops is through *mutual* reformulation and specification of questions, by which they take on particular and context-bound shades of meaning." Thus, a focus on interviews as speech events offers linguistic anthropologists further insights into local customs for accomplishing understanding thanks to this mutual, interactional dynamic between researcher(s) and respondent(s). Mainly inspired by Briggs's (1986) research, linguistic anthropologists and sociolinguists have turned their attention to the discursive dimension of the interview, rather than to its form, and have started to explore many of its facets by demonstrating that this interactional setting is key in many research processes (De Fina and Perrino 2011).

This chapter examines the discursive and interactional dimensions of interviews focusing especially on how linguistic anthropologists prepare and conduct their interviews during their fieldwork. More specifically, this chapter examines five key themes as they are related to interviews. First, I describe the value of interviews in linguistic anthropology by emphasizing the emerging interactional dynamics between researcher(s) and interviewer(s). I demonstrate that these speech events are inherently interactional and that this aspect contributes to linguistic anthropological research. Second, I highlight the creation, development, and solidification of *fluid* and *intimate* identities between interviewer(s) and interviewee(s). The interview is indeed an important site to study the developing and intricate rapport between interviewer(s) and interviewee(s). Third, I examine how the production and significance of narratives as they are told in interview settings are also emphasized as being integral part of this speech event. Fourth, I emphasize the main ethical issues that linguistic anthropologists face when they engage in interviews with their research consultants. While researchers need to submit their interview questions for ethics review (Black and Conley Riner, this volume), they might run into unpredictable ethical issues while their interviews take place, issues that often need to be resolved in situ. While it is impossible to create general rules to avoid ethical issues in interview settings, the two cases that I propose (together with other similar situations throughout the chapters of this collection) might serve as examples of fluid ethical situations. Finally, this chapter presents and analyzes two excerpts that are part of longer interviews that I collected in my two fieldsites: Senegal, West Africa, in 2001, and Northern Italy, Europe, in 2003.

6.2 Ethnographic Interviews in Linguistic Anthropology

Interviews are among the most heavily used methods of data collection across disciplines as diverse as anthropology, sociolinguistics, education, social history, and social psychology. Linguistic anthropologists mainly use three types of interviews, based on the questionnaires that researchers prepare prior to these speech events: (1) *structured interviews* with questionnaires organized with a list of fixed questions that are asked to all interviewees following the same order—something that might be key in certain linguistic anthropological projects; (2) *semi-structured interviews* with questions touching on general topics and novel questions that do not need to be asked in a particular order; and, finally, (3) *unstructured interviews* with very informal questionnaires that usually emerge from more or less casual conversations between researchers and their informants. In some research projects, all these interview formats are used. Linguistic anthropologists, like other anthropologists, rely heavily on unstructured interviews and are usually open to changing their interview questions during the course of the interview: some questions can be skipped while some others are reframed or changed during the interview. It is very common for linguistic anthropologists to follow their interviewees' leads and let them shift topic without interrupting the flow of the conversation that might arise. While I was conducting the first phase of my PhD dissertation research in Senegal, for example, I was interested in learning about the use of certain plants in Senegalese healers' ethnomedical practices. However, healers did not talk only about their ethnomedical practices when they were answering my questions. Rather, they would tell me many stories about the use of certain plants, sometimes taking up to two hours to tell a particular story. When this occurred, I learned to patiently listen to their narratives, changing the order of my interview questions accordingly, adding new questions, and sometimes skipping many of them. Some flexibility is then necessary when linguistic anthropologists engage in these interview practices, especially when they find themselves in the initial phases of their research and in contexts that are not as familiar as their own (Briggs 1986). The dynamics and content of interviews in linguistic anthropology are thus always fluctuating and greatly depend on speech participants' interactional moves as well as their sociocultural context.

6.2.1 The Interactional Nature of Ethnographic Interviews

Interviews are sites in which speech is "situated" (Fuller 2000) and are studied not just for the value of their content, the information that is collected, but also for their shifting, interactional nature (De Fina and Perrino 2011; Fontana and Frei 2004; Wortham et al. 2011). Research interviews are thus interactional encounters that are considered as a set of data besides the referential information (the content) that is collected during these speech events and that is very valuable. It is indeed through the careful analysis of interviews that linguistic anthropologists can learn key points related to their research such as subject matters that will develop their research topics, attitudes or beliefs about these topics, metadiscursive statements about them, and so forth. Even this referential information changes with the progress of the interaction in interview settings, and it can (or not) be in sync with the interactional moves of interviewer(s) and interviewee(s). As Briggs reminds us,

> [E]ven though the referential or cognitive function is generally dominant in interviews, this does not, as Jakobson (1960, 353) has noted, mean that other communicative functions are of no importance. [...] Speech also possesses a *performative* capacity, meaning that words are also means of *creating or transforming* a given state of affairs. The performative force of an utterance may include a transformation of the relationship between interviewer and respondent(s) or between the respondent(s) and other persons who are present.
>
> (Briggs 1986, 45–6, emphasis in original)

To better appreciate Briggs's and other linguistic anthropologists' perspective on the interactional nature of interviews, it is important to differentiate the "denotational text" from the "interactional text" of speech events. While the "denotational text" describes the reference and predication about "states of affairs" done in the interview, including the topics that are discussed, the stories that are told, and other content, the "interactional text" refers to interaction itself—the roles of the speech participants while the interview takes place, the actions being performed, and so forth (Perrino 2015b, 2019; Silverstein 1998; Wortham 2000, 2001). Thus, researchers need to analyze interviews not only for their content, but also for their interactional text, that is the various moves that interviewer(s) and interviewee(s) make during the interview, for example, variations in speakers' prosody (tone, rhythm, pitch), laughter, pauses, and other discursive maneuvers (Gumperz 1982) such as gestures, gaze, and movements (Goodwin 2015). These discursive strategies would remain unveiled by just looking at the content of the interview.

The dynamic and interactional nature of interviews emerges, for instance, when researchers prepare structured or semi-structured questionnaires for their interviews, and then they find themselves not following them or asking different questions during these speech events. This is actually part of the emergent nature of conversations, and interactions more generally. When I conducted my interviews both in Senegal and in Northern Italy, I had to continually adapt and change my previously prepared questions. In Senegal, I was interested in learning about the healing properties of particular plants and my questions were mostly centered around these issues. However, as I mentioned earlier, Senegalese healers tended to recount many stories about their experiences with plants rather than providing me with a list of the properties of the plants they used in their ethnomedical remedies. I had similar experiences in my other fieldsite, Northern Italy, where I conducted interviews with other researchers (group interviews) as well. While we prepared our questionnaires diligently, our interviewees were often taking our questions in different directions and we, as interviewers, tried to let the conversation go in those directions without forcing it back to follow the questionnaire script. It is indeed very important to understand that interview guides are just initial prompts to help linguistic anthropologists start an interview that can take various, unpredictable routes.

The interactional nature of ethnographic interviews clearly emerges when researchers decide, and manage, to audio- and/or video-record these events. In these cases, the audio or video recorder plays a key role in interviews (see Kohler and Murphy, this volume), since interviewees are aware of its presence and, as a consequence, might change their responses, the way they speak, and so forth, especially in the beginning of the interview. After a while, as linguistic anthropologists have classically argued, interviewees adapt to the presence of these devices and the conversation becomes more "natural" as a result (Ahearn 2017; Briggs 1986). With this in mind, it is clear that interviewer(s) and interviewee(s) co-construct the interview while their interactions unfold through the various questions that are asked and the many stories that are told (Perrino 2011; Talmy 2011). It is also important to remember that, as Briggs has pointed out, in many societies interviews might not be the preferred way to get the information researchers are seeking. Linguistic anthropologists, and researchers in other disciplines as well, should spend some time in the society they wish to study before utilizing their own research tools. In this way, they would develop an awareness of certain sociocultural patterns that might not emerge in the initial phases of fieldwork. It is thus key to "learn how to ask" (Briggs 1986) and be sensitive to the sociocultural and linguistic norms that are circulating in a community of practice before imposing interviews as ways to elicit information. Doing otherwise would mean to exert authority and power over research participants and not be able to collect valuable and accurate data. This is why Briggs's ethical argument is paramount for linguistic anthropologists: they need to learn from their research participants first, and then they can "interview" them. They also need to "learn how to ask" their questions in other ways if necessary. Thus, especially during the initial stages of fieldwork, it is important that ethnographers learn the relevant sociocultural conventions about interviewing and asking questions more generally so that they can gain the necessary sociocultural and communicative awareness and competence. This is, moreover, a key ethical point that every ethnographer should have on their agenda.

6.2.2 Fluid Identities and Knowledge Production in Research Interviews

As linguistic anthropologists have demonstrated, interviews are also key sites to study speech participants' identity (co)construction as it is connected to their interactional moves (De Fina 2011; De Fina and Perrino 2011; Modan and Shuman 2011; Perrino 2011; Perrino and Pritzker 2019; Wortham et al. 2011). This is possible, for example, when researcher(s) and interviewee(s) engage in long interview-conversations in which several personal narratives emerge. When speech participants assume certain positionings vis-à-vis each other to assert their points during their stories, for instance, they often also perform their identities. At times, their entire interaction can be suddenly reoriented and some of their participant roles can be reversed too. This is the case when interviewers and interviewees share similar life experiences or when they need to ask, and/or answer, sensitive questions. In her research on how sensitive disability questions are managed in interview settings, for example, Williams (2019) examines how interviewers ask questions about disability and how their co-constructed identities, shared between researcher and interviewee, can reorient the interaction. The fact that both interviewer and interviewee are disabled, for example, completely changes the dynamics of the interview. Williams thus argues that interviewees can respond to sensitive questions if they attend to certain interactional tasks. Focusing on both interviewers and interviewees, Williams's research thus offers new ways to think about how to ask, and respond to, sensitive issues in interview settings. Similarly, in her work on research interviewers as "Knowers" and "Unknowers," Roulston (2019b) analyzes interview transcripts in which interviewer(s) and interviewee(s) continuously fluctuate between known and unknown information and thus change their participation roles very often. This means that both interviewers and interviewees show their knowledge of certain topics that are brought up during the interview. As Roulston writes,

> [r]esearch interviewers must navigate the spectrum of potential relationships with interviewees from insider to a culture from which interviewees are drawn, to outsider. Since much qualitative interview research focuses on participants' lifeworlds, interviewers are routinely placed in a position of "unknowing" about participants' personal information preserves (Goffman 1971), while all the while having knowledge and expertise about particular research topics.
>
> (Roulston 2019a, 32)

Speech participants' role-shifts thus demonstrate not only that their identities continuously change but also that interviews are unpredictable and ever-changing interactional events. During my fieldwork in Senegal, for example, I had to adapt my questions to the various situations in which I found myself. In interviews with healers, for instance, since I was interested in learning about their ethnomedical recipes and practices, I was often put in the position of the "unknower." This meant that I listened to the healers' narratives and advice most of the time without adding any points to their stories. I was also doing so as a way to respect their high societal status. Healers are highly respected and honored in Senegal. Sometimes, I just needed to ask a couple of questions and they would offer their responses for hours. My list of prepared questions was not useful in those circumstances.

Some other times, I needed to prompt them with a lot of questions on their usage of plants and the Qur'an in their ethnomedical practices. Every interview is a unique experience.

The situation was different, however, in my interviews with other social actors in Senegal. In the summer of 2002, I interviewed a journalist, a man in his forties, Baye, in Dakar, the capital of Senegal, since I wanted to learn more about Senegalese practices both in ethnomedical centers, or as they refer to them, "traditional hospitals," and in Western biomedical hospitals. Upon a fine-grained analysis of this interview, I discovered that there were many shifts of participant roles at particular moments of the interview (Perrino 2005, 2007). At that time, Baye was recounting a story of a serious disease he had when he was a child and, interactionally, I was not paying enough attention to his telling. From the transcript, I noted that I was not offering minimal responses, engaging in small conversation, asking follow-up questions, and so forth. I was silent while he was telling me his sad stories. In brief, as Tannen (2007) would put it, I was not showing any kind of "involvement." That is why, as I show in a similar example later, Baye not only changed his interactional moves at particular moments of the interview, but he also changed the content of his story, the *denotational text*. More specifically, given my distraction while he was recounting his past stories, he transformed me into one of the main characters of his narrative so that I could "witness" more closely what he had gone through when he was a child. Through these interactional and denotational moves, Baye not only reclaimed my full attention in his story, but he also took control and authority over the rest of the interview, showing, once again, how fluid the roles inhabited by researcher(s) and interviewer(s) are. Stories in interviews are indeed key sites that need to be studied and analyzed with particular care.

6.2.3 Narratives in Interview Settings

Narratives in interviews have been rarely examined as speech events within the interview context (De Fina and Perrino 2011). Like interviews, as I mentioned earlier, narratives in interviews have been often considered for their content rather than for their complex and multiple interactional functions. As De Fina and I have contended:

> [t]his lack of attention to the interview context is partly the consequence of a treatment of the interview as a somewhat unnatural event, of an excessive

focus on genres such as the canonical story or the life story within interview narratives, and of a tendency to treat narratives in interview[s] as a much more homogeneous genre than they really are.

(De Fina and Perrino 2011, 7)

As research on this topic has demonstrated, however, interviews are key sites to examine the emergence of storytelling practices as well. In interview settings, speech participants usually end up telling stories of their past, present, or imagined future. As I noted earlier, during these speech events, participants can assume and reverse speech roles while they deliver their stories. Speakers' roles can shift, for example, from acting as a storyteller with full narrative authority, to being an audience member or a listener (De Fina and Georgakopoulou 2012). Narratives in interviews are thus very intricate as they offer the researcher access to the subtleties of participants' interactions at various levels (De Fina and Perrino 2011, 2). In storytelling events, speech participants continuously align and misalign with the various topics of the story and with each other. In this way, they engage in interactional positionings thus demonstrating, once again, how narratives simultaneously shape and are shaped by their surrounding context (Duranti and Goodwin 1992). As Briggs (1986) has suggested, it is better to wait and familiarize oneself with the new environment before interviewing research consultants and other ordinary speakers. With this in mind, it is important to recall what Briggs has advocated about the sensitivity that ethnographers collecting interviews need to exert. Interviews themselves, and the narratives enclosed in them, would lose all their value and utility if they were not collected with a certain sociocultural and ethical awareness by ethnographers. As Briggs keenly writes,

[t]he context in which a question is posed often affects the respondent's interpretation of the query and the nature of his or her response. Resultant variations in the received data thus range from the interviewee's intentional omission or falsification of material to subtle differences in pragmatic indexical meanings.

(Briggs 1986, 45)

Furthermore, continues Briggs, if the notion of the interview itself is not shared by the culture under study, interviewees might "apply norms of interaction and canons of interpretations that differ from those of the interviewer" (Briggs 1986, 48). That might be one of the reasons for which linguistic anthropologists might misinterpret the data obtained in these interviews if they don't exert caution and if they are not sensitive to the new sociocultural context when they conduct their interviews. All this entails multiple, intricate ethical issues as they are connected to interviews, as Briggs (1986) and others (Black 2017; see also Black and Conley Riner, this volume) have pointed out. Along these lines, before examining my examples of narratives in interviews that I collected in both my fieldsites, I briefly discuss some significant ethical issues that might emerge when ethnographers collect interviews.

6.3 Ethical Issues in Research Interview Practices

Before embarking in their research, linguistic anthropologists need to make sure that their projects follow some key ethical guidelines (see Black and Conley-Riner, this volume). First, their interview guides/lists of questions need to be approved by the Institutional Review Board (IRB), together with their project, before researchers can start any kind of interviewing activity. The IRB asks researchers to prepare a consent form that needs to be signed by the interviewee(s) before the interview begins. The consent form has some key clauses explaining the rights of the interviewee(s), the fact that the interview might be audio- and/or video-recorded, and the research project in general terms. If interviewees don't wish to answer a question, they have the right to stop the interview at any moment, as is usually noted in the consent form. Thus, interviews can take various directions also because interviewees might feel anxious or compelled to answer certain questions, especially being aware of the presence of an audio or, even more so, a video recorder (see Kohler and Murphy, this volume). These "transduction technologies," as Black (2017) calls them, can influence the trajectory of the interview and therefore act as affordances to researchers as well who can better understand the limits of their research in certain contexts and situations. Black indeed contends that these technological devices, or "transducers," are "prosthetic extensions of our selves" that "offer distinct possibilities for the ethnographic encounter in their simultaneous extension of and disconnect from the ethnographer's social self" (2017, 55). They transduce, or transport, information from one culture to another; they can thus be seen as extensions of ethnographers' eyes and ears, as it were. If interviews are not considered as such in a society, as Briggs (1986) has famously argued, they would not be productive since they would misrepresent the sociocultural aspects under study.

With this in mind, what happens when ethnographers realize that their interviews won't be possible or didn't go as planned? What alternatives do linguistic anthropologists have if, once in their fieldsite, they realize that using their audio and video recorders for their interviews would be inappropriate? These are key questions that ethnographers should keep in mind when they embark in a research project involving interviews with or without audio and video recording.[2] I often found myself in situations in which I had to negotiate between my research needs and the possibilities that I had available in the sociocultural setting in which I was conducting research. As Black (2017) has acutely noted, not using the audio recorder at particular times, as much needed as it was in his research, meant to be respectful of the sociocultural norms in the HIV community of practice he was studying and, ultimately, to gain respect and trust among his research participants.

Similarly, when I was in the process of conducting ethnographic research in Senegal, I often had to adapt my research to the wishes and needs of my research consultants. Several times, for example, healers didn't feel comfortable being asked questions in the classic "questionnaire" format. Rather, their preference was to be in control of the conversation and to teach me their ethnomedical recipes by offering their knowledge (*xam xam* in Wolof) in various forms. During these teaching moments, I was able to ask questions related to some plants that they used in their healing practices. This was a new interview format for me, but I adapted to it and I received a lot of benefits from adapting because I learned more than I expected about the use of plants in their medical recipes. Ethically, it was important to respect their wishes and not to interrupt them with other questions. Other times, there were some challenges in adjusting to Senegalese healers' wishes. Once, for example, I interviewed a healer in a village in inner Senegal, after several days of traveling in unsafe conditions. Once I arrived at his home, the healer asked me to stay at his door and to turn backward so that he could see just my back. He of course did the same; he was turned the other way, facing his wall. We were not looking at each other. He agreed on all my research terms, he happily signed the consent form, and so forth, he only asked me to be interviewed without looking at him. The interview lasted longer than three hours and it was an interesting, new format for me, which I respected. I turn now to two case studies that emphasize the emergent nature of interviews, and how they are context-bounded and always fluctuating. Without an attentive look at their interactional nature, many salient points would be entirely missed in interviews.

6.4 Intimacy in Interviews

6.4.1 Conducting Ethnographic Interviews in Senegal

While conducting interviews with healers and ordinary speakers in several villages in Senegal, my interviewees and I also started to construct our *intimate*, long-lasting relations (Perrino 2021). While grasping intimacy, intimate relationships and intimate identities might be challenging, Pritzker and I have recently proposed to define intimacy as

> an *emergent feeling of closeness* in combination with significant levels of *vulnerability, trust,* and/or *shared identities*, that can vary across cultures as well as in time and space. Intimacy, from this vantage point, is contingent and often precarious in that it must be constantly made and remade in specific contexts and interactional moments.
>
> (Perrino and Pritzker 2019)

In this perspective, intimacy is a fluid and ever-changing concept, which can be positive at times and negatives at other times. Intimacy is often an invisible, yet ongoing, social process that connects or disconnects people and that continuously influences their emotional stances (Garcia 2010; Mattingly 2014). Being part of our everyday lives, intimacy thus "permeates everyday interaction, creating the collaborative foundation for romantic and sexual, but also political, economic, and material relationships" (Perrino and Pritzker 2019). Many of my Senegalese informants, for example, shared many of their personal and illness stories with me during my interviews with them. Moreover, I noted that Senegalese narrators often included me, their interlocutor, "into" their past stories through a particular interactional move that I have named *participant transposition* (Perrino 2005, 2007). Some of my Senegalese consultants named it *démarche participative* ("participatory move") during my follow-up interviews with them. I would have never been able to fully understand this narrative practice without the assistance of my consultants during my follow-up interviews and playback experiments[3] with them. It was indeed during these follow-up interviews that I was drawn to think more about this narrative practice in terms of *participant transposition* (Perrino 2005, 2007) after a Senegalese collaborator and research assistant of mine used the verbs "transpose" and "transport," for example, to gloss *démarche participative*: "la *démarche participative*, pour te faire rentrer dans ce contexte-là. C'est comme si je t'avais transposée, transportée dans mon histoire-là" ("the participatory move [is done] in order to make you enter that context. It is as if I had transposed [or] transported you inside my own story"). Thus, Senegalese interviewees ended up telling me personal stories in which they established an alignment of their past story with our present interaction. In this sense, Senegalese storytellers often move their interlocutors into their stories, the denotational text, giving coherence to the interactional text as well. This discursive strategy is common in Senegalese everyday interaction, especially when they tell stories. In this case, as the example shows, the boundaries between past and present are blurred, while a particular cross-aligned configuration emerges during the telling. In my research, I have contended that these interactional movements create and reinforce intimate relations between speech participants, who thus become closer both intertextually and interdiscursively (Silverstein 2005) while their stories unfold.

These alignments clearly emerge in Example 1, in which speech participants enact intimate stances through various cases of participant transposition. I conducted this interview in Thiès (a small town in the vicinity of Dakar, the capital of Senegal), in June 2001, with a Senegalese collaborator of mine, a woman in her late forties at that time, whom I name Maimuna.[4] A combination of Wolof (the vehicular language of Senegal) and French (the former colonial language), which is a typical combination in urban centers in Senegal, emerged during the interview. I was conducting these interviews as part of my PhD dissertation project on Senegalese ethnomedicine, and my questions were centered on healers' use of plants in their medical recipes and on their illness stories. This interview lasted for more than an hour, during which Maimuna recounted three personal narratives. In these stories, she also engaged in participant transposition five times. In one of her illness narratives after thirty-five minutes into the interview, for example, she remembered that she had an unbearable pain in her legs and entire body one night and that her family wanted to take her to the healer.[5] In this excerpt, Maimuna enacted five cases of *participant transposition*:

Example 1: "*I was very scared of being paralyzed!*"

(M: Maimuna; S: Interviewer)
First Line: Original French and Wolof Version[6]
Second Line: English Translation[7]

Interviews in Linguistic Anthropology   **173**

1. **M:** […] c'étai::t en novembre e:::n 1991
    […] *it wa::s in November i:::n 1991*

2. mmhh e:::t j'étais très malade pendant la nuit d'un fin de semaine
    mhmm a:::nd I was very sick one might of a weekend

3. je ne pouvais pas bouger et mes jambes me faisaient très mal=
    I couldn't move and my legs hurt badly=

4. **S:** =Je suis désolée=
    =I am sorry=

5. **M:** =merci … j'avais trè:::s peur d'être paralisée
    =thanks … I was ve:::ry scared of being paralyzed

6. tout mon corps me faisait mal et tremblait, *xam nga*?
    my entire body hurt and was shaking, *you know*?

7. **S:** *waaw xam naa* je peux imaginer la douleur
    yes I know I can just imagine the pain

8. **M:** donc j'avais pris le *palu*, tu sais?
    so I got malaria, you know?

9. avec la fièvre *feebar* haute
    with high fever fever

10. *amoon naa feebar*, la fièvre était tell- tellement forte
    I had a fever, the fever was real- really high

11. **je ne pouvais pas** dormir
    I couldn't *sleep*

12. **je ne pouvais pas** bouger
    I couldn't *move*

13. **je ne pouvais pas** même penser, t'as-vu?
    I couldn't *even think, do you see?*

14. *gis nga palu boobu*
    <u>do you see the kind of malaria</u> [I had]?

15. pendant la nuit je dis à ma sœur **SABENA**[8]
    *during the night I say to my sister **SABINA***

16. "**Sabena**, excuse-moi, *je ne peux pas bouger*"
    "***Sabina**, sorry, <u>I can't move</u>*"
|

17. **S:** @@@@=

18. **M:** =et **Sabena::** ma sœur, elle dit
    *=and **Sabina::** my sister, she says*

19. "Maimuna, *ñu ngiy dem* chez le *seriñ*"
    "*Maimuna, <u>let's go</u> to the <u>healer</u>*"

20. elle donc va chez le guérisseur
    she then goes to see a healer

21. elle demande des médicaments pour mon palu mais les
    guérisseurs n'en donnent PAS!=
    *she asks for some medicines [to heal] my malaria but healers
    DON'T give them out!=*

22. **S:** =oui je le sais!
    =yes I know!
    |

23. **M:** **Sabena** *xamuma*@@@@
    ***Sabina** doesn't know*@@@@

24. ella y va également les chercher pour moi
    she goes there to look for them for me anyway

25. ma chère sœur **Sabena** […]
    *my dear sister **Sabina** […]*

After my first questions about her healing habits and about her family's
diseases, Maimuna naturally launches into a personal narrative without

me giving her any specific prompts. She starts her narrative with a classic Labovian orientation (Labov 1972; Labov and Waletzky 1966) to contextualize the disease she underwent when she was younger (lines 1–2).[9] She indeed situates her story in a spatiotemporal framework: she was sick in her bed and it was a weekend in November 1991. She recounts that one night she couldn't move in her bed and her legs were in terrible pain (line 3). After I instinctively show my sympathy for her by latching with her in line 4, she confesses that she was in fear of being paralyzed in her bed that night (line 5) and that her entire body was in terrible pain (line 6). That Maimuna tried to find sympathy and intimacy with me becomes clear intertextually and interdiscursively from line 6 until the end of her story. Intertextually, she often ends her lines with rhetorical questions for me, such as "you know?" (lines 6, 8), "did you see?" (line 13), and "do you see the kind of malaria [I had]?" (line 14) to find complicity, support, and understanding. After I show my sympathy with her in line 7, she asserts that she feared to have contracted malaria, *palu*[10] in Wolof, in line 8, since she also had a high fever. Maimuna also codeswitches from French to Wolof after line 6 and emphasizes the fact that she might have contracted malaria given the high fever and the pain in her body she experienced. As a discourse strategy (Gumperz 1982), *codeswitching*[11] can change speakers' participation roles and can thus project various interactional meanings (Bailey 2000; Heller 1988; Woolard 1995), such as more connection with the surrounding audience who is supposed to understand both codes (Perrino 2015b). Soon after these brief codeswitches to Wolof in lines 8 and 10, Maimuna codeswitches back into French and starts describing the terrible high fever she had that night. By codeswitching back to Wolof in line 14 she emphasizes, again, the gravity of her disease and wants to make sure that I understand what her past self went through ("*do you see the kind of malaria* [I had]?" [line 14]).

Maimuna's intimate and emphatic stance emerges even more clearly in lines 11–13, when she repeats the negative form of the French modal verb "pouvoir," conjugated in the first singular person, followed by three different verbal constructions: "*I couldn't sleep*" (line 11), "*I couldn't move*" (line 12), and "*I couldn't even think*" (line 13). This *poetic* form of repetition in speech has been studied as *parallelism* by several linguistic anthropologists. Parallelism can be simply defined as repetition with variation in discourse and has been examined extensively especially for its discursive intertextual effects (Silverstein and Urban 1996; Tannen 2007; Wilce 2001, 191). These parallelistic structures emerge several times in this interview, especially when I do not seem to be emotionally involved in the details of Maimuna's illness story. She tries to keep my attention focused on the hardship of her past self by repeating certain structures. I add my remarks to her storylines only three times, in lines 4, 7, and 22, thus acknowledging my attention, but they are probably not enough to show my full sympathy and support. The dynamic nature of the interview thus pulses at every turn showing that these speech events have a unique nature since participants often co-construct their stories in these settings.

It is precisely after Maimuna's second instance of codeswitching from French to Wolof in line 14, where she asks me if I realize the kind of malaria she had, that she engages in the first instance of participant transposition. By explicitly addressing me as if I were present in her past story in line 15 (*"[...] I say to my sister **SABINA**"*), she inserts, or *transposes*, me into her past self and I thus suddenly become one of her past addresses, her sister precisely. This transformation of me into one of her intimate family members indexes the level of intimacy that we enact as our interview progresses through her storytelling events. Her kin-related stance emerges, and becomes more prominent, at every turn, by including me in her past self, in her narrated event, and by uttering my first name loudly in lines 15–16. At that moment, she definitely gets my attention, and I start laughing in line 17 by being surprised of becoming, all of a sudden, her sister in her story. Through so doing, Maimuna makes me part of her reported speech, or "constructed dialogue" in Tannen's (2007) terms, in line 16, by sharing, again, the fact that she cannot move from her bed. Through this strategic narrative move, I suddenly become a witness of her serious health conditions when she addresses me in her reported clause sharing her inability to move in line 16. In these lines, Maimuna aligns her past self with the present interaction between the two speech participants, the two of us. At the same time, we actively co-construct an intimate rapport (Perrino 2021).

Maimuna sustains this case of *participant transposition* at every line from line 15 until line 25. At line 18, moreover, I am tropically transformed into Maimuna's sister who witnesses her immobilization and pain in her bed. I thus, unexpectedly, become her sister and I am then so close to her. In the story that Maimuna recounts, my past self offers that we go to the healer together to see if he can help her (line 18). However, my past self goes to the healer by herself in search of some medications for her (lines 20–21) instead. Maimuna uses the historical present ("she goes" [line 20], "she asks for" [line 21], "Sabina doesn't know" [line 23]) thus making her past self part of the present interaction (Perrino 2007, 2011, 2015a). Here, past and present become one; their boundaries are entirely blurred. With a wit of irony, indexed by her raised volume in line 21 and by four bursts of laughter in line 23, Maimuna recounts how, wrongly, my past self visited a healer to look for some medicines for her (lines 21, 23), even though my past self claims to know this fact in line 22. To keep my full attention focused on her story, Maimuna questions my real knowledge of Senegalese ethnomedical rituals. Healers usually don't dispense medicines; one needs to go to the pharmacy or to a Western biomedical doctor to find them. Through these discourse strategies (Gumperz 1982), Maimuna captures all my attention since I have become one of the main protagonists of her narrated event, a very close member of her family, her sister. At the same time, however, she also actively constructs a more intimate relation between us. At line 25, indeed, she expresses her intimate stance toward my past self by adding the adjective "dear," "chère" in French, when she refers to "her sister Sabina." Notably, four more instances of participant transposition together followed this interaction during this interview,[12] providing us with opportunities to enact and co-construct an intimate relationship.

Interviews are thus sites where interactional moves can take different directions depending on participants' multiple and various stances. Maimuna goes so far as to transpose me into a member of her family, her sister, an interactional move that invites me to witness the seriousness of her malaria and body pain in a way that would have otherwise been impossible. By making me into a witness in the denotational text, she creates a sense of obligation so that I become less distracted, and thus more present, in the interactional text. In the process, however, Maimuna promotes a closer rapport between us, since, as we have seen, more intimate relationships can develop and solidify during these narrating sequences.

6.4.2 Narrating Trauma in Ethnographic Interviews in Northern Italy

My second example is extracted from an interview that I collected in the small town of Treviso, in Northern Italy, in May 2003. At the time, I was studying the transnational circulation of Senegalese ethnomedicine in Italy, as well as researching migration more generally. My interviewee, Veronica, was an Italian schoolteacher who was in her fifties at the time. She accepted to be interviewed since she had a lot of experience as a volunteer assisting children, and occasionally migrants, in northern Italian hospitals during her free time. My interview with Veronica, which lasted almost two hours,

178   Research Methods in Linguistic Anthropology

focused on the issue of how Italian hospitals and hospital personnel had been reacting to new waves of migrants in Italy. At a certain point, however, when she was talking about the relationship between Italian doctors and migrant patients, she launched into three personal narratives during the interview. In one narrative, Veronica recounted the experience she had with a physician who directed the neurology department where her father had been hospitalized for possible brain cancer a couple of days before. Her narrative began with a description of how Veronica had gone to the neurology department to hear about her father's diagnosis after the doctors had performed a CAT scan on him. In Italy, doctors do not usually talk directly to patients about their diagnoses if they are serious. Rather, they first communicate with a close family member and leave the choice to that family member as to what, or how much, of the diagnosis to convey to the sick patient. As one of the daughters of this patient, then, Veronica was allowed to go to the doctor to hear her father's diagnosis results. Anxiously, as she recounted, she rushed to the hospital to hear the verdict about her father's brain problems.

Example 2: *"Here everyone has problems!"*

(V: Veronica; S: Interviewer)
First Line: Original Italian Version
Second Line: English Translation

1. **V:**   ehmm io- eh c'era mio padre ricoverato
     ehmm I- uh there was my father [who was] hospitalized

2. che aveva un tumore al cervello
     who had a tumor at his brain

3. e io ero andata il giorno dopo che gli avevano fatto la TAC
     and I went that day after they performed the CAT on him

4. per sapere di quale:- quale era il problema di cui era affetto
     to know of wha:t- what was the problem by which [he] was affected

5. e:h e avevo mio figlio Mauro a casa con mia sorella
     u:h and [I] had my son Mauro at home with my sister

Interviews in Linguistic Anthropology   **179**

6. e io non lo potevo lasciare mio figlio quindi è stata uhm
    and I couldn't leave my son so [it] was uhm

7. sì mia sorella era in grado di fare determinate manovre pe:::rché lui eh
    yes my sister was able to take certain steps be:::cause he [i.e., her son] eh
    |

8. **S:** per lui
    for him

9. **V:** e:h però:: io naturalmente ero venuta via col cuore in mano=
    u:h bu::t I of course had gone away with my heart in my hands=

10. **S:**   =eh
    =eh

11. **V:** perciò ero- mordevo anche un po' il freno
    so [I] was- '[I] was also a bit in a rush[13]

12. guardavo l'orologio
    [I] was looking [continuously] at my watch

13. ero ansiosa e preoccupata sia per mio figlio sia per mio padre perché non sapevo-
    [I] was anxious and worried both for my son and for my father because [I] didn't know-

14. e questo medico::: al quale io ho chiesto
    and this docto:::r to whom I asked

15. "scusi professore ma Lei" dico
    "sorry professor but you [formal]," [I] say

16. "pensa di poterci:: eh spiegare quanto prima
    "[you] think [you] can explain to us as soon as possible

17. sa ho dei problemi avrei dei problemi
    [you] know [I] have some problems [I] might have some problems

18. posso anche spiegarLe"
    [I] can also explain [them, i.e. the problems] to you [formal]"

19. "qua problemi ne abbiamo tutti"
    "here everyone has problems"

20. mi ha risposto mi ha inveito
    [he] responded to me, [he] railed against me

21. nel corridoio dicendo che lì: lì lavoravano
    in the hallway [he was] saying that there: there they were working

22. non è che:: stessero lì a grattarsi i cosiddetti
    it is not tha::t [they] were staying there scratching their you-know-what

23. e ehmm e questo mi ha trattato veramente in maniera:: molto molto aggressiva
    and uhmm and this [doctor] treated me really in a very very aggressive manne::r

24. cosa che io non gli ho mai perdonato
    something that I have never forgiven to him

25. e dopo che appunto ci ha spiegato, illustrato la situazione
    and after that [he] actually explained, illustrated the situation to us

26. che era drammatica appunto ho detto
    which was actually tragic, [I] said

27. "guardi:::: Lei si ricordi comunque ecco che è un esser umano anche Lei
    "liste:::n [you should] remember anyway well that you are a human being as well

28. che non debba mai provare le situazioni che io sto provando in questo momento
    [I wish] you never experience the situations that I am experiencing in this moment

Interviews in Linguistic Anthropology 181

29.   perché allora capirebbe" [...]
      because at that point [you] would understand" [...]

30.   ho preso e me ne sono andata
      [I] got together and [I] went away from there

31.   e non mi ha più visto questa persona
      and this person never saw me again

In this short, but intense, narrative, delivered during our interview, Veronica seems to be eager to tell me her personal experiences with an Italian neurologist who was overseeing her father's care. At the beginning of her narrative, Veronica keeps her past story separate from our present interaction. The two events, the *narrated event* (or denotational text) and the *narrating event* (or interactional text) (Jakobson 1957; Silverstein 1998; Perrino 2015b; Wortham 2000, 2001) are kept distinct and distant. That is, it is as if the narrator is standing back and recounting her past; the past does not overlap with the present. This is typical of a Labovian narrative. Like Maimuna in Example 1 presented earlier, Veronica begins her story with a classic Labovian orientation, in which she lays out the key contextual facts that she deems essential for understanding the rest of her narration. While this orientation extends from line 1 to line 13 in the current excerpt, in lines 1–2 Veronica informs the interviewer about the important fact that her father was hospitalized for brain cancer. The fact that this tragic statement is in the very first lines of her narrative indicates her disposition to emotionally involve the interviewer right at the outset of her story. Indeed, as Veronica continues in lines 2–3, at that point in her past story, she actually didn't know whether her father had brain cancer or not. She backs up in her past story to recount all the details to me, her interviewer.

The day after the CAT scan was performed on her father, she explains, Veronica went to the hospital to hear what the outcomes were (lines 3–5). Despite the fact that in the first 5 lines of the orientation, Veronica sets up a very dramatic situation, the interviewer seems to remain unresponsive verbally.[14] At line 6, Veronica then adds even more dramatic information when she states that, for this occasion, she had left her son at home with her sister. At first, this line does not seem to add anything dramatic or tragic to the story; however, if one looks at the interactional history between Veronica and me, her interviewer, things become more intricate. Indeed, during our previous interviews and conversations, Veronica had mentioned that her one-year-old son, Mauro, had been very ill for more than a year and that she could not leave him alone (line 6), not even for ten minutes.[15] If one looks at the interactional text then, one notices that Veronica accelerates her pace in line 6 when she says '*I couldn't leave my son so this was uhm*', which indicates a sense of anxiety in remembering those moments.

Her involvement becomes even more intense after I overlap with her at line 8. In line 7, Veronica explains that she left her son with her sister, who, at the time, was the only person who was able to help her son with his medical care. It is precisely at that point that I cooperatively overlap with her (Tannen 1984, 2007, 2012) to show not only solidarity with her past dramatic situation, but especially awareness of it at the moment of the narrated event. Soon after my overlap, moreover, Veronica adds more emotional details to her description when she says "*of course I had gone away with my heart in my hands,*" in line 9. She uses the Italian metaphor "col cuore in mano" ("*with my heart in my hands*") to show how much she cared that I understand the gravity of the situation when she left her son behind to go to the hospital. She then recounts how much in a hurry she was when she was waiting for the doctor at the hospital: in line 11, she uses another metaphoric phrase, "mordevo un po' il freno," which literally means "*I was biting the brake a bit.*" This tropic phrase is followed by a further explanation when she says that she was continuously checking her watch and that she was worried for both her son at home and her father at the hospital (lines 12–13). It is at this point of her narrative (at line 14) that Veronica aligns her past story with our present interaction by using certain discourse strategies (Gumperz 1982) to continue her story. In this way, Veronica makes some interactional moves that solidify her sense of trust and intimacy toward me, her interviewer.

As in the Senegalese interaction discussed earlier, Veronica's narrative alternates between moments of alignment between past and present and moments in which she keeps her past story more distant from the present interaction (especially the beginning of her narrative). The interview becomes emotionally more involved and dynamic in relation to shifts between Veronica's past narrative moments that she recounts and our present interaction when she accelerates her pace and shows how anxious she was. By using the Italian proximal deictic demonstrative adjective *questo* ("this") when referring to the doctor in her narrated event in line 14, for example, Veronica brings her past experience back to the present, to her narrating event. Her narration is marked by rapid shifts that create the impression of back-and-forth space-time movement. Soon afterward, indeed, still in line 14, by using the past tense (*passato prossimo*) of the Italian verbum dicendi "chiedere," that is "io ho chiesto" ("*I asked*"), her story is temporally relocated into her remote past. Past and present become, again, two separate realms. The two spatiotemporal realms conflate, again, in line 15, however, when Veronica starts a long stretch of direct reported speech. Her narrated event is aligned, again, with our narrating event, the here-and-now interactional framework.

Direct reported speech, or, as Tannen (2007) usefully defines it, "constructed dialogue," has particular interactional qualities when it is used in conversation. In her direct reported speech, starting in line 15, Veronica addresses the chief of the neurology department as if he were present in, and part of, our interactional text. As normally happens in Italian conversations between speakers who do not know each other or who have a different status, Veronica addresses the doctor by using the Italian polite form of address *Lei*. In the same line, moreover, she uses the historical present of the Italian verbum dicendi *dire* in the first-person singular form, "dico" ("*I say*"), and this, again, further decreases the spatial and temporal boundaries between narrated event and narrating event. Veronica continues by showing politeness in different ways in her constructed dialogue. In line 16, for example, she asks the doctor whether he thinks that he could inform her as soon as possible about the diagnosis of her father. She does so by politely saying "*[you] think to be able:: uh to explain to us as soon as possible*" and by lengthening the Italian final vowel "i" in the Italian verb "poterci" (which I translated "*to be able::*"), showing respect toward him, but perhaps some hesitation and trepidation as well.

In lines 15–18, Veronica maintains and projects a respectful and polite demeanor in her request to the doctor. In line 19, however, when she reports the doctor's response to her question, Veronica breaks register by saying "qua problemi ne abbiamo tutti" ("*here everyone has problems*"), and then she qualifies the doctor's behavior in her constructed interaction with him. By using the Italian proximal deictic *qua*, Veronica voices the doctor as a not well-behaved person. Indeed, in Italian, there are two proximal deictics for "here," that is *qui* and *qua*. According to some northern Italian consultants of mine, while *qui* and *qua* can be interchangeable (Renzi and Cardinaletti 1988), *qui* is stereotypically more refined than *qua*. During a follow-up interview, for example, Veronica herself stated that *qua* is used in more dialectal situations than *qui*, especially in her region, Veneto. Thus, by having the neurologist utter *qua*, she thus voices him negatively, as someone who is not as courteous as a doctor should be. In line 20, having completed her direct reported speech, Veronica shifts to the past tense again to reflect upon, and thus describe, the doctor's behavior by saying "*[he] responded to me, [he] railed against me.*" She first uses the verb "rispondere" ("*to respond*") which is a rather neutral verb, but soon afterward she uses the verb "inveire" ("*to rail against*") which is a much stronger verb indexing aggressiveness on the part of the other speaker (i.e., the doctor). Thus, Veronica seems to be completely dumbfounded by the doctor's response to her polite request, and she then gives more details about that particular moment by describing how he railed at her in the hallway of the hospital when he said that they were working very hard and that they didn't have any time to waste there (lines 21–22). She then adds, "*[T]his [doctor] treated me really in a very very aggressive manner,*" in line 23, where she uses the proximal demonstrative adjective "questo" ("*this*"), again, when she refers to the doctor. By using this proximal demonstrative pronoun, Veronica not only shifts back to the present narrating event and, again, makes the doctor be part of it, but also communicates her profound disrespect toward him to the interviewer. At the same time, she nourishes her intimate rapport with the interviewer, since she enacts her hidden emotions and looks for sympathy, as Maimuna did in Example 1 earlier.

Furthermore, Veronica also undergoes a sudden interactional transformation in this interview: from a remissive and polite relative of a patient of the neurology department she becomes a vindictive and aggressive speaker. After claiming that she would never forgive this doctor for his rude behavior in line 24, Veronica continues her sad story by stating that the doctor finally explained the clinical situation of her father to her and probably to her siblings (line 25),[16] and this happened a few hours after her request to the doctor, as she told me after our interview. The diagnosis of her father was really tragic, since she was informed that he suffered of brain cancer. It is at this moment of the narrated event, at the very peak of her complicating action (Labov and Waletzky 1966), that Veronica conflates the past with the present interaction again by resorting to a lengthy, uninterrupted, direct reported speech. She addresses the doctor by catching his attention with the polite form of the verb "guardare" ("to look"), which is conjugated in the present subjunctive (line 27). The Italian polite imperative "guardi," which I glossed in English as "listen," is mainly used in two ways in Italian: to show understanding and sympathy to a listener (as in the sentence, "guarda, ti capisco benissimo," "*look, I really understand you*") or to start an argument, as in Veronica's case, in her direct reported speech. By addressing the doctor with "guardi" ("listen") and by lengthening the final vowel *i*, Veronica immediately sets the tone of her upcoming statements.

At line 28, sarcastically, she uses another polite imperative of the reflexive verb *ricordarsi* which is also preceded by the polite third-person subject pronoun *Lei*: "Lei si ricordi comunque ecco" ("*you [should] remember anyway well*"). The explicit use of the polite third-person subject pronoun *Lei* further increases Veronica's unfriendly tone, especially if one considers the fact that subject pronouns are optional in Italian and they are often used to just add emphasis to one's speech. Here, in this stretch of this constructed dialogue (Tannen 2007), Veronica indeed uses the polite subject pronoun *Lei* repeatedly. In lines 27–29, she continues by saying that the doctor has to remember "*that you are a human being as well, I wish you never experience the situations that I am experiencing in this moment.*" By reminding him that even doctors are mortal, Veronica challenges his hierarchical position and thus downgrades him to the same level of all other human beings. In this way, through Veronica's direct reported speech, the doctor is not only part of her *narrated event*, the past story, but he has become part of her *narrating event*, the present interaction, as well. It is as if he were co-present, since she addresses him as if he were in the here-and-now interaction, he is the "real" addressee of her conversation, not the interviewer. Veronica then suddenly ends her stretch of direct reported speech at line 30 when she recounts that after the above reported conversation with the doctor, she quickly went away, and this person never saw her again (lines 30–31). With the use of the proximal demonstrative feminine adjective "questa" (in "questa persona," "*this person*") in line 31, Veronica briefly realigns her past story with the interactional text of the interview. The two stories become the same again, with the doctor being one of the interlocutors, although he is fading away, as it were, since Veronica leaves the scene.

The fleeting and ever-changing nature of interviews, particularly during storytelling events in these settings, thus clearly emerges in this example as well. Like in the interview with Maimuna in Example 1, the two speech participants, Veronica and I, get more intimate through the lines of her tragic story. While I overlap with Veronica only twice in the beginning of the interview, in lines 8 and 10, unlike my more involved participation with Maimuna's stories in Example 1, my silence during Veronica's storytelling indicates my sympathy, respect, and participation as well. Silence, as has been demonstrated (Basso 1979; Nakane 2012), can be very meaningful and can show involvement instead of indifference or disinterest. In both cases, then, *intimate relations* are foregrounded, showing how interviews can be transformed into *intimate* moments for speech participants. Both Maimuna and Veronica have cultivated close relationships with me which have lasted

Research Methods in Linguistic Anthropology

over fifteen years now. These two examples thus show how interviews can develop differently, depending on the various sociocultural contexts, speech participants, and, of course, the stories that are told during these events.

6.5 Concluding Remarks

While interviews are used in research across various disciplines, they are one of the most important methods of data collection for linguistic anthropologists. As I have discussed in this chapter, interviews are discursive and interactional events and need to be treated and analyzed as such in order to unveil some key, emerging interactional patterns, as the two examples show. In this respect, linguistic anthropologists should consider interviews as social practices rather than merely as research instruments (Roulston 2019a, 7) given their situatedness in context. They are thus a prominent part of their research not just as methods but also as data. Besides preparing questionnaires and IRB forms for their fieldwork, researchers also need to be ready to improvise during their interviews to adapt them to their research consultants' contexts, desires, and needs. Questionnaires are good starting points, but, as I describe in the two examples analyzed in this chapter, every interview is a unique speech event. Questions themselves can take very different directions. It is thus clear that the interactional context of the interview cannot be considered artificial or, worse, be erased, as some researchers still try to do. This is one of the most important points that linguistic anthropologists should keep in mind when they engage in interviews.

As the two examples presented in this chapter have shown, speech participants often, without being prompted by the interviewer, recount personal stories in interviews. Narratives emerging in these interactional settings are thus more common than one would think, as Maimuna's and Veronica's respective interviews indicate. In these cases, both interviewees shared personal narratives and also constructed and solidified an intimate rapport with the interviewer in the process. In Example 1, just thirty-five minutes into the interview, Maimuna shared a personal narrative about a serious past illness of hers, which almost paralyzed her in her bed. Through certain discursive strategies, such as participant transposition (Perrino 2007, 2011), the use of laughter, prosody, and codeswitching (Gumperz 1982) at particular moments of the interaction, she tried to recover my full attention when she felt that I was getting distracted or that I was not emotionally involved enough. Storytelling practices can thus do a lot of interactional work in interviews. Similarly, Veronica shared a very dramatic story about her father and son right at the outset of our interview. She immediately showed confidence and trust in her interviewer. She projected her intimate stances by sharing very personal moments of her past with me. In that case, however, I remained almost silent, yet very present, throughout her telling.

In closing, as linguistic anthropologists have recently argued, the interview can take different directions as conversations and stories can be more or less engaging, thus prompting different types of questions and sub-questions (Perrino 2011). Interviewees can talk for long stretches of time or just answer researchers' questions rapidly in a "yes-no" fashion. Researchers need to take all this into account when they engage in research interviews. Furthermore, as De Fina and I (2011, 8) have pointed out, researchers need to be aware of the fact that the narratives that they collect in interview settings are interconnected with speech participants' interactional roles in complex ways. In this way, as I have shown in my analysis of Examples 1 and 2, narratives are constantly redefined as the interview unfolds. Mishler's (1986, vii) early intuition that the interview is a "form of discourse" should now be taken as one of the main tenets for interviews not only in linguistic anthropology, or anthropology more generally, but across many other disciplines using these research tools as well.

Appendix. Transcription and Abbreviations Conventions[17]

||	Utterances starting simultaneously.
|	Overlapping utterances.
=	Latching, or contiguous utterances, with an interval of less than one-tenth of second between lines.
(00.00)	Time intervals within and between utterances (length of pauses in seconds, tenths and hundredths of seconds).
::	Syllable lengthening.
:::::	Prolonged syllable lengthening.
-	Syllable cut-off.
.	Stopping fall in tone.
,	Continuing intonation.
?	Rising intonation.

!	Animated tone.
____	Words with underline indicate stress.
CAP	Words in capitals indicate increased volume.
(…)	Talk between parenthesis indicates the transcriber's best guess at a stretch of discourse that is unclear on the original tape.
(???)	Question marks inside parenthesis indicate uncertain or unclear talk.
[…]	Three dots between square brackets indicate that some material of the original transcript has been omitted.
[[ ]]	The material inside double square brackets indicates transcriber's comments.

Regular font = French or Standard Italian.
Underlined Italics: Wolof.
Italics: English Translation.
Wavy underling: very fast speech.
Bold: Portions of transcripts discussed in the analysis.

6.6 Ethnographic Activities

Complete one or both activities:

1 Imagine being a researcher (or a member of a small team of researchers) involved in a linguistic anthropological project on narratives in interview settings. These are the required tasks for this activity:

   a) Prepare a 300-word description of your project.

   b) Prepare a basic questionnaire for your interviews.

   c) Find at least four or five friends (students on campus; family friends; friends of friends) or relatives (your close family members or more distant relatives) and set up some appointments to conduct interviews face to face or via FaceTime/Skype/Zoom.

   d) Audio- or video-record your interviews (see also Kohler and Murphy, Chapter 9, this volume).

   e) Transfer your audio and/or video data in your computer or tablet and back up all the files (on Google Drive/iCloud/Dropbox and on an external drive).

   f) Carefully listen to the collected interviews and indicate where interviewees launch into narratives/stories (long or short stories).

g) Write a short commentary/summary for each narrative that you find in these interviews. While you do so, answer the following questions: Why do you consider these excerpts as narratives? What do these narratives bring to the interactional dynamics of the interview?

h) Optional (extra-credit): Create your own transcription conventions and transcribe these narrative excerpts and make sure to follow what you learned on transcription in Chapter 13 (Shohet, this volume) and in the other chapters as well.

2 You are about to start a new linguistic anthropological project on medical practices in the United States. One of the first phases of this project requires you to interview doctors and patients in some selected US hospitals. What are the ethical issues that are key to consider before interviewing your research consultants? Write a 300–500-word statement indicating the various ethical issues involved in interviewing doctors and patients in hospitals in the United States. Why do linguistic anthropologists need to think carefully before engaging in interviews? More generally, are the IRB requirements (see Black and Conley Riner, Chapter 4, this volume) sufficient to protect your interviewees' identities and privacy? Feel free to discuss these issues with one of your classmates before writing your statement.

6.7 Questions to Consider

Answer the following questions (for a minimum of 300 words per question) and refer to this chapter to review some key concepts while writing your answers:

1 As described in the introduction of this chapter, how does Mishler conceptualize the interview? What does he mean when he states that the interview is a "form of discourse"? Support your answer with some detailed examples from the chapter or from your own experience.

2 In his book entitled *Learning How to Ask*, Briggs made some important anthropological and ethical steps vis-à-vis the interview as a research method/tool. What are his important contributions to this field? Why are they central in any anthropological research?

3 What are the three main types of *qualitative research interviews*? In your own words, describe each type in detail and explain what category

of interviews Perrino used in Examples 1 and 2. Can researchers use these three types of interviews altogether? If so, how? Would this be ethical?

4 Are narratives in interviews different from narratives emerging in other speech events, such as naturally occurring conversations? Why? Support your perspective with detailed examples from this or other chapters.

5 Are interviews replicable speech events or are they unique and thus different from one another? Support your answer with some examples from this chapter or from your own experience.

6 Consider one of the transcripts proposed in Examples 1 or 2 and explain why the interviews that the author conducted with Maimuna or Veronica are interactionally significant. Do you see any parallels between the *narrated event* and the *narrating event* in these interviews? Support your answer by referring to the lines of the selected transcript.

6.8 Notes

1 In this chapter, I refer to "surveys" as tools used to gather content-oriented interviews rather than yes/no, quantitative gathering tools.

2 These are the same questions that ethnographers should keep in mind when audio- and/or video-recording any types of discursive practices while conducting their fieldwork, such as naturally occurring conversations. Since this chapter centers on interviews, I mainly refer to interviewing practices in my examples and various theoretical points.

3 *Playback experiments* have been used extensively in linguistic anthropology, although their origin lays in other disciplines (McGregor 2000). They usually consist of follow-up interviews with previously interviewed research consultants during which portions of audio- or video-recorded materials are played back to them in order to glean more information on the topic or to resolve possible ambiguities. In my research, I have highly valued these types of follow-up interviews since scholars are often not aware of certain nuances of the phenomena they are studying. By playing back portions of audio and video data, I was able to gain deeper, and more valuable, insights rather than relying just on my own intuitions.

4 In this chapter, I use pseudonyms for all my research participants to protect their identity and privacy.

5 In many Senegalese families, herbal remedies are used to cure many diseases at home before going to a healer or to a Western biomedical doctor.

6   See Appendix for transcription conventions.

7   All translations from Wolof, French, and Italian to English are mine unless otherwise stated.

8   My Senegalese informants often pronounced my first name, [Sabɨna], as [Sabɛna].

9   In the 1960s, importantly, Labov and Waletzky (1966) elaborated their well-known narrative model in which narratives, to be considered as such, need to contain six units indicating the "necessary" progression of a narrative. The six Labovian narrative units are the *abstract*, the *orientation*, the *complicating action*, the *resolution*, the *coda*, and, finally, the *evaluation* (Labov and Waletzky 1966; De Fina and Georgakopoulou 2012, 27–9).

10 The Wolof term *palu*, which is widely used to indicate any disease with malaria-like feverish symptoms, derives from the French *paludisme*, "malaria." As many of my Senegalese consultants confirmed, unlike the French term (*paludisme*), *palu* is used to refer not only to cases of malaria, but also to other ranges of diseases as different as having a high fever, being unconscious or hallucinated, having a bad cold, suffering from extreme fatigue, to mention just a few.

11 While codeswitching takes many forms and involves different units, such as inter-sentential versus intra-sentential, when I mention this discourse strategy in this chapter, I only refer to its sociocultural and pragmatic functions in interaction.

12 Due to space limitations, in this chapter, only the above case of *participant transposition* is presented and analyzed.

13 Literally, "*[I] was also biting the brake a bit.*"

14 This interview was only audio-recorded.

15 Later I learned from Veronica that, after a couple of months, her one-year-old son tragically passed away.

16 In line 25, the Italian pronoun *ci* ("to us") indicates that Veronica received the information about her father's disease together with her siblings or other relatives.

17 Some of the transcription symbols described below are drawn from the works of Jefferson (1978; 1984), Schiffrin (1994), and Duranti and Goodwin (1992).

6.9 References Cited

Ahearn, Laura M. 2017. *Living Language: An Introduction to Linguistic Anthropology*. Oxford, UK: Wiley-Blackwell.

Bailey, Benjamin. 2000. "Social/interactional Functions of Code Switching among Dominican Americans." *Pragmatics* 10 (2): 165–93.

Basso, Keith H. 1979. *Portraits of "the Whiteman": Linguistic Play and Cultural Symbols among the Western Apache*. New York: Cambridge University Press.

Black, Steven P. 2017. "Anthropological Ethics and the Communicative Affordances of Audio-Video Recorders in Ethnographic Fieldwork: Transduction as Theory." *American Anthropologist* 119 (1): 46–57.

Briggs, Charles L. 1986. *Learning How to Ask: A Sociolinguistic Appraisal of the Role of the Interview in Social Science Research*. New York: Cambridge University Press.

De Fina, Anna. 2011. "Researcher and Informant Roles in Narrative Interactions: Constructions of Belonging and Foreign-Ness." *Language in Society* 40 (01): 27–38.

De Fina, Anna, and Alexandra Georgakopoulou. 2012. *Analyzing Narrative: Discourse and Sociolinguistic Perspectives*. New York: Cambridge University Press.

De Fina, Anna, and Sabina Perrino. 2011. "Interviews vs. 'Natural' Contexts: A False Dilemma [Special Issue]." *Language in Society* 40 (1): 1–11.

Duranti, Alessandro, and Charles Goodwin. 1992. *Rethinking Context: Language as an Interactive Phenomenon*. New York: Cambridge University Press.

Fontana, Andrea, and James H. Frei. 2004. "Interviewing: The Art of Science." In Norman K. Denzin and Yvonna S. Lincoln eds., *Handbook of qualitative research*, 361–76. Thousand Oaks, CA: Sage.

Fuller, Janet. 2000. "Changing Perspectives on Data: Interviews as Situated Speech." *American Speech* 75 (4): 388–90.

Garcia, Angela. 2010. *The Pastoral Clinic: Addiction and Dispossession along the Rio Grande*. Berkeley: University of California Press.

Goffman, Erving. 1971. *Relations in Public: Microstudies of the Public Order*. New York: Basic Books.

Goodwin, Charles. 2015. "Narrative as Talk-in-interaction." In Alexandra Georgakopoulou and Anna De Fina eds., *The Handbook of Narrative Analysis*, 197–218. Malden, MA: Wiley-Blackwell.

Gumperz, John J. 1982. *Discourse Strategies*. New York: Cambridge University Press.

Heller, Monica. 1988. *Codeswitching: Anthropological and Sociolinguistic Perspectives*. Berlin, New York: Mouton de Gruyter.

Jakobson, Roman. 1957. "Shifters and Verbal Categories." In Linda R. Waugh and Monique Monville-Burston eds., *On Language*, 386–92. Cambridge, MA: Harvard University Press.

Jakobson, Roman. 1960. "Linguistics and Poetics." In Thomas A. Sebeok ed., *Style in Language*, 350–77. Cambridge, MA: Massachusetts Institute of Technology Press.

Jefferson, Gail. 1978. "Sequential Aspects of Storytelling in Conversation." In J. Schenkein ed., *Studies in the Organization of Conversational Interaction*, 219–48. New York: Academic Press.

Jefferson, Gail. 1984. "On the Organization of Laughter in Talk about Troubles." In J. Atkinson and J. Heritage eds., *Structures of Social Action: Studies in Conversation Analysis*, 346–69. New York: Cambridge University Press.

Labov, William. 1972. *Language in the Inner City*. Philadelphia: University of Pennsylvania Press.

Labov, William, and Joshua Waletzky. 1966. "Narrative Analysis: Oral Versions of Personal Experience." *Journal of Narrative & Life History* 7 (1–4): 3–38.

Mattingly, Cheryl. 2014. *Moral Laboratories: Family Peril and the Struggle for a Good Life*. Berkeley: University of California Press.

McGregor, Peter K. 2000. "Playback Experiments: Design and Analysis." *Acta Ethologica* 3: 3–8.

Mishler, Elliot George. 1986. *Research Interviewing: Context and Narrative*. Cambridge, MA: Harvard University Press.

Modan, Gabriella, and Amy Shuman. 2011. "Positioning the Interviewer: Strategic Uses of Embedded Orientation in Interview Narratives." *Language in Society* 40 (01): 13–25.

Nakane, Ikuko. 2012. "Silence." In Christina Bratt Paulston, Scott F. Kiesling, and Elizabeth S. Rangel eds., *The Handbook of Intercultural Discourse and Communication*, 158–79. Malden, MA: Blackwell.

Perrino, Sabina. 2007. "Cross-Chronotope Alignment in Senegalese Oral Narrative." *Language and Communication* 27 (3): 227–44.

Perrino, Sabina. 2011. "Chronotopes of Story and Storytelling Event in Interviews." *Language in Society* 40 (1): 91–103.

Perrino, Sabina. 2015a. "Chronotopes: Time and Space in Oral Narrative." In Anna De Fina and Alexandra Georgakopoulou eds., *The Handbook of Narrative Analysis*, 140–59. Malden, MA: Wiley-Blackwell.

Perrino, Sabina. 2015b. "Performing Extracomunitari: Mocking Migrants in Veneto Barzellette." *Language in Society* 44 (2): 141–60.

Perrino, Sabina. 2019. "Narrating Migration Politics in Veneto, Northern Italy." *Narrative Culture* 6 (1): 44–68.

Perrino, Sabina. 2021. "Intimacy through Time and Space in Fieldwork Interviews." In Zane Goebel ed., *Reimagining Rapport*, 73–95. New York: Oxford University Press.

Perrino, Sabina, and Sonya Pritzker. 2019. "Language and Intimate Relations." In Kira Hall and Rusty Barrett eds., *Handbook of Language and Sexuality*. New York: Oxford University Press (Oxford Handbooks Online).

Perrino, Sabina M. 2005. "Participant Transposition in Senegalese Oral Narrative." *Narrative Inquiry* 15 (2): 345–75.

Rapley, Timothy John. 2001. "The Art(fulness) of Open-Ended Interviewing: Some Considerations on Analyzing Interviews." *Qualitative Research* 1 (3): 303–23.

Renzi, Lorenzo, and Anna Cardinaletti. 1988. *Grande Grammatica Italiana Di Consultazione*. Bologna [Italy]: Il Mulino.

Roulston, Kathryn. 2019a. *Interactional Studies of Qualitative Research Interviews*. Amsterdam/Philadelphia: John Benjamins Publishing Company.

Roulston, Kathryn. 2019b. "Research Interviewers as 'Knowers' and 'Unknowers'." In Kathryn Roulston ed., *Interactional Studies of Qualitative Research Interviews*, 59–78. Amsterdam/Philadelphia: John Benjamins Publishing Company.

Schiffrin, Deborah. 1994. *Approaches to Discourse*. Cambridge, MA: Wiley Blackwell.

Silverstein, Michael. 1998. "Improvisational Performance of Culture in Realtime Discursive Practice." In Keith Sawyer ed., *Creativity in Performance*, 265–312. Greenwich, CT: Ablex Publishing Corp.

Silverstein, Michael. 2005. "Axes of Evals." *Journal of Linguistic Anthropology* 15 (1): 6–22.

Silverstein, Michael, and Greg Urban. 1996. *Natural Histories of Discourse*. Chicago: University of Chicago Press.

Talmy, Steven. 2011. "The Interview as Collaborative Achievement: Interaction, Identity, and Ideology in a Speech Event." *Applied Linguistics* 32 (1): 25–42.

Tannen, Deborah. 1984. *Conversational Style: Analyzing Talk among Friends*. New York: Oxford University Press.

Tannen, Deborah. 2007. *Talking Voices: Repetition, Dialogue, and Imagery in Conversational Discourse*. Cambridge: Cambridge University Press.

Tannen, Deborah. 2012. "Turn-Taking and Intercultural Discourse and Communication." In Christina Bratt Paulston, Scott F. Kiesling, and Elizabeth S. Rangel eds., *The Handbook of Intercultural Discourse and Communication*, 135–57. Malden, MA: Blackwell.

Wilce, James MacLynn. 2001. "Divining Troubles, or Divining Troubles? Emergent and Conflictual Dimensions of Bangladeshi Divination." *Anthropological Quarterly* 74 (4): 190–200.

Williams, Valerie. 2019. "'Like Us You Mean?': Sensitive Disability Questions and Peer Research Encounters." In Kathryn Roulston ed., *Interactional Studies of Qualitative Research Interviews*, 37–57. Amsterdam/Philadelphia: John Benjamins Publishing Company.

Woolard, Kathryn A. 1995. "Changing Forms of Codeswitching in Catalan Comedy." *Catalan Review* IX 2: 223–52.

Wortham, Stanton. 2000. "Interactional Positioning and Narrative Self-Construction." *Narrative Inquiry* 10 (1): 157–84.

Wortham, Stanton. 2001. *Narratives in Action: A Strategy for Research Analysis*. New York: Teachers College Press.

Wortham, Stanton et al. 2011. "Interviews as Interactional Data." *Language in Society* 40 (01): 39–50.

6.10 Further Reading

De Fina, Anna, and Sabina Perrino. 2011. "Interviews vs. 'Natural' Contexts: A False Dilemma [Special Issue]." *Language in Society* 40 (1). (Read all the articles of this special issue.)

Roulston, Kathryn. 2019a. *Interactional Studies of Qualitative Research Interviews*. Amsterdam/Philadelphia: John Benjamins Publishing Company. (Read all the chapters of this edited volume.)

7

Audio-Video Technology for and in the Field: A Primer

Gregory Kohler and Keith M. Murphy

7.1 Introduction

This chapter is designed to do two things at once. First, we present some of the main considerations and methodological rationales involved with using digital audio and video for data collection in ethnographic fieldwork, mostly from the point of view of linguistic anthropology or for the benefit of someone who is interested in linguistic anthropological insights and methods. Second, we critically discuss some of the most common considerations actually entailed in using audio recorders and video cameras in fieldwork. But before we start, there are some caveats.

It is difficult to discuss recording technologies with any enduring precision because the technology changes so quickly. This is less true with digital audio formats and equipment than it is with video, which changes quite rapidly, but nonetheless, it is important to bear in mind that formats and device form factors are often made obsolete. Thus, our goal in this chapter is to unpack some of the basic requirements and contingencies that apply to almost all audio- and video-recording scenarios in fieldwork, regardless of the technologies that happen to be available.

7.2 Audio and Video Data: Some Bugs and Features

Recordings of naturally occurring human speech and face-to-face interaction offer a kind of concrete, sharable, and reviewable ethnographic data that typically invites very close inspection—and as with all forms of data, they require some consideration in terms of both their limitations and affordances. As Alessandro Duranti (1997) has argued, we should think of audio and video recordings as *inscriptions* of otherwise ephemeral instances of social action. We can write down a verbal description of an observed social moment in the field or audio-record the sounds of that moment (and then transcribe them) or create video recordings of that moment— each of which is a kind of stabilized (though not necessarily always stable) representation of a situation that happened in the social world. Video recordings, because they include so much multimodal information, often feel like especially robust or "more objective" representations of "reality" than other kinds of inscription, and in some respects, that might not be wrong. It is important to bear in mind, however, that inscriptions of all types, even video, are always limited because they are always *versions* of moments in the world, and thus they are always selective, biased, and infinitely subject to interpretation.

The first basic limitation of recording technologies is that it is impossible to record everything, so one must be selective in terms of what to record or which particular technology to use. It is possible to structure recordings— for example, recording a set number of times, for a set number of minutes, on a set number of days—but even choosing how to arrange this structure is itself always selective. In general, it tends to be easiest to record things that are recognizably "worth recording"—usually activities, performances, and other organized or semi-organized kinds of events—where the worthiness is determined either by the ethnographer or the people we work with (or both). This selectiveness produces a sort of bias, though, meaning that this orientation toward bounded activities privileges organized kinds of action and de-emphasizes recording spontaneous and less-organized situations. Often the audio recorder or video camera will come out when a fieldworker senses that "something is going on," but even these cases are largely based on anthropological intuition—or, sometimes, on a person nudging the ethnographer with something like, "you should record this." There is no inherent methodological problem with such selectiveness, but nonetheless it is important to remember that because this approach is significantly driven by intuition, then recordings are rarely "representative" in a *statistical* sense. Instead, they are representative in an *ethnographic* sense—based on the embedded and immersive experiences of the fieldworker—and the researcher should make sure that when analyzing a given recorded event, a reasonable assessment of how common or uncommon the situation is should be provided.

Second, audio and video recordings are always partial and sometimes deceptively so (see Black 2017). The easiest way to experience this partialness is to pay attention to the frame, in a very literal sense, when recording video. The camera's ability to capture video information is always limited by the size and shape of the lens, as well as the particular mode the user sets on the camera (some modes are wider or narrower or squarer than others). This means that whatever visual information lies just beyond the frame at any given point will always be left out, and while it is usually possible to move the camera around to capture more visual information, the problem does not go away—it just shifts along with the motion of the camera. In other words, the camera's gaze will always be incomplete. But rather than trying to overcome this limitation, which is essentially impossible to do, it is important for the ethnographer to supplement video recordings with fieldnotes that provide a different description of the wider scene. Indeed, it is very tempting to let video recordings substitute for observation-based fieldnotes, but it is best to use both methods together, allowing each to support the other.

Third, audio and video recordings are always mediated by particular technologies and specifications, and even the very device the ethnographer uses. Everything from the data-processing firmware, to the microphone, and even the form factor and weight of the device—plus the lens and light sensor on a camera—can impact the recording process and data quality in some way. One camera might excel in low-light contexts but have an inadequate internal microphone. Another camera might have advanced audio features but lower video resolution or a short battery life. Even a camera with perfect specs may be so unwieldy or heavy that it gets left at home more often than not. All of these factors and more will impact the kind and quality of recordings produced, and while there is not a single set of factors that always matters more than others when working with recoding technologies in the field, there are some definite preferences to consider, which we discuss below.

Limitations like these can be frustrating, but they are certainly outweighed by some distinct advantages of working with audio and video data. First, audio and video recordings are essentially *infinitely reviewable*. One of the most glaring deficiencies of observation-based fieldnotes is that analysts only really get one shot to see a situation unfold, and their description of it, often written down after the fact, is heavily dependent on memory, a notoriously unreliable cognitive faculty. Recordings, in contrast, can be listened to or watched repeatedly without any loss of quality. They can be slowed down, sped up, or paused, while audio volume can be increased and video images can be expanded in size to provide a closer look at smaller details, depending on the quality of the original file.

Recordings are also easily *sharable*. For reasons that are not entirely clear, anthropologists tend to treat fieldnotes as private and inviolable rather than data that can be shared with colleagues and students. One explanation that is often invoked is "to protect anonymity," but this is mostly a red herring: we know how to anonymize data, and besides, most ethnographic fieldnotes are not inherently sensitive, which means that this practice is more of an unquestioned convention among ethnographers than a requirement (Clemente 2013). Audio and video data, however, are designed to be shared. Digital files can be sent or transferred with ease to collaborators nearby or across the world. Video can be displayed on screens of almost any size, to groups of almost any size who can watch video segments together, either in each other's presence or remotely. And the central benefit of this shareability is the opening up and redistribution of interpretation. Rather than one person maintaining sole control over the data and its meanings, recordings, when shared, invite multiple possible perspectives to be brought to bear on the data.

These first two advantages lead to a critical third: interpretations of recordings are *revisable*. It is often the case that after repeated listenings of a recorded scenario, or viewings of video clips—or when reviewing a recording after a period of time has elapsed, or once multiple collaborators have voiced their perspectives—that the analysis of a recorded situation changes, sometimes even drastically. This could be for any number of reasons, from the relatively basic—like someone else can hear a word or phrase that the ethnographer never picked up—to the relatively profound—like after gaining more familiarity with some cultural domain, a recorded interaction feels completely different from the time it was originally recorded. This ability to subject recorded data to revision and reinterpretation after leaving the field—sometimes years later—is a critical benefit that almost no other kinds of primary ethnographic data share.

7.2.1 But There Are Objections to the Use of Video

Despite relatively inexpensive video-recording technology being available for many decades, the majority of cultural anthropologists, and even many linguistic anthropologists, still do not use it in their fieldwork. Resistance to video inevitably generates a small set of objections, to which there are easy responses.

Won't the camera change people's behavior? This is by far the most common objection, but it relies on at least two inaccurate premises about how people act. First, it presumes that people always behave in some static, "normal" way that is then subject to disruption at the exact moment a camera is introduced. Second, it presumes that the presence of an observing ethnographer does not change a person's behavior, but the presence of a camera absolutely does. A more realistic premise is that behavior is always context-dependent, and people's self-consciousness shifts regularly in everyday life, according to many different factors. This means there is not some general norm that is being changed by the use of a camera in ethnographic fieldwork, but that the presence of the camera creates a specific kind of context, and that context will affect people differently. Of course, it is always important to pay attention to how the camera might be affecting people—but ethnographers should also pay close attention to how *they themselves* are affecting people, because an ethnographer, too, creates a specific context that will affect people in different ways. The basic solution to this problem is to draw on multiple methods over a period of time so as to accurately assess people's actions in the video recordings through comparison with other observed situations. In almost all cases there will not be a big difference between on-camera and off-camera behavior. In almost all cases, people will adjust to the presence of a camera very quickly.

Isn't the video camera intrusive? The short answer is yes—although again, the ethnographer is also intrusive—and the longer answer is that the camera's intrusiveness can be mitigated through careful consenting processes and general ethical consideration of the people being recorded (see Black and Conley-Riner, this volume). It is important to bear in mind that the incorporation of cameras into mobile phones, along with the proliferation of social media apps and platforms that encourage sharing images and videos, has rapidly shifted people's exposure to and comfort with the presence of video technologies in everyday life—and this is increasingly the case in most regions of the world. Discomfort with video recording is, paradoxically, often felt more strongly by the ethnographer, who is anxious that using video might be "asking too much" of people. The worst that can happen, though, is that someone says no—though so long as one follows good procedure by asking permission, receiving informed consent, and being clear about what the video is for and how it will be used, then it is quite common that people will agree.

In certain ethnographic contexts, won't video recording put people at risk? Maybe, but in all kinds of cases this applies to many other ethnographic methods, too. It is up to the ethnographer to weigh the costs and benefits of using video in a particular setting or with particular people; to decide whether broaching the possibility of using video is worthwhile; and to go through the informed consent process with people, after which a shared decision about using video can be made. Of course, sometimes neither ethnographers nor their collaborators fully understand the possible risks involved with video—but again, this is true for all ethnographic work, so it is important for fieldworkers to carefully use their training, professional judgment, and interpersonal intuition in making the call.

7.3 Working with Audio in the Field

In shifting to specifics, we will start with audio recording, because it is slightly less complicated than video recording. There are three broad scenarios in which audio recorders are typically used in linguistic anthropological fieldwork. The first, and probably the most common, is for recording interviews. The second is for recording an ongoing activity for which capturing turn-taking and participation is critical. The third is for recording instances of speech for which phonetic clarity and fidelity are the priority. While these scenarios might not be mutually exclusive in actual ethnographic practice, they do involve some different considerations, including the kinds of required equipment and the setup of the data-collecting situation.

Prior to about the year 2000, most of the audio-recording technology available to ethnographers relied on electromagnetic tape to capture analog sound signals on portable machines. Over time the fidelity—that is, the degree of match between an original sound and its recording—steadily improved, but there were strong limitations to the quality that this technology could produce, since analog recordings always involve some amount of loss in the sound data. For a brief period digital audio tapes (DAT), a format developed by Sony, provided lossless digital recordings on tape—meaning the recordings were exact replicas of the original sounds—surpassing the fidelity of every other early digital recording technology (like, for example, MiniDiscs, which recorded compressed, "lossy" files onto small compact discs). After the development of solid-state recording devices, which digitally capture sound directly onto flash memory without moving parts like tape or discs, along with the creation of several high-fidelity, lossless audio file formats, it is now easier than ever to introduce very high-quality audio recording into almost any ethnographic project.

7.3.1 Recording Interviews

Recording interviews is the easiest task for an audio recorder to accomplish, and almost any stand-alone device will work. There are some specific features that do matter more than others, however. First, recording devices will have options for either internal storage or external storage through removable flash memory, like secure digital (SD) cards. In general, the more storage to work with, the better. Second, a good audio recorder should include an input for an external microphone. In most cases the built-in microphone will work fine for interviews, but there may be situations in which an external microphone is necessary. Third, the device should have an easily navigable user interface. Locating recorded files and being able to play them back, move them into folders, and transfer them easily are critical to the overall usability of the recorder. Fourth, the file formats the recorder uses—and the recorder hardware itself—should be compatible with other devices used in the project, especially a laptop or desktop computer. Fifth, the device should have sufficient battery life for lots of recording. Devices with swappable batteries (rather than non-swappable rechargeable ones) are ideal, especially for fieldwork where electricity is less reliably available.

It has become quite common to use smartphones to audio-record interviews, but we do not recommend this practice. A dedicated audio recorder is designed to do one job, and do it well, while the phone—even though the sound quality can often be quite high—is intended to do many different tasks. Crucially, several of those other tasks can unexpectedly arise during the interview session, like when the researcher receives a phone call or SMS or needs to look up information on the web. When this happens during an interview, it unnecessarily disrupts the ongoing audio recording, which can in turn introduce uncertainty (like accidentally ending the recording) into the rest of the interview.

In the interview situation, the recorder (or the external microphone) should be placed as close to the interviewee as is comfortable. Lapel mics (also known as lavalier mics) that attach to an interviewee's clothing generally provide higher-quality audio, but they sometimes feel awkward to wear, especially for interlocutors with whom researchers have not developed strong rapport. After the recording has been started, the recorder should be tested to ensure it is working either by listening through headphones plugged into the device or by watching the level bars move on the recorder's screen, if it has that feature. Quiet locations are obviously better, but more often than not, they might be hard to find, so we advise testing the recorder in different environments before going to the field.

7.3.2 Recording Interactions

The second fieldwork scenario in which audio recorders are useful is in recording specific multiparty, face-to-face activities. We recommend that, whenever possible, such interactions be recorded with video, which we discuss in detail below, but there are, of course, circumstances in which that is not possible. All of the above points also apply here, but with some extra considerations.

For stationary situations in which participants are gathered around a relatively small shared space, an omnidirectional stand microphone that can be placed in the center of the group is a simple solution. Some external microphones are unidirectional—they only record sound from a source placed directly in front—and some are omnidirectional—they record everything in the surrounding environment. Using an omnidirectional mic to capture a relatively intimate group interaction can easily account for multiple speakers at once but will usually produce lower-quality data than that produced by individual mics. A better option is to set up participants with their own lavalier microphones. This can be done with each participant's audio recorded to separate recorders, and all of those files later synced up with software or with individual wireless transmitters for each participant connected to a single receiver that is plugged into the recorder (and thus the multiple channels are synced in real time on the device itself).

Naturally occurring, multiparty interactions are hard to control or contain, so it may be difficult to manage the quality of the recordings. In our own research, we have used high-quality omnidirectional mics to great effect in such scenarios; however, they will not provide optimal recordings of phonetic detail.

7.3.3 Recording for Phonetic Analysis

Again, in terms of basic device features, all of the above considerations apply for recorders used for capturing fine-grained phonetic details, but there are a few additional complications involved.

Since phonetic analysis requires very high-quality audio, the recorder should have some specific features that are easily adjustable by the researcher. First, the researcher should be able to switch between mono and stereo recording easily. Most recorders have this option, though some are easier to toggle than others. For phonetic analysis, the mono setting will reduce the possibility of unwanted noise in the recording. Second, the device should allow the researcher to adjust the gains and levels—basically, the loudness of the recording as sound is being captured—easily and, preferably, on the fly. Third, the device should allow for adjustments in sampling frequencies in order to record the highest-quality audio possible. Compact discs are sampled at 44.1 kHz, which has become a standard for digital audio, but some devices allow for raising the sampling rate to as high as 48 kHz, which significantly increases recording fidelity, but also file sizes. Finally, while most audio recorders can usually work with multiple file formats, WAV files are high quality and lossless, and thus preferable to compressed formats, like MP3.

Equally important here is an external microphone. Each of the three main form factors—stand mics, lavalier mics, and head-mounted mics—has pros and cons, but head-mounted mics, which position the diaphragm closest to the speaker's mouth, are the best for high audio quality. In addition, while omnidirectional mics may pick up some unwanted sounds, they are generally preferred because they can compensate for a speaker's fidgety body movements. There are other factors that can contribute to the functionality of microphone, like whether it requires its own power source or not, but it is always important that the microphone used keeps the overall signal-to-noise ratio as low as possible.

Recording for phonetic analysis is usually much more formal than recording interviews or multiparty interactions. The microphone should be placed close enough to the speaker's mouth to capture a significant range of sound, but not so close that breathing and other small noises end up muddying the recording. The environment should be as quiet as possible, which means rooms with carpets and soft, padded furniture work better than empty rooms that echo. If recording outside, windy places or areas with ambient noises (like the sounds of birds or insects) should be avoided.

7.4 Working with Video in the Field

While the use of video in linguistic anthropological fieldwork continues to expand, a number of other subfields, as well as disciplines outside of anthropology, have also enthusiastically brought video into ethnographic practice. These include visual anthropology (where ethnographic film has historically been situated), and more recent fields like multimodal anthropology, visual ethnography, and digital ethnography, all of which work with visual data. There are a number of resources geared toward these other disciplines that are also useful for linguistic anthropological work (see Bates 2015; Pink 2012; Redmon 2019; Shrum and Scott 2017), as well as others more closely aligned with what linguistic anthropologists are interested in (e.g., Erickson 2006; Jewitt 2012; Ochs et al. 2006; Rusk et al. 2015).

7.4.1 A Very Brief Timeline of How Video Came to the Field

Two of the first ethnographers to use film in fieldwork were Margaret Mead and Gregory Bateson, during their stays in Bali and Papua New Guinea in the 1930s (Jacknis 1988). From that fieldwork they produced a number of ethnographic films, which set an early standard for working with visual ethnographic data. In these early days it was not yet clear how (or whether) to resolve the tension between using film as a data-collection tool and using film to create a piece of cinematic art. Mead and Bateson themselves certainly found value in using film to conduct comparative studies of everyday practices, as with the footage used in "Bathing Babies in Three Cultures" (1954), a cross-cultural study of child-rearing practices, alongside creating more spectacular pieces for popular audiences, like "Trance and Dance in Bali" (1951), a documentary about Balinese ritual. But in the decades that followed their pioneering efforts, the inclination toward data-oriented projects would be overshadowed by a stream of powerful audience-oriented films, and soon enough, works by filmmakers like Jean Rouch, John Marshall, and Tim Asch, three early advocates of using film in anthropology, would solidify the status of ethnographic film as both a legitimate form of anthropological representation (if not exactly a source of primary data) and a significant cinematic genre unto itself. Meanwhile, data-oriented visual work would spend several decades either in hibernation or developing on its own outside the field of cultural anthropology.

Capturing complex phenomena or fleeting behavior has always been a vexing problem for ethnographers and other social scientists. The human power of observation is limited, as is memory and the capacity of words to sufficiently represent what is observed. David Efron, a student of Franz Boas—who had himself experimented with film on an expedition to Kwakwaka'wakw territory in 1930 (Ruby 1980)—found an early non-filmic solution to the problem in his cross-cultural comparison of gestures by Sicilian and Jewish immigrants in New York City. For his book, published as *Gesture and Environment* in 1941 (republished in 1972 as *Gesture, Race, and Culture*), he enlisted artist Stuyvesant van Veen to draw vivacious illustrations of men moving their hands and arms as they talked. While this was not the most efficient way to address the issue, it was nonetheless an advancement in representing difficult-to-capture ethnographic details.

By the 1950s clinical psychologists had also developed an interest in studying "nonverbal behavior" in individuals and groups, but they, too, lacked means to do so in any rigorous way. As with ethnography, observations in clinical settings proved difficult to capture and manage systematically. Then in the 1960s a psychologist named Paul Ekman, who was himself interested in nonverbal behavior, happened to cross paths with anthropologist Gregory Bateson while the two were both working at the Veterans Administration hospital in Palo Alto, California (Ekman 1987). Bateson had been interested in nonverbal communication since his days in Indonesia, and he encouraged the young psychologist to keep pursuing the topic—going so far as to lend Ekman the camera he and Mead had used back in Bali. Bateson later gave Ekman some of the footage from those earlier ethnographic projects, for the purposes of conducting some cross-cultural comparison (though, according to Ekman [1987], Bateson eventually grew disillusioned with the psychologist's turn toward universals). Once introduced to the power of film for research on embodied communication, Ekman would go on to revolutionize the study of facial expressions and emotion (of course not without critique within anthropology).

By the late 1960s helical-scan videotape—first in a reel-to-reel format, then as cassettes—was widely available as a cheaper and more robust research technology than film: magnetic tape allowed for synchronous recording of both audio and video information in a single device, whereas film required a separate contraption for capturing sound. One of the earliest large-scale projects to take advantage of this technology was conducted by Donald Fiske and Starkey Duncan in the early 1970s, both then in the Department of Psychology at the University of Chicago. For this project, which resulted in the book *Face-to-Face Interaction: Research, Methods, and Theory* (Duncan and Fiske, 1977), the researchers staged and recorded short conversations between graduate students from different programs at the university. The interactions were then transcribed (first by hand, then coded on punch cards) and analyzed in detail by a team of researchers. The well-known conversation between "Mr. A and Mr. B" analyzed by linguistic anthropologist Michael Silverstein (1997, 2004)—as well as by psychologist David McNeill (1992), though he names them "H" and "O"—was originally drawn from this corpus.

Around this same period in the early 1970s, two married graduate students at the University of Pennsylvania—Marjorie Goodwin in anthropology (M.H. Goodwin 1990) and Charles Goodwin in communication studies—began experimenting with video for recording nonverbal communication in everyday (that is, non-staged) settings. Since the late 1960s, Harvey Sacks, Emmanuel Schegloff, and Gail Jefferson had been developing techniques for examining the mechanics of social interaction through data derived from audio-recorded telephone calls, initiating what would become the field of conversation analysis (CA). The Goodwins had also been working with naturally occurring interaction, and soon got their hands on samizdat copies of Sacks's lectures from William Labov (C. Goodwin 2018; see also Sacks 1992). One key difference in the approach the Goodwins were experimenting with, however, was the use of video for exploring the complex relation between moving bodies and spoken language in multi-party interaction. Working under the informal guidance of Erving Goffman (note, that Goffman had previously been a mentor of Sacks and Schegloff at Berkeley), and using the newly available Sony Portapak video recorder, Charles Goodwin recorded family therapy sessions at the Philadelphia Child Guidance Clinic, and soon enough the Goodwins began bringing the recorder to ordinary events, like family barbecues. This move proved to be revolutionary: pointing the camera toward, and keeping it focused on, situated mundane interactions, not for cinematic purposes but for illuminating what Goffman (1964) had earlier termed "the neglected situation"—that is, the stuff of daily life in which social reality is actually created and lived—would usher in a brand-new era for ethnographic analysis.

7.4.2 Some Technical Considerations for Video Equipment

Before considering what specific video equipment is needed in the field, ethnographers should first think about the kinds of situations they intend to record, the wider context in which those situations occur, and the final form they want their work to take. While all of these considerations also apply to audio data, the devices used for capturing audio are much less technologically complex and prone to rapid change and obsolescence, which means that incorporating video in a research project requires a higher degree of planning. There are, of course, many options available for using video equipment in fieldwork, but within that range it is critical to consider some basic criteria that themselves do not change much or too quickly.

Cost. The amount ethnographers spend on a video-recording device should be somewhat proportional to the significance of video data in their overall project. If video recordings will be the centerpiece of their research, then it is worthwhile to spend more money on this equipment. If the video data ethnographers intend to collect are more supplementary to other kinds of ethnographic data, it would be appropriate to compromise on some camera features to lower overall costs. Luckily, the progression of video-recording technology since its introduction to mainstream consumers in the 1970s has moved toward higher-quality footage for less and less money, so finding a useable option should be a relatively easy task.

Outgoing versus Incoming Technologies. Precisely because video-recording technology is constantly advancing, at almost any point at which ethnographers decide to procure a camera, they need to make a decision between an older, usually cheaper, but also inferior (in some respect) technology, and a newer, usually more expensive, but also better (in some respect) technology. There is no always-correct choice to make, but both older and newer technologies do involve some risk. Older technologies face the possibility of disappearing, or at least becoming more difficult to work with, within the timeframe of a research project—especially if the same data are used for a long period of time (say, ten years or more). This was particularly a problem during the videotape era (from the 1980s until the very early 2010s), when machines capable of playing a specific cassette-tape format would regularly be discontinued and replaced by machines for a new tape format (or, eventually, by solid-state digital recording). But even in the post-cassette era, some of the features of video technology that we discuss below change in ways that make using older files more difficult over time. Adopting a newer technology at the start of one's research can alleviate this problem to some degree, but unfortunately not entirely. One of the biggest risks with newer technologies is corporate competition, which can produce multiple incompatible technologies that exist side by side for a while, but only one of which will end up lasting more than a few years. If researchers choose the one that does not survive, they will be in the same position as having chosen an outdated technology (but also having spent a lot more money in the process). None of these risks is ultimately unmanageable, but they all highlight that it is absolutely critical to think through and research the specific equipment well before setting off for the field.

Form Factor. There are two very basic categories of video-recording equipment: (1) devices that are primarily dedicated to video recording and (2) devices that do video recording along with some other function(s). In general, devices devoted to video recording will produce higher-quality video data, but non-dedicated devices can also produce impressive results.

The two most common dedicated devices are camcorders and what are known as "action cameras." Camcorders are the descendants of film cameras and the old Portapak cameras from the 1970s. They are usually longer than they are wide, designed to be held in one hand or mounted to a tripod, and they often allow external audio attachments—but they do not typically allow the use of different lenses (unless a very high-end device is used). Action cameras, on the other hand, come in many shapes—some are cubes, some are more rectangular, some are mounted to a handle, some are long and thin—and they are all relatively small, lightweight devices. Their ability to take attachments varies, but very few allow swappable lenses, and the quality of the video they produce is lower than that of camcorders.

Most digital still cameras also have the ability to record video, and this is becoming an increasingly common device for research. These cameras are usually designed to be held in two hands, and they are typically wider than they are long. One of the main advantages to using this kind of camera is that they are made to work with many kinds of interchangeable lenses. Many still cameras even have inputs for attaching external microphones. Note, though, that there are two different digital still camera technologies. The older and more common is the digital single-lens reflector (DSLR) camera, which uses an optical viewfinder, and the "mirrorless" digital camera, which uses only a digital viewfinder. There are other technical differences between these cameras, but for research purposes they function almost exactly the same. What matters is that the attachments for each type may differ—and differ by manufacturer, as well as by technology—so it is important not to confuse which type of camera is being used.

Smartphones are another example of non-dedicated video technology available for researchers. While smartphones have had video-recording capabilities from their earliest days, only since the late 2010s has the video they produced been good enough to use as ethnographic data. Fieldwork is often unpredictable, and transporting video and audio equipment requires time and effort. Smartphones have lower-quality video and audio than the other cameras, but they provide portability and easy accessibility, and they are likely to be with the researcher most of the time. They are also very effective research tools beyond video and audio recording, making great cameras for still photography and for scanning documents. Voice memos and other note-taking tools can help out in a pinch for fieldnotes when a computer is not available. A smartphone should probably never be the main video-recording device—see our warning about using them for interviews above—but as a backup, the higher-end models are definitely more than adequate.

Overall, the most suitable form factor for a device will depend on the specific contexts in which it will be used—for instance whether the researcher will be moving or standing still while recording. Things like the weight and relative bulkiness of this equipment will have a major impact on one's ability to use the camera in certain situations and even to transport this equipment to different activities. Plus, there is always a trade-off with regard to the obviousness of a camera. In our experience, most interlocutors quickly adjust to having video and audio equipment in their environment; however, equipment that requires constant attention will become more distracting to the people we are working with and might disrupt the recorded interaction. To avoid this issue, researchers are often tempted to use smaller cameras, or cameras that are easier to cover or disguise, because they seem less intrusive. While this may be an advantage in some cases, it should not be the default option. In fact, it is often easier and more ethical (see Black and Conley-Riner, this volume) to use a conspicuous and visible (though not intrusive) camera (this also applies to audio recorders) precisely because the camera's presence reinforces the researcher's role as *someone conducting research,* which is a status we should embrace rather than conceal.

Research Methods in Linguistic Anthropology

All cameras are designed to work within specific sets of constraints, regardless of their form factors. Choosing the right device for one's fieldsite and research goals is largely a process of balancing the capabilities for managing these constraints against one another. The following are the most important factors to pay attention to.

Resolution: Image resolution is the feature that accounts for the level of detail revealed in a video (or still) image. In general, the higher a camera's resolution, the sharper its images will appear. Resolution tends to be given as a number, which counts the columns (width) and rows (height) of pixels in each video frame. Before the advent of digital video, most footage was shot in standard definition, which measures 480 pixels wide. Since the 2000s, high definition (HD) video has become the norm, with available resolutions steadily growing larger and larger. Full high definition (FHD) resolution is 1920 x 1080 or 1920 columns of pixels by 1080 rows of pixels. Ultra high definition (UHD), also known as 4K, is four times as large, at 3840 columns of pixels by 2160 rows of pixels.

Higher resolution does not just make videos look better and provide more detail. It also gives more flexibility after the fact. For instance, if ethnographers shoot video in 4K instead of FHD, they would be able to crop a quarter of the frame size and still maintain a high-quality FHD resolution. Higher resolution also allows researchers to pull high-quality screen grabs from video footage and to digitally zoom-in without much loss of detail. This can be beneficial for cropping specific objects or people or body parts, such as gesturing hands, in a given frame, which can increase the analytical strength of the data and also help produce better quality images for presentations and publications.

But there are some things to note. First, resolution is one of the features of video recording that is most subject to the "outgoing vs. incoming technology" problem. As of the early 2020s, 4K cameras are widely available and not too expensive, but 8K, 16K, and even 64K resolutions are on the horizon. What is more, the resolution of cameras is only as useful as the resolution of the screen on which the footage is later viewed. For both data analysis (working through your video data) and data presentation (showing it to an audience), if the resolution of the screen is lower than that of the camera, then most of the benefits of the higher resolution disappear. Thus, if a video is recorded at 4K resolution but the computer monitor is an FHD monitor, or the projector used at a conference is only standard definition, then the details captured by the 4K camera will not be obvious to a viewer.

Lighting: While most linguistic anthropologists will not need to invest in separate lighting equipment for their recordings, they should still consider the different lighting scenarios they are likely to encounter in the field. While most cameras excel at capturing video in well-lit circumstances, many struggle in situations in which there is a drastic contrast between highlights and shadows (known as "dynamic range"), or in low-light situations. If ethnographers know ahead of time that they will be recording in low-light or high-contrast situations, they should opt for a camera that specializes in those contexts.

Image Stabilization: During filming with a video camera, stabilization is a critical consideration to plan for. There are a few methods and technologies that exist for helping calm a shaky camera. For situations in which ethnographers are not moving around much, tripods are the most common video stabilization technology. They can range in price, depending on their height, materials, and build-quality. While it is easy to find many inexpensive tripods, the danger is that a cheap one might collapse mid-shot and damage more expensive video equipment, so it is often worth spending a little more money on a higher-quality model. Researchers should also consider which tripod heads to invest in. While ball heads are generally the cheapest, they are also the least versatile for video work, as they are designed to be fixed in one position. Pan-and-tilt heads were designed for video work, but they can only move in one direction at a time—either vertically or horizontally. In addition, it can be difficult to achieve smooth movement from one position to the next. Fluid heads are the most versatile for video, but they are also the most expensive. They have almost 360 degrees of rotation, so videographers can easily move the camera from one shot to the next. In addition, fluid heads have variable resistance that counterbalances the jerkiness of one's hand while the camera moves.

Monopods are similar to tripods, but with only one foot instead of three. This makes monopods much more versatile for capturing video on the move. While a tripod allows one to place a camera in a position and leave the camera unattended, one will always need to hold the monopod in place. Even the most stable monopods will easily fall without support.

Gimbals can provide the best stabilization for constant movement, but they tend to be expensive and unwieldy. There are two types of gimbals— mechanical and motorized. Both types aim to offset the movement of the camera to maintain a steady shot. Mechanical gimbals counterbalance hand movements with a system of weights, which are very heavy alongside the weight of the camera equipment. Motorized gimbals use small, lightweight motors to counterbalance movement, but they are more expensive. Also note that gimbals require a lot of attention from the ethnographer, making them very invasive while recording an ongoing interaction.

Camera manufacturers also provide in-camera software stabilization in their devices. Even top-of-the-line action cameras include in-camera stabilization that rivals the best gimbals. The downside to in-camera stabilization is that the process involves camera software modifying the actual image by trimming each frame to make it appear similar to the previous and subsequent frames in the video. This results in a smaller image resolution and a slightly zoomed-in image compared to the maximum angle of the lens. The advantages of smooth, in-camera stabilization without a gimbal often outweigh these disadvantages, though, because the difference in image size is often too small to matter for research purposes.

Audio: All video recording devices are able to record sound alongside a moving image, but currently no devices have built-in microphones that surpass the quality of audio produced by external equipment. If using a built-in microphone is the only option in a given situation, that is usually adequate. Some newer technology is specifically designed with low-quality audio in order to pack better video quality into a smaller device. This technology will require external audio that you sync later. But no matter how good a camera's audio is, it would be best to prepare ahead of time by bringing external microphones to use with a video recording device.

External microphones can connect to a video recorder through several different inputs, though the most common by far is a standard 3.5 mm stereo input, which allows for analog (non-digital) audio recording. Some high-end cameras also connect through what's called a "hot shoe," which allows for attaching a range of external equipment to the camera, including professional-grade XLR-cabled microphones, which capture extremely high-quality, balanced audio. Most researchers, even linguistic anthropologists, will be satisfied with medium-grade audio technology that connects through a stereo jack. Some low-end cameras do not include an input for an external mic, however.

The two most common external microphone formats for capturing audio with video are lavalier microphones and shotgun microphones. Lavalier mics generally produce higher-quality audio for recording an individual's speech, as they are attached directly to a speaker—usually to a piece of upper-body clothing, and extending with a wire to a battery pack and wireless transmitter clipped to lower-body clothing. Lavaliers are designed to isolate only one speaker's speech, so they do not capture ambient noise very well, including the speech of other people. Thus, they can be a bit unwieldy, as all the lavalier mics worn by different speakers will need to be synced together, either by connecting all the microphones to a single audio receiver with cords or by using a more expensive set of wireless lavalier transmitters and receivers. Needless to say, while the quality of speech recordings that lavalier mics produce is very high, they tend to work best in situations in which there is time for pre-planning and setup.

For most other situations, especially naturally occurring ones, shotgun microphones are usually better alternatives. They have the advantage of providing relatively high-quality audio of everything that happens directly in front of them. For video, their biggest advantage is that they generally require fewer cords and peripheral equipment: they can slot directly in the hot shoe, and an attached 3.5 mm cord can easily plug directly into the camera's audio input. Researchers can also use a mix of shotgun mics and lavaliers to provide the benefits of gathering more ambient noise with the shotgun mic and clear audio from speakers with the lavalier mics.

Finally, it is also possible to use the old film method and record audio on a completely separate device—especially external audio recorders that capture high-quality digital audio—and then sync the audio and video later in post-production. This method is extremely labor-intensive, and we do not recommend it unless there is a need for very high-quality digital audio.

Battery life: While battery life can at first seem like a trivial concern, it is one of the most important points for considering a video camera for field research. Many DSLR and mirrorless cameras only have a thirty-minute battery life while recording video, while camcorders and action cameras can last much longer. How long the battery lasts before needing a recharge also depends on the kinds of recording, the quality settings for the audio and video, and other factors that are often hard to predict. The bottom line, though, is that it is critical to be prepared for powering recording devices and for dealing with the inevitable situation in which a battery dies right when it is needed most.

For devices that use interchangeable batteries, including most camcorders, DSLRs, and mirrorless cameras, it is imperative to have more than one battery. One or two extra, fully charged batteries should be in every researcher's camera bag, along with the one that came with the device. Many manufacturers also offer higher-capacity battery packs, which can sometimes double the possible recording time. Before buying a camera, researchers should consider how long they expect to film in any given situation and how often they will be near an outlet to charge batteries or cameras.

Some recording devices have built-in batteries rather than swappable ones, so if the device needs recharging, it must be plugged in to the wall, which can limit the ability to move the device around. In such cases, a fully charged high-capacity portable charger can be used.

Finally, note that fieldsites differ with regard to access to electricity sources, so it is critical that researchers determine early on, preferably before going to the field, how they will be able to charge their devices (this is of course also true for laptops, phones, still cameras, and audio recorders).

Data storage: Digital video files take up a lot of memory, so it is vital to account for video storage along with video recording in project planning.

On-camera. Most devices contain some amount of built-in flash memory for storage. Internal storage is workable, of course, but it is not expandable, so it would be best to use a device that allows for external storage through removable flash memory media, like secure digital (SD) cards, which come in many different capacities. One should be careful, however, because not all memory cards are the same, even if they look like they are compatible. While many DSLRs and camcorders can use standard SD cards, for optimal performance they will usually require very fast SD cards that can be more expensive than low-speed versions. Action cameras often take microSD cards but again require faster speeds than most budget cards. Higher-end cameras can require more advanced flash memory options, such as XCD cards, which are fast and high capacity, but also expensive. Whichever device researchers select, it would be ideal to investigate the specific memory options it allows and to always consider higher capacity storage for longer continuous recording without having to switch out cards.

Off-camera: Long-term data storage is also key in ethnographic research. High-capacity hard drives are the cheapest and most stable way to store data for future use. It is important to have backups of these files on separate hard drives, and it is good practice to keep the hard drives in separate locations, to avoid losing everything in cases of fire, theft, or some other misfortune. Another option is cloud storage, which eliminates the need to transport hard drives and allows for easy access through the internet. Cloud storage can pose ethical challenges, however, as it is more susceptible to hacking, corporate shutdowns that could compromise the data, and even possible government surveillance.

7.4.3 Some Lessons We Have Learned

In his research on the island of Sardinia, Italy, where he conducted a total of thirty months of fieldwork between 2013 and 2019, Gregory

Audio-Video Technology For and In the Field

Kohler video-recorded interviews, walk-throughs on farms, and various interactions between farmers and farm inspectors. From his preliminary fieldwork in the summers of 2013, 2014, and 2015, he knew many of the interactions that he wanted to record would take place in poorly lit, cramped spaces with little access to power outlets or stable surfaces on which to place a camera. This meant that battery life, dynamic range (for poorly lit spaces), wide-angle lenses (for small spaces), portability (for walk-throughs), and camera stabilization gear would be the most important aspects to consider for a video camera. He ultimately opted for a mix of video and audio equipment to serve different purposes in his research. A small-form GoPro Hero4 action camera ended up being the most affordable way to achieve portability, stabilization, and a wide-angle lens for use in tight spaces. While the camera struggled with dynamic range and poor lighting, its advantages outweighed its limitations. He also used a Panasonic Lumix DMC-GH4, a mirrorless digital still camera that also recorded video. This camera was useful for higher-quality recordings of in situ interviews, and because it was capable of managing a high dynamic range, it was well suited for the open-air walk-throughs that he conducted with famers, but it lacked the portability of the GoPro and created much larger video files that are more difficult to work in the post-production editing process.

While the GoPro provided the best quality video for much of Kohler's research, it posed many challenges in terms of audio quality. The built-in microphone produced low-quality recordings—a problem further compounded by the camera's protective plastic shell. He tried solving this problem by plugging in an external microphone. While the external microphone provided higher-quality recordings, the videos included a mysterious mechanical buzz. After some research, he discovered that this buzz was caused by the camera's internal hardware getting picked up by the external mic. In the end, Kohler opted for a separate audio-recording device — the Zoom H2n digital audio recorder—and then synced the audio and video in post-production. To do this, he used one of the oldest and easiest tricks—he clapped at the beginning of each video recording and then used the audio spike from the clap to sync the separate audio recording to the video device's internal recording.

In some situations, Kohler found it easier to record quick conversations with his smartphone rather than with a dedicated device. Smartphones pose some ethical challenges, however. They often have weaker data protection than encrypted hard drives, so ethnographers should be careful about how much data they store on their smartphones, and they should delete any sensitive data as soon as possible. In addition, smartphones can affect how interlocutors perceive the recording situation, since they lack the formality of standalone devices. This is a case in which using a recorder that is too familiar, or too "informal," to people might throw them off guard in unintended ways.

Keith Murphy has been working with video for many years and has seen many formats and technologies come and go. For an undergraduate research paper that he wrote in the late 1990s, he used video data originally collected by Duncan and Fiske (1977) for their research on face-to-face interaction, and he had hoped to keep working with that data over time. After locating the original helical-scan video reels at the University of Chicago, he transferred that video to Hi-8 cassette tapes. Unfortunately, Hi-8 tapes would be obsolete within a few years, so he later converted those tapes to Mini-DV tapes, a more enduring format. Of course, this format was not quite enduring enough, and it, too, died off. He thus digitized the Mini-DV tapes into digital QuickTime files, finally moving away from physical media, although by then, after so many transfers, the quality of both the audio and video had been significantly degraded. In subsequent research projects Murphy tried to learn from this experience by choosing video equipment and video formats that would last, but even purely digital files are subject to format rot over time, as software changes and developers abandon older video encoding standards in favor of more modern approaches. The lesson learned is this: if linguistic anthropologists want to keep using a particular piece of video data, or at least have it available for reference or comparison in the future, they need to keep converting it to formats that newer computers can work with. Otherwise, the file might remain, but the data it contains will simply disappear.

7.5 Final Words

In this chapter, we have highlighted the most significant aspects of this technology, without getting too bogged down by the details of specific devices, because the details that matter to some researchers might be different than those that matter to us or to another researcher. Instead we have laid out the parameters within which linguistic anthropologists can conduct their research for the equipment they need for their projects. Video recording is a particularly powerful method for linguistic anthropologists and one that is increasingly cheaper and easier to use in all sorts of scenarios. As we have discussed, though, it still deserves a tremendous amount of consideration, both conceptual consideration as a data-collection method within a larger research project, and practical consideration as a basic tool with advantages and disadvantages in its basic operations. Key considerations for buying equipment are, what data are needed to answer research questions? Which methods are best for collecting those data? Which tools are best suited towards those methods? One should only then start researching what equipment to get, read reviews, explore where technology is going, and ask colleagues for recommendations. It is definitely a fair amount of additional work to do, but it is worth it, because in the long run it will save time, energy, and headaches. Despite the effort video requires, it will provide some of the best ethnographic data available, especially for linguistic anthropologists.

7.6 Ethnographic Activities

1. Make a data backup plan for your research. What kinds of data will you collect (fieldnotes, audio and video files, photocopies/PDFs of documents, etc.)? How will you store/back up these data? How could you make the data more accessible to research collaborators? What might be some ethical considerations to your data backup plan?

2. Think about the various methods you want to use in your field research and the role technology plays in facilitating that research. Prepare a list of three or more research methods and how you might incorporate different technology into those methods. Think about the considerations listed in this chapter (cost, form factor, resolution, battery life, etc.) while outlining your project.

7.7 Questions to Consider

1 What types of technology are commonly used in linguistic anthropological methods? How does the use of video technology in linguistic anthropology differ from the use of video in other disciplinary fields?

2 What is the relationship between video recordings and objectivity (think also about the ways video is manipulated in social media)?

What are some ways that we as researchers can better use video in order to portray our fieldsites?

3 What are some common objections to the use of video as an anthropological method? Brainstorm some responses to those objections.

4 Think about the things you would take into consideration before buying video or audio technology. What factors would be most important to you in your research?

5 Consider the ways that video and/or audio technologies have changed in your lifetime. What advantages and disadvantages do these changes pose for anthropological research methods? What research possibilities do you see with recent technological advancements?

7.8 References Cited

Bates, Charlotte. 2015. *Video Methods: Social Science Research in Motion.* Abingdon-on-Thames: Routledge.

Bateson, Gregory, and Margaret Mead. 1951. *Trance and Dance in Bali.* New York: New York University Film Library.

Bateson, Gregory, and Margaret Mead. 1954. *Bathing Babies in Three Cultures.* New York: New York University Film Library.

Black, Steven. 2017. "Anthropological Ethics and the Communicative Affordances of Audio-Video Recorders in Ethnographic Fieldwork: Transduction as Theory." *American Anthropologist* 119 (1): 46–57.

Clemente, Ignasi. 2013. "Conversation Analysis and Anthropology." In Jack Sidnell and Tanya Stivers eds., *Handbook of Conversation Analysis*, 688–700. New York: Wiley-Blackwell.

Duncan, Starkey, and Donald W. Fiske. 1977. *Face-to-Face Interaction: Research, Methods, and Theory.* Mahwah: Lawrence Erlbaum Associates.

Duranti, Alessandro. 1997. *Linguistic Anthropology.* Cambridge: Cambridge University Press.

Efron, David. 1941. *Gesture and Environment: A Tentative Study of Some of the Spatio-Temporal and Linguistic Aspects of the Gestural Behavior of Eastern Jews and Southern Italians in New York City, Living under Similar as well as Different Environmental Conditions.* New York: King's Crown Press.

Efron, David. 1972. *Gesture, Race and Culture.* Berlin: Mouton de Gruyter.

Ekman, Paul. 1987. "A Life's Pursuit." In Thomas A. Sebeok and Jean Umiker-Sebeok eds., *The Semiotic Web '86: An International Yearbook*, 4–46. Berlin: Mouton de Gruyter.

Erickson, Frederick. 2006. "Definition and Analysis of Data from Videotape: Some Research Procedures and Their Rationales." In Judith L. Green, Gregory Camilli, and Patricia B. Elmore eds., *Handbook of Complementary Methods in Education Research*, 177–91. Mahwah: Lawrence Erlbaum Associates.

Goffman, Erving. 1964. "The Neglected Situation." *American Anthropologist* 66 (6): 133–6.

Goodwin, Charles. 2018. *Co-Operative Action*. Cambridge: Cambridge University Press.

Goodwin, Marjorie Harness. 1990. *He-Said-She-Said: Talk as Social Organization among Black Children*. Bloomington: Indiana University Press.

Jacknis, Ira. 1988. "Margaret Mead and Gregory Bateson in Bali: Their Use of Photography and Film." *Cultural Anthropology* 3 (2): 160–77.

Jewitt, Carey. 2012. "An Introduction to Using Video for Research," Working Paper, NCRM, http://eprints.ncrm.ac.uk/2259/.

McNeill, David. 1992. *Hand and Mind: What Gestures Reveal about Thought*. Chicago: University of Chicago Press.

Ochs, Elinor, Anthony P. Graesch, Angela Mittmann, Thomas Bradbury, and Rena Repetti. 2006. "Video Ethnography and Ethnoarchaeological Tracking." In Marcie Pitt-Catsouphes, Ellen Ernst Kossek, Stephen Sweet eds., *The Work and Family Handbook: Multi-Disciplinary Perspectives, Methods, and Approaches*, 387–409. Mahwah: Lawrence Erlbaum Associates.

Pink, Sarah. 2012. *Advances in Visual Methodology*. New York: SAGE Publications.

Redmon, David. 2019. *Video Ethnography*. Abingdon-on-Thames: Routledge.

Ruby, Jay. 1980. "Franz Boas and Early Camera Study of Behavior." *Kinesics Report* 3 (3): 6–11, 16.

Rusk, Fredrik, Michaela Pörn, Fritjof Sahlström, and Anna Slotte-Lüttge. 2015. "Perspectives on Using Video Recordings in Conversation Analytical Studies on Learning in Interaction." *International Journal of Research & Method in Education* 38 (1): 39–55.

Sacks, Harvey. 1992. *Lectures on Conversation*. Hoboken: Blackwell.

Shrum, Wesley, and Greg Scott. 2017. *Video Ethnography in Practice: Planning, Shooting, and Editing for Social Analysis*. New York: SAGE Publications.

Silverstein, Michael. 1997. "The Improvisational Performance of Culture in Realtime Discursive Practice." In R. Keith Sawyer ed., *Creativity in Performance*, 265–312. Greenwich: Ablex Publishing Corp.

Silverstein, Michael. 2004. "'Cultural' Concepts and the Language-Culture Nexus." *Current Anthropology* 45 (5): 621–52.

7.9 Further Reading

Kohler, Gregory. 2017. "'Gregory Dry': Parody and the Morality of Brand". *Language in Society* 46 (05): 719–37.

Murphy, Keith M. 2012. "Transmodality and Temporality in Design Interactions." *Journal of Pragmatics* 44: 1966–81.

Murphy, Keith M. 2017. "Art, Design, and the Ethics of Ethnographic Encounter." In G. Bakke ed., *Between Matter and Method: Anthropology and the Arts*, 97–115. New York: Bloomsbury.

8

Video Ethnography: A Guide

Teruko Vida Mitsuhara and
Jan David Hauck

8.1 Introduction

The collection of video data is becoming increasingly common in ethnographic fieldwork, not least because technological developments have streamlined the filming process and made equipment more affordable. In linguistic anthropology in particular, the use of video has become a sine qua non, as it enables a layered analysis of talk in interaction including gestures, gaze, facial expressions, corporeal alignments, and bodies moving in space, alongside the wider semiotic environment in which they take place and which they help constitute (M. H. Goodwin 2006; C. Goodwin 2009, 2018). But even in other disciplines and when language and communication are not the primary focus of a study, video data can add important information. A hand gesture during an interview may convey a subtle but indispensable message that can change the meaning of the words uttered. A facial expression or a quick glance during a ritual performance may hint at other social dynamics at play yet may only be noticed by the analyst after repeated viewing of video footage. Nevertheless, video is not a crystal ball able to reveal everything—it can record a congregation, but it cannot explain who the participants are or why they are there; it cannot capture impressions, scents, the atmosphere, and other aspects of a scene required for thick description (Geertz 1973). A good understanding of the particular affordances of video recording and what video ethnography may add to a particular project is therefore essential (see also Kohler and Murphy, this volume).

Our goal in this chapter is to provide guidelines for addressing ethical, technological, and practical questions of video ethnography to prospective and established ethnographers in order to ensure its successful employment in fieldwork. Documenting people's everyday lives in their homes, workplaces, neighborhoods, villages, or schools with video cameras and sound equipment can add valuable insights to ethnographic research and yet may also be intrusive and disrupting to participants if not done properly, ethically, and professionally. Appropriate procedures to obtain consent before the beginning of fieldwork and the ongoing monitoring of research activities during fieldwork are of utmost importance.

We have divided the chapter into three sections that address issues to consider before going to the field, during fieldwork, and beyond, respectively. Each section walks the reader through a number of "steps," roughly following the sequence that a researcher should expect to follow from devising a project to its completion, starting with determining whether video recording is necessary and possible, and if so, how to proceed with obtaining consent, choosing equipment, creating a database, and what to pay attention to during day-to-day filming. We note here that there is some overlap between sections and that while some steps may address primarily either technological, or practical, or ethical questions, these are always intertwined. Different recording technologies afford different ways of collecting data and entail different ethical questions (Black 2017; Black and Conley-Riner, this volume).

Our chapter is explicitly meant as a guide, which, we hope, will not only assist in designing a project with video but also be a resource to look for help while in the field—the guide we wish would have existed when we both started our first video ethnographic projects. We will be drawing extensively on our experience from these projects in order to illustrate general scenarios and point out issues that will be relevant in a wide variety of contexts. Mitsuhara (2019) carried out two years of fieldwork in Mayapur, a rural village composed of religious migrants in West Bengal, India, working primarily with mothers and their children. She filmed everyday interactions in the peer group and with caregivers at family's homes, on the playground, in a school, and while transiting through the village. Hauck (2016) has been working for many years among indigenous former hunter-gatherers in eastern Paraguay, the Aché. He has been filming community members across generations in a language documentation project and has also carried out a socialization study with children, filming everyday interactions with caregivers and in the peer group at home, in open spaces in the village, in a school, and on multiday hunting treks in a forest reserve.

8.2 Before the Field

Video ethnography begins long before the researcher sets foot at the site they have chosen for their fieldwork and has practical, technological, and ethical implications that must be considered at every stage of the planning process. The steps in this section will address the main questions to consider before departing for the field.

8.2.1 Step 1: Determining If You Need Video

Before purchasing a camera or budgeting one into an application for research funding, it is important to reflect upon why obtaining video is necessary for a given project. Purchasing the right equipment and planning daily research routines require a precise understanding of what video adds to a given case study and what its limitations are. There are good reasons for why video has become a key component of research in linguistic anthropology. It is not only integral for documenting the embodied, multimodal character of talk in interaction (M. H. Goodwin 2006; M. H. Goodwin and Cekaite 2018; C. Goodwin 2009, 2018; Katila et al. forthcoming; Heath et al. 2010; Kissmann 2009; Smith 2018); it also allows for repeat viewing, reanalysis, and the joint exploration of data with other researchers (Duranti 1997, 116–7; Heath et al. 2010, 55) as well as the research participants themselves (Schieffelin 1990, 100).

Kohler and Murphy (this volume) provide an overview of the use of audio and video technology for research and we refer to their chapter as a resource that will help in answering the question what video does and what it does not do. It bears reiterating here, though, that as Kohler and Murphy note any and all video data are necessarily selective, biased, and partial. Video does not "objectively" represent reality; rather it *constitutes* phenomena in particular ways and makes them available to our reflexive awareness, both in the field as well as after (C. Goodwin 1994; Mondada 2006; Speer and Hutchby 2003). Moreover, the particular affordances of different recording devices will impact how research is conducted (Black 2017). These aspects of video should not discourage researchers from using it in ethnography. But they also mean that video is a *supplement*—not a substitute—for other established ethnographic techniques. For example, taking fieldnotes while filming in order to contextualize the recording is imperative (Duranti 1997, 115–6; C. Goodwin 1993, 193).

We are completing this chapter during the global COVID-19 pandemic through which possibilities for in-person ethnography have been reduced as a result of social distancing measures. It will take some creativity to imagine and reinvent ways to conduct ethnography from afar while adhering to such measures, and video may be an avenue through which to continue research under such conditions. Video ethnographers may look for inspiration from the fields of remote, digital, and virtual world ethnography, all of which have experimented with conducting research that is not in person for many years. In the specific case of linguistic anthropologically informed video ethnography with its attention to embodied, face-to-face interaction, solutions could take different forms. For example, in a fixed setting such as a dinner table or kitchen, an ethnographer could set up a camera, set the frame, leave, and pick up the equipment later without closely interacting with participants. One could also mail a camera and remotely train participants to set it up and film themselves, as has been done in the entertainment industry where directors send equipment and train actors in setting up the shots as they direct from afar. Lastly, social scientists conducting market research have used remote qualitative research software (e.g., dscout, https://dscout.com/) that allows participants to record themselves using their mobile phone. Such software may be another avenue to explore for remote video ethnography. As all these options require more involvement from research participants, ethnographers will need to address the question of compensation and (co-)authorship of data and publications produced in this way. Training of assistants to film in the researcher's stead must also include awareness of ethics and consent procedures. While the main focus of this chapter is how to conduct in-person ethnography, much of what we discuss will be relevant for remote projects as well.

8.2.2 Step 2: Determining If You Are Able to Use Video

Gaining consent for video recording is a related but separate issue to gaining general consent for conducting research (see Black and Conley-Riner, this volume), as there will always be recognizable people in recorded data. Even when faces are blurred or voices distorted in data, which are made public for conference presentations or as multimedia resources for students to use in class, body language is often identifiable to those who know the participants. Consent for video recording must therefore be thorough and clear regarding who will be filmed, why, how such recordings or video stills will be used in the future, and whether the data will be destroyed or stored somewhere, such as in a public archive, on a secure cloud server, and/or on the ethnographer's own hard drives (see Heath et al. 2010, 14–36).

Obtaining consent is a complex and ongoing process. Usually, there are some aspects of the consent process that must be initiated before arriving in the field or during a pilot study (institutional access, permission by community leaders), while others can only be obtained at the beginning of fieldwork (consent from individual participants). In her research in India, Mitsuhara gained consent from community leaders and the school administration one year prior to beginning her fieldwork with children. Upon arriving in the field a year later for the main phase of the research, she underwent consent and assent procedures with individuals as she recruited families and children to her study. Regarding consent procedures with minors, do note that "consent" is not something children can grant in a legal sense, but they can assent or not to participation in research, while the researcher obtains consent from parents or legal guardians (see Black and Conley-Riner, this volume).[1]

8.2.3 Step 3: Purchasing Equipment

Different fieldsites, fieldwork scenarios, and research questions call for different filming equipment. Anticipating the situations one is likely to encounter is key for choosing the right technology, yet such anticipation may not be easy. Pilot phases of research are the best way through which to gauge what to invest in. In what follows, we offer a number of general points on the affordances of different types of cameras and accessories, but also some specific observations on small features that can make a big difference (see also Kohler and Murphy, this volume, for further technological details).

No matter what equipment one chooses, there are inevitable trade-offs in the choice of a device regarding price, quality, ease of use, complexity of setup, and intrusiveness. Is it advisable to save on accessories when faced with a constrained budget in order to be able to buy a more expensive camera? Is it worth it to install multiple cameras in order to capture a scene from multiple angles, or is this too intrusive for the participants? Is a dedicated device necessary at all, given that some smartphone models offer lenses that can compete with those of consumer camcorders in many regards? There are no straightforward answers to such questions; they will depend to a large degree on specific research scenarios. We hope that the following pages will be of help in the search for the right equipment.[2] We distinguish three categories of devices, each producing different kinds of data: (1) handheld cameras (including consumer and semi-professional camcorders, digital photo cameras with video-recording capabilities, and smartphone cameras), (2) POV (point of view) cameras, and (3) 360-degree omnidirectional cameras.

Handheld Cameras

For most projects, a consumer electronics *handheld camcorder* with a camera-mounted *external microphone* will be the go-to choice. Their relatively small form factor and ease of use make consumer camcorders popular and versatile. We both used a handheld camcorder extensively in our respective fieldwork activities, as a handheld device as well as mounted on a tripod, which we will discuss later. Before settling on a particular device, we highly recommend going to a dedicated camera retail store, playing around with different models, and consulting with an expert explaining one's research project. Many features of a camera—such as lenses (for view angles and zoom factors), low light modes, or image stabilization—will depend on the specific research scenario and it is crucial to have a good idea of the range of scenes one might be filming in the field when purchasing equipment.

In terms of camera resolution researchers should orient themselves on current standards,[3] yet we highly recommend to ensure that the camera has *removable batteries* and slots for *external memory cards* (SD cards). Backup batteries are crucial even in settings where frequent recharging is possible, as charging always disrupts the research process. Internal memory can be useful if large enough but has the drawback that it takes significantly more time to transfer data from a camera's internal memory to a computer or hard drive in comparison to simply replacing an SD card. Unless battery capacities improve significantly in the coming years or reliable automatic wireless transmission of video data from the camera to an external hard drive becomes feasible, we consider removable batteries and SD cards to be nonnegotiable features. Another highly useful feature is the ability to *capture stills* during video recording, as it allows the videographer to keep a separate picture index of different scenes, which will greatly help finding particular videos in the database.

With a larger budget one may also consider *semiprofessional* or *pro consumer video cameras*, as their image quality and range of features outrival consumer models considerably, especially when the goal is to be able to transform the footage into an ethnographic film, or for long-term archiving purposes, such as in language documentation work, but larger cameras are also more obtrusive and harder to handle.

One alternative to video camcorders is a *digital photo camera* with video-recording capabilities (DSLR or mirrorless), which are very popular among filmmakers for low-budget video projects, as they often have better lenses and sensors compared to consumer camcorders. There are a number of drawbacks when considering them for ethnographic fieldwork as their recording time is usually limited and they lack many of the features of a camcorder. But for certain low light conditions or when a photo camera may be perceived as less intrusive they may be an option. It is important to be very explicit in the consent procedures here, as one certainly does not want to lead research subjects into thinking that they are being photographed while one is actually filming them. As cameras are becoming smaller, it is the researcher's responsibility to make sure participants are aware that they are being filmed so that they may opt out of it if they wish. This applies especially to the use of *smartphone cameras* for filming.

Without a large budget, a researcher might not have another option but to use their smartphone and higher-end models today do shoot quite decent video. But they also have numerous drawbacks: Smooth zooming is difficult through a smartphone's touch screen, batteries and memory cards are usually not replaceable, and audio quality is often inadequate, all points that call for a dedicated camera. If using a smartphone, we highly recommend using it with a hand grip or video rig (a frame to mount the phone in) or mounting it on a tripod and connecting an external microphone.

Irrespective of the kind of device, handheld and tripod-mounted cameras are mostly used to capture social interaction from a *third-person perspective*, here referring to the perspective of an observer who is not involved in the interaction being filmed. Of course, in most cases a researcher is all but another participant, so the camera's (third-person) perspective is also the researcher's own first-person perspective (see Pritzker and Perrino, this volume). Only when mounted on a tripod the camera does not film from the perspective of any of the interactants, which also allows the researcher to enter the frame in order to participate in activities.

Point-of-View Cameras

By contrast to cameras that capture a third-person's or researcher's perspective, so-called *point-of-view (POV) cameras* (often marketed as *action cameras)* can be used to capture the *first-person perspective* of the research

Figure 8.1 Girl wearing GoPro with chest harness in conversation with her friend

subjects.[4] These can wear the cameras with specific harnesses, usually either on the chest (see Figure 8.1) or on the forehead, while going about their everyday activities. They are thus filming from their own subjective "point of view," that is, what they are attending to at any particular moment, such as the interlocutor of a conversation or the object that is being handled, providing a unique perspective on human interaction.

Among the benefits of a POV camera are that they give the participant wearing it control over what is being recorded—they may turn the camera on and off as they please. At the same time, these devices allow participants to record scenes in the researcher's absence, providing data from settings that might otherwise not be accessible.[5] In her research, Mitsuhara gave the children she was doing research with GoPro cameras and chest harnesses and asked them to record their rides to and from home as well as in school during recess. POV cameras can, of course, also be worn by the ethnographer themselves, allowing them to actively participate in ongoing interaction together with research subjects (Edmonds, forthcoming).

Most POV cameras record at wide angles with a fixed fish-eye lens, providing up to a 170-degree field of view, much wider than regular cameras and thus providing a fuller picture of the scene the subject is attending to. There is, however, also a serious drawback to the fact that they have fixed lenses, which is the lack of optical zoom. Different fields of view, i.e., different angles at which a scene is recorded, are achieved digitally and thus lossy and may distort or stretch the frame at the edges.

Another drawback of POV cameras, especially when worn with a harness, is that there is no way to monitor what is being captured in ongoing interaction. Some models have (or allow for the installation of) an LCD monitor, yet, given their small size, they do not afford the same precision of a larger screen or viewfinder. The number of other controls is also severely limited and while they are an excellent addition to handheld cameras to capture supplemental video, we would not recommend them as primary cameras—at least not yet.

A specific type of POV camera developed in social psychology already in the 1990s is the "subcam," a miniature camera worn with specific glasses, which records the precise field of view of who is wearing it. Subcams are used primarily in "Subjective Evidence-Based Ethnography" (Lahlou 2011), a research procedure that involves reviewing the recordings together with the research subjects, asking them to reconstruct and describe their psychological states at every moment, which gives access to their subjective experience of the activities they are engaged in.

360-Degree Cameras

A relatively new technological development that can provide exciting opportunities for research in linguistic anthropology is that of omnidirectional cameras, which record a 360-degree field of view. When filming with a traditional camcorder, the scope of the recording is predetermined by the width of the frame and thus the decision of what is relevant in an interaction and what is not is always made in advance—it is in the hands, literally, of the videographer. A POV camera places that decision in the hands of the participant wearing it—the frame is determined by their head or body movement—but it is still predetermined. An omnidirectional camera, by contrast, allows for changing the field of view *after the fact*, providing a range of new possibilities for visual analysis. Similar to a POV camera, it may also be useful when the presence of the researcher is not desired or possible.

The most common (and affordable) types of these cameras are those that record through two lenses at opposite sides of the camera, each recording at an angle of more than 180 degrees. The camera automatically "stitches" the two images together through software, producing a continuous 360-degree image. Once uploaded to a computer, one can watch the video at any angle and move the image around dynamically during playback, just as one would be able to turn around when actually being present at the scene. With corresponding 360-degree spatial audio this can create a credible sense of immersion in the video, of "inhabiting" the scene filmed (McIlvenny 2019).

A 360-degree camera is particularly beneficial for a relatively fixed setting, especially when people are facing one another. For example, when recording a group of people sitting around a table for a meal, with a regular camcorder it is impossible to always keep every participant's face in the frame. A 360-degree camera placed in the middle of the table records the entire scene from the perspective of the table and allows for accurately tracking everyone's eye gaze at all times, analyzing gestures, or the handling of objects (İkizoğlu 2020). During analysis, one can either look at the footage as flat spherical image (see Figure 8.2), for example, for the simultaneous

Figure 8.2 Full spherical video still image from footage of a dinner table conversation filmed with a 360-degree camera. Courtesy Didem İkizoğlu

Figure 8.3 A zoomed-in section of the same still. Courtesy Didem İkizoğlu

analysis of activities at opposite sides of the camera, or one can zoom in and narrow the field of view, such as to focus on two people next to one another in conversation (see Figure 8.3). McIlvenny (2019) discusses software currently in development that enables the analyst to annotate and analyze 360-degree video in virtual space itself.

Recording with Multiple Devices

In some cases, it may be useful to record with multiple devices simultaneously (C. Goodwin 1993, 191–2; Heath et al. 2010: 53–5), be it to record from different angles, to record with different types of cameras, or to record high-quality audio with separate *solid-state audio recorders*. For example, Mondada (2006, 56), filming agronomists and computer scientists discussing farmland maps, used one camera pointing down from the ceiling, providing a detailed view of pointing and other gestures, and another one from the side recording participants waist up showing body posture and gaze. Being able to draw from both cameras proved crucial for analysis since "the alternation between mutual gazes and a common focus of attention on the artefacts is a key feature that neither one nor the other image alone can capture."

With the rise of mobile video calling, video conferencing, and other forms of computer-mediated communication, *screen recordings* of smartphone or computer screens can provide valuable insights into participation frameworks mediated by a technological interface, revealing what participants are attending to on the screen. In her work in rural China on video calls between migrant parents and their "left-behind" children, Gan recorded the child and a co-present adult who was facilitating the video call,[6] as they were interacting with the smartphone during the call. Simultaneously she recorded a screen capture of that smartphone's screen, providing the image of the remote parent as well as a thumbnail inset of the video of the child (the latter representing the image that the parent sees on their screen). Both video streams were then synchronized into a combined video showing them side by side for analysis (Gan et al. 2020).

Synchronization is a challenge in all cases of multiple recordings. This can be accomplished with traditional video editing or transcription software.[7] A more advanced solution, budget permitting, is to choose a setup with devices that start recording simultaneously and/or to use devices that can record a universal time code, allowing video software to easily synchronize recordings.

Microphones

The audio quality of most built-in microphones of video cameras (not even speaking of smartphones) is far too low for accurate recording of talk to be transcribed. We strongly recommend investing in an external microphone no matter what camera type a researcher has settled for. The best choice for camcorders is camera-mounted *stereo shotgun microphones* that combine the benefits of a shotgun microphone (i.e., partially isolating sound coming from the source the camera is focusing on) with the ability to capture a stereo image of the entire scene. For recording everyday interaction, we highly recommend a stereo microphone (over mono shotgun microphones usually used in filming) as it preserves the natural soundscape of the scene and will greatly assist in transcribing (see Shohet and Lloyd, this volume). Especially when transcribing recordings with multiple participants it is extremely helpful to be able to detect the direction a sound is coming from in scenes where people might have turned away from the camera or moved out of the frame.

Some camcorder manufacturers will offer microphones that are mounted onto the camera with specific *brackets*, with the benefit that sound data and power are transmitted from and to the microphone without the need of extra cables or batteries. Microphones that are not designed to be mounted on a camera require a *shockmount* to minimize noise from handling the camera and normal camera operations, especially in the case of handheld devices. When filming outdoors, wind noise can also seriously distort the audio and make transcribing talk difficult, so any microphone should always be fitted with a "*dead cat*," a fuzzy artificial fur windshield.[8]

Semi-professional cameras usually have dedicated audio inputs with XLR connectors that allow for the use of professional microphones and also record Linear PCM audio signal, two features that should be considered when high-quality audio is required. Weight is a factor to bear in mind here, however, as heavy microphones mounted to a camera make it difficult to handle. Placing the microphone on a handheld boom pole or, in stable settings, on a separate stand next to the camera may also help to minimize camera noise.

With few participants and if the activities being filmed allow for it, *lavalier* or *lapel microphones* clipped to each participant's shirt and recording separate audio tracks are a great option, especially when filming in a large crowd or at a playground with a lot of background noise or when clear audio from individual participants is required. These types of microphones require a wireless system receiving the individual signals or individual audio recorders, however.

Tripods

Whether to film from a fixed angle with a camera installed on a tripod or to follow participants around with a handheld device depends to a large extent on the particular activities being filmed (see Heath et al. 2010, 38–42 for discussion). However, since most cameras can be easily mounted on a tripod and unmounted again, for most purposes we would recommend a hybrid approach. The benefit of a tripod is obvious when filming from a fixed angle, such as at a dinner table, but even when filming outdoors and in mobile settings they should not be discounted. Even if one is confident in their steady hand while filming, the slightest movement can later be seen as an abrupt jolt on the video recording and a monopod or a tripod helps in creating smooth and steady footage. While monopods still require the researcher to hold the camera, tripods have the additional benefit that they allow the researcher to engage more freely in interaction with research participants—or to fully absent themselves from the scene (Heath et al. 2010, 44).

In his research with Aché hunter-gatherers, for example, Hauck recorded video on hunting treks in a forest reserve as well as in a village and a primary school. Filming was done with a handheld camera, which was mounted on tripods in different settings. On hunting treks, Hauck used a small tripod that was strapped to the side of his backpack. While not walking through the forest, Hauck installed the camera on the tripod at one end of camp to film activities around the campfires. This also enabled him to partake in activities. Participation in common activities such as meals may be expected from the researcher in many communities where it would be considered rude to reject an offer of food or a conversation while filming (see Pritzker and Perrino, this volume). A tripod may help in such a situation. In the village, especially to record in school classrooms, Hauck used a larger and more stable tripod.[9]

Power Supply

A sufficient number of backup batteries are a must, no matter if research is carried out in a remote area with unstable electricity or in a setting where power outlets are available for frequent recharging, because charging a battery will always disrupt the research and takes time. When going on hunting treks that lasted for up to five days, Hauck carried six separate battery packs but still ran out of power occasionally. Some camera manufacturers offer batteries with capacities higher than the one included in the camera, which are always preferred.[10] Good options are also portable power banks, as they allow for the recharging of different devices and cut down on the number of different batteries to purchase. Hauck used a GoPro in one research trip and successfully recharged its batteries with a power bank overnight and while he was trekking. Researchers working in remote areas that are not connected to the national power grid often purchase mobile solar panels for recharging of recording devices.

Data Storage and Computers

SD cards have become the default storage medium for video recording. While there are cards with a capacity of up to 1 TB, we suggest buying several smaller cards (e.g., 64 or 128 GB, depending on the quality one plans to record at) and swapping them at regular intervals. This ensures that less data are lost should something go wrong with one card and encourages frequent uploading to the computer.

Most people will have a laptop computer with them in the field, which is especially important in the case of video recording for backing up recordings.[11] Two external hard drives capacious enough to each hold an entire backup of all data are also highly recommended and must be encrypted with a password (see Black and Conley-Riner, this volume). If there is a stable internet connection in the field, cloud backups are possible too, as long as the files are encrypted. Given the sensitivity of video data, we suggest "zero knowledge" services that encrypt data locally *before* uploading.

Other Accessories

Other accessories will depend on one's particular research setup, such as a professional camera bag to fit extra batteries, microphone, or headphones, a case or pouch to keep SD cards organized, or a rain cover for outdoor conditions. In warm humid settings, bug repellent should not be discounted as an essential accessory so that one can steadily film without swatting mosquitoes.[12]

8.2.4 Step 4: Familiarizing Yourself with the Equipment and Devising a Recording Schedule

To the extent that it is possible, a recording schedule specifying what, when, and where to record should be outlined before going to the field—likely also required for research proposals or submissions to funding agencies or institutional review boards (see Das, this volume). While it will likely change once in the field and researchers must be flexible to accommodate unforeseen events, having clear goals of what to film and when, and when *not* to film, greatly helps in the everyday research process. General advice we would like to give is to be specific about the intervals at which one will aim to film and to schedule breaks and days where no filming or other research activities are to be carried out (see Jones and Gershon, this volume, for more details on planning your research).

In the religious village school where she was doing research, Mitsuhara filmed morning scripture classes and lunch periods three times a week. Once a month she recorded morning routines of focal families and filmed playtime in the neighborhoods twice a month for two hours. She filmed temple visits and pilgrimages that her focal families went to whenever they occurred throughout her fieldwork. Hauck recorded everyday interactions in the indigenous village on two days every other week. Every six weeks he recorded at timed intervals for one full day. He went on hunting treks to a nearby forest reserve with his focal families once a month on which he recorded during all four days.

Before departing for the field, it is also crucial to study the manuals and test all equipment to know how each device works and interfaces with the computer or hard drive that data are uploaded to. We recommend setting aside a full test day at a location that mirrors the recording environment expected at the fieldsite. No matter if filming inside or outside, equipment should be tested for a substantial period of time in order to preempt potential problems. Does the camera bag fit all necessary equipment, including microphone and enough batteries? How fast does the camera drain the battery when actually filming for a few hours? Does the microphone produce good audio? Other logistical issues may pop up at this time, and it is better to catch these at home rather than in the field where it may be difficult or more expensive to obtain additional items needed or to troubleshoot with help from IT assistance at the university or equipment shop.

The first thing when setting up the camera is to set the correct date and time. One should keep in mind that when doing fieldwork in a different time zone from one's home, this must be adjusted accordingly. The right data and time settings are indispensable when handling large numbers of video files or when combining video data with other types of recordings (see Pritzker, this volume). We recommend experimenting extensively with different camera settings. Usually automatic focus and exposure work well for most purposes. Most cameras with touchscreen LCD monitors allow for adjusting focus/exposure while filming by tapping on a desired region of the screen. Most should also have a setting that recognizes faces automatically and attempts to focus those whenever possible. Such functions can be helpful especially for those projects recording everyday interactions, as one will not have time to quickly readjust manually every time participants move. What is often problematic is automatic white balance, and we suggest testing this extensively when filming inside, outside, in the shade, on a rainy day. Many cameras offer specific presets for different scenarios that are often better than letting the camera do it automatically. When filming in the forest, Hauck experienced that neither the automatic white balance setting nor any of the standard presets did a decent job given the amount of green in the surroundings. He therefore had to create his own preset specifically for this environment. When using a POV camera, we suggest trying out different field-of-view settings together with different harnesses and angles in order to make sure to have the best possible frame.[13] Familiarizing oneself with the equipment also means knowing how to upload recordings onto a computer and organize them into a database.

8.2.5 Step 5: Creating a Database Structure and Import Workflow

An often overlooked yet vital component to video ethnography is database management. Fieldwork usually being understood primarily as the period of data *collection*, the question of how to organize data on a computer may come only as an afterthought. However, without a clear structure in place to store recordings under, even after a few days of filming, it may become difficult to sustain an overview of the data one has laboriously collected. Especially given that video or audio recordings are not easily searchable before having been transcribed, organizing them in a way that keeps them accessible, using a common naming scheme, and assigning metadata will greatly facilitate subsequent retrieval for analysis.

Creating a database is actually quite simple. The main thing is to create a hierarchical folder structure on the computer or hard drive that will hold all video recordings and to use a common and meaningful naming scheme for all files upon importing (see Figure 8.4). In both of our research projects that

Figure 8.4 Screenshot of folder structure on computer hard drive. Each folder contains a video file, an extracted audio file, an ELAN transcription file, a file for ELAN settings, and a subtitles file

we have discussed here, we have created one folder for each day of recording and then separate subfolders in which we have placed each individual video. Keeping each video file in a separate folder may seem expendable, but as soon as further files such as transcription files are added to it, having too many files in the same folder may complicate accessing them. Most camcorders create a single file for each clip (i.e., each time the recording is paused a new file will be started), thus, when filming extensively, one may end up with hundreds of files for a single day of filming and an equal number of transcription files.

To import recordings from a camera or SD card we strongly recommend using software or a script that can automatically rename files based on the recording date and time—this will make it a much easier task for the exhausted researcher after a day of filming. While date and time information is also part of each video file's embedded metadata that can be accessed in video players, if doing research in a time zone different from one's home, one would constantly have to add or subtract the time difference, and to avoid confusion it is best to have it fixed as part of the filename (yyyy-mm-dd_hh.mm.ss.mp4). This, moreover, makes the information immediately available. In addition to the date and time of recording, Mitsuhara has also added an abbreviation containing information about camera type (as she collected data with a camcorder and a GoPro), key participants, and location (yyyy-mm-dd_hh.mm.ss_GP_xyz.mp4).

The researcher should also make sure to import the data with the same quality it was recorded. Some programs, especially specialized video editing software, will reencode video files by de- or recompressing them. This may result in much bigger file sizes and should be avoided (unless one has sufficient hard drive space and the video needs to be edited anyways).[14]

At least as important as a folder structure is to keep *metadata* on the recordings.[15] Metadata is data about data. It includes information as to the day, time, and location the video was filmed; its participants, context, activities, topics; things such as the progress of the transcription, what projects or publications a given recording may be used for, or any other information that is important for a given project. Metadata is crucial as it ensures a specific video can be easily located so the researcher does not have to rewatch entire videos in order to find a particular episode. Global initiatives among language researchers have devised common metadata schemes to make language data exchangeable.[16] If collaborating on a project with others, or when the goal is to share data later, it is certainly worth it to familiarize oneself with and adopt a common framework.

There are dedicated programs to create databases that include files as well as metadata.[17] For most individual projects it may be sufficient to use the

Session	Date	Duration	Setting	Context	Activity	Description	Comments	Participants	Video
2013-08-16_12.52.32	2013-08-16	02:52	forest	trekking, resting	walking, shouts, conversation	shouts across distance, conversation		adults, children	mp4
2013-08-16_12.58.52	2013-08-16	05:26	forest	trekking, resting	walking, conversation	hunters join the group, children present monkey to camera		adults, children	mp4
2013-08-16_13.04.54	2013-08-16	11:34	forest	resting	conversation, gathering	sitting resting, children conversation, extracting palm hearts close by		adults, children	mp4
2013-08-16_13.49.08	2013-08-16	06:47	forest	resting, trekking	sitting, walking			adults, children	mp4
2013-08-16_14.02.25	2013-08-16	30:58	forest	trekking, arriving	walking, setting up, conversation	arrival at campsite,		adults, children	mp4
2013-08-16_14.43.28	2013-08-16	04:36	forest	at camp	conversation			adults, children	mp4
2013-08-16_15.54.57	2013-08-16	01:20	forest	at camp	food-prep, conversation	children helping prepare food		adults, children	mp4
2013-08-16_16.02.27	2013-08-16	02:24	forest	at camp	food-prep, conversation	children bringing dead monkeys, hunters arrive		adults, children	mp4
2013-08-16_16.18.37	2013-08-16	04:29	forest	at camp	food-prep, conversation			adults, children	mp4
2013-08-16_17.31.13	2013-08-16	08:57	forest	at camp	eating, conversation	getting dark		adults, children	mp4
2013-08-17_07.46.41	2013-08-17	19:37	forest	at camp	conversation, leaving	morning conversations, leaving campsite		adults, children	mp4
2013-08-17_08.59.26	2013-08-17	01:22	forest	trekking	walking	passing over bridge		adults, children	mp4
2013-08-20_08.05.56	2013-08-20	03:34	homespace	play area	playing, sibling caretaking	playing, caretaking of younger sibling, children interacting with tapir		children, tapir	mp4
2013-08-20_15.57.33	2013-08-20	11:30	homespace	at home	conversation		terere w/ mbtp, antn, clbt	adults, children	mp4
2013-08-25_09.15.06	2013-08-25	09:05	homespace	play area	peer-group-inter., singing	children singing song		children, tapir	mp4
2013-08-25_09.25.47	2013-08-25	01:40	homespace	at home	peer-group-inter., child-animal-inter.	children talking about and interacting with tapir		children, tapir	mp4
2013-08-25_09.27.42	2013-08-25	13:38	homespace	at home	playing	soccer		children	mp4
2013-08-25_10.09.39	2013-08-25	16:38	homespace	at home	playing	playing with beads		children	mp4

Figure 8.5 Screenshot of a section of an Excel spreadsheet formatted as data table with multiple columns for different categories of metadata. Each entry (row) refers to one "session," i.e., a video file with its respective transcription and subtitle files

data table function of Microsoft Excel or similar software and link it to the files on the hard drive (see Figure 8.5 and the exercise at the end of the chapter).[18]

Parallel to the video database, we also recommend keeping a database with photographs, including stills from the videos. Any photo software should be sufficient for this, but we suggest utilizing the same naming conventions used with the videos, as this can help locate particular videos later.

8.3 In the Field

Despite one's best efforts to test equipment beforehand, devise a research schedule and workflow, and obtaining institutional consent at a distance, there are a number of issues that can only be fully addressed once in the field, including obtaining individual consent from participants and familiarizing them with research technology. Certain issues may only arise from the contexts of filming, such as informed consent for bystanders being filmed.

8.3.1 Step 6: Consent as an Ongoing Process

Even if general consent has been obtained from the administration of an institution or community leaders beforehand, consent from individual participants can only be obtained during recruitment. Not everyone will consent to being filmed even if they are fine with other aspects of the research such as being interviewed. Moreover, consent is a component of research that is ongoing and requires the ethnographer's judgment about whether or not what is being filmed falls under the agreement for what should be recorded in the first place (see Black and Conley-Riner, this volume).

In order to minimize causing offense or overstepping boundaries for content filmed or time spent filming, it is advised that researchers note in the consent phase of research what types of scenes would be recorded and for how long. For example, one could outline that "recording meals" means recording dinner-time meal preparation, dinner conversations, and cleanup, all of which could take one to three hours. In Mitsuhara's consent forms for filming, she gave sample scenarios of the settings she would film such as the morning routine (6:00 a.m. to 8:30 a.m.), children's religion classes, and playtime. This opened conversation about the purposes of filming conversation and everyday activities among recruited families.

Participants do object to being filmed at times, but one must be aware that more often than not, participants with whom an ethnographer has established a relationship or those receiving compensation for participation in the research may not feel comfortable vocally objecting to recording. This is especially the case with research with minors. As part of her consent and assent procedures, Mitsuhara attended a school meeting where she explained her research and showcased her video camera and tripod. She made clear that no one was obliged to be recorded. "If you see the camera and don't want be recorded, move your head, or give me a funny face, and I'll know you don't want to be filmed." Mitsuhara did the funny face herself and imitated what it would look like to refuse the camera's lens at any point during the study. Children utilized this "funny face" tactic later to refuse being filmed. Making sure children feel they can refuse an interaction with an adult and her technology (journals, camera, and her very ethnographic gaze) is an important point to make clear with all research subjects, especially when recording video.

8.3.2 Step 7: Becoming a Video Ethnographer within the Site

Imagine, after having established themselves in the field, the researcher attends an important event, takes out their camera, and begins recording. Instead of being able to capture the event, all of the participants stop and look at the researcher, as they are not used to seeing them record. The dilemma here is that the camera has become a marked object because the researcher failed to establish the camera as part and parcel of their presence. Key to becoming a video ethnographer in the field is to make the camera a third arm. This means walking around with recording equipment whenever at the site, regardless if there is a plan to record or not. Being seen with a camera or camera bag keeps the camera's presence unmarked, that is, not an object of interest.

García-Sanchez (2014, 61–2), for example, walked around her fieldsite in Morocco with a camera and tripod every day of fieldwork, even when she was not going to use them. Mitsuhara's consent and assent procedures in India took one month to complete. During that time, as she could not record people, she walked around with a photo camera, taking pictures of the environment, buildings, and documented scenes at public events. She opted to purchase a professional camera for photography instead of utilizing a cellphone not only to gain quality images, but mainly to help associate a camera with her identity in the field.

If researchers decide to use smartphones to film, they should be aware that although this technology is less marked in everyday settings and use, a phone is not normally associated with "research." Using it therefore as one's personal communication device as well as professional recording equipment can sometimes produce unease as participants are unclear whether the recording is part of research. Curating one's image as a video ethnographer while also collecting optimal video and sound makes choosing a professional camera a worthwhile investment if possible.

8.3.3 Step 8: Familiarizing Participants with Equipment and Research Process

Given the high use of photography and video use in the twenty-first century, recording devices do not generate the same awe that perhaps they would have in former times. Nevertheless, we suggest holding a forum or other meeting at one's fieldsite(s) at the beginning of fieldwork to introduce not only oneself and one's research interests, but also any equipment and what it will be used for. This will allow research participants (or potential participants if they have not been recruited yet) to ask questions about and interact with the devices in order to see for themselves what technologies are being used to record them. It may greatly reduce the number of conversations about why one might be filming at someone's home or workplace, while also putting the ethnographer more at ease when filming human subjects as it helps ensure that consent or assent granted is informed.

To familiarize school children with her presence and that of a recording device, Mitsuhara also let the children she worked with take pictures and record videos with both the photo and video cameras. She had a standing policy that teenagers and adults in the community were welcome to borrow her cameras if she was not using them. Once the novelty and exclusivity of the items disappear, participants are more likely to be at ease with cameras in everyday settings.

When participants are required to operate recording devices themselves, such as is the case with the use of POV cameras, enough time should be allocated for multiple camera test days for participants to become familiar with the new technology.[19] In Mitsuhara's research, children played with a GoPro quite a bit in the beginning, which also made the camera more familiar and less of a foreign object on their body. Figuring out how much autonomy to give the children with regard to the camera's eye yielded very odd and sometimes intrusive shots. Mitsuhara eventually was able to learn where the camera should be placed and how to secure it tightly at whatever angle given the focal child's height. Children were taught how to turn it on and off and how to remove the harness. After a period of getting used to the camera, children became skilled videographers. They gave Mitsuhara walking tours with a voiceover telling her what they were doing and why.

What this example illustrates is the degree to which the presence of a camera can impact an interaction or become the primary focus of an interaction. This, however, should not be seen as a problem. Both researcher and research subjects are a community of practice, constituted to not an insignificant degree around the presence of a video camera, while also participating in other communities simultaneously. Just as people's attention shifts continuously throughout the course of regular activities so does their attention shift to the recording process and back to other things (Black

2017; Speer and Hutchby 2003). If anything, the presence of a camera makes ethnographic research more explicit and transparent to the participants. Familiarizing them with recording technology does therefore not mean making them unaware of its presence and rather making it available to them in such a way that they feel comfortable to engage with it on their own terms.

8.3.4 Step 9: A Day in the Life of the Video Ethnographer

Once consent and/or assent has been granted and participants and researcher have familiarized themselves with the equipment and the research process, filming can begin. While equipment should have been thoroughly tested before arriving at one's fieldsite, it is nonetheless advisable to devise a test day (or days) for testing whether one's planned routine is indeed feasible and whether adjustments are necessary—at least one should not start filming on a day when one anticipates to collect particularly important data, such as an important ritual or gathering. Footage from such a testing period should not be discarded, however, as it can offer important insight into the community, culture, or language. If researching in a different time zone, date and time of the equipment must be adjusted before beginning to film. The following paragraphs address the issues to attend to on any particular day of filming, more or less in the order that they appear throughout the day.

The Night Before

Any given day of video recording starts the night before, when all batteries and other devices must be charged. Once data from the previous day have been uploaded to the computer, SD cards must be erased to make room for new data. Nothing is more disruptive than having to stop filming because the camera ran out of power and there is no fully charged backup battery, or because there is no space left on the SD card.

Starting the Day

At the start of a filming day, the camera should be briefly turned on to ensure it is working well. Batteries, SD cards, and headphones should be packed in the camera bag, alongside other accessories. Every day is different so one should always check the white balance before starting to film, as well as sound. As lighting conditions change throughout the day these settings might need to be adjusted. Headphones are crucial for checking and monitoring the sound before beginning to film. As recording schedules may be very different in different projects, each researcher's day will start out very differently, and what they will record, on what days, and at what intervals will vary greatly. General advice we can give is to be prepared that things may not go as planned and to be flexible to change course, but this should not lead one to improvising day to day.

Where to Film

If a researcher can choose the location where to film, for example, when recording an interview or story, they should be mindful of possible interference of noise. For example, when filming inside, the noise of a refrigerator or other appliance can be extremely disturbing on the recording. Minimizing background noise is particularly important for projects that have phonetic or prosodic analyses as components.

What to Film

The particular activities to be filmed will depend to a large extent on the individual project (see Hall, this volume). Many researchers in linguistic anthropology will be focusing on what Goffman ([1961] 1972, 84–5) calls "situated activity systems," i.e., "somewhat closed, self-compensating, self-terminating circuit[s] of interdependent actions," such as a game, a meal, the production of an artifact, a school exercise, or a bedtime routine.

However, in the future one's research interests may change or one may wish to keep a record for the community or future researchers. If possible and if consent for extensive filming has been granted the ethnographer should aim for recording a comprehensive picture of diverse practices at their fieldsite(s). Especially in contexts of rapid cultural change, researchers may happen upon practices that, while not their primary research interest, may be of great importance to the local community and their audiovisual documentation for posteriority can provide a valuable resource not least to future generations of the community itself. In Hauck's research on children's language practices, for example, he also spent considerable time filming elders weaving baskets and doing other handicrafts. It is thus important to be open to filming unexpected activities and events as well.

Filming Activities

Whatever situated activities are being filmed, it is important to provide a full record of them. Researchers should ensure that they always *record the beginning and end of an activity* when possible. For instance, in the case of dinner-time conversations, filming should begin before people sit down to dinner and also capture the moment when they leave. On hunting treks with the Aché, Hauck always tried to film the arrival at a campsite as well as when the group left the site for the next trek through the forest. At the same time, important information can also be contained in between activities. In his research with geologists, Smith (2018, 17–9) recorded them continuously, not just when stopping at a given site to be inspected but also while walking across the terrain in order to gain a "micro-longitudinal" perspective on participants' decision-making in transit.

How to Film

At the beginning of a scene, and at intervals in between, it is recommended to *pan over all participants* present. Especially in the case of many participants and frequently shifting participation frameworks such as playgrounds, this will greatly help later on when transcribing to identify speakers that might have moved offscreen.

While video ethnography for analysis is different from footage collected for an ethnographic film, basic principles of videography still apply, in particular *slow and steady* camera movements. Panning (moving the camera sideways) or tilting (moving the camera up and down) should be smooth, avoiding hard stops. *Zooming* should be kept to a minimum. It may sometimes be helpful to zoom in to capture a particular detail of the interaction, but generally one should aim for the widest shot possible in order to capture body language and surroundings of participants. Peripheral vision and frequently looking beyond the LCD monitor help greatly for *anticipating movements*, such as a new participant entering or someone leaving the frame.

The *length* of recordings is an important point to consider. A greater number of shorter clips will make accessing data easier in one's database (as well as transcribing less of a daunting task). Some cameras will have a function to manually split recordings while filming (starting a new file by pressing a button without interrupting the recording). This can also be accomplished by briefly stopping and restarting the recording; however, one may lose important information in the intervening seconds.

Monitoring the state of the battery and remaining space on the memory card is important while filming in order to switch them at opportune moments. One should plan ahead what to film when working with a limited set of batteries or limited power supply. Keeping the camera in standby, turning it completely off while not recording, and turning the LCD monitor off when recording a stable scene from a tripod are simple ways to prolong battery life.

Taking Video Stills

As opposed to text, which can be searched for particular words, and photos, which are usually easily identifiable through thumbnails, the content of a video file is only accessible when watching the file. Capturing stills at regular intervals while filming will greatly assist later when trying to find a particular scene, as the still can be easily searched for in a photo database. We both have made use of our camera's function to take stills extensively and archived them in a photo library, using parallel naming conventions (letting the photo software title the images automatically using the "yyyy-mm-dd hh:mm:ss" scheme). When trying to find the video of a particular scene, we can now first search for a still from the scene in our photo database. Assuming the photo still has the title "2020-01-25 10:19:20," we can then look for the corresponding video file, which will start with "2020-01-25 10 …" in our video database.

Taking Fieldnotes

Video stills, however, do not contain any information that is not already in the video. Just as any other product of the ethnographic encounter, be it a transcript, a photograph, or a material object, video will be meaningful only if properly contextualized and many aspects of context cannot be extracted from the recording after the fact. While handling the camera, taking fieldnotes (see Pritzker and Perrino, this volume) may not be possible, yet we strongly recommend keeping a notebook in or with the camera bag at all times and jotting down contextual information and other observations in between filming, when the camera is installed on a tripod, and immediately after a filming session (see Duranti 1997, 115–6; C. Goodwin 1993, 193).

Ethnoarchaeological Tracking

Video recording may also be used in the field for timed observations as part of scan sampling or ethnoarchaeological tracking (Ochs et al. 2006), i.e., documenting participants' location, the activities they are engaged in, and with whom they are interacting at fixed intervals throughout a period of time. This is usually done with specific devices (see Ochs et al. 2006, 397); however, lacking these, one can also use the video camera for the same purpose. Once every six weeks in the village and on one day on every other hunting trek, Hauck followed key participants a full day, filming them briefly at ten-minute intervals. From those videos, information about the location of the participant, their activity, and whom they were interacting with at each instant of assessment was entered into a database, giving insight into the communicative ecology in which children are embedded in their everyday lives.

Ongoing Awareness of Participants' Assent

Throughout the video-recording period, awareness that consent and assent are ongoing processes is important. Participants might voice not wanting something to be filmed or "on record," or the researcher may decide to shut the camera off for context-specific considerations. Recall the episode from Mitsuhara's assent procedure where she suggested that children make a "funny face" to deny being filmed for an activity or day or entirely throughout fieldwork even if parents had granted consent for research. When working with children especially it is important to try to always be aware of signs that might hint at discomfort being filmed. A child might appear fine with it one day or for one activity, but not other days or activities. Mitsuhara had to turn the camera off, using her personal judgment that something was not okay or necessary to document (such as a child vomiting from sickness) while keeping it on for other moments (such as bullying).

When using POV cameras, children who are wearing them can decide for themselves what they want to film. However, this type of filming presents an additional challenge as it puts the onus of deciding what and who is appropriate to be filmed on the children. In reviewing GoPro footage, Mitsuhara found one instance where the child wearing the camera was being bullied and the bully was unaware they were on camera. The child then announced to the bully that Mitsuhara would see the footage, mobilizing the camera as a tool for documentation and reporting of their behavior. Interesting as such data are, recordings obtained when the anthropologist is absent present additional challenges for informed and aware assent, as in the example of a particular bully being unaware they were being filmed until announced, after which the bullying ceased.[20]

8.3.5 Step 10: Archiving and Backups

A recording day is not over before the data are uploaded to a computer or hard drive and backed up—one should never wait till the next day. Files must be dated immediately after transferring. We reiterate our suggestion to use software that can automatically name files by date and time or using a script for it. The most basic metadata, such as the location of the recording or the participants, should be added right away into the database, but generally speaking, the more metadata one adds up front, the better, as it is much easier with fresh memory of the recording event than to extract the information from the video and fieldnotes later. At the same time, photos should be imported into the photo archive. Backups of the entire database should be made at regular intervals, ideally running them overnight after every day of recording.

Once all data are securely uploaded and backed up, SD cards can be erased to make room for new data. Batteries must be recharged overnight, yet be mindful when using external chargers to not leave the camera without any battery for too long. Some cameras may lose their settings, in particular time and date. It can be frustrating when, after import, one notices that half of the videos are dated five years prior to the actual date and one has to recalculate date and time and rename the files.

8.4 Beyond the Field

Adding information to the database, and transcribing, translating, annotating, and analyzing recordings are activities that should commence while in the field, ideally as soon as one has gathered the first videos, and will continue throughout the years that a researcher is engaging with their data. Transcribing and analyzing in the field allows for checking data and interpretations with participants and research assistants, and new questions that may arise can be discussed directly. Playing back recordings to the research subjects enables the researcher to ask specific questions about their interpretation of the events or subjective experience (Schieffelin 1990; see also Lahlou 2011).

We both used the free ELAN software[21] for transcription (see Shohet and Lloyd, this volume). We recommend keeping the transcription file in the same folder as the video file and using the same filename (see Figure 8.4). There are, of course, other ways to do it (such as a parallel folder structure for transcription files), yet we have found that keeping all data derived from or associated with a given clip together, including subtitle files, works best for large archives. We both also trained local research assistants in ELAN, and after leaving our respective fieldsites, we left videos to be transcribed with them. Given that ELAN transcription files do not import but rather link to video files, completed transcriptions could easily be emailed to us by the transcribers. Placing them in appropriate folder automatically relinked them to the correct video.

Participant names should be anonymized already in the transcription file, not just when preparing data for publication. We recommend an easy scheme of pseudonyms that is meaningful to the researcher, as well as storing the key in an encrypted file. Depending on the type of consent granted by research participants, researchers might need to blur faces or otherwise render participants unrecognizable in video data or stills that are to be presented, published, or sent to transcriptionists.

Since the researcher will present on and write about the issues captured in the videos in places far away from where these were recorded, in this way too, gathering video data inevitably points beyond the context in which fieldwork takes place. While this must have been addressed in consent procedures, if at all possible researchers should also continue to keep research participants informed about results of their analyses. In many cases, "after the field" becomes "before the field" as researchers will return frequently for follow-up visits to their fieldsites, and it is good practice to continue to keep participants involved in the research.

This is particularly true when doing research in contexts far removed from academic settings in Western countries. Can we still speak of "informed" consent if those giving it do not have a clear idea of what presenting the data elsewhere might entail? For obtaining consent, strategies have been suggested such as asking whether research participants to be recruited would agree to have their videos shown in a neighboring village or to people from a different ethnic group. However, it is still a different issue to present data to complete strangers in a different country (see Black and Conley-Riner, this volume).

Hauck addressed this issue in his research with the Aché in the following way: After returning from the field for the first time, he presented excerpts of the videos filmed in the community in a research lab to an academic audience at his home university. He filmed this session. The video shows himself, the Aché videos projected onto a screen, as well as other researchers watching and commenting on the videos. Three months later he returned to the field and showed this video to all of his research participants, including the children and their parents, explaining the purpose and activities of the lab, in order to give them a better understanding of how video data are being used in an academic setting. At this occasion he asked again for confirmation of participants' permission to use the data in similar settings. While the understanding that the research participants have of the research is of course still different from that of an academic audience, this is one way of minimizing the gap between these two different contexts and to make sure that participants are aware how their data are being used. Keeping an open discussion about the purpose and life of video data throughout fieldwork and after is essential to maintain an ongoing ethical relationship with research participants.

8.5 Ethnographic Activities

Activity 1

In this activity you will test your equipment by choosing to film a setting that resembles your ethnographic site. For example, if your site is outdoors and your research focuses on human–nonhuman interactions, perhaps choose a dog park as your test site. If your research is in a home environment you might want to film a dinner at home. Have a friend or family member help out for testing sound and image if possible.

1 Charge your batteries the night before filming.
2 Set up your camera with the SD card and battery. Bring your tripod and prepare the camera bag with the additional equipment you need (microphone, "dead cat" if filming outdoors, headphones, backup batteries, and SD cards).
3 When you arrive at your site set the white balance and, as you observe the lighting around you, check how light is captured on screen and make appropriate adjustments. This step takes trial and error and may take a while until you arrive at the desired film quality.

Video Ethnography: A Guide   253

4   If you have a friend with you, begin filming them as they walk around and talk, and notice the levels of sound on the camera LCD screen and through headphones to ensure that everything is being optimally recorded. This is where you can figure out how far from the action the camera can be before you lose sound clarity.

5   Now that your camera and sound are set up and tested, let's move on to frames of filming. Pick a scene to film with your friend in it and film at the widest angle (fully zoomed out). Depending on the aim of your research you may need a wide frame but be aware of losing clarity on the face and eyes. Next, zoom in to a medium shot (waist up) and then do a close up (face and neck). Notice how your camera handles zoom and what type of automatic refocusing occurs. When filming stationary settings such as a dinner table you will most likely keep the camera at medium shot, yet make sure that all of your participants are in the frame. For outside filming, you might need a wider shot. If you are planning to analyze gestures and facial expressions, you will need a much closer take of your participants, but will lose the context of the environment as well as what is happening with the rest of the body. Play around with these settings and become very familiar with the particulars of your camera.

6   You have now concluded your testing equipment day. Depending on how it went, you may decide that different equipment is better suited for the interactions and settings you aim to film. Refer back to this chapter as you decide which equipment you might need and make sure to set aside another test day before beginning your research.

Activity 2

Now that you have tested your equipment and filmed a couple of scenes, you will need to import the video and place it into an organized database so you can locate your video clips later.

1   Create a folder that will contain your database and subfolders for each recording.
2   Upload the video clips to your computer.
3   Place the video clips into their respective folders.
4   Name folder and clip in a unique way, for example, yyyy-mm-dd_hh.mm.ss_XX_YY, where XX is a code for the location (e.g., DP for dogpark) and YY is a code for a participant.
5   Create a new file in Excel (or a similar spreadsheet application) and write the word "Session" in cell B3. In subsequent cells in row 3 write

254   **Research Methods in Linguistic Anthropology**

"Date," "Duration," "Location," "Participants," "Context," "Activity," "Description," and "Transcription Status." Add further categories relevant for your project (see Figure 8.5 from our discussion in Step 5 for an example).

6   Copy and paste the unique name of your video file into cell B4.

7   With cell B3 selected, click "select all," which should select all cells in row 3 with data and the row below them (B3 to J4).

8   Click on "Format as Table" to create a data table.

9   Fill in the metadata of your first entry and add new entries. You can add new rows by hitting the tab key when in the last cell of the last row (see Figure 8.5).

10   Congratulations! You have now created a database. You might add further columns for more metadata when you are in the field depending on your needs, but the important thing is to create the infrastructure before entering the field to avoid getting overwhelmed with data during fieldwork. It will help you keep your data organized and make research, analysis, and write-up much easier.

8.6 Questions to Consider

1   Discuss the pros and cons of using video in ethnographic research. Consider the possibilities that video affords for analyzing data and presenting it to other researchers and what budgetary factors need to be considered.

2   How would you explain what a video database is and how video can be used for "science and educational purposes" to someone outside of the academy?

3   How might informed consent change when it comes to consenting to have one's video-recorded data be part of a scientific archive?

4   Write out a few sentences to add to an existing consent form regarding video ethnography. Give an example of something that could be filmed with time frames for how long one might film. Refer to the short example from "Step 6: Consent as an Ongoing Process" for an idea of how to phrase this.

5   What are some reasons a researcher would want to use a point-of-view camera or a 360-degree camera? What can these cameras add to research?

8.7 Acknowledgments

We thank Candy Goodwin, Michael S. Smith, and our editors, Sabina Perrino and Sonya Pritzker, for valuable comments on earlier drafts of this chapter, any shortcomings remaining our own responsibility.

8.8 Notes

1   We discuss assent further in the section "In the Field."
2   Due to rapid changes in technology we will not refer to specific models, as they will likely become obsolete in a few years. For these details, we suggest consulting online sources—such as websites dedicated to videography, forums, and blogs—as well as one's professional network for people who have recently used video in their fieldwork.
3   A resolution of 4K (UHD) is definitely recommended at the time of writing (see also Kohler and Murphy, this volume).
4   Most widely known are GoPros, but many other manufacturers offer POV cameras as well.
5   Especially in situations when an ethnographer's physical presence is not desired or possible (such as due to COVID-19), a POV camera may be a good option to be used by research participants in the researcher's absence.
6   The children are raised by other adults, usually grandparents, who also facilitate the video calls with the remote parents.
7   Final Cut Pro, Adobe Premiere, or Avid are the standard choices for professional video editing software, but we also highly recommend DaVinci Resolve (https://www.blackmagicdesign.com/products/davinciresolve/), which has the complete set of features for complex video editing but is available for free. The ELAN transcription software (https://archive.mpi.nl/tla/elan) has a dedicated media synchronization mode and can display up to four videos simultaneously. And if participants are recorded on separate audio tracks, some can be muted during transcription, thus allowing the transcriber to focus only on one recording.
8   Foam pop filters that usually come with a microphone are often insufficient.
9   Smaller tripods are often much less stable, and smooth panning over a scene may be virtually impossible; larger tripods usually have better heads that allow for smoother camera movements but are also considerably heavier.
10 While there are some third-party batteries compatible with a given camera offered often at significantly cheaper prices, we have had negative

experiences with those and recommend only purchasing batteries from the camera manufacturer.

11 If it is not feasible to bring a computer we strongly suggest looking into other backup options on external drives that can receive data directly from the camera.

12 Since mosquito buzzing will be picked up by the microphone and can be very disturbing on the recording, Hauck also sprayed the dead cat with bug repellent.

13 At the end of this chapter in the section "Ethnographic Activities" there is an outline of how to test the equipment and engage in a "mock" filming day prior to leaving for the field. Ideally ethnographers will do this before fieldwork, but it is advisable to have another day or days when in the field to see which light and sound issues need to be attended to in a specific setting.

14 Those who are familiar with the command line should look into ffmpeg for importing and renaming of video files. For the less computer-savvy, we found out that Apple's Photos app imported original videos directly, while iMovie inevitably reencoded them, so we recommend using the former to Mac users.

15 At the end of this chapter in "Ethnographic Activities" there is an outline of how to set up a database in Excel.

16 See, for instance, the TalkBank project <talkbank.org/>, in particular its Child Language Data Exchange System (CHILDES) <childes.talkbank. org/>, the Component MetaData Infrastructure (CMDI) from the CLARIN project <www.clarin.eu/content/component-metadata>, and the Open Language Archives Community (OLAC) <www.language-archives. org/documents.html>.

17 MySQL Workbench <www.mysql.com/products/workbench/> is the only open source solution yet requires some programming knowledge. Claris FileMaker Pro <www.claris.com/filemaker/> does not require programming knowledge but is relatively expensive. Some transcription programs also offer database management solutions, e.g., Transana <www. transana.com/> and Dedoose <www.dedoose.com/>, but they also have quite high price tags.

18 In our databases we have added one column with the paths to the folders containing each video file that worked as hyperlinks opening that folder when clicked.

19 In the case of a project that is fully remote where participants themselves act as videographers (such as may be required due to COVID-19), it is even more important to allocate sufficient time for extensive preparation, testing, and troubleshooting.

20 Such issues necessarily arise in the case of remote projects when relying on research assistants to be in charge of filming and must be addressed accordingly.

21 ELAN (see https://archive.mpi.nl/tla/elan) is one of the most efficient, reliable, and versatile software available for transcription, annotation, and coding of video data, whether one is interested in interlinear glossing for fine-grained linguistic analysis, phonetics, gesture, and body language, or for the coding of interviews and even visual documents. Being in continuous development at the Max Planck Institute for Psycholinguistics by now it has become an all-in-one tool for producing transcripts, subtitles, and exporting data in a variety of formats for further analysis.

8.9 References Cited

Black, Steven P. 2017. "Anthropological Ethics and the Communicative Affordances of Audio-Video Recorders in Ethnographic Fieldwork: Transduction as Theory." *American Anthropologist* 119 (1): 46–57. https://doi.org/10.1111/aman.12823.

Duranti, Alessandro. 1997. *Linguistic Anthropology*. Cambridge: Cambridge University Press.

Edmonds, Rosalie. 2021. "Balancing research goals and community expectations: The affordances of body cameras and participant observation in the study of wildlife conservation." In "Researchers' Participation Roles in Video-based Fieldwork," special issue, *Social Interaction: Video-Based Studies of Human Sociality* 4 (2).

Gan, Yumei, Christian Greiffenhagen, and Stuart Reeves. 2020. "Connecting Distributed Families: Camera Work for Three-Party Mobile Video Calls." In *Proceedings of the 2020 CHI Conference on Human Factors in Computing Systems*, 1–12. Honolulu, HI: Association for Computing Machinery. https://doi.org/10.1145/3313831.3376704.

García-Sánchez, Inmaculada M. 2014. *Language and Muslim Immigrant Childhoods: The Politics of Belonging*. Chichester, West Sussex: Wiley-Blackwell.

Geertz, Clifford. 1973. *The Interpretation of Cultures: Selected Essays*. New York: Basic Books.

Goffman, Erving. (1961) 1972. *Encounters: Two Studies in the Sociology of Interaction*. Harmondsworth, Middlesex: Penguin.

Goico, Sara, Katila, Julia, Yumei Gan, and Marjorie Harness Goodwin, eds. 2021. "Researchers' Participation Roles in Video-based Fieldwork." Special Issue, *Social Interaction: Video-Based Studies of Human Sociality* 4 (2).

Goodwin, Charles. 1993. "Recording Human Interaction in Natural Settings." *Pragmatics* 3 (2): 181–209.

Goodwin, Charles. 1994. "Professional Vision." *American Anthropologist* 96 (3): 606–33.

Goodwin, Charles. 2009. "Video and the Analysis of Embodied Human Interaction." In Ulrike Tikvah Kissmann ed., *Video Interaction Analysis: Methods and Methodology*, 21–40. Frankfurt: Peter Lang.

Goodwin, Charles. 2018. *Co-Operative Action*. Cambridge: Cambridge University Press.

Goodwin, Marjorie Harness. 2006. *The Hidden Life of Girls: Games of Stance, Status, and Exclusion*. Malden, MA and Oxford: Blackwell.

Goodwin, Marjorie Harness, and Asta Cekaite. 2018. *Embodied Family Choreography: Practices of Control, Care, and Mundane Creativity*. London and New York: Routledge.

Hauck, Jan David. 2016. "Making Language: The Ideological and Interactional Constitution of Language in an Indigenous Aché Community in Eastern Paraguay." PhD diss., University of California, Los Angeles.

Heath, Christian, Jon Hindmarsh, and Paul Luff. 2010. *Video in Qualitative Research: Analysing Social Interaction in Everyday Life*. London: Sage.

İkizoğlu, Didem. 2020. "Agency and Participation in Multilingual Family Interaction." PhD diss., Georgetown University.

Kissmann, Ulrike Tikvah, ed. 2009. *Video Interaction Analysis: Methods and Methodology*. Frankfurt: Peter Lang.

Lahlou, Saadi. 2011. "How Can We Capture the Subjects Perspective? An Evidence-Based Approach for the Social Scientist." *Social Science Information* 50 (3–4): 607–55. https://doi.org/10.1177/0539018411411033.

McIlvenny, Paul. 2019. "Inhabiting Spatial Video and Audio Data: Towards a Scenographic Turn in the Analysis of Social Interaction." *Social Interaction: Video-Based Studies of Human Sociality* 2 (1). https://doi.org/10.7146/si.v2i1.110409.

Mitsuhara, Teruko Vida. 2019. "Moving toward Utopia: Language, Empathy, and Chastity among Mobile Mothers and Children in Mayapur, West Bengal." PhD diss., University of California, Los Angeles.

Mondada, Lorenza. 2006. "Video Recording as the Reflexive Preservation and Configuration of Phenomenal Features for Analysis." In Hubert Knoblauch, Bernt Schnettler, Jürgen Raab, and Hans-Georg Soeffner eds., *Video Analysis: Methodology and Methods; Qualitative Audiovisual Data Analysis in Sociology*, 51–67. Frankfurt: Peter Lang.

Ochs, Elinor, Anthony P. Graesch, Angela Mittmann, Thomas Bradbury, and Rena Repetti. 2006. "Video Ethnography and Ethnoarchaeological Tracking." In Marcie Pitt-Catsouphes, Ellen Ernst Kossek, and Stephen

Sweet eds., *The Work and Family Handbook: Multi-Disciplinary Perspectives, Methods, and Approaches*, 387–409. Mahwah, NJ: Lawrence Erlbaum.

Schieffelin, Bambi B. 1990. *The Give and Take of Everyday Life: Language Socialization of Kaluli Children*. Cambridge: Cambridge University Press.

Smith, Michael Sean. 2018. "Constituting Interaction and Phenomena in Geological Practice: A Study in the Interactive Organization of Talk, Bodies, and Phenomenal Landscapes and Their Public Revealing as Consequential Worlds in Geological Fieldwork." PhD diss., University of California, Los Angeles.

Speer, Susan A., and Ian Hutchby. 2003. "From Ethics to Analytics: Aspects of Participants' Orientations to the Presence and Relevance of Recording Devices." *Sociology* 37 (2): 315–37. https://doi.org/10.1177/0038038503037 002006.

8.10 Further Reading

Black, Steven P. 2017. "Anthropological Ethics and the Communicative Affordances of Audio-Video Recorders in Ethnographic Fieldwork: Transduction as Theory." *American Anthropologist* 119 (1): 46–57. https://doi.org/10.1111/aman.12823.

Heath, Christian, Jon Hindmarsh, and Paul Luff. 2010. *Video in Qualitative Research: Analysing Social Interaction in Everyday Life*. London: Sage.

Mondada, Lorenza. 2006. "Video Recording as the Reflexive Preservation and Configuration of Phenomenal Features for Analysis." In Hubert Knoblauch, Bernt Schnettler, Jürgen Raab, and Hans-Georg Soeffner eds., *Video Analysis: Methodology and Methods; Qualitative Audiovisual Data Analysis in Sociology*, 51–67. Frankfurt: Peter Lang.

9

Transcription and Analysis in Linguistic Anthropology: Creating, Testing, and Presenting Theory on the Page

Merav Shohet and Heather Loyd

9.1 Introduction

Data are the bread and butter of linguistic anthropologists' craft, just as they are for any scientist. In the process of collecting and interpreting data, linguistic anthropologists create theory and expand on existing theories. We gain new insights about the phenomena we observe and the concepts we develop, come to question, refine, or extend by closely working with the data we collect and transcribe in the field and long after returning "home." Previous chapters walked readers through the process of initiating research and collecting the data necessary to answer significant and interesting questions in linguistic anthropology. This chapter focuses on *what to do with the data collected*. Transcription and analysis, we emphasize throughout, constitute an iterative process of selection and interpretation.

Advances in technology have made it easier and cheaper to collect ever more comprehensive corpora of audiovisual material to be analyzed. These data help scholars answer their original research questions and generate new ones. Just as the process of collecting data is selective—in the sense that one must always choose which events to attend, which practices to observe and record, and whom to talk to—transcription is even more so, in turn spawning further analyses and interpretations. Geertz's (1973) truism that layers of meaning multiply "turtles all the way down" the deeper we dig means that we have to be selective about where to stop and analyze, knowing that there is always more to observe and interpret.

One feature that distinguishes linguistic anthropologists from sociocultural theorists may be our approach to what and how to transcribe. Seeing language as constitutive of the sociocultural worlds we inhabit, we take communication as a prime lens for accessing experience, from our most minute, phenomenologically-oriented being-in-the-world, to the larger structures of power that constrain and afford (but never fully determine) social groups' relations. Through transcripts, linguistic anthropologists translate the rich cornucopia of semiotic resources that constitute participants' social environment—and thus experience—into a two-dimensional space. In Alessandro Duranti's (2006) formulation, transcripts are "like shadows on a wall": they are skeletal, selective representations of a rich phenomenal world that allow ethnographers to draw their audience's attention to specific features of that world in order to make convincing claims about it.

Ethnographers might ask if the transcript of a recorded slice of an interview or interaction should simply capture what was vocalized. Why might that not be enough? In the following pages, we address this by walking readers through key steps for logging, transcribing, and coding data to build theory. In line with linguistic anthropologists (e.g., de León 2015; C. Goodwin 1994; M. H. Goodwin and Cekaite 2018) and conversation analysts (e.g., Mondada 2016, 2019), we suggest that attending to the rich, multimodal features of interactions, including, for example, participants' gestures, movements, eye gaze, facial expressions, pacing, pitch, and a plethora of other communicative cues that generate and encode meaning in their worlds, we become better positioned to make claims about those worlds which we seek to study. In this sense, it is useful to think of transcription and analysis as a series of funnels and spirals: funnels that, through selection, translate the rich world of experience onto the two-dimensional space of a page (whether paper or digital), and spirals that, in the recursive process of selecting and analyzing data collected and coded, generate ever-more expansive layers of meaning comprehensible to our various audiences, from the people engaged in the phenomena we study, to our varied readers (See Figure 9.1).

How do we go about this process? First, the anthropologist must decide what to collect and how to collect it, as discussed in earlier chapters. This of

Figure 9.1 A funnel–spiral illustrates the recursive nature of collecting, selecting, transcribing, and analyzing data

course relates to the kinds of questions with which we set out into the field, which entails making further decisions and adjustments in the course of fieldwork. Ideally, one should begin transcribing—and therefore analyzing—data while still in the field, preferably with the aid of the people whom we study. And even before rendering speech and other features of interaction into a transcript, it is useful to continually listen to, watch, or otherwise review the data that have been collected and to begin logging these. Not the devil, but delight, is in the data!

9.2 Taking Stock of What We Have and What More We Need: Logging

Logging—whether by activity, theme, place, or another code—is an intermediary step between data collection and analysis (Ochs and Kremer-Sadlik 2013). Logging streamlines the process of transcription and is indeed a key precursor activity that helps us initiate a transcript: a text object that we can further analyze. As we collect, log, and transcribe data, we generate hypotheses, questions, interpretations, and, ultimately, theory. The amount of data collected can feel overwhelming when we consider the countless pages of participant-observation notes, photographs, audio, and video

264   Research Methods in Linguistic Anthropology

recordings that a linguistic anthropologist might collect during fieldwork. Logging these data helps researchers to

1. get a sense of what has been collected (so far) and get an idea about what we still need, as well as possible follow-up questions to ask participants, if possible;
2. begin to organize the corpus by generating themes and questions; and
3. select the "juicy bits" of data to examine in more detail and to more fully transcribe those bits.

What do we mean by "juicy bits"? As we log, we start seeing things that excite us, surprise us, or spawn new questions. The juicy bits are the things that stick out and make us want to dig deeper and analyze. They are also the instances we want to collect more of and that get us to ask more questions and ultimately expand upon or develop new theory (for more on linking research questions to theory, see Richland, this volume). As we take stock of the juicy bits, we start to see patterns. These patterns may be gendered, situational (e.g., distinct phonology, gestures, or clothes and speech in formal versus informal settings), or in other ways addressee-related (e.g., distinctions emerge based on the addressee's age, race, social role, etc.), and a combination of these. Patterns may also vary by the types of activities and linguistic or other semiotic elements at hand. We mark these as the portions to transcribe first, whether with analytical software (e.g., NVivo, Dedoose, Transana, ELAN) or using our own color-coding or other system.

Logging and selecting are iterative and recursive processes, where we choose what categories are most relevant to our study and specific analysis. Some possibilities include logging the data according to the activity, participants, themes, location, or scene. Codes used—that is, the labels we deploy to categorize our data—can refer to both activities and topics of discussion. Ideally, logs should note timestamps for each item, to help us easily locate scenes of interest to return to and expand on.

Logging is not simply listing. It is already an analytic and interpretive step. It requires making decisions about what to log, what might be categorized together under the same code, how to delineate when an activity begins or ends, or even what is worth noting down. It is often a good idea to do this with a language assistant or expert who can provide an emic understanding of the activities examined, particularly when working with languages that researchers are still learning, as we further discuss below (see also Schieffelin 1979, 1990).

Consider the following examples, which demonstrate how one could go about creating an activity log and definition of its codes. Note how this log provides both the file time and clock time for when the recording was made, and how it includes codes about where the activity took place (in which room) and what type of activity or sets of activities were observed (see Figures 9.2 and 9.3). This helped the UCLA Center on Everyday Lives of Families (CELF) team of multidisciplinary analysts working on the same data corpus to select relevant scenes of interest to their respective projects (Ochs and Kremer-Sadlik 2013).[1]

Activity Log	Participants Codes	Location Codes
Videofile#	Father: Chris	LV = living room
F23_02_04_04_A09	Mother: Luisa	PBR = parent's bedroom
Day of the Week:	Child 1: Linda, 10	CBR = child's bedroom
Wednesday	Child 2: Luke, 8	KT = kitchen
Date: August 24, 2004		GR = garage
Family: Richardson		FR = family room
		DR = dining room
		BTH = bathroom
		BY = backyard
		FY = frontyard

[FOOD, HUMOR, PLAY, RESEARCHER, HOUSEHOLD, ARRIVAL, DISCIPLINE, CONFLICT, FOOD, RECREATION, TV, GROOM, READ, RELIGION, SCHOOL, STORIES, HEALTH, JOB]

Time Code	Clock Time	Activity
00:00:00	17:52	KT/ Father cutting food in the kitchen and children are singing a song. [FOOD, HUMOR]
00:00:31	17:53	Father joins children in re-enacting a scene from a movie. [HUMOR]
00:01:34	17:54	Linda and Luke pretend they are a character from *Lord of the Rings*. [PLAY]
00:02:15	17:55	KT/ Father explains *Lord of the Rings* to researcher. [RESEARCHER]
00:03:21	17:56	Linda and Luke continue to talk about *Lord of the Rings*. [PLAY]
00:03:59	17:56	KT/ Father begins cooking dinner. [FOOD]
00:04:22	17:57	Father asks Luke to play piano.
00:04:38	17:57	DR/ Luke and Linda wrestle at the dinning room table. [PLAY]
00:05:08	17:58	KT/ Father cleans off cutting board. [HOUSEHOLD]
00:06:27	17:59	DR/ Luke and Linda play rock, paper, and scissors to decide who plays piano first. [PLAY]
00:07:13	18:00	Mother arrives at home. [ARRIVAL]

Figure 9.2 Excerpt from the CELF study's activity logs

UCLA Center on Everyday Lives of Families
Activity Log Categories

These codes refer to activities as well as topics of discussion:

1. **Food** – meal, snack, eating, cooking
2. **Play** – games, pretend play
3. **Affection** – hugs, kisses, pats
4. **School** – homework, talk about school
5. **Household** – cleaning, washing, taking out garbage, going through mail, work in yard
6. **Job** – work brought home from parent job, talk about parent job
7. **TV** – watching TV, talk about TV
8. **Computer** – email, games, internet, etc.
9. **Phone** – any talking on phone
10. **Groom** – washing, bathing, brushing teeth, dressing, fixing hair, etc.
11. **Conflict** – arguing, clear difficulty in family interaction
12. **Bedtime** – bedtime activities, getting ready for bed, talk about bedtime, bedtime stories
13. **Read** – reading mail, newspapers, magazines, books
14. **Home** – home decorating, beautification, improvement, remodeling, upgrading
15. **Health** – illness, medication, injury

Figure 9.3 Excerpt from the CELF study's code definitions of activity logs

9.3 Decisions, Decisions: What and Why to Transcribe

At the same time that we strive to collect and log as much data as possible, we also begin the process of transcribing, ideally when still in the field. Like other research activities, transcription is an iterative and recursive process that will continue long after data are collected, and it entails both coming armed with and building theory (Ochs 1979). We first select segments of recorded data by asking what is interesting or provocative about them, and then we make decisions about how to represent them. Our decisions are political acts, as we elaborate below.

At the initial stage, it is better to select more than what we will end up representing to our target audiences, since we have yet to discover the patterns that will ultimately be the crux of our analysis. Yet, already, there are scenes that either affirm what we were expecting to find or that contradict our initial hunches and hypotheses. Both confirmatory and contradictory data are important to select, transcribe, and code (as discussed below) to create or refine our theories and answer our original and new or emerging research questions.

In an ideal world, we would transcribe *everything*, while continuing to highlight segments of particular interest. Unfortunately, we do not always have enough resources to transcribe all our data immediately, especially when there is the added layer of translation from another language to the target audience's language. The good news is that, depending on the type of ethical approval one has received (see Black and Conley-Riner, this volume), ethnographers may keep their recorded data for future transcription and (re)analysis. As a rule, it is a good idea—and even imperative—to have multiple copies of collected data, labeled in a systematic fashion, that we may access in the future, even as technology continues to change. At the same time, it is important to protect these data from breaches of confidentiality in our increasingly mediatized world (for more on video ethnography and recording technologies in the field, see Kohler and Murphy, this volume; Mitsuhara and Hauck, this volume).

Bridging our time spent in the field and conversations with our various future audiences, transcripts are multilayered products. They allow us to see a whole world in a little grain of sand, for it is often in small strips of interaction that we glimpse cultural patterns of hierarchy, morality, ways of being a person, or enacting conflict, community, and belonging. Yet transcripts cannot stand alone: for others to comprehend what we "see" and find significant in our transcripts, we must pick transcript segments and layouts that are particularly illustrative of the phenomena we wish others to learn from, and we must explicate these segments and our decisions to represent them in these ways (Ochs 1979).

How do we choose which parts of the world to represent and how to represent them? In the beginning, we rely on inklings and hunches based on what we learned through reading relevant literature, engaging with other theories, and conducting ethnographic fieldwork, where we can see the cultural universe and sets of power dynamics at play (see Richland, this volume). Alternatively, selected strips of interaction may contradict what we thought was happening and allow us to see things in a new light. Collaboration with participants is key: they are the experts of their own lives, and it is a good idea to ask them what is going on in the recordings.

Early linguists and anthropologists developed the IPA transcription system to ensure phonetic accuracy. Yet this is not always what linguistic anthropologists and other analysts are most interested in, since another consideration is whether the transcript will be accessible to a wider audience and to the participants themselves (assuming they are literate). Further, different languages have different ways of representing sounds, as well as standards for what a word "ought" to sound or look like, which may not be how it actually sounds (Boas 1889; Bucholtz 2000; Duranti 1994). This can be of analytic interest, for example, when considering different registers of speech that are associated with different statuses within a given society, including, for example, gender, race, class, age, and so on. Moreover, as linguistic anthropologists, we rely on much more than words alone to grasp how people act, think, and feel. We also pay attention to features of delivery and poetics within speech segments and across interactions. As such, even silence is potentially meaningful and analyzable in its own right, as Norma Mendoza-Denton (1995) demonstrates in her analysis of pregnant pauses during the 1991 Anita Hill-Clarence Thomas senate hearings.

In short, "transcription involves both interpretive decisions (What is transcribed?) and representational decisions (How is it transcribed?)" (Bucholtz 2000, 1439). Minimally, a transcript tends to include which participant said what and in what sequence and notes about the context of the utterances, such as the setting of the scene, including when and where the interaction took place and who was present. At times, linguistic anthropologists may attend closely to the phonetic and syntactic features of speech, and to distinct metapragmatic usages such as pitch, elongation, or phonemic productions, as these may reveal differences between groups of speakers' social statuses and roles. Additionally, we may also attend to overlaps, pauses, false starts, (self-)repair, and so forth when analyzing how the delivery of talk and uses of the body construct specific actions in interaction with others.[2] To this end, when the data consist of audiovisual materials, it is often productive to note non-vocalized features of the interaction, such as eye gaze, facial expressions, gestures, touch, body posture, movements through space, and so on. This is not simply to try to represent "everything" that was happening, since such a wish is an impossibility, and likely unwise because it would make the transcript unwieldy. Rather, the analyst selects segments of perception to highlight as evidence for the claims being advanced in the analysis. Still, because transcription and analysis are iterative processes, there are certain "best practices," such as transcribing as much as possible in as much detail as possible and placing each action and sub-clause within a turn at talk on a separate line, to allow the analyst to visualize embedded, if less than fully conscious, features of the discourse, as we discuss further below.

As linguistic anthropologists transcribe and review linguistic data, we write additional notes and memos (annotations) to ourselves about insights into the cultural dynamics that we gain from the transcripts. Memos might address questions such as the following:

- Which practices do we need to pay more attention to?
- What patterns are starting to emerge?
- Is there situational variation?
- What are the social functions of particular practices?
- What meanings do practices hold for the participants?
- How are practices interconnected?
- How are the (micro) language and communication practices connected to (macro) cultural frameworks?

As noted earlier, transcribing recordings with the help of participants and other native experts (when not working in our own language) is especially important, since they provide insights and metalinguistic commentary on what constitutes particular speech acts and normative ideas about how people do and ought to talk. Collaborative annotation is often the basis for generating further questions about communicative practices and events and allows us to create and test theories with participants in the annotation process. As Bambi Schieffelin (1990, 30–1) notes, the activity of listening to recordings with participants and observing their reactions helped her

> understand the roles that prosody, voice quality, affect-marked affixes and expressives, and formulaic expressions played in conveying affect, and how the pragmatic use of word order disambiguated utterances and indicated what was at issue. These transcripts of situated speech plus the elicitation sessions based on them, focusing on verb morphology, the case-marking and pronominal systems, syntactic variation, and metalinguistics, provided the data for a linguistic sketch of Kaluli and an analysis of children's psycholinguistic development.

In short, annotating transcripts with participants is key for extending the contextualizing ethnographic and linguistic information, which allows us to interpret the significance of interaction. A key step in this work of interpretation is coding, which helps us figure out what are the interesting things to show in our data, as we discuss next.

9.4 Coding: How We Continually Build and Refine Theory

Throughout the research process, anthropologists rely on empirical data to try to figure out what is going on, what is at stake for research participants, and how cultural practices and patterns relate to larger-scale structures of power. We label, or code, these relations, just as we label the smaller chunks of evidence that we marshal to formulate and support our theories. Sifting through and transcribing our data help us to identify themes and patterns that seem worth writing about and investigating further. We begin this process by logging and continue to organize and reorganize the data throughout, since cutting up slices of life into categories and themes presents an ongoing challenge, calling us to define and delimit what constitutes given phenomena, and how to work through the many layers of meaning (Geertz's "turtles") that we come to see in our corpora. Qualitative analysis typically consists of building grounded theory (Corbin 2015), where we let the categories emerge from the data, even as we also come equipped with preconceived labels for how to categorize those data.

All data—observations, fieldnotes, naturally occurring linguistic recordings, interviews, informal conversations, newspaper articles, website contents, photographs, and so on—can be used to create grounded theory. As we pore over these, we begin to organize them into categories, sorting sets into smaller, interconnected piles that we label and code. Acts of labeling and organizing allow us to discover patterns and themes in the data and to link them with other patterns and themes (LeCompte and Schensul 1999, 3). We do not code all piles of data with the same level of granularity, just as we may not log or transcribe everything with the same level of detail: we always have to be selective, while trying to be as thorough as possible, for example, by reading and rereading our transcripts, re-watching and re-listening to our recordings, discussing them with participants, field assistants, colleagues, mentors, and so on.

Coding involves attaching names or labels to (segments of) interviews, conversations, or fieldnotes and describing events and incidents, words, sentences, or phrases that recur or stand out for us. These labels consist of the concepts and ideas that we single out for analysis and elaboration. Gradually or quickly, we have "ah-ha moments" where we begin to abstract a number of ideas contained in a single concept or small set of related concepts (DeWalt and DeWalt 2011). This allows us to identify patterns, such as the rhetorical strategies of resilience identified by Loyd (2012) and asymmetrical reciprocity and sacrifice theorized in Shohet (2021), as we will discuss below. Our labels typically come from both the literature we read in preparing our projects and from our participants themselves. Additionally, as analysts, we come up with our own labels, drawing on our experiences of the world and in the field. We repeatedly test our concepts and labels, to determine if they can apply more broadly to other events, practices, situations, people, and so on.

For linguistic anthropologists, coding data is not solely focused on cultural categories and verbalized content (*what* people say or do), but also on form (*how* they say and do it). For example, we can attend to grammatical, prosodic, or discursive features within particular utterances, genres, conversational sequences, or other communicative encounters, including written texts such as social media posts and public inscriptions (e.g., posters, advertisements, instructional material, or prayers) and other semiotic acts and embodied practices like makeup, tattoos, clothes, movements, and so on (see e.g., Ahearn 2001; Bucholtz 2011; de León 2017; García-Sánchez 2014; Gershon 2010; Harkness 2014; Hillewaert 2016; Jacobs-Huey 2006; Jones 2011; Keane 1997; Mendoza-Denton 2008; Nakassis 2016; Shankar 2015). Attending to such features can also clue us in to when participants may joke or hold back to leave things unsaid and theorize these silences and omissions as well (see e.g., Black 2019; Samuels forthcoming; Shohet 2021).

To establish her grounded theory of Neapolitan girls' "Rhetoric of Resilience" in Italy, for example, Loyd began by reading and rereading her fieldnotes and coding them for recurring themes that were relevant to the everyday lives of her participants. For each paragraph, she added relevant thematic labels in brackets with an asterisk after each item so she could easily search for it later on (e.g., ROMANCE*; CONFLICT*). These thematic categories emerged from the data, as throughout fieldwork, Loyd noticed the importance of both romance and conflict in the girls' lives. Whenever Loyd had the girls interview each other as part of her child-centered methodology (Hecht 1998), the first question they asked was, "Do you have a boyfriend?" They initiated interviews in this way even when they already knew whether or not the interviewee had a boyfriend and then continued to ask questions about relationships past and present. This interest in romance similarly appeared any time Loyd was introduced to another woman, as the first question women and girls would ask her was, "Are you married" or "Do you have a boyfriend?," which was also a question that they asked if they ran into a girl or woman in the neighborhood that they had not seen in a while. Similarly, Loyd noted the prevalence of conflict talk ("*appiccecarse*") in the neighborhood, both among girls' peer groups and within their families. Loyd observed that participants were frequently involved in conflicts (exemplified by Excerpt 3 below, in the next section) and loved to talk about their own and others' conflicts, taking pleasure in reporting to her about these events in exacting detail.

Around the same time as coding her fieldnotes, Loyd started logging her video-recorded data with a research assistant who helped translate the girls' and their families' interactions from Neapolitan into Italian. Here, too, she noticed that conflict talk often centered around romance and relationships, including flirting, courting, stealing boyfriends, or cheating on partners. Logging and coding these data helped Loyd realize that there was something interesting happening at the intersection of romance and conflict in her fieldsite, so when transcribing with her assistants, she made sure not to miss any conversations involving either or both of romance and conflict.

Loyd initially went into the field searching for problem-solving practices that children employed to secure their social networks, gain prestige, and handle life predicaments in an area known for its high rates of unemployment, school dropouts, and underground economy. She unexpectedly discovered that orientations toward romance and conflict were precisely how girls carved out status in a place that does not offer many avenues for women to gain power or control (for more on how questions and projects shift in the field, see Jones and Gershon, this Volume). From literature and her own southern Italian family, Loyd knew that Neapolitans were renowned for their theatricality, wit, and verbal prowess. It was not until she started to transcribe in great detail both verbal and embodied practices, however, that she came to realize just how rhetorically skilled Neapolitans were—even at the age of five.

Loyd coded all conflict- and romance-talk transcripts for cultural themes and rhetorical practices. Following Elinor Ochs and Lisa Capps (2001), who analyze narrative in interaction, Loyd coded the transcripts for participants' transgressions and moral assumptions, to decipher what was at stake (i.e., *why* the girls were fighting), and called this the "moral logic of conflict." Loyd's codes included such themes as "Rights, Power & Control," "Boys, Romance, & Femininity," "Honor & Respect," and "Belonging and Exclusion." Secondly, following Marjorie H. Goodwin (1990, 2006), Loyd analyzed *how* the girls were fighting and handled transgressions (i.e., she coded for their "rhetorical practices of resilience"). Here, she coded for such practices as threats, directives, insults, justifications, and negative person descriptors, as well as gestures, eye gaze, and prosody. As typically happens in the analysis process, Loyd (2011) ended up lumping some codes together while taking others apart. For example, she lumped "honor" with "respect" while splitting "conflict" into such sub-codes as "threats," "bald directives," "rhetorical questions," and so on. She then further split the code "threat" into "unmitigated threats," "conditional threats," "ambiguous threats," and "threats through rhetorical questions."

Loyd's coding process entailed printing out all of her transcripts. She then used highlighters and colored sticky tabs to denote the different themes and rhetorical practices within the conflicts. She also wrote memos about the practices and relations between them, which formed the genesis of the analysis that became her dissertation and future publications. In retrospect, Loyd might have benefited from coding her data in a qualitative analysis software program such as NVivo, ATLAS.ti, Dedoose, Transana, ELAN, or MAXQDA, which allow researchers to organize their data digitally by logging, coding, and adding memos within the program, and then generating visualizations of key themes that emerge. For example, NVivo generates graphs of the most used codes and lists which terms emerge around another term—images that can be included in support of the analytic focus put forth in a given publication.

In her study of anorexia (discussed subsequently), Shohet followed a similar coding and analysis process. She arrived at her conclusions about extremely slim and (self-)starving women's illness and recovery genres as discursively consequential for their experience with eating disorders by modeling the dimensional approach to narrative analysis devised by Capps and Ochs (1995) and Ochs and Capps (2001), who examine the relationship between grammar and psychological dispositions. This approach demonstrates that the ways in which people linguistically formulate their thoughts and feelings shape their experiences of the world (see also Ochs 2012). In their study of an agoraphobic woman named Meg, Capps and Ochs identify grammatical features and semantic constructions that lead Meg to narrate herself as "helpless" and "abnormal." She does so by non-self-consciously using such grammatical resources as reason adverbs and adverbials (e.g., "all of a sudden, I realized"), try constructions (e.g., "the more I tried the worse it became"), and intensifiers and de-intensifiers (e.g., "It was *SO:::* awful" and "That was kind of how I coped"), as well as semantic constructions of herself as a non- or diminished agent (e.g., "anxiety just overtook me" or "I can't leave") that narratively frame her as an inevitably helpless victim of panic (see Capps and Ochs 1995, 56–75).

Shohet loosely followed this model to code for the narrators' degrees of certainty (e.g., using "I know" and "I realized" versus "I don't know" or

"I think"); affiliation with institutional accounts of eating disorders (e.g., deploying biomedical, psychodynamic, or feminist tropes); porousness between their past and present narrated selves (e.g., "recovery is always gonna be a defeat" versus "before my anorexia, I was a façade [...] *but*, when I came out, I was a real person, [...] I'm *not* a façade"); and temporal and moral linearity (e.g., presenting events as having a clear beginning, middle, and end or as cyclical, and voicing assuredness or ambivalence and contradiction) (see Excerpt 1). In closely reexamining her detailed transcripts, Shohet discovered that the very grammar and interactional features of the women's narratives, including such elements as adverb and verb phrases, progressive tense verbs, and direct reported speech clustered together to constitute the genres that she identifies, namely, the "fully recovered," "struggling to recover," and "eluding a diagnosis" genres (see summary in Shohet 2007, 249; 2018b). As in Loyd's case, the process of coding and adapting previous scholars' codes and analytic frameworks to make sense of (new) patterns embodies ethnographic theory-building: we examine new data and arrive at new theoretical insights and concepts (e.g., "the logic of conflict" or "genres of illness and recovery") by linking micro practices to macro processes that we and others document, interpret, and theorize, continually moving between adopting, refining, or extending conceptual frameworks to explain our findings (Fife 2005).

Shohet carried her interest in genres of discourse to fieldwork in Vietnam, where she examined both ordinary and ritual life events. While ritual analysis typically attends to what people say and how they use their bodies in space, it can sometimes be important to "transcribe" the written signs that shape participants' worlds and constrain their engagements with that world, as the following example illustrates.[3] For instance, Shohet discovered that the multitude of photographs she snapped of funerary inscriptions outside and inside a participant's home following his death revealed an intricate story about how the dead are to be mourned and remembered inside the home (among kin and close friends), versus outside the home (in front of more diverse public audiences of fellow citizens) in Vietnam. These insights were not gained by interviewing mourners in the midst of their grief, for this seemed insensitive and unethical to do. Rather, they were gained through a close examination, and coding, of the photographs' communicative qualities after Shohet presented a more psychologically oriented paper on how grief is managed in the wake of a loved one's death, and audience members asked questions about the pictures' written contents.

In the field, Shohet observed that funerals bore seemingly standardized inscriptions that announce the identity of the deceased and their mourners and the schedule of rituals that would lead to the burial. Having documented the various text artifacts and participants involved at such an event at the mourning family's request, Shohet ultimately coded for the different inscriptions' location and placement, materiality, colors, scripts, and message contents, as well as who viewed which artifact (see, e.g., Figure 9.4 in Shohet 2018a, 63).

In this Vietnamese funeral example, linguistic analysis focused less on people's utterances and modes of speaking than on the semiotic-material artifacts that framed and proscribed spaces for the expression of emotion by mourners. Written forms, in their varied materiality, are

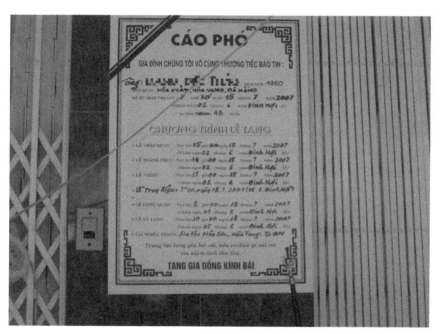

Figure 9.4 A funerary inscription coded for its placement (indoor or outdoor); material (paper or cloth); color (black and white or colorful); medium (printed or embroidered); script (Traditional Chinese, Romanized Vietnamese, or Sino-Romanized script); and audience (close family and friends or broader public).

evidently rich sites not only for sociocultural knowledge, but also for affect production that exceeds their semantic content, as Shohet details in an article that connects Vietnamese burial practices, historical legacies of war, and past and new usages of Traditional Chinese, contemporary standard (Romanized) Vietnamese, and a new script that has emerged to mark life cycle rituals such as weddings and funerals in Vietnam (see Shohet 2018a).

9.5 The Insights and Ethics of Representation: What Is Illuminated in Different Transcript Designs

Having begun to transcribe and code data, we must continually consider how best to present our analyses. Different transcription formats will be appropriate depending on which questions we are trying to answer and depending on other constraints, such as issues of confidentiality and technology used for recordings. Published transcripts also sometimes differ from the transcripts we use in the course of analysis, since different publication venues impose their own sets of constraints. In general, it is a good practice to transcribe more layers than we initially think we need, as the different layers may illuminate additional sets of connections or insights that we may not have anticipated when just listening to or watching a given recording. We can think of this as a "master transcript" that will be modified according to different analytic and representational concerns, since at a later stage in the process it will be important to prune some of the layers to make the transcript as clear as possible for our intended audience. Alternatively, researchers may construct a first-pass, bare bones rudimentary transcript and later build up segments from it for further analysis. This approach may be particularly productive when researchers farm out the transcribing process to assistants or even technological tools such as close-captioning or Rev.com, where accuracy can be quite poor but may substantially cut down the time and labor of initial transcription. With either strategy, it is important to read and reread transcripts for further insights (and accuracy) and to continually make decisions about how best to present our claims to intended audiences.

The following examples illustrate different types of analyses undertaken with different data sets that we and others collected for different projects. We begin with a corpus where interviews with (self-)starving women were only audio-recorded, which means that apart from her interview notes, the analyst was only able to attend to the auditory communicative channel. And yet, as we illustrate below (and began to discuss in the previous section of this chapter), there are many layers to uncover through narrative analysis (see, e.g., Buchbinder 2015; Carr 2011; Mattingly 2010; Samuels 2019).

Intuiting that the variable ways women told their illness and recovery stories signified different ways of experiencing an eating disorder, Shohet devised transcription conventions to depict different features of women's recorded narratives. For example, she marked self-interruptions, long or short pauses, utterances delivered with more emphasis, or in a louder, faster, or slower tone of voice. These transcription conventions, in combination with the decision to break up each monologue into clause-by-clause lines for analysis (see Excerpt 1), helped Shohet "hear" the contours of each woman's story as it was delivered, as well as "see" the different poetic and argumentative structures that emerge. Accordingly, Shohet coded for the significance of rhetorical strategies such as parallelism and repetition (e.g., "I live a life based on **my** terms, **my** beliefs, **my** values"), causal step-like progressions (e.g., "**Before** my anorexia I was a facade [...] And **then** the eating disorder happened, [...] and I almost died, **and but, when I came out** I was a real person"), or equivocation (e.g., "**Parts of me** want to stop this whole night*mare*, ... **but part of me** loves it, you know?") (Shohet 2007, 357, 365, 367). Including line numbers and bold-facing features of analytic interest were yet other transcription conventions geared to help readers follow her lines of argument.[4]

Even long after the audio-cassette recordings were damaged, Shohet's detailed transcripts have allowed her to reanalyze the data and argue that women at different stages of an illness and recovery continuum recount their experiences using distinctly different genres. Specifically, those who call themselves "fully recovered" narrate more linearly structured accounts that represent the descent to and ascent from illness as a set of steps with a clear delineation of stages marked with strong evidential verbs of knowledge and certainty and lists of typifications that mark affiliation with master narratives about anorexia. Alternatively, women who describe themselves as "struggling to recover" or as overlooked and not diagnosed ("eluding a diagnosis") resort to more hedges and markers of doubt and ambivalence (Shohet 2007, 2018b). For example, "Kaye," a white American college student who struggled with eating, uses trail-offs and hedges (e.g., " ..., " "guess," "just," "kind of," "maybe" in lines 1, 3, and 10), subjunctive constructions (e.g., "I would be" in line 4, "if I were" in line 5), and self-interruptions (lines 7–9) to express ambivalence over her pediatrician's lack of concern about her precipitous weight loss (Shohet 2018b, 505).

Excerpt 1. Example of audio-recorded data transcribed clause by clause, bolding features of analytic interest

1 K: I **guess** it's **just** because ...
2   since I *had* been 140,
3   and like, 20 pounds is **kind of** a significant amount of weight,
4   so I **would think,**
5   **if I were** a doctor–
6   *((chuckles))* which I hope to be one day–
7   I **would be,**
8   I **mean,**
9   I **would think,**
10   **maybe** between 130 and 140 is normal, **but** ...

As discussed earlier, Shohet coded each woman's narrative practices to argue that the women's different discursive strategies are consequential not just for reflecting, but also shaping their illness and recovery experiences.

These days, linguistic anthropologists often collect video-recorded data and consequently may choose to represent a far richer slice of the sensorium recorded, as we see in the following extract from Marjorie Harness Goodwin, Asta Cekaite, and Charles Goodwin (2012, 18–19). In their transcript excerpt below, the authors use line drawings to represent each girl's face and body in relation to others (lines 10–13); pitch contour graphs to reveal the girls' vocal reactions to others (lines 10 and 12); squiggly boxes to represent intonation especially salient in the transcript (lines 9–10 and 12–13); circles to note actors' salient movements (line 11); and arrows and lines pointing to actors' evaluative stances toward one another or joint alignment against each other's utterances (lines 10–11).

Excerpt 2. Example of video-recorded data transcribed to illustrate the wide range of semiotic resources involved in interaction as it unfolds moment by moment

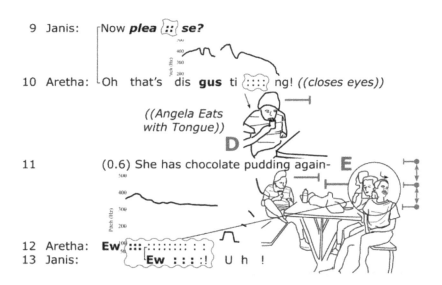

Goodwin et al. (2012) use this elaborate set of annotations to argue that emotions are not simply the internal properties of individuals who externalize them with the use of words or facial expressions. Rather, emotions are an intersubjective achievement produced second by second in the flow of everyday interaction, as participants use a wide range of semiotic resources to display their affective stances (see also Goodwin and Goodwin 2001; Wilce 2009). Goodwin, Cekaite, and Goodwin's transcript design allows us to visualize and almost viscerally hear how girls at a school lunch table position themselves to exclude and marginalize one participant who is poorer and not a part of their in-group. The girls do so not just by refusing to sit next to their classmate (Angela) and suggesting that she sit elsewhere (lines 2–3, not shown here), but also with their vocalized and other embodied expressions of disgust at her food choices and manner of eating.

This rich example demonstrates that analysts can call out a wide variety of verbal and nonverbal communicative elements in a transcript to build their argument and provide evidence for their claims. In this case, the authors link micro-communicative actions detailed in the transcript to larger-scale processes that reinforce social inequality and exclusion. Clearly, there are infinite details to draw readers' attention to in any given interaction, just as happens in our unfocused perception of the world. Left as a stream of consciousness, we may risk the opportunity to gain insight from the dense forest of details. To help readers follow along, then, scholars should (a) offer a clear legend explaining their transcription conventions; (b) explain why they chose to highlight those features specifically; and (c) be mindful of what they choose to represent, prioritizing elements that push the argument forward.

Indeed, in the interest of directing audiences to a specific analytic focus, linguistic anthropologists can select a sparser range of semiotic resources that participants use to construct meaning. For example, to demonstrate how Neapolitan girls (similar to the American ones represented by Goodwin et al. [2012]) use a rich array of communicative resources to competitively insult one another and thereby assert a sense of control over each other and over their own lives, Loyd (2012) delineates participants' rhetorical strategies. Following Goodwin and Goodwin's (2000) method of transcription, Loyd labels the rhetorical strategies line by line in capital letters, in the far-right column of the transcript, and adapts conversation analysis conventions developed by Sacks et al. (1977)—including capital letters to mark increased volume, brackets ([) to mark speech overlap, and italicized comments in parentheses to represent the girls' embodied actions—to help the reader envision the moment-by-moment unfolding of status-building acts (see Hepburn

Transcription and Analysis   281

and Bolden [2013] for a review of the conversation analytic approach to transcription). Together, these transcription decisions help Loyd construct her argument by breaking down each utterance to highlight participants' trajectory of actions.

Excerpt 3. Example of translated, multilingual transcript highlighting participants' rhetorical strategies

1. Susy: Ahh, va' ccà va llà, va' ccà!   ACCUSATION
            Ahh, you go here, you go there, you go here!
            ((*pointing each way*))

2. Marta: Mammà! C' sta facenn' vutà 'a cap'.   ACCUSATION/
            My god! She is making my head spin.   FORMAT TYING

3. Adele: No, ma chell' m' fà girà propri' ll'uocchi'.   ACCUSATION/
            No, but she is making my *eyes* spin.   FORMAT TYING
            ((*making circles around her eyes with index
            finger*))

4. Susy: A me, mi fa' girà- mi fa' girà ll'uocchi' re pall',   ACCUSATION/
            ['e pall' miez' all' uocchi'   FORMAT TYING
            **To me, she is making- she is making my eyes
            of balls- [*eyeballs* spin!**

5. Marina: [Aggi' stà immobile?   RHETORICAL Q
            [Am I supposed to stand still?   AS DEFENSE

6. Adele: Eh! [Stai immobile!   BALD DIRECTIVE/
            Yeah! [Stand still!   FORMAT TYING

7. Susy: [NUN T'HE A MOV'R'! NUN T'HE   BALD DIRECTIVES
            A MOV'R'!
            [DON'T YOU MOVE! DON'T YOU MOVE!
            ((*puts hand around mouth like a megaphone and
            screams in Marina's face*))

Including illustrations of the girls' postures, gestures, and facial expressions could have further enhanced the interaction's legibility. However, since Loyd was restricted by the publication's editor to only include two images (used elsewhere in the chapter), here, she decided to rely on the conversation analysis convention of putting contextual visual semiotic information in double parentheses. Further prioritizing readability while facing the challenge of providing an English-language gloss or translation for participants' uses of both Neapolitan and Italian, Loyd also decided to underline Neapolitan-language utterances to mark them off from those in Italian. She then placed English glosses underneath each original utterance.

Transcribing the two languages (Neapolitan and Italian) presented yet another challenge, since there are multiple ways of representing the phonological combinations produced in each language. This was especially true for Neapolitan, which carries less status than Italian. For purposes of readability, Loyd consequently decided to adapt the orthographic system developed by Neapolitan linguist Nicola De Blasi (2000) to represent speakers' use of Neapolitan as opposed to using participants' writing conventions.

In her ethnographic depictions of Black American communities and their folklore in the 1930s, Zora Neale Hurston (2008 [1935]) made similar choices, insisting on using Black American English (BAE) rather than Standard American English (SAE) orthography to represent her interlocutors' tales. These were political acts, choosing to legitimate and publish a way of speaking devalued by mainstream, dominant (White) society.[5] Indeed, there is no neutral, objective way of transcribing or translating a language, since "all transcripts take sides, enabling certain interpretations, advancing particular interests, [and] favoring specific speakers" (Bucholtz 2000, 1440). Transcribers will differ on which "side to take" and what to foreground or background in relation to the analytic point they seek to advance. These decisions can be quite fraught, since the ethics of representation involves vexing questions to which there is no absolute one right answer. For example, linguistic anthropologists may ask whether we have a responsibility to cast participants in the "best possible light" or not, what that means, to whom, and under what circumstances?

Sometimes, transcribers prefer to privilege legibility for their intended audiences over and above accurate phonological representation or detailed morpheme-by-morpheme linguistic analysis. In the transcript above, for example, Loyd presents idiomatic glosses in English underneath each line of Neapolitan speech. In contrast, Alessandro Duranti (1994) creates a three-line gloss in his discussion of the ways in which senior political orators in Samoa use features of their grammar to mark and sustain their relative statuses.

Samoa is a hierarchical society with an ergative language: speakers use a morpheme, "*e*," to mark human agents as subjects of transitive clauses (i.e., noting direct causality of a subject doing something to a direct object). Duranti noticed, however, that only senior orators used ergative markers, and did so to blame, accuse, or praise others directly, while others in the community were prohibited from doing so. Senior orators' privileged use of ergative markers reinforced systems of power and authority in their hierarchical social system. To illustrate this selective use of ergativity in Samoan, it was essential for Duranti to highlight it in the transcript through a morpheme-by-morpheme gloss in the line between the original Samoan and the English gloss (1994, 122).

Excerpt 4. Example of morpheme-by-morpheme transcription and gloss

Iuli;   mea   lea   'ua   fai   e   Loa.
           thing this PST do ERG Loa
           This is what Loa has done.

Alternatively, when transcripts are directed to a less linguistic (and more sociocultural or religious studies) audience, as in Ayala Fader's discussion of Brooklyn Hasidic girls' use of Yiddish and English, the author may prefer to provide blocks of texts in the original language(s), followed by the English translation as a block of text underneath. As we see in the following excerpt, Fader (2009, 46) italicizes participants' recorded utterances, underlines English words in the majority-Yiddish text and then provides the English gloss as a block of text underneath the entire sequence.

Excerpt 5. Example of translated, multilingual transcript presented as blocks of text

MORAH CHAYA: *Vus maynt a <u>policeman</u> iber de yaytser-hure? A <u>policeman</u> iber de yaytser-hure maynt az indz zol me trakhtn far zikh alayn.* […]

MORAH CHAYA: What does a policeman over the evil inclination mean? A policeman over the evil inclination means that we should think for ourselves.

This transcription design allows Fader to call linguistic anthropologists' attention to instances of code-mixing among Yiddish-speaking women and girls, while allowing other audiences simply to focus on the semantic contents of the participants' speech.

The process of transcription evidently has a double role for linguistic anthropologists. The act of transcription affords scholars the opportunity to see grammatical patterns and their social force, while completed transcripts in turn provide tangible evidence to support the analyst's arguments. In her work on moral personhood and the disposition to sacrifice as an asymmetrically reciprocal relationship in Vietnam, for example, Shohet (2013) arrived at many of her insights in the process of transcribing interactions between caregivers and very young children.

Shohet organized some transcripts as tables with five columns, where the columns represent (from left to right) the line number of interest, the speaker, the English gloss, metapragmatic (nonverbal) features of the interaction, and finally the original Vietnamese utterance. This mode of representation at first was simply an aesthetic solution to two challenges: how to pay simultaneous attention to verbal and nonverbal actions and how to represent English glosses of the Vietnamese utterances.[6]

The table layout made visible the unsurprising observation that adults take many more turns at talk than the toddler and that the vast majority of these turns are directives that index their authority over the toddler. Yet, alongside these directives, the nonverbal channel represented in a second column afforded Shohet the novel insight that adults were not simply demanding respect from the toddler, but also yielding to her. The nonverbal column shows how the toddler's mother firmly demands correct performance, but does this lovingly, by gently molding her daughter's body into the right (normatively expected) embodied position of respect and issuing her commands in a sing-song tone of voice that mitigates the stern force of the directive. Looking at the columns together, Shohet saw how Vietnamese family members enact the mantra to "respect those above and yield to those below" in minute routines such as the leave-taking one represented in the table (Shohet 2021, 88). The architecture of the transcript helped Shohet visualize the connections between the architecture of the interaction and broader sociomoral frameworks that inform enactments of hierarchy and reciprocity in Vietnam.

Excerpt 6. Example of translated, multilingual transcript presented as a table to illustrate the multimodal nature of interaction

Table 1. "Perform Respect to the Neighbors" Transcript

Line #	Speaker	English gloss	(Meta)pragmatic features	Vietnamese
1	Mom	Enough, [let's] go back	*Looking at Em*	Thôi về
2		Ready to go back?	*Matter-of-fact tone*	Về được chưa?
3		[Perform] *ạ* to Minh [before we] go back	*Minh walks over to stand next to Mom*	ạ Minh về
4		*ạ* to Minh [before we] go back	*Minh turns around to look at Em*	ạ Minh về
5	Neighbor Minh	Go "*ạ:*," "*ạ-ạ:::*"	*Nods his head, as does Mom*	A: đi, ạ-ạ:::
6	Em	*ạ::: ạ:*	*Bowing head down, Mom and Minh looking at her*	ạ:::ạ:
7	Mom	Also *ạ* to Vi	*Pointing to Vi*	Ạ Vi nữa lại
8		*ạ* to Vi too [before] going back	*Em turns around to face direction Mom is pointing in*	ạ Vi nữa về
9		*ạ* to Vi over there	*Pointing to Vi*	ạ Vi kìa
10	Em	*Ạ:: =*	*Bending low to bow*	A:: =
11		*ạ:::: ạ:*	*Almost falls, catches balance with her hands, Mom bends over laughing*	ạ:::: ạ:
12	Mom	Enough	*Em gets up*	Thôi
13		Go "*ạ*"	*Mom steps toward Em and flicks her gently*	Ạ đi
14		Fold your hands to perform *ạ* again	*Steps back as Em begins to bow again*	Dòng [vòng] tay lại ạ
15	Em	*Ạ:::*	*Bowing so low that has to balance on hands, hat falls, Mom steps forward*	A:::
16	Mom	Bow to [perform] *ạ* just halfway of course	*Bends by Em, flicks her back lightly but firmly, picks up and puts Em's hat back on*	Ạ dừa dừa [vừa vừa] thôi chớ

Another representational (transcript) choice that proved key in Shohet's analysis was to retain in the English column the Vietnamese particle ạ to parsimoniously represent the gloss "pay respect [using a baby language register] and simultaneously perform a half bow." By looking at the small details of the transcript line by line and in its totality in relation to other observed interactions, we see how repeated daily rituals establish and reinforce larger-scale dispositions and rituals in a community's life. It was the insights gained in the process of transcription that led Shohet to call the combination of respect and yielding "asymmetrical reciprocity" and further theorize it as part of Vietnamese sociomoral organization and the expectation to "sacrifice" (Shohet 2013; 2021).

To allow audiences to see and hear for themselves how the sequences unfold, Shohet decided to include frame grabs and short video clips of the interactions discussed in published materials.[7] In addition, per publishing conventions, she provided a caption ("Em's objectionable compliance with Mom's directives to perform respect") to the series of photos to succinctly describe the social acts being displayed in the images and their direct relevance to the main argument (see Figure 9.5 in Shohet 2021, 92):

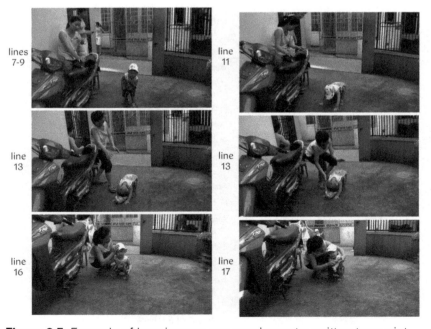

Figure 9.5 Example of how images can supplement a written transcript

Note that although Shohet first secured participants' permission in the field to record them and use these materials in future presentations and publications, for each publication, she has recontacted them to verify that they still agree to being featured. We consider this repeated securing of consent standard ethical practice in anthropology, since the decision to include visual materials risks breaching participants' privacy. Especially in published materials, it is important to try to hide or disguise a participant's identity and refrain from using images that may stigmatize them in some way. It is also important to be reflexive and explicit about the representational choices that we make, including not to disguise participants' identities in some cases (e.g., Briggs and Mantini-Briggs 2016).

Whether highlighting rhetorical strategies in Napoli and Samoa, verbal and nonverbal respect markers in Vietnam, or stances of emotion in Los Angeles, deliberate choices were made by the analyst to move their argument forward. While it could seem completely unremarkable to the person performing the actual act (e.g., mom directing child to use a respect marker plus bow), a linguistic anthropologist's magnifying glass links the on-the-ground micro-interaction to the sociocultural-historical macro-phenomenon, calling the reader's attention to larger issues of morality, hierarchy, asymmetrical reciprocity, socialization into sacrifice and resilience, and so on, with just a short transcript and/or sets of images. In presentations and publications, we show how seemingly abstract cultural frameworks and processes work in everyday life as phenomenologically emergent collaborations between interlocutors. These frameworks and processes are not self-evident. We need to show our audiences how ostensibly banal encounters in participants' lives reflect and constitute the workings of power, hierarchy, and morality in their social worlds.

9.6 Conclusion

As we hope to have shown, analyzing and transcribing data are circular, yet iterative processes. They work like a funnel to select *what* to transcribe and then generate, like spirals, more and more layers of meaning the more we transcribe. These layers can emerge from transcribing a short strip of interaction in increasing detail or accruing sets of similar interactions. The layers combine to paint meaningful and more or less granular patterns that we observe during fieldwork and long after, as we continue our analyses.

Oftentimes, insights emerge from our conversations with others: with participants, field assistants, colleagues, the texts we read, and the various audiences to whom we present our analyses. Interpretation is thus a never-ending process, where we continually go back to the data to re-mine and reanalyze segments. Consequently, it is imperative to re-listen, re-watch, and sometimes re-transcribe data in light of our new questions or insights. In this sense, transcribing and analyzing are bricolage works that are never complete, and always collaborative and redolent with the residues—and sometimes explicit—contributions of others.

In our published works, it is important to be as explicit as possible in noting why we made the selections and decisions that we did, always keeping in mind that data could be interpreted and elaborated in numerous other ways. Further, since analyzed data become the heart of our dissertations, articles, and ethnographic monographs, as we use transcripts to support our arguments, we must select layouts that are detailed enough to evidence our claims and that are clear enough for our different audiences, as well as sensitive to the wishes and needs of fieldwork participants. To find the right balance, it helps to be reflexive and transparent about our choices, as discussed in Bucholtz (2007), to consult with fieldwork participants or assistants if possible and appropriate, and to provide a legend to help our audiences make sense of our transcripts. In these ways, linguistic anthropologists can become ambassadors of sorts between fields like cultural anthropology and linguistics. Our linguistically attuned analyses and transcripts show the former how language works as a rich domain of meaning in its own right and show the latter why ethnography matters for understanding the grammar and pragmatics of the language(s) at hand. In attending to the multimodality of social action and emotion evident in our data collections, we can link these up to the sociocultural processes and power dynamics constituting participants' worlds through detailed (and ever mutable) transcripts.

9.7 Ethnographic Activities

1 Audio- or video-record a fifteen-minute conversation or find a video on YouTube and transcribe it in two different ways. What transcription choices did you make? What are the implications of the choices you made? For example, what did you foreground by doing it in each of

the two ways? What is revealed about the larger sociocultural context by transcribing the segment in those ways? What have you left out by doing so?

2 Using the transcript that you created above, code it for its linguistic and embodied practices. For example, look for displays of politeness and respect, epistemic certainty and authority, power, agency, and community-building through such rhetorical practices as kinship terms, honorifics, animation, insults, cursing, innuendo, metaphors, humor, sarcasm, compliments, hedges, intensifiers, diminutives, silence, laughter, gesture, eye gaze, vowel lengthening, pitch, tone, etc.

9.8 Questions to Consider

1 Consider your intended fieldwork site(s). What are some of the possible categories you would use to initially log activities in your data? What are some of the possible cultural themes that you could code for?

2 What are the benefits of annotating transcripts with participants and other local experts? How might social politics shape what you could or ought to transcribe in the field? What are some consequences for not annotating transcripts with participants or other local experts?

3 What features of discourse, the body, and the built environment might you code for in different types of data (e.g., fieldnotes, interviews, naturally occurring interaction, photographs, social media posts)?

4 When collecting data that include language(s) that differ from the intended audience's target language, what are the advantages and disadvantages of different types of transcript layouts—e.g., two-line versus three-line gloss, side-by-side, or block quotation—for presenting the languages under consideration?

5 What are some of the differences and similarities between testing and creating theory? How would you go about these processes?

9.9 Notes

1 The CELF project was a nine-year interdisciplinary research collaboration between linguistic, sociocultural, medical, and archaeological

anthropologists, applied linguists, clinical psychologists, sociologists, and education specialists that studied how dual-earner, middle-class working families manage their home life. CELF researches (including Loyd and Shohet) collected between 30 and 40 hours of videotaped everyday family interactions for each of the participating thirty-two families between 2002 and 2005. Research methods also included psychological questionnaires (e.g., marital quality, depression, self-esteem); in-depth interviews (e.g., health, education, social networks, and daily routines); measuring, mapping, and photographing the home; home tours recorded and narrated by family members; scan-sampling that systematically tracked participants across time and space; and saliva collection that measured family members' stress levels throughout the day. Logging of the video recordings began soon after each family's data were collected and digitized, before initiating transcription.

2 For more on the symbiotic relationship between linguistic anthropology and conversation analysis, see, e.g., C. Goodwin (2018); M. H. Goodwin (1990); Sidnell (2009).

3 For additional examples of this type of analysis, see also Chumley (2016); Hillewaert (2015); Murphy (2015).

4 Adding line numbers to published transcripts is common but not standardized. Some analysts start from the number 1 for all transcript excerpts, while others use the line numbers from their master transcripts or omit them completely.

5 Whether or not to capitalize Black and/or white as labels for US population segments is a contentious, inherently political/politicized issue, particularly since "White" (with a capital W) indexes White Supremacists, as Kwame Anthony Appiah (2020) and John McWhorter (2020) explain.

6 Since Vietnamese is an isolating language (commonly described as "monosyllabic"), the English language gloss often requires more space, making the placement of English glosses right below or above the Vietnamese aesthetically impractical. In her working transcript, Shohet placed the original Vietnamese in the middle column (3) and the English gloss in the last column (5), but for publication purposes, she realized that readers find it easier to have the English come first, next to the speaker's column (2).

7 To view the clip, see. https://anthrosource.onlinelibrary.wiley.com/action/downloadSupplement?doi=10.1111%2Faman.12004&file=aman12004-sup-0001-MovieS1.mov under "Supporting Information" on the *American Anthropologist* website. The clip has subtitles, but these are unfortunately only viewable with QuickTime Player 7, which is no longer supported by Apple (macOS10.15 and higher can no longer view the subtitles).

9.10 References Cited

Ahearn, Laura M. 2001. *Invitations to Love: Literacy, Love Letters, and Social Change in Nepal*. Ann Arbor: University of Michigan Press.

Appiah, Kwame Anthony. 2020. "The Case for Capitalizing the 'B' in Black." *The Atlantic*, June 18. https://www.theatlantic.com/ideas/archive/2020/06/time-to-capitalize-blackand-white/613159/.

Black, Steven P. 2019. *Speech and Song at the Margins of Global Health: Zulu Tradition, HIV Stigma, and AIDS Activism in South Africa*. New Brunswick: Rutgers University Press.

Boas, Franz. 1889. "On Alternating Sounds." *American Anthropologist* A2 (1): 47–54. https://doi.org/10.1525/aa.1889.2.1.02a00040.

Briggs, Charles L., and Clara Mantini-Briggs. 2016. *Tell Me Why My Children Died: Rabies, Indigenous Knowledge, and Communicative Justice*. Critical Global Health. Durham: Duke University Press.

Buchbinder, Mara. 2015. *All in Your Head: Making Sense of Pediatric Pain*. Oakland, CA: University of California Press.

Bucholtz, Mary. 2000. "The Politics of Transcription." *Journal of Pragmatics* 32 (10): 1439–65. https://doi.org/10.1016/S0378-2166(99)00094-6.

Bucholtz, Mary. 2007. "Variation in Transcription." *Discourse Studies* 9 (6): 784–808. https://doi.org/10.1177/1461445607082580.

Bucholtz, Mary. 2011. *White Kids: Language, Race and Styles of Youth Identity*. Cambridge: Cambridge University Press.

Capps, Lisa, and Elinor Ochs. 1995. *Constructing Panic: The Discourse of Agoraphobia*. Cambridge: Harvard University Press.

Carr, E. Summerson. 2011. *Scripting Addiction: The Politics of Therapeutic Talk and American Sobriety*. Princeton: Princeton University Press.

Chumley, Lily. 2016. *Creativity Class: Art School and Culture Work in Postsocialist China*. Princeton: Princeton University Press.

Corbin, Juliet M. 2015. *Basics of Qualitative Research: Techniques and Procedures for Developing Grounded Theory*. 4th ed. Los Angeles: SAGE.

De Blasi, Nicola. 2000. *Il Napoletano Parlato e Scritto Con Note Di Grammatica Storica*. Napoli: Libreria Dante & Descartes.

de León, Lourdes. 2015. "Mayan Children's Creation of Learning Ecologies by Initiative and Cooperative Action." In Maricela Correa-Chávez, Rebeca Mejía-Arauz, and Barbara Rogoff eds., *Advances in Child Development and Behavior*, 49:153–84. Burlington: Academic Press. https://doi.org/10.1016/bs.acdb.2015.10.006.

de León, Lourdes. 2017. "Texting Amor: Emerging Intimacies in Textually Mediated Romance among Tzotzil Mayan Youth." *Ethos* 45 (4): 462–88. https://doi.org/10.1111/etho.12183.

DeWalt, Kathleen Musante, and Billie R. DeWalt. 2011. *Participant Observation: A Guide for Fieldworkers*. 2nd ed. Lanham, MD: Rowman & Littlefield.

Duranti, Alessandro. 1994. *From Grammar to Politics: Linguistic Anthropology in a Western Samoan Village*. Berkeley: University of California Press.

Duranti, Alessandro. 2006. "Transcripts, Like Shadows on a Wall." *Mind, Culture, and Activity* 13 (4): 301–10. https://doi.org/10.1207/s15327884mca1304_3.

Fader, Ayala. 2009. *Mitzvah Girls: Bringing up the Next Generation of Hasidic Jews in Brooklyn*. Princeton: Princeton University Press.

Fife, Wayne. 2005. *Doing Fieldwork: Ethnographic Methods for Research in Developing Countries and Beyond*. New York: Palgrave Macmillan.

García-Sánchez, Inmaculada Ma. 2014. *Language and Muslim Immigrant Childhoods: The Politics of Belonging*. Chichester, UK: Wiley-Blackwell.

Geertz, Clifford. 1973. *The Interpretation of Cultures: Selected Essays*. New York: Basic Books.

Gershon, Ilana. 2010. *The Breakup 2.0: Disconnecting over New Media*. Ithaca, NY: Cornell University Press.

Goodwin, Charles. 1994. "Professional Vision." *American Anthropologist* 96 (3): 606–33. https://doi.org/10.1525/aa.1994.96.3.02a00100.

Goodwin, Charles. 2018. *Co-Operative Action*. Learning in Doing. New York: Cambridge University Press.

Goodwin, Marjorie Harness. 1990. *He-Said-She-Said: Talk as Social Organization among Black Children*. Bloomington: Indiana University Press.

Goodwin, Marjorie Harness. 2006. *The Hidden Life of Girls: Games of Stance, Status, and Exclusion*. Malden, MA: Blackwell.

Goodwin, Marjorie Harness, and Asta Cekaite. 2018. *Embodied Family Choreography: Practices of Control, Care, and Mundane Creativity*. London: Routledge. https://doi.org/10.4324/9781315207773.

Goodwin, Marjorie Harness, Asta Cekaite, and Charles Goodwin. 2012. "Emotion as Stance." In Anssi Peräkylä and Marja-Leena Sorjonen eds., *Emotion in Interaction*, 16–41. Oxford: Oxford University Press. https://doi.org/10.1093/acprof:oso/9780199730735.003.0002.

Goodwin, Marjorie Harness, and Charles Goodwin. 2001. "Emotion within Situated Activity." In Alessandro Duranti ed., *Linguistic Anthropology: A Reader*, 1st ed., 239–57. Malden, MA: Blackwell.

Harkness, Nicholas. 2014. *Songs of Seoul: An Ethnography of Voice and Voicing in Christian South Korea*. Berkeley: University of California Press.

Hecht, Tobias. 1998. *At Home in the Street: Street Children of Northeast Brazil*. Cambridge, UK: Cambridge University Press.

Hepburn, Alexa, and Galina B. Bolden. 2013. "The Conversation Analytic Approach to Transcription." In Jack Sidnell and Tanya Stivers eds., *The Handbook of Conversation Analysis*, 57–76. Malden, MA: Blackwell.

Hillewaert, Sarah. 2015. "Writing with an Accent: Orthographic Practice, Emblems, and Traces on Facebook." *Journal of Linguistic Anthropology* 25 (2): 195–214. https://doi.org/10.1111/jola.12079.

Hillewaert, Sarah. 2016. "Tactics and Tactility: A Sensory Semiotics of Handshakes in Coastal Kenya." *American Anthropologist* 118 (1): 49–66. https://doi.org/10.1111/aman.12517.

Hurston, Zora Neale. 2008. *Mules and Men*. New York: Harper Perennial.

Jacobs-Huey, Lanita. 2006. *From the Kitchen to the Parlor Language and Becoming in African American Women's Hair Care*. Oxford: Oxford University Press.

Jones, Graham M. 2011. *Trade of the Tricks: Inside the Magician's Craft*. Berkeley: University of California Press.

Keane, Webb. 1997. *Signs of Recognition: Powers and Hazards of Representation in an Indonesian Society*. Berkeley: University of California Press.

LeCompte, Margaret Diane, and Jean J. Schensul. 1999. *Designing & Conducting Ethnographic Research*. Walnut Creek, CA: AltaMira Press.

Loyd, Heather. 2011. "Growing up Fast: The Rhetoric of Resilience among Inner City Neapolitan Girls." PhD diss., University of California Los Angeles. http://search.proquest.com/docview/923060615/?pq-origsite=primo.

Loyd, Heather. 2012. "The Logic of Conflict: Practices of Social Control among Inner City Neapolitan Girls." In Maryanne Theobald and Susan Danby eds., *Disputes in Everyday Life: Social and Moral Orders of Children and Young People*, 15:325–53. Bingley, UK: Emerald Books. https://doi.org/10.1108/S1537-4661(2012)0000015017.

Mattingly, Cheryl. 2010. *The Paradox of Hope: Journeys through a Clinical Borderland*. Berkeley: University of California Press.

McWhorter, John. 2020. *Defund Karen: On the Insults and Acronyms of America's Racial Reckoning*. Podcast. Lexicon Valley. https://slate.com/podcasts/lexicon-valley/2020/07/blm-bipoc-defund.

Mendoza-Denton, Norma. 1995. "Pregnant Pauses: Silence and Authority in the Anita Hill-Clarence Thomas Hearings." In Kira Hall and Mary Bucholtz eds., *Women and Language*, 51–66. London: Routledge.

Mendoza-Denton, Norma. 2008. *Homegirls: Language and Cultural Practice among Latina Youth Gangs*. Malden, MA: Blackwell.

Mondada, Lorenza. 2016. "Challenges of Multimodality: Language and the Body in Social Interaction." *Journal of Sociolinguistics* 20 (3): 336–66. https://doi.org/10.1111/josl.1_12177.

Mondada, Lorenza. 2019. "Rethinking Bodies and Objects in Social Interaction: A Multimodal Multisensorial Approach to Tasting." In Ulrike Tikvah Kissmann and Joost van Loon eds., *Discussing New Materialism: Methodological Implications for the Study of Materialities*, 109–34. New York: Springer.

Murphy, Keith M. 2015. *Swedish Design: An Ethnography*. Ithaca: Cornell University Press.

Nakassis, Constantine V. 2016. *Doing Style: Youth and Mass Mediation in South India*. Chicago: University of Chicago Press.

Ochs, Elinor. 1979. "Transcription as Theory." In Elinor Ochs and Bambi B. Schieffelin eds., *Developmental Pragmatics*, 43–72. New York: Academic Press.

Ochs, Elinor. 2012. "Experiencing Language." *Anthropological Theory* 12 (2): 142–60. https://doi.org/10.1177/1463499612454088.

Ochs, Elinor, and Lisa Capps. 2001. *Living Narrative: Creating Lives in Everyday Storytelling*. Cambridge: Harvard University Press.

Ochs, Elinor, and Tamar Kremer-Sadlik. 2013. *Fast-Forward Family Home, Work, and Relationships in Middle-Class America*. Berkeley: University of California Press.

Sacks, Harvey, Emanuel A. Schegloff, and Gail Jefferson. 1977. "The Preference for Self-Correction in the Organization of Repair in Conversation." *Language* 53 (2): 361–82. https://doi.org/10.2307/413107.

Samuels, Annemarie. 2019. "Narrative Navigation: HIV and (Good) Care in Aceh, Indonesia." *Culture, Medicine, and Psychiatry* 43 (1): 116–33. https://doi.org/10.1007/s11013-018-9602-y.

Samuels, Annemarie. forthcoming. "Strategies of Silence in an Age of Transparency: Navigating HIV and Visibility in Aceh, Indonesia." *History and Anthropology*. https://doi.org/10.1080/02757206.2020.1830384

Schieffelin, Bambi B. 1979. "Getting It Together: An Ethnographic Approach to the Study of the Development of Communicative Competence." In Elinor Ochs and Bambi B. Schieffelin eds., *Developmental Pragmatics*, 73–108. New York: Academic Press.

Schieffelin, Bambi B. 1990. *The Give and Take of Everyday Life: Language Socialization of Kaluli Children*. Cambridge: Cambridge University Press.

Shankar, Shalini. 2015. *Advertising Diversity: Ad Agencies and the Creation of Asian American Consumers*. Durham: Duke University Press.

Shohet, Merav. 2007. "Narrating Anorexia: 'Full' and 'Struggling' Genres of Recovery." *Ethos* 35 (3): 344–82.

Shohet, Merav. 2013. "Everyday Sacrifice and Language Socialization in Vietnam: The Power of a Respect Particle." *American Anthropologist* 115 (2): 203–17. https://doi.org/10.1111/aman.12004.

Shohet, Merav. 2018a. "Two Deaths and a Funeral: Ritual Inscriptions' Affordances for Mourning and Moral Personhood in Vietnam." *American Ethnologist* 45 (1): 60–73. https://doi.org/10.1111/amet.12599.

Shohet, Merav. 2018b. "Beyond the Clinic? Eluding a Medical Diagnosis of Anorexia through Narrative." *Transcultural Psychiatry* 55 (4): 495–515. https://doi.org/10.1177/1363461517722467.

Shohet, Merav. 2021. *Silence and Sacrifice: Family Stories of Care and the Limits of Love in Vietnam*. Oakland: University of California Press.

Sidnell, Jack. 2009. *Conversation Analysis: Comparative Perspectives*. Cambridge: Cambridge University Press.

Wilce, James MacLynn. 2009. *Crying Shame: Metaculture, Modernity, and the Exaggerated Death of Lament*. Oxford: Wiley-Blackwell.

9.11 Further Reading

Goodwin, Charles, and Goodwin, Marjorie H. 2004. "Participation." In Alessandro Duranti, ed., *A Companion to Linguistic Anthropology*, 222–43. Oxford: Blackwell.

- Argues for "participation" as an analytic concept by demonstrating how in the midst of doing things together, participants coordinate their bodies and talk with that of their co-participant to build actions that define and shape their lifeworld.

Mondada, Lorenza. 2007. "Commentary: Transcript Variations and the Indexicality of Transcribing Practices." *Discourse Studies* 9 (6): 809–21.

- Considers the indexical nature of social actions and practices and offers examples for how transcriptive decisions and layouts are not merely textual ones but are at the heart of interpretive activities across fields.

Ochs, Elinor. 2004. "Narrative Lessons." In Alessandro Duranti, ed., *A Companion to Linguistic Anthropology*, 269–89. Oxford: Blackwell.

- Summarizes key insights and strategies for analyzing and theorizing narrative-based interactions, including elicited and naturally occurring collaborative ones.

10

Online Research and New Media

Archie Crowley and Elaine Chun

10.1 Introduction

Linguistic anthropologists have recently grappled with various theoretical, methodological, and ethical questions relevant to conducting research in the online realm, where linguistic and sociocultural processes, including socialization and social connection, language shift and innovation, discourse circulation and ideological regimentation, are increasingly taking place. Given the present ubiquity of online interactions, some scholars have argued that "virtually all ethnographies of contemporary society should include technologically mediated communication, behavior, or artifacts" (Garcia et al. 2009, 57). In this chapter, we offer an overview of the main issues that have emerged in linguistic anthropological research in online spaces, specifically focusing on *new media practices*, as we point to methodological and ethical considerations that arise and highlight areas of inquiry that provide insight.

New media practices involve the distribution of media objects across public space via computers or the internet, and like other forms of computer-mediated communication,[1] they allow individuals who are in disparate geographical *offline* places to convene in a shared *online* space. Yet, more specifically, these practices are characterized by their dependence on digital platforms, whether social media platforms, such as YouTube, Instagram, or Twitter, or peer-to-peer platforms, such as Airbnb and Kickstarter (de Reuver et al. 2018), and their association with specific genres, including blogs, vlogs, tweets, and memes. Our discussion includes practices that have emerged as part of "Web 1.0," involving the digitization of content in more-or-less static forms, as well as those that developed as part of "Web 2.0," which has arguably transformed communicative practices through the collective creation and dynamic distribution of content, respectively, by and among multiple users.

Despite its implicit temporal contrast with practices of *old media*, such as television, radio, and newspaper, new media practices are hardly new to some users, in terms of how they may simulate long-existing genres of communication (e.g., newspaper articles) and how they may feel outdated when associated with platforms that are waning in popularity among youth (e.g., Facebook) or even defunct (e.g., Friendster). In fact, Gershon (2017, 16) argues that "the newness of new media lies not in the technology but in the sociomaterial practices that linguistic anthropologists' analytical concepts render visible." For example, she shows how a familiar concept such as "participation structure" can be applied to precisely illustrate how participants coordinate their communicative practices across online contexts.

One of the goals of our chapter is to articulate the concerns that may arise, specifically for linguistic anthropologists, when pursuing digitally based research, while also shedding light on the promise that such analyses may offer. Conducting research in digital contexts may require us to rethink our analyses, giving attention to semiotic objects that extend beyond the traditionally "linguistic," including visual images and written texts. It may also require us to reconsider key concepts, including *language, interaction, identity, community,* and *ethnography,* given their seemingly flexible manifestations in online settings. Among key concerns that linguistic anthropologists may raise in the study of online discourse is the potential barrier to developing meaningful relationships between researchers and participants when interactions are neither face-to-face nor confined to a specific place. As such, for linguistic anthropologists trained in ethnographic methods, it may not be obvious that the types of interactions that emerge on mediated online platforms lend themselves to "thick descriptions" of fieldsites that provide nuanced and situated understandings of sociocultural and linguistic processes (Geertz 1973). Likewise, particular ethical dilemmas of privacy, consent, and anonymity may arise due to the relative ease of capturing and searching online content. While these concerns are rooted in long-standing disciplinary assumptions about how best to study the relationship between language and culture, there are many reasons to be optimistic about our discipline's burgeoning acceptance of online research.

Digital discourses do not merely provide a "window" into communities and ideologies but are the very vehicle of some of these cultural constructs, for example, by offering marginalized communities an opportunity to newly imagine themselves and by potentially challenging and reshaping the importance of linguistic and national boundaries. Ultimately, linguistic anthropologists are well positioned to provide insights about contemporary sociocultural processes and ideologies as they become shaped via digital means.

10.2 Areas of Inquiry

10.2.1 Sociocultural Questions

As computers have come to mediate many aspects of everyday life, researchers have explored the sociocultural significance of digital practices, specifically, how digital discourse practices have shaped and have become shaped by locally and widely circulating ideologies. In some cases, digital practices have become incorporated into everyday routines, requiring the coordination of online and offline environments. For example, Sunakawa (2012) has explored webcam conversations between Japanese individuals living in the United States and their family members in Japan and has illustrated how children have been socialized into familial interactions through "show and narrate" activities of reporting everyday life. Likewise, researchers have also shown how gamers, connected in virtual space yet located in the same physical room, used participation cues such as deixis and repetition to organize roles and actions within the two spatial environments (Keating and Sunakawa 2010). In other cases, virtual space itself may serve as the primary site of cultural practices, prompting researchers to ask, "How does 'culture' work in virtual worlds?" (Boellstorff et al. 2012, 52). These studies have required an ethnographic lens in order to understand how people use online technology and how these practices shape local understandings.

A pair of related questions that researchers have continued to grapple with is whether we can understand online discourse practices as qualitatively distinct from offline ones or whether they can inform our understanding of discourse more generally. On the one hand, online practices may diverge from offline ones, bearing sociocultural dynamics that are seemingly novel. For example, subcommunities (e.g., ASMR, K-pop fans) and genres (e.g., vlogs, memes) have emerged in ways that have produced local norms and ideologies. On the other hand, digital discourse sometimes presupposes evaluations of language that we might hear or see in offline contexts, such as adherence to prescriptive ideologies. While the online and offline worlds are distinct in some respects, the idea that online worlds entail losing awareness of the real world may be an "immersive fallacy" (Boellstorff 2008, 113), as one of the appeals of virtual worlds is the user's meta-awareness and mediation of what may be called an "intertextual gap" (Briggs and Bauman 1992)—that is, a sense of both co-existence yet divergence—between offline and online worlds (Manning 2009). For example, despite the fact that users may be engrossed in an online platform, they typically maintain an awareness of the ways in which technology mediates their experience through a device, a screen, or an interface. Additionally, as Boellstorff (2008) discusses, the gap between the offline and online worlds becomes saliently invoked in virtual world concepts such as "afk" (away from keyboard), whereby an avatar may be "present" in the online world but "immersed" in the offline world.

The growing cultural significance of new media practices has arisen in part because new media users encounter fewer gatekeeping mechanisms than those attempting to participate in old media, such as television and radio production. As such, marginalized communities that had been excluded from traditional media institutions have greater access to tools for disseminating their own content, providing public visibility to sociopolitical issues, and building communities that orient to perspectives that had been erased in public space. For example, on Twitter, users have performed acts of "hashtag activism" to document and challenge police brutality, and researchers have employed "hashtag ethnography" as a method for studying such activism. In their analysis of *#Ferguson*, a hashtag that invited a collective critique of a white police officer's murder of a Black man, Bonilla and Rosa (2015, 12) suggest that "social media participation becomes a key site from which to contest mainstream media silences and the long history of state-sanctioned violence against racialized populations."

Of interest to language scholars is how language ideologies circulate in online spaces, as illustrated in the early work on Mock Ebonics (Ronkin and Karn 1999) and Mock Spanish (Hill 2005) that employed a method of "Google intertextuality" (Bauman 2005) to identify how linguistic forms reproduced racist linguistic stereotypes in the United States. Recent work has additionally focused on the uptake of media objects, such as how commenters contextualize videos that they have watched. As noted by scholars, such uptake often reproduces hegemonic ideologies, such as when viewers embraced "lingwashing"—that is, the learning of indigenous African languages by Cape Town whites as a superficial "moral cover for enduring inequities" (McIntosh 2018)—and when they responded to a Northern Italian politician's racist story that was reported on in a news story (Perrino 2017). In many cases, the ideological effects are complex, involving both the reproduction and contestation of hegemonic ideologies, such as in a comedic performance of East Asian Orientalism in the Arab world (Chun and Walters 2011), the circulation of ironically stereotypical representations of Black language by an Asian American (Chun 2013) and K-pop fans' prescriptive evaluations of pronunciations of Korean performers' names as "incorrect" and "hybrid" (Chun 2017). In other cases, hegemonic ideologies may be more successfully challenged, as noted by linguistic anthropologists who have explored how digital discourse can serve as a political or cultural resource for linguistically marginalized communities (Smalls 2018). For example, Hillewaert (2015) shows how Lamu youth from Kenya used orthographic representations of the KiAmu dialect on Facebook to challenge stereotypes of the variety and to reclaim a local identity, and Calhoun (2019) illustrates how Black racial comedy on the video platform Vine can offer anti-hegemonic potential. As these studies illustrate, research on new media has been fruitful in answering important sociocultural questions concerning how digital discourse practices shape and become shaped by community ideologies. In the next section, we address the complex semiotic processes and nuanced meanings that emerge in the context of these ideologies.

10.2.2 Semiotic Questions

Given that retrievable traces of discourse (e.g., visible text and images as well as replayable moments of video and audio) circulate in digital space, many linguistic anthropologists have come to recognize the potential that these traces offer for exploring semiotic processes, that is, how linguistic signs become interpreted by media users. Crucially, online discourse, which is often "time-stamped," allows researchers to identify "pathways of discourse" (Wortham and Reyes 2015), or the shaping of discourse meanings along a range of temporal scales. This shaping sometimes occurs through discursive links created at the interactional scale, such as when a stretch of discourse becomes treated as an extractable text, extracted from one context, and reinserted into a new context (*entextualization-decontextualization-recontextualization*) (Bauman and Briggs 1990). In other cases, a moment of discourse may repeat a prior moment (e.g., a retweet) (Johnstone 1994; Tannen 2007) or precontextualize, or anticipate, future contexts (e.g., a Facebook request that precontextualizes the recipient's acceptance) (cf. Ochs 1992). At a wider scale, discourse events across an individual lifespan can represent moments of socialization (Schieffelin and Ochs 1986), such as being socialized into the norms of an online discussion board; they can also represent the process of social identification (Wortham 2006), such as recurring moments of self-positioning as an avid K-Pop fan. Finally, at the broadest scale, researchers can observe community-wide or sociohistorical processes, such as the adoption and diffusion of semantic and social meanings of words, such as "lady Pond" on Twitter (Squires 2014), and the emergent regimentation of registers (Agha 2005) or genres, such as the establishment of a local communicative repertoire as users post remakes of a viral YouTube video (Rymes 2012). Likewise, Bax (2018) has examined how media circulations of "the C-word" not only produced the recognizability of "cracker" as an anti-white slur but also indexed particular "stance cohorts," or those who hold the same stance toward a particular stance object, whether as "euphemizers" and as "reverse racists."

As noted by Agha (2011), discourse is not merely mediated, producing communicative links between senders and receivers, but "mediatized," or actively commodified for circulation. During these processes, linguistic signs are often circulated and interpreted in combination with non-linguistic ones, such as in Calhoun's (2019) analysis of how spoken and embodied signs, in combination with video captions, work together to create local interpretations of racial comedy on Vine, as well as Slobe's (2018) analysis of how critiques of "white girls" are wielded through both aural and visual signs, including rising intonation, creaky voice, and blonde hair. In these ways, new media spaces provide researchers with an opportunity to explore how multiple kinds of signs can become meaningful within and across contexts of time and space.

10.2.3 Metadiscursive Questions

Another important strand of research has examined reflexive ideologies that media users share about online discourse and media. Following the lead of other scholars, we refer to these discourses that comment on discourse practices as "metadiscourses," as a parallel to the concept of "metalanguage," or language used to talk about language. Metadiscourses that are specifically about new media reflect "media ideologies"—for example, beliefs about how different forms of media are used and how the medium shapes the message—that can influence how individuals engage with platforms. For example, college students' media ideologies about different forms of media, such as texting, calling, emailing, or conversing over social media, might shape how they flirt and break up with their significant others (Gershon 2010a). Media ideologies can also shape how users view and use a particular medium via a process called "remediation" that produces connections between older and newer forms of media (Gershon 2010b) and thus "shared understandings of oldness, newness, and nostalgia" (Gershon 2017, 20). For example, Bauman (2010) shows how the adaptation of live oral storytelling to audio recording leads to a co-present performance that maintains a continuity with past forms of the media and produces a "mediatized nostalgia."

Media ideologies may also pertain to how users connect media and varied modalities, as in the case of Jones and Schieffelin's (2009) study of quotative *like* in text messaging among US college students who align this medium more closely with verbal rather than written forms, despite the fact that metadiscursive enregisterments of "internet language" presuppose a prescriptive standard language ideology (Squires 2010). Using comparative approaches, researchers have pointed to similarities between online registers and offline ones, noting how the former incorporates elements of both traditional writing and face-to-face discourse (Baron and Ling 2003). Likewise, conversation analysts have examined the openings and closings in synchronous instant messenger conversations, finding that they resembled those used in verbal phone conversations (Raclaw 2008). Yet some have warned against explicit comparisons of this kind, as they fail to treat online interactions as "social practices in their own right" (Lamerichs and Molder 2003, 469). Perhaps, more importantly, they presuppose a fundamental distinction between "online" and "offline" language that can erase the fact that discourse, regardless of their mediation, involves a shared set of semiotic characteristics and processes.

10.3 Rethinking Concepts

Relative to traditional face-to-face discourse, online discourse arguably "compresses" offline dimensions of time and space and depends more heavily on visual texts (e.g., videos, images, written text), given that participants commonly engage in discourse both asynchronously and remotely from one another. As such, linguistic anthropological research within a digital landscape requires that we rethink long-standing concepts, including *language, interaction, identity, community,* and *ethnography.*

10.3.1 Language

Digital research requires an inclusive understanding of how we conceive of *language.* Despite the speech-centered history of our discipline, linguistic anthropologists have long recognized that linguistic phenomena are tightly connected to semiotic phenomena that extend well beyond spoken discourse; not only is language sometimes visually based, as in the case of signed languages, but it is inseparable from "discourse" broadly conceived (Gee 2014; Johnstone 2017), including gestures (M. H. Goodwin and C. Goodwin 1986), stylistic and corporeal displays (Bucholtz 2010; Eckert 2004; Mendoza-Denton 2008), and public performances (Bauman and Briggs 1990; Bucholtz 2011; Coupland 2001). As such, while the study of language in the digital realm might be less amenable to uptake in the neighboring discipline of linguistics, which remains largely committed to an idealization of speech over writing, linguistic anthropologists are well prepared to confront the analytical challenges presented by semiotic complexities in the digital realm, including overlaps between text- and speech-based discourse (e.g., comments posted in response to media objects) as well as visually rather than aurally salient signs (e.g., memes, emojis, videos).

10.3.2 Interaction

The notion of the *interaction,* as a core unit of analysis in linguistic anthropology, presents important potential in analyses of digital discourse. Traditional analyses of interactions have tended to be face-to-face, yet traditional interactional units remain relevant even in online contexts in which participants are spatially or temporally distant. For example, in a thread of comments on YouTube or Reddit, users take "turns" by posting comments, often producing "sequential pairs" by using the "reply" or "like" functions and engaging in "repairs" via editing or reposting. While the scale of time for interactions may be relatively wide—spanning between minutes to years—and while participant roles may be relatively more fluid than when face-to-face, online interactions involve familiar processes of recontextualization (via retweeting and creating memes) and negotiation (via discussion threads and comment chains) that are similar to offline discursive processes.

Studies of interaction have been attuned to the ways in which embodiment and gaze are crucial parts of interactions (C. Goodwin 2000; Bucholtz and Hall 2016). When users experience a computer-mediated gaze, language may be embodied differently from when they are face-to-face. While corporeal gestures or orientations tend to have important significance in face-to-face settings, "the perception of an image provided by the computer screen is not similarly affected when a person moves [their] own body" (Keating 2015, 255). Additionally, when compared to a face-to-face gaze, some research has shown that a computer-mediated gaze is not as effective in getting attention and establishing joint attention to a task (Heath and Luff 1993). However, users develop innovative strategies for collaboration in these online spheres within the unique properties of different digital software. For example, in online games, players utilize the cursor to manipulate and move the virtual space to draw attention to certain areas (Keating and Sunakawa 2010), or participants in online video calls make exaggerated gestures when they know their interlocutor's video is on (Mol et al. 2011). Furthermore, as many in-person interactions have come to be replaced with virtual ones during the COVID-19 pandemic, computer-mediated interactions on platforms such as Zoom have become deeply embedded in everyday lives, simulating aspects of face-to-face experiences (e.g., a "raise hand" feature as a bid for the floor; private chats as non-disruptive "sideplay" [Goffman 1981] or breakout groups that shift the participation framework) while also inviting creative possibilities of interaction (e.g., backgrounds that seemingly transport participants to imaginary locations or participant usernames that serve as digital name tags). In these ways, online interactions provide a new perspective on important linguistic anthropological questions about language and interaction.

We suggest that the notion of *interaction* remains highly relevant in online settings, even if participation structures (M. Goodwin 1990) and participant frameworks (Goffman 1981), which shape communicative networks and discursive flows, qualitatively diverge from those found in offline communities. On the one hand, forms of Web 1.0 media, such as online newspapers and blogs, are typically understood as based on a unidirectional distribution model, whereby language largely flows from a central set of producers to a broad audience of consumers. Through these mediatizing practices (Agha 2011), communities are imagined (cf. Anderson 1983) by

Table 10.1 Types and examples of new media characterized by participation structure

Type of new media	Web 1.0	Web 2.0 (consumer-oriented social media)	Web 2.0 (network-oriented social media)
Discourse structure	Mostly unidirectional, regulated flow from *few* producers to *many* consumers	Partially bidirectional, semi-regulated flow from *some* producer/consumers to *many* consumers	Bidirectional, largely unregulated flow from *many* producer/consumer to *many* producer/consumers
Examples	Fox, CNN, CNET, PC World, Merriam-Webster, NIH, Britannica, Netflix	YouTube, Instagram, Twitter, Urban Dictionary, Wikipedia, CraigsList, Etsy	Twitter, Snapchat, Facebook, NextDoor, Tumblr, Reddit, Slack, LinkedIn, Steam, Roblox

producers who shape how consumers may come to imagine themselves. On the other hand, forms of Web 2.0 media are felt to be produced through the collective contribution and distribution of content, such that consumers themselves can be producers as well. Table 10.1 represents how Web 1.0 and Web. 2.0 discourses vary in terms of their degree and direction of discursive flow, including spaces that are relatively unidirectional and those that are relatively bidirectional.

10.3.3 Identity

Even if attention to the concept of *identity* has waned in some parts of anthropology (Brubaker and Cooper 2000), linguistic anthropological research has long been invested in examining the relationship between language and acts of identification, or how language can position selves and others within a broader sociocultural landscape, for example, in terms of race, gender, sexuality, or class (Bucholtz and Hall 2004). Studies of digital discourse have required researchers to reexamine their assumptions about the social construction of identity, namely its potential multiplicity, its necessary intersubjectivity, and its relation to the body. The relationship between a person's online and offline identities raises important questions: *Can researchers know who a specific user is? To what extent can we expect alignment between online and offline identities? Do offline identities matter?*

Contrary to what has generally been assumed in face-to-face ethnographic research contexts, it may not, in fact, pose a problem if a researcher never "knows" how a user identifies in offline contexts. If identity is a situated and emergent construct rather than an intrinsic truth about an individual (Bucholtz and Hall 2005), researchers may find it productive instead to focus primarily on the identity that emerges online—that is, what is presented, perceived, and ratified—instead of attempting to figure out the "truth" of a person's offline identity. At the same time, even if linguistic anthropologists understand that offline identities are no more intrinsically authentic than online ones, local ideologies may sometimes assume alignment between the two. For example, when media users make claims of race and gender (e.g., "as an Asian person" or "as a trans person"), the presupposition may be that this online declaration of identity maps on to an offline identity. Yet in other cases, such alignment does not hold, such as when gamers create an avatar or when Twitter users become identified as attempting unsuccessfully to "pass" as member of a group to which they are not read as belonging (Robinson n.d.).

The body plays an important role in signaling an individual's identity. While offline embodiments of skin color, vocal quality, or hexis may be understood as habituated practices of identity (Bourdieu 1977), online forms of embodiment can be relatively flexible, with some forms of discourse even "re-embodied" (cf. Bucholtz 2011), as signs beyond the corporeal serve as vehicles of communication. Such is not to say that representations of the body are not important in digital forums, for example, when users display avatars, or pictorial "head and shoulders" used to represent online characters, but that the relationship between an individual's body—as displayed online—and their identity—whether online or offline—is less likely to be assumed by others to be necessarily and naturally aligned. Furthermore, online video games, in which the avatar is not merely an image that is controlled and voiced by the user, provide a fruitful lens through which to explore Goffman's (1981) observation that "the speaker" can be divided into potentially distinct roles, namely the speaker who is held responsible for the words (principal), the speaker who creates the words (author), the speaker who articulates the words (animator), and the character whom the words represent (figure).

10.3.4 Community

Another linguistic anthropological concept that may require reconceptualization in digital settings is *community*, a construct that has often entailed—at least within language-oriented studies—particular temporal and spatial characteristics, such as interactional frequency, membership consistency, and geographical proximity, and that has sometimes been defined along shared sociocultural axes, such as age, race, or gender, a mutual orientation to a set of goals (Eckert and McConnell-Ginet 1992), or a collective repertoire of linguistic forms and norms (Gumperz 1982). Some online communities are aligned with traditional conceptions, for example, when members are engaged in joint gameplay (Newon 2015) or shared fandom (Chun 2017) or when a community is felt to be intimate, such as a Facebook group whose members share knitting memes and are admitted only by permission devoted to knitting memes, whose members are admitted only by permission and who share memes.

Yet in other online spaces, traditional notions of community may be difficult to maintain, given the infrequency of participation, inconsistency of membership, and disparateness of goals and perspectives, encouraging us to consider what community membership entails. For example, subscribers to a YouTube channel arguably belong to a "community" even if its membership is vague, including even those who watch videos only sporadically, never interacting with other members. In addition, the boundaries between communities may be overlapping, such as group of school friends who play video games online together, or they may be ambiguous, as in the case of "Black Twitter," which exhibits porous boundaries between those who participate on Twitter as well as other platforms (Smalls 2018).

Perhaps what is minimally required is the reflexive recognition that members constitute a community, even if it is largely an "imagined" one (Anderson 1983). While it might be assumed that the relative anonymity maintained in online spaces leads to shallow interpersonal connections, members can become "intimate strangers" (Tomita 2005), engaging with "hybrid forms of sociality between stranger contemporary and intimate consociate" (Manning 2009, 314). Although not always geographically oriented to the same place, online communities are often felt and understood by users as based in some "place"; for example, virtual worlds," for example, in the case of virtual worlds, which are felt to constitute "new kinds of places" (Boellstorff 2008, 91). In these ways, digital media and technology both overlap with broader linguistic anthropological understandings of understandings of how linguistic anthropologists understand how notions like *place*, *locality*, and *intimacy* are connected to a sense of community.

10.3.5 Ethnography

A final concept that has important implications in digital contexts is that of *ethnography*. Linguistic anthropologists typically seek to identify "emic" interpretations by identifying local categories and ideologies as well as situated meanings within a community. To do so, they typically spend extended periods of time engaging in ethnographic fieldwork, conducting long-term participant observation, and producing "thick descriptions" (Geertz 1973). While the technologically mediated nature of the contact that digital researchers have with community members may diverge in character from traditional, face-to-face ethnographic encounters, it is possible for familiar methodological tools of ethnography to be adopted when studying online communities. To this end, sociologists and anthropologists (Horst and Miller 2012; Pink 2016) have developed methods of "digital ethnography," sometimes called "netnography" (Kozinets 2007), as they treat the digital realm as one of the worlds that people inhabit.

We use the phrase "digital ethnography" to refer to the array of frameworks that researchers use to incorporate ethnographic methods when exploring and understanding participants' digital lives. It involves many of the same methods of inquiry that face-to-face ethnographers use, such as spending time in a community and working to understand practices and interactions through observations of and conversations with community members. Digital researchers can engage in participant observation, or "the embodied emplacement of the researching self in a fieldsite as a consequential social actor" (Boellstorff et al. 2012, 65), examining and engaging with communities using an anthropological lens. When doing so, they maintain a mindful awareness of interactional processes, including a reflexive consideration of their own positioning, and they pay systematic attention to sociocultural dimensions. This process is aided by the writing of fieldnotes and purposeful engagement with the community in order to elicit local understandings. Researchers can also conduct interviews, via video calling tools, such as Zoom or Skype, or in person, allowing them to pose questions that are not immediately answerable by observation alone, such as participants' interpretations of their own and others' online linguistic practices, their ideologies about language or media, or information about their background that may bear contextual relevance. Some digital ethnography incorporates observation and interaction with the participants in both online and offline settings, yet most give primary focus to online lives and interactions.

While a potential overlap exists between researchers and participants even in face-to-face settings, for example, in the case of "native ethnographers"

(Narayan 1993) or participant observers more generally, ambiguities seem to be augmented in digital research contexts, given that participatory modes are multiple and fluid. For example, a researcher, when initially learning the norms of a community, might engage in methods of observation that can be locally classified as "lurking," or spending time in an online community without posting or engaging. Some participants may feel "spied on" when researchers spend time lurking in online communities (LeBesco 2004), yet despite the pejorative undertone of the label, this "passive" form of participation can be an acceptable practice in some digital communities. Similarly, some researchers who engage in online linguistic anthropological research might describe themselves as casual users, if not active participants, of an online platform that they are studying. Importantly, online communities have varied conceptions of who counts as a "participant" and what counts as "participation"—for example, a participant in an online video game might be expected to take part in gameplay, whereas a participant in a message board forum might merely read and "like" posts. It is crucial to maintain reflexivity with respect to how the researcher engages with a community as a participant observer, taking into account the norms of that community.

As noted above, one of the goals of ethnographic research is to collect and analyze data in ways that capture the local experiences of participants. However, if user experiences are varied, for example, between those who primarily produce content and those who consume them or those who actively engage and those who passively observe, the question remains as to which particular set of users' experiences are to be foregrounded. In addition, while a large corpus of digital data can represent a wide range of interactional encounters, it is unlikely to represent the experiences of any single user. Of course, similar quandaries arise in offline research, as no single speaker has awareness of the various kinds of information that a conversation analyst might transcribe. Perhaps what researchers should aim to do is to identify not only which aspects of the data are relevant but also for which participants these data are relevant and for what processes and projects.

10.4 Data Collection and Data Analysis

The rise in digitally based linguistic anthropological research is likely to produce both curiosity and concern in a discipline that has long valued face-to-face, long-term methods of participant observation that researchers typically associate with an ethnographic approach. In general, a shift to the digital has required researchers to consider a wider set of data types while still assuming the goals of traditional methods of data collection and analysis. Given the range of types of discourse practices that exist in the digital realm, the affordances and constraints of each platform, and the variety of research questions that might be asked, methods of data collection and analysis vary widely. Our discussion engages with both the possibilities that arise when analyzing new media data while also attempting to address the worries of skeptics.

10.4.1 Data Collection

Data collection decisions depend on the research questions that are being posed, while also shaping these questions. For example, a researcher might seek to understand how a particular linguistic sign—a word, its pronunciation, or its orthographic representation—has become conventionalized or contested over a period of months or years, in which case, it may be useful to "scrape" a large archive of textual data over this time span, organizing the corpus of data systematically in a digital spreadsheet tool and coding for uses of the sign as well as metalinguistic evaluations of its manifestation (e.g., Chun 2013; Jones and Schieffelin 2009). A researcher might wish to explore the nuanced semiotic process by which such discursive objects can be recontextualized, replicated, and contested (e.g., Rymes 2012; Perrino 2017), in which case, capturing individual tokens, or instances of a specific linguistic phenomenon (e.g., a particular word or phrase), through a manual search, or taking screen captures of how tokens are visually contextualized may be most useful. Alternatively, analysts might be interested in how new media users interface with digital tools, in which case, video-recording users in their physical environment (e.g., Keating and Sunakawa 2010), capturing audiovisual streams of on-screen discourse in real time, and interviewing them afterward might be beneficial. Other researchers might choose to depend on more traditional tools of anthropological inquiry, such as participant observation, in order to capture the situated experiences of community members over a longer scale of time. In other words, a wide array of types of data can be collected online.

An elusive aspect of online research is the shifting nature of the internet landscape. It is important to assume that online content will eventually become no longer accessible through a web link, even if some websites are saved in the Internet Archive. As such, practices of documentation are crucial, whether by taking screenshots of online interactions, copying the text of posts into a separate document, or exporting data scraped from a website. If video or audio files exist, they can be downloaded for archival and transcription. When storing potentially large amounts of online data, it is important to consider practical issues regarding storage space on computers and using external hard drives for storage. Ethical considerations about anonymizing data will be discussed below in our "Ethics" section.

One of the alluring aspects of working with digital data may be the ease with which large amounts of data from an expansive community of users can be collected. Discourse that individuals have produced and circulated over the course of several months or years can be retrieved in the span of a day, for example, by searching for a specific hashtag (e.g., *#BlackLivesMatter*, *#COVID19*) that users themselves have generated as a topic tag, by relying on a platform's algorithm for keyword searches (see Crowley's analysis below), by using software that "scrapes" content from a webpage, or by distributing a survey to a large number of participants via a social media platform. Without leaving home, interviews can also be conducted with those in distant locations, and without committing significant time and money, researchers can gain access to the kind of relatively unvarnished discourses that those in face-to-face settings might have access to only after significant participant trust has been gained.

Yet we heed the warning that "big" data are not necessarily better data (Reyes 2014), given that it discourages, or at least diminishes, a qualitative understanding of how discourse is situated in particular contexts and how language shapes and becomes shaped by these contexts. When multiple "tokens" are collected, their decontextualization and recontextualization as a "data set" or "corpus" also make less visible those temporal dimensions of language that have long been of interest to linguistic anthropologists, namely how tokens are sequentially located in relation to others along various scales (Wortham 2003): an interactional scale (e.g., as moments of alignment, contestation, or correction), an ontogenetic scale (e.g., as moments of socialization or identification), or a sociohistorical scale (e.g., as cases of shift or enregisterment). They may also obscure footings and voicings, such as whether these tokens are performed, as well as interpreted, as moments of irony, parody, or sincerity. Finally, they can obscure an understanding of the ideological significance of language, as the formal elements of tokens (whether a lexical or phonemic variant is present/absent) are prioritized over their situated semiotic meanings (how ideologies are invoked, which social meanings are indexed, and what sociocultural actions are achieved).

10.4.2 Data Analysis

Digital data offer many possibilities for the analysis of sociocultural and linguistic processes, including enregisterment, language shift, socialization, community formation, and cross-ethnic encounters, to name just a few. We provide below a list of questions that may be asked during the process of analyzing online discourse. While researchers need to only address those that are relevant to their theoretical objectives, we provide an inclusive list of directions for guiding inquiry. In general, these questions reflect linguistic anthropological goals: providing a description of discourse events, situating the meanings of discursive tokens in relation to one another, identifying discursive processes across multiple tokens, and maintaining a reflexive lens.

1 Describe the structural characteristics of events.
   - What discursive elements—including linguistic features, discourse genres, and other semiotic resources—are used and how? Examples include *likes, comments, repostings, avatars, summaries*, and *subtitles*.
   - How does the use of these resources allow users to perform stances and acts? Examples include *alignment, disalignment, praise*, and *critique.*
   - How does the use of these resources allow users to enact roles and identities? Examples include *regular member, newcomer, troll*, and *racialized/gendered positions.*
2 Situate the significance of discourse tokens via their relationship with other tokens.
   - How are discursive elements spatially and temporally structured? Examples include *videos embedded in another video, chains of comments*, and *lists of similar videos.*
   - How are tokens sequentially organized and contextualized in relation to one another? Examples include *responses, repetitions*, and *parodies.*
   - How do tokens participate in broader discourse practices? Examples include *discursive reproduction* and *contestation.*
3 Identify discursive processes emerging across multiple tokens.
   - How have tokens become mediatized as commodifiable objects for broad circulation?
   - How do chains of discourse tokens reflect local negotiations of meaning?

- How do media users eventually establish themselves as particular social types?
- How do genres, styles, or registers become recognizable?

4 Maintain a reflexive lens.
- What kinds of ideologies of media discourses and language locally circulate?
- How is the researcher's analysis shaped by their own perspective of observation and participation? How might this perspective diverge from those of media users?
- How does the researcher's analysis itself shape or contest broader political agendas and interests?

10.5 Ethics

Online research faces ethical concerns that mirror those found in offline settings, such as what kind of consent is necessary, how personal privacy may be compromised, and how individuals and communities, particularly those in vulnerable positions, may be harmed (see also Black and Conley-Riner, this volume). However, there are unique considerations that arise within a digital landscape, where the lines between what is public and private are sometimes unclear, where individuals participate in public discourse spaces without full awareness of the consequences, and where efforts to anonymize data can sometimes be undone. This section discusses additional ethical issues that must be taken into consideration, while still noting that the diversity of platforms, communities, and data types requires that each project be taken on a case-by-case basis in order to best protect individuals and communities from harm.

In general, the discourse of public figures, such as politicians, news anchors, or television hosts, is typically considered part of the public domain, such that researchers are not expected to obtain consent from these language users nor do they need to anonymize the data (e.g., Hall et al. 2016). Yet in the present era of "digital influencers," or individuals who commoditize aspects of their personal lives for profit on platforms such as Instagram or Twitter, there can exist an ambiguity with respect to their "public" status. It may be argued that influencers willingly and knowingly provide personal information in exchange for fame and profit, or symbolic and economic capital (Bourdieu 1991). Yet it may also be argued that some of these individuals are not fully aware of the consequences of their mediatized content. For example, small-scale internet "celebrities" with relatively modest followings may be shaping their discourse on the assumption that they are performing for a limited—perhaps even in-group—audience. In such cases, researchers should consider the risks for specific individuals and communities whom they are observing in making these decisions. For example, L. Jones (2019) uses pseudonyms in her discourse analysis of two trans teens' online video blogs, noting that although both vloggers have over 10,000 subscribers each and although the videos are publicly available, "[these] young people may not have considered their potential reach [and] may also be potentially vulnerable" L. Jones (2019, 4).

In addition to producers of mediatized content, millions of users communicate in "public" online forums typically without the expectation that their words will be read widely, such as when commenting on a YouTube video, Instagram post, or news article. Yet as boyd and Crawford (2011) note, "[j]ust because data is accessible doesn't mean that using it is ethical" (boyd and Crawford (2011, 36). Some questions that might be considered when assessing the public nature of discourse include the following: *Do authors know that their posts are publicly accessible? Who is their intended audience? Is there a risk of harm to individuals or other community members as a result of a researcher's use and circulation of discourse data unbeknownst to the author of that data?* These questions are aligned with the guidance of the American Anthropological Association's Statement of Ethics (2012) that suggests that the three most important principles of professional responsibility are to refrain from doing harm, to be transparent about research, and to obtain consent.

If a researcher assesses that a risk of harm exists, there are several options for obtaining consent in online spaces. When looking at online content creators on platforms such as Instagram or YouTube, researchers may choose to reach out via email or direct message to ask for consent in participation in the research. A researcher who is already a member of a private online community (e.g., a Facebook page) can post a request for members to "opt in" as a participant of the study, analyzing only those posts that are authored by those who have consented. D'Arcy and Young (2012) outline steps and considerations when using Facebook for recruitment, such as messaging group members or posting in the group to obtain informed consent. Once a researcher has become connected through social media to their participants or collaborators, various steps can be taken to ensure that participants are aware of what the researcher's goals are, when their posts are being collected and viewed as part of the research project, and when the collection period has ended. In particular, Modan (2016) notes that the relationships that researchers build with participants using social media may present ethical dilemmas, including the blurring of professional and personal lines when researcher and participant become "friends" on platforms, the possibility of producing tensions when a researcher's social media network includes "those who are at odds with each other," and the voyeuristic nature of social media, which contrasts with traditional participant observation settings where of "an ethnographer's bodily presence is usually on the radar of informants" (104).

However, when conducting research on a public page or a large forum, obtaining informed consent of social media users might be challenging. In such cases, considerations of anonymity are important. If media users are personally identifiable, the best course of action may be to anonymize any identifying content; for example, usernames can be changed and icons or avatar photos can be blurred or excluded. If the platform uses what appears to be the offline names of individuals, removing these or assigning pseudonyms or numbers is appropriate. In the case of visually based online platforms such as Instagram, TikTok, or YouTube, blurred images or line drawings are ways of anonymizing content, though keeping in mind that while searchability may be significantly diminished, it may never be completely erased. As such, researchers can consider strategies to reduce the risk of others identifying individuals in the data, for example, by replacing keywords that prevent searches or changing non-crucial content words, without compromising the integrity of the analysis (e.g., changing a comment such as "I like hotdogs" to "I like hamburgers"). Finally, as noted by the Linguistic Society of America's "Revised Ethics Statement" (2019), "[a]nonymous observations of public behavior, which often cannot involve full knowledge of the potential consequences [of] consent, should be thoroughly vetted with research ethics boards; if allowable, such research should include no information that could inadvertently identify individuals or, where sensitive, the community."

10.6 Case Study

In this section, we illustrate how the issues discussed above bear relevance to a specific case, namely the discursive pathway produced by YouTube vlogs (video blogs) that address language practices and ideologies within English-using transgender communities in North America. During the 2010s, trans people began to gain recognition in mainstream media, such as television shows, films, and the news, and trans advocates worked to educate cisgender audiences on "appropriate" language to use when talking about trans people, including in online spaces. Vlogs in particular served as a crucial resource for community-building (Raun 2016) and information-sharing for members of the transgender community who engaged in discussions of self-identification, labels, and community language practices. Additionally, vloggers often positioned themselves as authorities or experts who gave advice on various topics to their audiences (Dame 2013; Konnelly 2018). These metalinguistic discourses reflected the trans community's engagement with linguistic activism as a key component of the broader movement for trans rights in the United States.

Although YouTube was an important space for trans people during this time, this public platform also led to the circulation of aggressive transphobic or transnormative discourses both from within and outside the community. In part, this discourse was the result of a gap between an "imagined audience," composed of those who were open to learning from or aligning with the videos, and a far more heterogeneous "actual audience," which included those who expressed transphobic sentiments. Ironically, many of these trans vlogs became interdiscursively linked to transphobic videos via YouTube's algorithm of juxtaposing "related videos," thus inviting viewers to post "hate" comments. One important outcome was that the videos of many trans YouTubers—as well as LGBT YouTube creators more generally—were demonetized. Without a source of income, many left the platform for other sites, such as Instagram. Since then, YouTube has become a relatively unpopular media space for trans content creators.

This analysis explores the specific discursive process that may point to why the trans community eventually made its way from YouTube to other sites. Specifically, we show that a media space such as YouTube may seemingly provide opportunities for trans community members to invite shared understandings among both trans and cis viewers, as their videos widely circulate in public space. We discuss the tensions that arise when trans creators' videos in fact come to circulate among disparate audiences, entering pathways of uptake among viewers who engage in "hate" discourse that is openly vitriolic. In other words, new media spaces may give a previously marginalized community a platform to be heard, but discursive trajectories—possibly unanticipated by video creators—can lead to the community's continued marginalization. This snapshot also demonstrates some of the methodological, ethical, and analytic possibilities and challenges that online platforms present and that we have discussed in this chapter.

As a nonbinary researcher who had participated in a range of online and offline trans communities, Crowley was aware of how various language ideologies mediated members' negotiations of language use, and they sought to understand how terminology of specific relevance to nonbinary members came to be chosen as well as how these members rationalized these choices. Their methods of data collection were thus shaped in part by their prior experiences of participating in online community spaces, including YouTube. Further, these methods aligned with their research goals of understanding both the range of language ideologies that members invoked as well as the ways in which these language ideologies were situated in specific moments of discourse as rationalizations for terminological choice. Their methods of data collection were also shaped by their research goals of identifying both broad patterns of language ideologies across the trans community on YouTube and contextualizations of these ideologies within specific moments of discourse, such as during narratives of "coming out." They thus assembled a small corpus of videos posted between 2015 and 2019 by initially using a keyword search of the phrase "how I knew I was nonbinary" on YouTube's main page. In order to explore discourse within a similar set of widely viewed videos, from among the top twenty search results, Crowley selected the twelve videos that featured a single person talking to the camera in a vlog style and that included narratives of coming out as well as discussions of nonbinary identity and gender labels. The resulting videos were between five and twelve minutes in length.

Given Crowley's interest in the vloggers' orientations to trans community linguistic practices, they transcribed the selected vlogs and copied and pasted viewer comments that allowed them to trace how the vloggers' discourses were taken up, whether in acts of alignment or disalignment. A corpus of transcribed video transcripts as well as text comments were systematized and maintained in a spreadsheet tool, which allowed for convenient coding, searching, and analysis.

It should be noted that the videos, despite being ostensibly "public," were not widely circulating. Each had view counts under 150,000 and comments numbered under one thousand; these are small figures when compared to "viral" videos that can have over a billion views and over tens of thousands of comments. Additionally, in the current landscape of YouTube, popular channels can have millions of subscribers, but within this subcommunity of trans YouTubers, it was more common for a channel to have between one thousand to ten thousand subscribers. While vlogs might be thought of as public presentations, easily retrievable by anyone with a quick keyword search, not all the vloggers and commenters were active "public figures." Given the personal risks that exist for trans people in many public spaces, Crowley assigned pseudonyms to the vloggers and commenters as a means of maintaining their personal privacy.

The present analysis focuses on two excerpts from a video posted in 2017 by Taylor, a prominent nonbinary vlogger, who discusses their use of the term "trans" to refer to themself as a nonbinary person. As of May 2020, there were 15,755 views and 134 comments on the video, many of which directly engaged with Taylor's language ideologies. Crowley chose the following excerpts from the vlog because they each invited explicit uptake from commenting viewers. While both cases involved comments that did not wholly align with Taylor, they differed in their implications for trans discourses in public space, the first illustrating the possibilities of creating a shared understanding among trans and cis communities and the second appearing to preclude this possibility.

The first excerpt comes from the opening of the vlog, when Taylor explains their reason for deciding to refer to themself as *trans*, despite previously being hesitant to do so. Specifically, they "didn't want to deal with people who had a different perspective about what it means to be trans than I do" (line 5), namely those who did not recognize the validity of nonbinary gender identities or who did not consider nonbinary people to be "authentically trans."

Example 1a

1	trans (.) It most simply means
2	that you do not identify with the sex that you were assigned at birth
3	based on that definition I'm about as trans as it gets
4	I realized that I wasn't using this language not because I didn't identify with it
5	but instead because I didn't want to deal with people who had a different perspective about what it means to be trans than I do
6	and then I realized it's important that I be able to identify myself in the way that feels best to me

At the start of the video, Taylor presents a widely accepted definition of the label *trans* (lines 1–2) as a person who does "not identify with the sex that [the person was] assigned at birth." They then assert that they clearly meet this definition (line 3).

Research Methods in Linguistic Anthropology

While Taylor may imagine their discussion of labels to be directed primarily to members of the *trans* community who are viewing their video because they are grappling with similar issues, the video has become accessible to overhearers outside the community, who position themselves as addressees. The following example illustrates the uptake of one viewer who seemed to concede agreement with the point that Taylor makes.

Example 1b

> **Commenter 95** I do not agree with many things you have said on this channel or in this video, however, I appreciate the opportunity to understand where you are coming from with your views. I was glad you defined the word trans before you insisted non-binary was trans because I could now understand how you came to that conclusion.

This commenter recognizes that they do not agree with all of Taylor views, but they accept Taylor's claim that nonbinary people should be included under the trans umbrella, given the clear definition of the term "trans" that they have provided. Among the 134 comments that were posted, 72 reflected a positive uptake, including from those who may not have been trans themselves. Here, we see some evidence that discursive bits of this video have been taken up in positive ways that open up the possibility of legitimizing a nonbinary trans perspective in public space.

However, as the video circulated along pathways that were further from the trans community, it became vulnerable to openly negative uptake. As we noted above, videos such as this one came to be interdiscursively linked to transphobic videos via YouTube's algorithm of juxtaposing "similar" videos. In the next pair of examples, we show a viewer responded to a moment of the video when Taylor adopts what Zimman (2019) calls a "neoliberal ideology of selfhood," according to which the individual is prioritized as the ultimate authority with respect to the language that should be used for them.

Example 2a

1 every person has the ability and the right to label their own experience

2 to use words that make sense to them

3 I've said this before and I'll say it again

4 language is a tool is meant to help us describe our experiences and not meant to be something that feels like a box

5 or something that you feel like you must live up to in order to identify that way

Taylor explains that using language to label oneself is a personal "right" (line 1), and speakers are understood as agents who should be able to use language as a "tool" rather than feeling boxed in by it (line 4). This understanding of language, which prioritizes a person's self-identification, has been central to trans individuals' struggle for linguistic recognition. In response to this specific moment, a viewer raised their objection, challenging this understanding of how language works.

Example 2b

> **Commenter 54** You're very right saying that language is a tool. But you have to consider that people have to be able to understand what you're saying. The listener is the king, and if he doesn't understand you you have to use other words. How you feel can never be the one and only criterion for the applicability of a word.

The commenter rejects Taylor's claim on a few levels. First, their use of generically masculine forms "he" and "king" indexes their disalignment with gender-inclusive language. Second, they reject Taylor's view of language users as agents who have the right to label themselves, privileging instead "the listener" who is "the king" as the arbiter of what words are intelligible and appropriate. It should be noted that while the commenter seems to imply that trans community members fail to recognize that language must be interpreted, trans people tend to be, in fact, very aware of the dialogic nature of the self (Zimman 2017): having one's gender identification recognized and respected by others is crucial. As we saw above, Taylor expressed their acute awareness of how others might interpret their language use: "I didn't want to deal with people who had a different perspective about what it means to be trans than I do" (Example 1a line 5).

The close analysis of these two video excerpts offers a snapshot of how the discourses representing a marginalized community may meet both acceptance and contestation in online public space. In fact, with the passage of two years, the video was met with increasingly negative uptake by viewers, which was likely a reflection not of increasing transphobia but of how the video came to circulate among viewers outside of the trans community. In this way, YouTube offered a space for providing visibility to trans communities and encouraging discussions within them, yet unanticipated pathways of circulation and uptake also led to discourses of trans marginalization, which, in turn, led to a trans migration to more accepting new media spaces.

10.7 Conclusion

Studies of language in the digital realm may entail methods that sometimes diverge from those used in traditional ethnographic settings. As we have discussed earlier, this research raises particular ethical and intellectual concerns. At the same time, we have shown how the wide array of platforms, genres, and communities explored in online contexts can provide many opportunities to answer key linguistic anthropological questions. When this research is conducted with reflexivity, it can only enhance understandings of how new media discourses shape contemporary life as well as how discursive processes materialize more generally.

10.8 Ethnographic Activities

1 Compare two online communities that orient to, each of which defines itself in relation to the other, and orients to specific topics, hobbies, or activities that may define itself in relation to the other (e.g., fans of BTS versus EXO, knitters on Facebook versus Pinterest, YouTube commenters responding to the same news item on CNN versus Fox News). In each community, identify the roles of participation in this community (whether active or passive), the norms of communication (including linguistic and other semiotic forms), and relevant social types and cultural ideologies.
2 Choose a trending topic (e.g., a hashtag or keyword) on Twitter, Instagram, or some other digital platform and conduct a search of this topic. Describe how the "results" yield linguistic characteristics, including forms (words, orthographic representations) and voicing (repetitions, parodies), that are both similar and different. Observe how linguistic elements are juxtaposed on the visible page and consider how interdiscursive links produce interpretive effects for users of this platform.

10.9 Questions to Consider

1 Online communities have different ideas of what constitutes "public" or "private" posts, content, and personal information. Consider a

specific case in which the line between what is "public" and "private" is unclear. Would you choose to collect data in such spaces? If so, how would you choose to anonymize the author or content of a post? What risks and worries arise in processes of anonymization?

2 What challenges exist when representing multimodal data (videos, reaction images, gifs) in academic publications? Consider the ethics of searchability and the ephemerality of web links. What are some solutions to these challenges?

3 Communication in online spaces is "interactional" despite not bearing the same characteristics as face-to-face interaction. What platform tools are modeled on face-to-face interaction? What tools allow interactional moves that are distinct from those found in face-to-face interaction? Why might there be limits to treating online discourse as involving "interactions"?

4 Researchers may be tempted, if not encouraged, to study online communities in which they have minimal experience. Given that modes of participation in online communities can vary (from passive "lurkers" to active "contributors"), is a researcher who has not actively participated in a community justified in conducting research in it? What arguments might be presented for or against conducting researcher as a "lurker" from theoretical and ethical standpoints?

5 "Pathways of discourse" (Wortham and Reyes 2015) may be relatively visible in an online setting, where tokens are often temporally marked, whether through spatial placement or time stamps. Consider a discursive pattern that emerges in a series of tweets that respond to a single tweet—for example, tweets that shift from one stance to another over the course of a year. What conclusions might we draw from this pattern?

10.10 Note

1   This chapter focuses primarily on practices that are part of "new media," rather than addressing all forms of computer-mediated communication. However, we do consider some forms of telecommunication, such as instant messaging and video chatting, which are not canonically new media forms, given that this work has had important implications for new media practice as well.

10.11 References Cited

Agha, Asif. 2005. "Voice, Footing, Enregisterment." *Journal of Linguistic Anthropology* 15 (1): 38–59. https://doi.org/10.1525/jlin.2005.15.1.38.

Agha, Asif. 2011. "Meet Mediatization." *Language and Communication* 3 (31): 163–70.

American Anthropological Association. 2012. "Statement of Ethics." https://www.americananthro.org/LearnAndTeach/Content.aspx?ItemNumber=22869&navItemNumber=652.

Anderson, Benedict. 1983. *Imagined Communities: Reflections on the Origin and Spread of Nationalism*. London: Verso Books.

Baron, Naomi, and Rich Ling. 2003. "IM and SMS: A Linguistic Comparison." *Fourth International Conference of the Association of Internet Researchers, Toronto, Oct, 16–19.*

Bauman, Richard. 2005. "Commentary: Indirect Indexicality, Identity, Performance." *Journal of Linguistic Anthropology* 15 (1): 145–50.

Bauman, Richard. 2010. "The Remediation of Storytelling: Narrative Performance on Early Commercial Sound Recordings." In Deborah Schiffrin, Anna De Fina, and Anastasia Nylund eds., *Telling Stories: Building Bridges among Language, Narrative, Identity, Interaction, Society and Culture*, 23–43. Washington, DC: Georgetown University Press.

Bauman, Richard, and Charles L. Briggs. 1990. "Poetics and Performances as Critical Perspectives on Language and Social Life." *Annual Review of Anthropology* 19 (1): 59–88.

Bax, Anna. 2018. "'The C-Word' Meets 'the N-Word': The Slur-Once-Removed and the Discursive Construction of 'Reverse Racism.'" *Journal of Linguistic Anthropology* 28 (2): 114–36.

Boellstorff, Tom. 2008. *Coming of Age in Second Life: An Anthropologist Explores the Virtually Human*. Princeton: Princeton University Press.

Boellstorff, Tom, Bonnie Nardi, Celia Pearce, and Tina L. Taylor. 2012. *Ethnography and Virtual Worlds: A Handbook of Method*. Princeton: Princeton University Press.

Bonilla, Yarimar, and Jonathan Rosa. 2015. "# Ferguson: Digital Protest, Hashtag Ethnography, and the Racial Politics of Social Media in the United States." *American Ethnologist* 42 (1): 4–17.

Bourdieu, Pierre. 1991. *Language and Symbolic Power*. Cambridge: Harvard University Press.

Bourdieu, Pierre. 1977. *Outline of a Theory of Practice*. Cambridge: Cambridge University Press.

boyd, danah, and Kate Crawford. 2011. "Six Provocations for Big Data." Paper presented at *A Decade in Internet Time: Symposium on the Dynamics of the Internet and Society*. Rochester, NY: Social Science Research Network, https://doi.org/10.2139/ssrn.1926431.

Briggs, Charles L., and Richard Bauman. 1992. "Genre, Intertextuality, and Social Power." *Journal of Linguistic Anthropology* 2 (2): 131–72.

Brubaker, Rogers, and Frederick Cooper. 2000. "Beyond 'Identity.'" *Theory and Society* 29 (1): 1–47.

Bucholtz, Mary. 2010. *White Kids: Language, Race, and Styles of Youth Identity*. Cambridge: Cambridge University Press.

Bucholtz, Mary. 2011. "Race and the Re-embodied Voice in Hollywood Film." *Language & Communication* 31 (3): 255–65.

Bucholtz, Mary, and Kira Hall. 2004. "Theorizing Identity in Language and Sexuality Research." *Language in Society* 33 (4): 469–515.

Bucholtz, Mary, and Kira Hall. 2005. "Identity and Interaction: A Sociocultural Linguistic Approach." *Discourse Studies* 7 (4–5): 585–614.

Bucholtz, Mary, and Kira Hall. 2016. "Embodied Sociolinguistics." In Nikolas Coupland ed., *Sociolinguistics*, 173–98. Cambridge: Cambridge University Press.

Calhoun, Kendra. 2019. "Vine Racial Comedy as Anti-hegemonic Humor: Linguistic Performance and Generic Innovation." *Journal of Linguistic Anthropology* 29 (1): 27–49.

Chun, Elaine. 2013. "Ironic Blackness as Masculine Cool: Asian American Language and Authenticity on YouTube." *Applied Linguistics* 34 (5): 592–612.

Chun, Elaine W. 2017. "How to Drop a Name: Hybridity, Purity, and the K-Pop Fan." *Language in Society* 46 (1): 57–76.

Chun, Elaine, and Keith Walters. 2011. "Orienting to Arab Orientalisms: Language, Race, and Humor in a YouTube Video." *Digital Discourse: Language in the New Media* 251: 273.

Coupland, Nikolas. 2001. "Dialect Stylization in Radio Talk." *Language in Society* 30 (3): 345–75.

Dame, Avery. 2013. "'I'm Your Hero? Like Me?': The Role of 'Expert' in the Trans Male Vlog." *Journal of Language and Sexuality* 2 (1): 40–69.

D'Arcy, Alexandra, and Taylor Marie Young. 2012. "Ethics and Social Media: Implications for Sociolinguistics in the Networked Public." *Journal of Sociolinguistics* 16 (4): 532–46.

Eckert, Penelope. 2004. "The Meaning of Style." In Wai Fong Chiang, Elaine Chun, Laura Mahalingappa, and Siri Mehus eds., *Proceedings of the Eleventh Annual Symposium about Language and Society—Austin, Texas Linguistic Forum 47*, 41–53, Austin, TX: Department of Linguistics, University of Texas at Austin.

Eckert, Penelope, and Sally McConnell-Ginet. 1992. "Think Practically and Look Locally: Language and Gender as Community-Based Practice." *Annual Review of Anthropology* 21 (1): 461–88.

Garcia, Angela Cora, Alecea I. Standlee, Jennifer Bechkoff, and Yan Cui. 2009. "Ethnographic Approaches to the Internet and Computer-Mediated Communication." *Journal of Contemporary Ethnography* 38 (1): 52–84.

Gee, James P. 2014. *An Introduction to Discourse Analysis: Theory and Method.* New York: Routledge.

Geertz, Clifford. 1973. "Thick Description: Toward an Interpretive Theory of Culture." *Turning Points in Qualitative Research: Tying Knots in a Handkerchief* 3: 143–68.

Gershon, Ilana. 2010a. "Media Ideologies: An Introduction." *Journal of Linguistic Anthropology* 20 (2): 283–93.

Gershon, Ilana. 2010b. *The Breakup 2.0: Disconnecting over New Media.* Ithaca, NY: Cornell University Press.

Gershon, Ilana. 2017. "Language and the Newness of Media." *Annual Review of Anthropology* 46: 15–31.

Goffman, Erving. 1981. *Forms of Talk.* Oxford, UK: Blackwell.

Goodwin, Charles. 2000. "Action and Embodiment within Situated Human Interaction." *Journal of Pragmatics* 32 (10): 1489–522.

Goodwin, Marjorie Harness. 1990. "Byplay: Participant Structure and Framing of Collaborative Collusion." *Réseaux. Communication—Technologie—Société* 8 (2): 155–80. p. 410.

Gumperz, John J. 1982. *Discourse Strategies.* Cambridge: Cambridge University Press.

Hall, Kira, Donna M. Goldstein, and Matthew Bruce Ingram. 2016. "The Hands of Donald Trump: Entertainment, Gesture, Spectacle." *HAU: Journal of Ethnographic Theory* 6 (2): 71–100.

Heath, Christian, and Paul Luff. 1993. "Interactional Asymmetries in Video Mediated Communication." In Graham Button ed., *Technology in Working Order: Studies of Work, Interaction, and Technology,* 35–54. New York: Routledge.

Hill, Jane H. 2005. "Intertextuality as Source and Evidence for Indirect Indexical Meanings." *Journal of Linguistic Anthropology* 15 (1): 113–24.

Hill, Jane H. 2008. *The Everyday Language of White Racism.* Malden, MA: Wiley-Blackwell.

Hillewaert, Sarah. 2015. "Writing with an Accent: Orthographic Practice, Emblems, and Traces on Facebook." *Journal of Linguistic Anthropology* 25 (2): 195–214.

Horst, Heather A., and Daniel Miller, eds. 2012. *Digital Anthropology.* New York: Routledge.

Johnstone, Barbara. 1994. *Repetition in Discourse.* Norwood, NJ: Ablex Publishing Company.

Johnstone, Barbara. 2017. *Discourse Analysis*. Malden, MA: Blackwell.

Jones, Graham M., and Bambi B. Schieffelin. 2009. "Talking Text and Talking Back: 'My BFF Jill' from Boob Tube to YouTube." *Journal of Computer-Mediated Communication* 14 (4): 1050–79.

Jones, Lucy. 2019. "Discourses of Transnormativity in Vloggers' Identity Construction." *International Journal of the Sociology of Language* 2019 (256): 85–101.

Keating, Elizabeth. 2015. "The Role of the Body and Space in Digital Multimodality." In Alexandra Georgakopoulou and Tereza Spilioti eds., *The Routledge Handbook of Language and Digital Communication*, 259–72. New York: Routledge.

Keating, Elizabeth, and Chiho Sunakawa. 2010. "Participation Cues: Coordinating Activity and Collaboration in Complex Online Gaming Worlds." *Language in Society*, 331–56.

Konnelly, Lex. 2018. "'I'm Just Making an Update Video': Stylistic Use of Creaky Voice in Non-binary Transition Vlogs." Paper presented at Lavender Languages and Linguistics Conference (LavLang) 25. Rhode Island College.

Kozinets, Robert V. 2007. "Netnography." *The Blackwell Encyclopedia of Sociology*, 1–2.

Lamerichs, Joyce, and Hedwig F. M. Te Molder. 2003. "Computer-Mediated Communication: From a Cognitive to a Discursive Model." *New Media & Society* 5 (4): 451–73.

LeBesco, Kathleen. 2004. "Managing Visibility, Intimacy, and Focus in Online Critical Ethnography." *Online Social Research: Methods, Issues, and Ethics*, 63–79. New York: Peter Lang.

Linguistic Society of America. 2019. "Revised Ethics Statement." https://www.linguisticsociety.org/content/lsa-revised-ethics-statement-approved-july-2019.

Manning, Paul. 2009. "Can the Avatar Speak?" *Journal of Linguistic Anthropology* 19 (2): 310–25.

McIntosh, Janet. 2018. "Listening versus Lingwashing: Promise, Peril, and Structural Oblivion When White South Africans Learn Indigenous African Languages." *Signs and Society* 6 (3): 475–503.

Mendoza-Denton, Norma. 2008. *Homegirls: Symbolic Practices in the Making of Latina Youth Styles*. Malden, MA: Blackwell.

Modan, Gabriella. 2016. "Writing the Relationship: Ethnographer-Informant Interactions in the New Media Era." *Journal of Linguistic Anthropology* 26 (1): 98–107.

Mol, Lisette, Emiel Krahmer, Alfons Maes, and Marc Swerts. 2011. "Seeing and Being Seen: The Effects on Gesture Production." *Journal of Computer-Mediated Communication* 17 (1): 77–100.

Narayan, Kirin. 1993. "How Native Is a 'Native' Anthropologist?" *American Anthropologist* 95 (3): 671–86.

Newon, Lisa. 2015. "Online Multiplayer Games." In Alexandra Georgakopoulou and Tereza Spilioti eds., *The Routledge Handbook of Language and Digital Communication*, 289–304. New York: Routledge.

Ochs, Elinor. 1992. "14 Indexing Gender." *Rethinking Context: Language as an Interactive Phenomenon* 11: 335.

Perrino, Sabina. 2017. "Recontextualizing Racialized Stories on YouTube." *Narrative Inquiry* 27 (2): 261–85.

Pink, Sarah. 2016. "Digital Ethnography." *Innovative Methods in Media and Communication Research*, edited by Sebastian and Anne Kaun, 161–5. Los Angeles: SAGE. https://www.palgrave.com/gp/book/9783319406992

Raclaw, Joshua. 2008. "Two Patterns for Conversational Closings in Instant Message Discourse." *Colorado Research in Linguistics* 21.

Raun, Tobias. 2016. *Out Online: Trans Self-Representation and Community Building on YouTube*. New York: Routledge.

Reuver, Mark de, Carsten Sørensen, and Rahul C. Basole. 2018. "The Digital Platform: A Research Agenda." *Journal of Information Technology* 33 (2): 124–35.

Reyes, Angela. 2014. "Linguistic Anthropology in 2013: Super-New-Big." *American Anthropologist* 116 (2): 366–78.

Robinson, Bianca. n.d. "Black Twitter, White Supremacists, and AAE." Unpublished manuscript.

Ronkin, Maggie, and Helen E. Karn. 1999. "Mock Ebonics: Linguistic Racism in Parodies of Ebonics on the Internet." *Journal of Sociolinguistics* 3 (3): 360–80.

Rymes, Betsy. 2012. "Recontextualizing YouTube: From Macro–Micro to Mass-Mediated Communicative Repertoires." *Anthropology & Education Quarterly* 43 (2): 214–27.

Schieffelin, B. B., and E. Ochs. 1986. "Language Socialization." *Annual Review of Anthropology* 15 (1): 163–91. https://doi.org/10.1146/annurev. an.15.100186.001115.

Slobe, Tyanna. 2018. "Style, Stance, and Social Meaning in Mock White Girl." *Language in Society* 47 (4): 541–67.

Smalls, Krystal A. 2018. "Languages of Liberation: Digital Discourses of Emphatic Blackness." In Netta Avineri, Laura R. Graham, Eric J. Johnson, Robin Conley Riner, and Jonathan Rosa eds., *Language and Social Justice in Practice*, 52–60. New York: Routledge.

Squires, Lauren. 2010. "Enregistering Internet Language." *Language in Society* 39 (4): 457–92.

Squires, Lauren. 2014. "From TV Personality to Fans and Beyond: Indexical Bleaching and the Diffusion of a Media Innovation." *Journal of Linguistic Anthropology* 24 (1): 42–62.

Sunakawa, Chiho. 2012. "Japanese Family via Webcam: An Ethnographic Study of Cross-Spatial Interactions." Edited by M. Okumura, D. Bekki, and K. Satoh. *Lecture Notes in Computer Science* 7258: 264–76.

Tannen, Deborah. 2007. *Talking Voices: Repetition, Dialogue, and Imagery in Conversational Discourse*. Vol. 26. New York: Cambridge University Press.

Tomita, Hidenori. 2005. "Keitai and the Intimate Stranger." In Mizuko Ito, D. Okabe, and M. Matsuda eds., *Personal, Portable, Pedestrian: Mobile Phones in Japanese Life*, 183–201. Cambridge, MA: MIT Press.

Wortham, Stanton. 2003. "Accomplishing Identity in Participant-Denoting Discourse." *Journal of Linguistic Anthropology* 13 (2): 189–210. https://doi.org/10.1525/jlin.2003.13.2.189.

Wortham, Stanton. 2006. *Learning Identity: The Joint Emergence of Social Identification and Academic Learning*. New York: Cambridge University Press.

Wortham, Stanton, and Angela Reyes. 2015. *Discourse Analysis beyond the Speech Event*. New York: Routledge.

Zimman, Lal. 2017. "Trans People's Linguistic Self-Determination and the Dialogic Nature of Identity." In Evan Hazenberg and Miriam Meyerhoff eds., *Representing Trans*, 226–48. Wellington, New Zealand: Victoria University Press.

10.12 Further Reading

Boellstorff, Tom, Bonnie Nardi, Celia Pearce, and Tina L. Taylor. 2012. *Ethnography and Virtual Worlds: A Handbook of Method*. Princeton: Princeton University Press.

This book provides useful guidance on conducting ethnography in virtual worlds, drawing on the authors' varied ethnographic experiences in game and non-game online contexts. It offers practical advice and discusses potential ethical issues.

11

Mixed Methods and Interdisciplinary Research in Linguistic Anthropology

Sonya E. Pritzker

11.1 Introduction

Linguistic anthropologists arguably already draw upon a range of diverse methodological approaches in any given study. Most studies thus often include participant observation (see Pritzker and Perrino, this volume), ethnographic interviews (see Perrino, this volume), sociolinguistic interviews, and video recording (see Kohler and Murphy, this volume; Mitsuhara and Hauck, this volume). Researchers also often draw on methods in visual anthropology (Morphy and Banks 1997). In interpreting data, moreover, ethnomethodological and conversation analytic traditions have played an enormous role in shaping the methods linguistic anthropologists use (Clemente 2013, M. Goodwin and Cekaite 2018, 24; see also Shohet and Lloyd, this volume).

Individual scholars or teams of linguistic anthropologists have also incorporated methods from other anthropological subfields and outside disciplines into their research, however, including quantitative survey methods (e.g., Bacon 2020), Participatory Action Research (e.g., Daniels 2018), archival methods (e.g., Hosemann 2019), and person-centered ethnography (e.g., Pritzker 2014; Shohet 2013). The argument could thus be made that the field of linguistic anthropology is already constitutive of a "mixed methods" subfield. Linguistic anthropology, in other words—to borrow the metaphor invoked by Weisner when he writes that "[m]ethods and research designs are *languages* understood across the social sciences" (2012, 3, emphasis mine)—could arguably be said to be fluent, or at least conversant, in multiple-language methods.

Deciding which methods to mix into studies in linguistic anthropology, however, can be a complex decision involving many considerations:

- When, for example, does it makes sense to incorporate mixed methods into a specific study?
- What are the benefits and drawbacks in developing a mixed methods approach to linguistic anthropology?
- And what kinds of considerations must we make in representing linguistic anthropology within a larger study that may also include researchers in other disciplines or anthropological subfields?

In reflecting upon such questions, this chapter takes a primarily conceptual approach to developing mixed methods studies in linguistic anthropology. While offering examples of studies using mixed methods where relevant, the overall focus of the chapter is primarily on developing an understanding of mixed methods *as* method. For reference, however, Table 11.1 provides an overview of some of the specific quantitative and qualitative methods that researchers may consider combining with the standard methods of linguistic anthropology, including a brief description of the procedures as well as the value and limitations of the method, especially with regard to the primary concerns of linguistic anthropologists.

Rather than discussing the pros and cons of specific methods, the remainder of this chapter thus emphasizes issues in the design and implementation of mixed methods studies. The central importance of study design cannot, in my opinion, be overemphasized. As one biostatistician dramatically put it, "[t]o consult the statistician after an experiment is finished is often merely to ask him to conduct a post-mortem examination. He can perhaps say what the experiment died of" (Fisher 1938, 17).[1] Though one may also want to ensure that those who collaborate with mixed methods research share an ethical orientation toward basic human rights and social justice, e.g., one would likely *not* want to collaborate with Fisher himself (see note 1), this life-or-death perspective provides insight into the importance of appropriately incorporating expert perspectives into the design of any study that involves mixed methods.[2] Highlighting the importance of integrating both data-collection and data-analysis strategies from the very outset of a study's conceptualization, the argument underscores several key points that I will be returning to throughout this chapter. First, it foregrounds the fact

Table 11.1 Selected Methods

Method	Definition and procedures	Value	Limitations and challenges	Sources
Archival methods	Collection and analysis of government or private sector administrative records	Helps historically, geographically, or socially contextualize primary data	Data are not always accurate or comprehensive; data not originally collected for research purposes; can take a long time to sort through; data triangulation often challenging	Schensul (2013) Hosemann (2019)
Cultural domain and/or cultural consensus analysis	Elicitation and measurement of the salient cognitive categories people in a community or society have (domains) and the extent to which they agree on the meaning of such domains (consensus); conducted using freelist and/or pilesort exercises	Can help researchers get a sense of shared meaning in society, e.g., what it means to be successful or what an ideal relationship consists of; may provide insight into how participants articulate meaning and/or vocalize the decision-making process to the researcher during freelisting and pilesorting exercises	Focused on cognition rather than practice: does not necessarily give us a lot of detail on why there is (dis)agreement on certain domains; often carried out with individuals on a one-by-one basis so not necessarily appropriate for gathering data on interaction among participants	Romney et al. (1986) Borgotti and Hagin (2013)

Method	Definition and procedures	Value	Limitations and challenges	Sources
Digital ethnography	Often referred to as virtual ethnography (Hine 2011), netnography (Kozinets 2015), and social media ethnography (Postill and Pink 2012), among other terms; digital ethnography involves the collection of ethnographic data in online environments either through observation ("lurking") only or in combination with some form of participation, either synchronous or asynchronous	Understanding how people engage with the internet; examining how people develop and maintain social relationships online, especially within and across racialized populations (e.g., Calhoun 2019; Smalls 2019); allows researchers to study multimodal communication that involves text, emojis, photos, videos, etc., as well as the creative use of punctuation (Deumert 2014); can be done completely virtually or can involve both online and offline interactions with participants	Challenges anthropologists to reconsider the notion of participant observation; requires understanding online interaction in terms of self-representation beyond the duality of "authenticity" and "performance" (Gershon 2015); requires researchers to rethink the ways in which they understand "participation" (Bonilla and Rosa 2015; Durrani 2018) and "authorship" (Deumert 2014); may be challenging to gather enough cultural background knowledge or the personal history of conversational partners (Jones and Schieffelin 2016)	Deumert (2014) Bonilla and Rosa (2015) Gershon (2015) Kozinets (2015) Jones and Schieffelin (2016) Durrani (2018) Calhoun (2019) Smalls (2019)

Method	Definition and procedures	Value	Limitations and challenges	Sources
Ethnoarchaeological tracking	Follows participants closely in space over time, noting location, activity, and objects involved at regular intervals	"[W]ell-suited to research in which intra- and intergroup comparisons of activities, uses of objects, and uses of space are an analytic goal" (Ochs et al. 2006, 391); can generate quantitative data	Tracking deters researchers' attention away from participation; making sense of this data in relation to other data can be challenging	Ochs et al. (2006)
Focus groups	Consists of interviewing a group of participants at once; should be based on representative samples; commonly used to ascertain social norms, attitudes, perspectives on products or phenomenon	Generates a lot of data, including interactions among participants; can be useful at the beginning of a study (to form research questions/hypothesis) or at the end of a study to confirm findings	Not necessarily generalizable; for linguistic anthropologists, these data may not be as compelling because the group often brings people together who normally wouldn't interact	Schensul and LeCompte (2013)
Mapping/GIS	Involves digitally or manually maps the space where a community is located, including the overall geography, the location of services and institutions, and the "activity spaces" and/ or "time budgets" of participants	Used to understand the ways in which participants relate to space in and over time, or the ways in which access to services and institutions is mediated by geography; can give insight into participants' "sense of place"	The researchers' production of maps may affect communities in unexpected ways; with activity space as the focus, data are often limited to the "gross allocation of time to different classes of activity" rather than a detailed understanding of activities (Cromley 2013, 147)	Cromley (2013)

Method	Definition and procedures	Value	Limitations and challenges	Sources
Microphenomeno-logical interviews	Interviewing participants in order to capture their "lived experience" through detailed questions about timing, location, and process of felt sensations	Produces fine-grained descriptions of embodied and emotional experience; may support linguistic anthropologists in gathering data on the ways in which experience is described in a given community or site (or by individuals)	Very individually focused; may not satisfy requirements for recording interaction. Like all interviews, microphenomenological interviews also must be analyzed in terms of the interaction between the researcher and participant	Petitmengin (2006) Petitmengin et al. (2019)
Participatory action research (PAR)/ collaborative ethnography	Involves the inclusion of research participants in the research process: including project design, data collection, data analysis, and final presentations in texts and other forms	Well suited to projects that aim toward producing results that affect the world in ways that align with community interests and social justice; also valuable in supporting self-awareness, e.g., teachers' awareness of language ideologies (Daniels 2018)	Establishing an equal balance of power in the research relationship can be challenging; may sometimes need to be adapted as appropriate; entails risks in terms of academic prestige of results, requests, and/or demands that participants make	Lassiter (2005) Daniels (2018)
Person-centered interviews	Involves asking about participants' experience over the course of their lives; often involves multiple interviews with the same person	Engages the interviewee as both "expert witness" and object of study (Hollan 2005, 463); offers an opportunity to explore the relationship between cultural context and personal meaning	Interviewee must feel comfortable enough to candidly express sometimes very personal experiences and feelings; generates a huge amount of data that must be triangulated with other material	Levy and Hollan (1998) Hollan (2005)

Method	Definition and procedures	Value	Limitations and challenges	Sources
Phenomenological/ embodied methods and autoethnography	Involves formal reflection, among researchers, upon their embodied and affective experience in the field, including their memories	Allows researchers to formally engage with their fieldwork experience as data; contributes to analyses that move away from trying to be "objective" and is more honest in terms of showing how findings emerge as a situated conversation in space and time	May not always be taken seriously by readers, especially outside of anthropology; careful balance is needed not to over-center the research on one's own experience; in linguistic anthropology, may not have similar data from participants if only collecting conversation/interviews	Desjarlais (1992) Collins and Gallinat (2010) Skinner (2010) Stodulka et al. (2018)
Photovoice	Entails giving participants cameras so they can document their lives in meaningful ways; once photographs are collected, group interviews are set up for participants to discuss and interpret the images	As a form of PAR, photovoice is oriented toward social justice: it gives participants a voice and is often useful in generating data that can be used to appeal to institutional and government powers; can function to generate dialogue in a community (Liebenberg 2018)	Same challenges as any form of PAR (see above); may not necessarily achieve the results hoped for in terms of reaching institutions and/ or effecting change; can be difficult to protect privacy and confidentiality of people who are photographed (Castleden et al. 2008)	Wang and Burris (1997) Castleden et al. (2008) Harper (2012) Liebenberg (2018)

Method	Definition and procedures	Value	Limitations and challenges	Sources
Psychophysiological methods	Involves the measurement of physiological arousal in various forms (heart rate variability, electrodermal skin conductance, etc.)	Can reveal momentary or habitual patterns of physiological arousal in participants; can be paired with video recordings of interaction or other ethnographic observations to get a sense of what is occurring physiologically during communication (e.g., Mendoza-Denton et al. 2017; Eisenhauer 2019; Pritzker et al. 2020)	Requires technological skill in different forms of data collection and analysis; may be costly or increase burden on participants; triangulation with other types of data can be challenging; researchers must be cautious in attributing results to revealing an underlying biological substrate that is more "real" than interaction	Seligman (2014) Mendoza-Denton et al. (2017) Eisenhauer (2019) Pritzker et al. (2020)
Social network analysis	Involves identifying people within a group, their perceptions of others in a group, and the connections between people; can be done with a single individual or across multiple groups	It can be used to identify patterns of interaction within and among groups; to track the ways in which knowledge or ideas travel through social groups; to identify cultural differences in social groupings; conducting social network analyses often have the advantage of helping anthropologists in recruitment.	Requires systematized sampling strategies; researchers need to be careful not to reduce participants to "nodes" in a network as opposed to individuals with complex lives and complex relationships	Trotter (2013)

Method	Definition and procedures	Value	Limitations and challenges	Sources
Ethnographic Surveys	Involves the structured collection of data through closed-ended questions (yes/no; Likert scale) which yield quantifiable results; can be administered face to face or online	Can be used to gather data that are representative and generalizable (depending on sample); can be used to gather information to adapt other aspects of research to a local population	Results limited by closed-ended nature of questions; question design depends on researcher knowledge of the site/topic; requires further collection of data to make sense of the results	Schensul and LeCompte (2013)
Video recall	Involves playing back previously recorded video to participants in order to elicit their ideas about what occurred in the interaction, what they were feeling, and anything else they would like to share; can be continuous or based on researcher-selected clips	Allows researchers to confirm or refute researcher codes and interpretations; offers perspective into the "subjective" experience of interaction; offers participants the opportunity to be self-reflective	May place increased burden on participants by taking additional time and/or making them revisit potentially emotional episodes; may be challenging to keep participants focus on process rather than content; conflicts between participant impressions and researcher observations may result	Welsh and Dickson (2005) Larsen et al. (2008)

that the best mixed methods or interdisciplinary research, in any field, adopts an integrative perspective from the very outset of study conceptualization. Rather than simply "adding on" methods that seem potentially valuable, careful consideration of how each new method is connected to the overall research question is critical, as is either the guidance from expert or a concerted effort to find training in a given method. Second, it foregrounds the considerable challenges that face researchers attempting to make sense of data collected with divergent methods. It also, however, suggests the value that researchers from different backgrounds with diverse skill sets can work effectively together in ways that breathe "life" into the study.

This chapter thus foregrounds a discussion of what it means for linguistic anthropologists to develop a mixed methods approach in their work, whether independently or as part of a larger team. The following section provides an overview of important considerations in crafting mixed methods studies in linguistic anthropology, including a discussion of the definition of "mixed methods research," the value of mixed methods research, and the challenges involved in implementing a mixed methods study. Section 11.3 then describes ethical issues in mixed methods and interdisciplinary research involving linguistic anthropology. Here, I focus on the ways in which mixed methods studies may increase the burden on participants. In this section, I also turn a critical lens back upon the ethics of mixed methods by posing questions about how one maintains fidelity to the core methods of linguistic anthropology in interdisciplinary research. In Section 11.4, I offer a short case study of a mixed method study that integrates linguistic anthropology with biocultural anthropology and communication studies. I conclude with a short review of the main "take-aways" of the chapter as well as several ethnographic activities and discussion questions.

11.2 Mixed Methods in Linguistic Anthropology: Issues and Considerations

11.2.1 Defining Mixed Methods

Many scholars adopt a definition of "mixed methods" as necessarily involving a combination of qualitative and quantitative methods (e.g., Weisner 2012; Fetters et al. 2013). While I highlight key perspectives from those who embrace this definition throughout the following sections, my stance in this chapter is that many of the core principles regarding the value, meaning, and challenges of conducting mixed methods research pertain to the incorporation of divergent quantitative as well as qualitative methods. Here, it may further be helpful to think about the ways in which "mixed theory" is itself a form of mixed method. While reading outside the field may also lead one to decide to implement explicit methodological expansions, in other words, it is also important to recognize the ways in which theoretical insights and perspectives from beyond linguistic anthropology can play a significant role in shaping one's research questions. Reading theory from other anthropological subfields and other disciplines thus arguably constitutes one of the most rudimentary ways in which one can begin to think about a project using mixed methods. As Richland (this volume) discusses, it often behooves linguistic anthropologists to develop their own work in conversation with scholars and researchers in other fields. A mixed theory approach might, for example, begin with the refinement of one's research question—and hence, one's methods—through immersing oneself in the theories and perspectives of scholars outside linguistic anthropology. In a study of everyday interaction at a Cherokee rock art site in the United States, for example, Manns (2020) built upon an in-depth reading of contemporary archaeological literature to engage with the language displayed on signage and the conversations of visitors to show how both often conflict with Cherokee ideologies of language and time. If we take "methods" to mean only the way Manns set about gathering and analyzing her data—specifically using handheld audio recorders to capture the dialogue of spectators engaging with the rock; conducting interviews with visitors and caretakers of the site; and developing detailed line-by-line analyses of conversations—it would be easy to conclude that the study represents mainly linguistic anthropological research. The ways in which she conceived of the study as well as the way she interpreted the data and framed the value and contributions of the research, however, reveal the important influence of archaeological theories in her study. "Mixed methods" can thus arguably point to a wide range of different interdisciplinary and cross-subfield approaches to research in linguistic anthropology.

11.2.2 The Value of Mixed Methods

In comparing methods to languages, Weisner points to the ways in which methods "speak" about human life and human behavior using various terminologies and jargons. The metaphor also suggests the ways in which methods, like languages, pragmatically achieve divergent understandings of human experience and human activity. When we draw on multiple and diverse methods in our research, Weisner suggests, it is like learning different languages, a skill that allows us to "draw those in other disciplines into conversations with us" (2012, 3). The resulting conversation, moreover, addresses the gaps between disciplines or what Levine (2016) discusses as a scientific "Tower of Babel." "The social sciences today are divided into research communities that cherish their separation from each other," Levine writes, arguing that mixed methods thus constitute "the essential basis for building substantive connections across disciplines" (2016, 8). Creswell et al. (2011, 4) take this a step further, suggesting that the use of mixed methods by diverse researchers has the capability of generating "a more just and democratic society that permeates the entire research process, from the problem to the conclusions, and the use of results." The transformative possibilities for mixed methods research to bridge vast conceptual divides are thus frequently touted as one of its foremost values.

Echoing this argument, linguistic anthropologists have likewise argued that the value of using mixed methods "challenges singular ways of producing and expressing knowledge—both linguistically and methodologically" (Bacon 2020, 174). In linguistic anthropology, what Bacon (2020) identifies as the "strict separation of research paradigms as philosophically incompatible" (2020, 174) thus often hampers the development of mixed methods studies. As I discuss further in Section 11.3, such "bias" can also be framed as a kind of ethical commitment to the core principles of one's discipline, both theoretically and methodologically. Advocating for mixed theory or mixed methods, importantly, does not necessarily mean that researchers must always compromise such principles. Das (2013) points out, for example, that linguistic anthropologists are often critical of quantitative approaches that are perceived, by many, to "privilege scientific knowledge in the service of state governance" (2013, 222). Das argues, however, that this bias not only occludes the fact that linguistic anthropologists often incorporate what Hymes called a "qualitative and discrete mathematics" (1977, 166, as cited in Das 2013), but also obscures the reality that many quantitative studies, particularly in sociolinguistics, "sometimes apply these methods to processes of identity formation as well" (2013, 222). Das thus concludes that an increased openness toward multiple different perspectives on methodologies contributes significant value to studies of linguistic anthropology.

Facing such biases, Weisner argues, can not only contribute to the breaking down of disciplinary boundaries, but can also "improve core theory" in a specific subfield or discipline (2016, 394). Indeed, there have been many examples of researchers using both qualitative and quantitative methods to develop theory in linguistic anthropology. Bacon (2020), for example, argues that the theory of language ideologies, in particular, benefits from a mixed methods approach. "Language ideologies … can never be fully observed through empirical means," he writes (2020, 174), concluding that the more and varied types of data we bring to the task of studying language ideologies, the better. In his study of language ideologies among K-12 teachers engaged in monolingual English immersion, he thus drew upon a three-phase design combining both qualitative and quantitative methods in order to develop a fine-grained theory that appreciates what he calls the "trajectory" of language ideologies (Bacon 2020, 184). Phenomenological approaches to the study of embodiment have likewise contributed to structuring the core research questions and methods in several projects conducted over the past several decades, for example (e.g., Wilce 2011; Corwin 2012; Shohet 2013; Pritzker 2014; Goodwin and Cekaite 2018; Pritzker and Perrino 2020). This body of work demonstrates how a nuanced approach to measuring people's felt experience deepens theories of interaction, indexicality and intertextuality (see, e.g., Ochs 2012). Collaborative research methods, finally—though often met with resistance in the academy for not meeting the demands of academic rigor (Lassiter 2005, 149)—have also expanded theory in linguistic anthropology. Daniels (2018), for example, drawing on the method of participatory action research (PAR), conducted research on how white teachers unknowingly perpetuate racialized language ideologies in the classroom by teaching children to codeswitch. Working closely with teacher-participants in the analysis and interpretation of data gathered during classroom sessions, Daniels was able to integrate white teachers' "embodied understandings of the relationship between race and language" (Daniels 2018, 169) with the developing theory of raciolinguistics (Flores and Rosa 2015; Alim et al. 2016). This work thus further demonstrates how a range a methodological approaches contributes to the development of core theory in linguistic anthropology.

In terms of the presentation and durability of research findings regarding their efficacy in the world, Weisner argues that mixed methods in anthropology specifically can support a robust *public anthropology* that contributes "to policy, practice, or current issues" (2016, 394; see also Hay

2016b, Worthman 2016). Mixed methods research can thus enrich analysis, bolster the "reach" of a project in terms of presentations and publications, as well as contribute meaningful solutions for public or social issues. Phillips notes that in order to accomplish this in linguistic anthropology, however, "it is necessary to have evidence for our claims, to give those claims authority and reliability" (Phillips 2013, 93). Phillips thus argues that the incorporation of empirically driven comparative methods—sometimes quantitative—is often necessary.

11.2.3 When to Mix Methods

Especially when there is a legitimate fear that such approaches might necessitate a dilution of the core theoretical commitments of linguistic anthropology, the question of when and to what extent to take a mixed methods approach to a given project is not always an easy one to answer. The methods one chooses in a given study should therefore emerge from an in-depth consideration of what kinds of data are needed in order to answer a particular research question. The range of methods one chooses should further ideally be decided at the design phase of one's project. As much as is realistically possible, then, methodological decisions should therefore be driven by the research question(s) and the design of the study rather than one's preferences or the demands (real or perceived) of advisors, collaborators, or funding institutions.

The size and extent of the study also matters when deciding when to use mixed methods. Weisner (2016, 403), for example, distinguishes between single mixed methods studies and "research programs." Whether one is considering using mixed methods in single studies or research programs, general guidelines are available to support the decision-making process based on objective criteria pertaining to the goals of the research. Mixed methods are a good fit, for example, when,

- researchers would like to converge different methods or use one method to corroborate the findings from another about a single phenomenon (triangulation);
- researchers would like to use one method to elaborate, illustrate, enhance, or clarify the results from another method (complementarity);
- researchers would like to use results from one method to inform another method, such as in creating a measure (development);

Mixed Methods and Interdisciplinary Research   **345**

- researchers would like to use one method to discover paradoxes and contradictions in findings from another method that can suggest reframing research questions (initiation);
- researchers seek to expand the breadth and depth of the study by using different methods for different research components (expansion).

(Wisdom et al. 2012, 723)

Though specifically talking about the integration or mixing of quantitative and qualitative methods, the distinctions between what Wisdom and colleagues refer to as "triangulation, complementarity, development, initiation, and expansion" thus offers a valuable overall perspective on when and why to mix methods.

It is also important to acknowledge, however, that in reality the processes described in generalized guides may not necessarily always be as distinct or clear-cut as they appear. The question of when to use mixed methods in a project is furthermore not always straightforward. Among both students and established scholars, moreover, the best-laid plans in terms of research design are often derailed in the course of research for a range of both pragmatic and ethical reasons. The plan to use a method that requires use of a complex internet-based software program, for example, might be determined to be impossible once one reaches the field and discovers that they cannot reliably find a decent Wi-Fi connection. Other restrictions encountered over the course of developing a project might require a kind of "pivot" *into* rather than *out* of a mixed-methods territory. In a recent study that I conducted in China, for example, I had secured funding and IRB to video-record interactions in the psychology clinic at a large hospital as well as among participants at a Beijing "mind-body-spirit" center that regularly held workshops and retreats focusing on self-development and personal growth (see Pritzker 2016, Pritzker and Duncan 2019). Both the hospital and retreat center were aware of my project and had approved of my being there. While the video recording proceeded smoothly at the hospital, however, it turned out that the center staff had decided that I could attend but not record the sessions. Though I was distressed by this turn of events, I went forward with the project anyway. Relying on my training in participant observation and person-centered ethnographic approaches to guide my research at the center and to make sense of it alongside video from the hospital, the study became—in one instant—decidedly more mixed methods than I had designed it to be. This occurred again in my own and many of my students' and colleagues' research in the midst of the COVID-19 pandemic of 2020,

346 Research Methods in Linguistic Anthropology

when many scholars had to quickly change tracks in order to incorporate remote or online research methods to ongoing fieldwork. Both examples underscore the need for methodological flexibility in addition to careful planning.

11.2.4 How to Mix Methods: Processes and Challenges

The "how" of mixing methods differs depending on who you ask. For researchers in many disciplines, it is important to develop a precise, step-by-step method to developing mixed methods projects in advance of collecting any data. Several researchers and methodologists have thus designed explicit guidelines for doing mixed methods (e.g., Fetters et al. 2013; Creswell et al. 2011). Tables 11.2 provides an overview of the ways in which Fetters et al. (2013), for example, delineate between various approaches to the design, implementation, and reporting of mixed methods studies.

Instead of providing a strict or restrictive map for doing mixed methods studies, and despite the fact that their categories are explicitly oriented to the integration of qualitative and quantitative approaches, the explanations developed by Fetters and colleagues offer a great deal of insight into the multiple ways it is possible to organize a mixed methods study. Their notions of "exploratory sequential" and "explanatory sequential" studies, for example—which in their definition involve the initial collection of qualitative data in order to inform the development of quantitative tools and vice versa—help us think about the ways in which one might structure a projects in time and

Table 11.2 Designs for mixed methods studies (adapted from Fetters et al. 2013, 2136–7)

Design	Definition
Exploratory sequential	Qualitative data collected first, informs later quantitative data collection
Explanatory sequential	Quantitative data collected first, informs later qualitative data collection
Convergent	Both/all kinds of data collected concurrently and systematically
Multistage	Studies move systematically between exploratory sequential, explanatory sequential, and convergent designs in multiple stages

Mixed Methods and Interdisciplinary Research   347

space. For instance, one might first use the primarily quantitative methods of cultural consensus analysis to conduct a study on people's attitudes toward retirement (Arnold 2019), followed up by participant observation or video recording of naturally occurring conversations in sites where it is likely that people will be talking about such topics or in an informal video-recorded group interview among people in another community who are close to retirement age. The first portion of such a study would generate quantitative data regarding people's shared ideals regarding successful retirement, while the latter portion would generate rich qualitative data showing how such ideals are discussed, disputed, or modified in situated interactions. In contrast, another study focused on, say, the experience of religion might combine two types of qualitative approaches in a "convergent" design that incorporates person-centered interviews with ethnographic observation and video recording of naturally occurring interaction among members of a certain church or other organization. Both kinds of data would provide important insights into the everyday enactment of religious experience in interaction as well as over the life course of individual members.

If one were to try to take these or any other mixed-methods approach to doing research, however, there are multiple other issues relating to the pragmatics of carrying out any study that combines methodological approaches. *Expertise*, as mentioned above, is one of the primary hurdles (Creswell et al. 2011). Unless one is situated in a department or other environment where there happens to be colleagues or advisors who are supportive in learning the ins and outs of conducting research using a particular methodology—or who can collaborate on the project—the study may be overwhelming to plan and conduct. It may also generate results that are not only uninterpretable but are not taken seriously by experts in the relevant fields. Manns (2020), whose research at a Cherokee rock art site is described above, worked diligently to create a dialogue between linguistic anthropology and archaeology, for example. This integration proved challenging, however, as she confronted divergences in core theoretical perspectives. From ideas about what the language on museum signage "does" to notions of what constitutes an archaeological "object," crafting a narrative that successfully incorporated perspectives from each field (while also taking care to center the Cherokee ways of knowing conveyed by her interlocutors) required many consultations with experts across subfields.

Even if one has adequate resources in terms of collaborators and/or advisors, however, conducting a mixed-methods study requires considerable time and effort to become familiar with new methods and overcome differences in theoretical approach, as well as to carry out all the pieces of the research. *Sampling* concerns may further be an issue when incorporating methods that require different numbers of participants in order to be considered valid (Creswell et al. 2011; see Section 11.4 for a case study in which this issue was of primary concern). By far the most challenging issue in addressing the "how" of mixed-methods research, however, is the question of *data analysis*. This only begins with what different members of a team or different fields would even consider "data." The informal conversations that emerge during a focus group, for example, may not be considered valid data by some researchers, nor might the prompted ratings offered in a closed-ended survey be considered useful by some linguistic anthropologists. Even if all members of a team agree that different types of data are valid, however, or even if an individual researcher comes to appreciate the unique ways in which different types of data contribute to the study, there is the issue of making sense of all the collected material. Table 11.3 details the strategies that Fetters et al. (2013) offer as guides to triangulating or linking the data collected in a mixed methods study.

Although again the authors are focused on the combination of qualitative and quantitative data, their strategies help us think about how different types of data can be connected, built upon, merged, or embedded. Strategies of "connecting" and "building" correspond to the different designs outlined by the authors, wherein one type of data analysis informs the design and enactment of other, later aspects of the study. In my earlier example of research on retirement, results from cultural consensus analysis might

Table 11.3 Strategies for triangulating data in mixed methods studies (adapted from Fetters et al. 2013, 2139–41)

Strategy	Definition
Connecting	Data linked in sampling, such as interview participants selected from among initial survey respondents
Building	Results from the analysis of one type of data inform design of later methods, such as observation or open-ended interview data used to build closed-ended survey questions
Merging	Data, once collected and analyzed separately, are merged together for concurrent analysis (often requires data transformation)
Embedding	Data are linked in multiple ways during both collection and analysis phases, e.g., when qualitative and quantitative data are connected or merged in the development of further measures

inform choices of where (and when) to try to collect observations and recordings.

The reality of most anthropological fieldwork, however, is that studies rarely proceed according to strict timelines and phases, especially among individual researchers who may have limited time at a fieldsite. In a study using a convergent design—and indeed, even in the final stages of a study using a sequential design—one will eventually have to figure out how to merge the data. Fetters et al. (2013) thus suggest that, regardless of the order in which data are collected, some sort of "data transformation"—which involves the conversion of one type of data into the other—must usually occur in mixed methods research. In mixed quantitative/qualitative research, for example, data transformation might involve "transforming the qualitative data into numeric counts and variables" or vice versa, e.g., "[transforming] quantitative data ... into a qualitative format that could be used for comparison with qualitatively accessed data" (Fetters et al. 2013, 2143). Data transformation, the authors suggest, has the potential to yield truly integrative results that can be reported in multiple different ways.

Regardless of whether and to what extent researchers go through the process of full data transformation, however, drawing meaningful conclusions from the findings is often a complex task. Fetters et al. describe many different ways this could shake out. Data from different methods, they explain, might confirm, expand, or contradict findings from other methods (2013, 2144). One can imagine, in the case of my earlier example combining person-centered interviews with observation and recording in a study of people's religious experience, that what people say in interviews might correspond to what they say in interaction, considerably helping to expand one's analysis of particular conversations. In any kind of study combining methods, however, results can also be what Fetters et al. call "discordant." If people say one thing during interviews and something completely different when they are interacting with their peers, for example, how might one make sense of this? "Authors deal with this conundrum," write Fetters and colleagues, "by discussing reasons for the conflicting results, identifying potential explanations from theory, and laying out future research options" (2013, 2144). While these are valid and reasonable approaches to dealing with discordant data, it is also important to consider the ways in which certain methods might have shaped the data. This may further open the space up for a theoretical conversation across subfields or disciplines in terms of the ways in which often taken-for-granted perspectives about what "agreement" or "meaning" consists of.

Research Methods in Linguistic Anthropology

Finally, the issue of presenting one's data in a format that makes sense to a variety of audiences can also provide a significant challenge when conducting mixed methods research. Table 11.4 again draws from Fetters et al. (2013) in terms of the ways in which it is possible to report findings from mixed methods studies.

One option, they note, is to report findings in a "narrative" format. Here, a researcher constructs a coherent story that variably moves back and forth between different types of data that confirm, expand, or even contradict each other or alternatively "weaves" them together. Fetters et al. (2013) also include "contiguous" reporting, in which all types of data are included but in different sections of a paper or presentation. This format, especially for anthropologists, still requires that authors craft a coherent narrative to make sense of the data as a whole. "Staged" reports, on the other hand, involve the writing up of findings from different portions of a project separately, often sending them off to different journals or bringing them to different conferences. A "joint display" approach, finally, involves the creation of a graphic or other visual for helping readers understand the ways in which data are seen as informing one another to yield a final result. Again, however, figuring out how to report data from mixed methods studies is not always as straightforward as the guidelines suggest. Depending on the selected publication venue, for example, what may seem like acrobatic feats of explanation are often required in order to concisely summarize divergent methods, often requiring further consultation with relevant experts. When viewed as a conversation across difference, however—returning to Weisner's metaphor of methods as languages—the careful integration of

Table 11.4 Approaches for reporting data in mixed methods studies (adapted from Fetters et al. 2013, 2142–3)

Approach	Definition
Narrative	Both/all kinds of data are reported alongside one another in a coherent narrative
Weaving	Reports weave findings from disparate types of data together based on different themes or concepts
Contiguous	Reports include both/all types of data, but in different sections
Staged	Findings from each stage of the project involving one type of data are reported separately as they are analyzed
Joint display	Reports create a graphic for visualizing how the data integrate and/or inform each other

data in various formats can contribute to the kind of "interdisciplinary methodological pluralism" that Weisner (2012, 4) argues constitutes the future of anthropology.

11.3 Ethical Concerns in Mixed Methods Research

When considering the ethics of mixed methods research, it is first important to consider the basic requirements of research in the social sciences (e.g., informed consent, lack of deception, insurance of privacy and confidentiality, and the accurate reporting of results). As discussed by Black and Conley Riner (this volume), there are further ethical considerations when conducting research in linguistic anthropology. In terms of mixed methods research, however, one of the most glaring ethical issues is a consideration of *participant burden*. Mixed methods studies thus often require additional time, effort, and inconvenience for participants. Different methods, for example, may require participants to commit to numerous and/or time-extensive interviews (e.g., in microphenomenological or person-centered methods). They may ask participants to revisit potentially traumatic interactions and experiences (e.g., in video recall). Or they may require people to wear heavy equipment that involves electrodes and wires (e.g., in psychophysiology). In thinking about the issue of participant burden, it is important to consider the question of *why* certain methods are needed to answer a specific research question or set of questions or hypotheses. In the design of a mixed methods study, the appropriate linking of research question to methods is thus also always an ethical consideration. Is it worth increasing the burden on participants, one must ask themselves, to get the desired results?

The ethics of mixed methods can also be considered from the perspective of the researcher's own theoretical, methodological, and other disciplinary commitments. This relates to the kinds of obligations one feels regarding the often-divergent perspectives on everything from language to experience in different disciplines. This philosophical problem can thus also be parsed in terms of the *ethical* commitments that researchers have to the core tenets of their field. From this vantage point, the resistance to compromising core values is not necessarily "biased" or "resistant" but instead constitutes a kind of ethical advocacy in terms of one's convictions about what kind of research is appropriate in a given field or population and what kinds of results are meaningful in a given discipline or in society more broadly. If one is primarily a linguistic anthropologist, for example, where might one be willing to make compromises in terms of methodologies? Certain methodological trade-offs are often required to meet the demands of required sample sizes, for example (see Case Study, below), or to accommodate the presentation of findings to different audiences. In striking a methodological balance, mixed methods research "must aim to be fair," writes Weisner (2016, 405). "Being fair," for Weisner, points to the need for researchers to remain "truly open to the possibility that our prior expectations may be wrong or need revision" (2016, 405). Although I could not agree more with this statement, I would add that while "being fair" may sometimes mean being open to making compromises, it also can sometimes mean making the effort to drawing a firm boundary around one's commitments when it comes to adjusting the ways in which one collects, interprets, or presents research data.

11.4 Case Study: Combining Linguistic and Biocultural Anthropology with Communication Studies

In an ongoing study funded by the National Science Foundation (NSF), Jason DeCaro (biocultural-medical anthropology), Josh Pederson (communication studies), and I (linguistic anthropology) are combining methods from each of our subfields to research the ways in which moment-to-moment physiology affects and is affected by everyday communication among long-term couples. Inspired by the interdisciplinary model for conducting ethnographic research in the home developed at the UCLA Center for the Everyday Lives of Families or CELF study (e.g., Ochs et al. 2006; Goodwin 2007; Saxbe and Repetti 2010; Goodwin and Cekaite 2018) and seeking to build on short-term laboratory research demonstrating how couples' interactions mediate and are mediated by physiological activity (e.g., Gottman and Notarius 2002; Haase et al. 2016), our study uses a convergent mixed methods design that involves spending three to four consecutive days with couples in their homes. Over the course of this time,

Mixed Methods and Interdisciplinary Research 353

couples are invited to complete several self-report measures, including an initial questionnaire about their relationship (Cohen et al. 1983; Lock and Wallace 1959) and a daily diary form. The study also includes multiple semi-structured ethnographic interviews with the couple and with each individual, observation/video recording of naturally occurring interaction as couples go about their daily business, and close monitoring of physiological activity using a mobile device that continuously measures changes in arousal in the parasympathetic and sympathetic nervous system (Cacioppo et al. 1994; Porges 2011; DeCaro 2016).

Couples are recruited online as well as through flyers and face-to-face conversations and must pass an extensive phone screening before we schedule them as participants. Our first visit to the couples' home, which usually includes a team consisting of at least one of the principal investigators and one or more graduate and/or undergraduate research assistants, begins with a long conversation about the consent form that often takes place in the couples' living room or at their kitchen or dining room table. On these visits, we are acutely aware of the potentially overwhelming nature of having what amounts to a gaggle of researchers descend on one's home carrying not only piles of video equipment (camera, tripod, etc.) but also several large cases with two laptops, a Wi-Fi router, and our physiological data-collection equipment. Developing rapport with couples, and sometimes their young children, is thus critical during this first encounter.

After consents are complete, we then attach the Mindware electrodes to the bodies of each partner and proceed with a video-recorded couple's interview. Here, we inquire about how the couple met and what their first date was like, how long they have been together, their happiest moments together, and any challenges they may face, among other things. These interviews usually take about an hour, sometimes considerably longer. When they conclude, we remove the Mindware devices from participants, confirm scheduling for the following days, and depart back to the lab to download data, clear memory cards, and recharge equipment. On the following three days, we return to the couple's home for "observational" visits where we attach the Mindware, set up the video equipment, and invite couples to proceed as normally as possible with their daily activities. At the end of the final day of observation, we split off into separate rooms and conclude with an individual interview with each partner. Once we have reviewed and preliminarily coded video data, we invite couples to engage in a video-recorded video-recall interview in which we ask questions regarding their perspective on pre-selected clips of interaction, including what they were feeling or thinking or what they perceived to be happening during the encounter (Welsh and Disckson 2005; Larsen et al. 2008). During the COVID-19 pandemic of 2020, video recall was combined with a remote follow-up interview with couples regarding their experience during local shelter-in-place orders. Though we are unable to use psychophysiological equipment during these interviews, we draw on methods of microphenomenological interviewing in order to assess embodied experience (Petitmengin 2006; Petitmengin et al. 2019).

We have published preliminary results from the study in various formats. We've used our data to demonstrate, for example, how intimacy is negotiated in interactions that simultaneously mediate and are mediated by physiological changes in arousal and de-arousal (Perrino and Pritzker 2019; Pritzker et al. 2020). We have also examined how physiological patterns of co- and counter-regulation often correspond to couples' narratives of relational identity (DeCaro et al. 2019). For the remainder of this section, however, rather than focusing on empirical findings, my discussion focuses on the *process* of conducting the relatively large-scale mixed method, interdisciplinary project.

Beginning with the design of our study, the process of planning involved many meetings in which DeCaro, Pederson, and I discussed our ideas and formulated a set of possible research questions that would speak to literature in each of our primary fields. We further contemplated the methods that each of us could bring to the study. In doing so, we hashed out a number of details that immediately prompted us to consider what kinds of compromises we each might have to make in order to design a coherent and actionable study. Sample size was one of the most glaring issues that came to the fore immediately in these conversations. In a moment that both DeCaro and I often reflect back upon with amusement, we were discussing the proposed sample size. At almost the very same instant, DeCaro said, "About 100 couples should be fine," while I said, effectively, "Ten or twenty couples would be great." Pederson, glancing back and forth between us, saved the day with his unique ability to make sense of the vast divergence in numbers just proposed. As a scholar in communication studies, he recognized the validity of my linguistic anthropological perspective on the level of detail we would need to focus on within each couple with three days of video, plus video of couple's interviews and video of recall interviews. He also recognized, however, that DeCaro was approaching the issue from the perspective of generalizability, something that communication studies scholars also concern themselves with. "How about 50?" he suggested, and we all took a deep breath. To do this study among fifty couples were going to require a compromise for all of us, especially for the anthropologists. For DeCaro, the compromise was to be in terms of the study's potential generalizability. For me, on the other hand, the compromise related more to the overwhelming responsibility of gathering—let alone analyzing—more than 500 hours of video-recorded interaction with fifty couples. It was a compromise that we could agree upon, however, since this sample size would allow us each to make meaningful contributions to our respective fields as well as remain committed to at least the core of our ethnographic values. From the outset of the design of the study, then, the mixed methods and cross-disciplinary nature of the study compelled us to make significant concessions in our overall approach, which we ultimately decided were worthwhile given that the data would (we hoped) be an invaluable resource for understanding the multidirectional relationship between physiology and communication in human relationships over time.

In terms of data-*collection* methods, I would venture to say that at least in the beginning of the project, none of us made any extreme compromises in terms of our methods. We have learned, however, that our overall refusal to compromise the basic data-collection strategies in each of our fields has created a monster-size project that places a significant burden upon participants, who not only invite us into their private spaces but also must agree to filling out multiple surveys and wearing the Mindware device while being video-recorded. It is also a burden for researchers, especially student research assistants, who are often required to give up evenings and weekends to travel back and forth from our lab to couples' homes carrying and managing heavy equipment. Walking into new relationships, sometimes as often as once per week for several weeks in a row, while often exhilarating, is also often exhausting for everyone on the team. At the same time, the limited time spent with individual couples, we have realized, constitutes a major ethnographic compromise, especially in terms of linguistic anthropology's usual commitment to longer-term fieldwork in a given site. Our insistence on doing home interviews, finally, has proven challenging in terms of our commitment to inclusivity across couples with varying socioeconomic statuses. We have found, for example, that whether due to time pressures or limited space, many low-income couples are hesitant about inviting us into their homes. There have also been several cases where we've been invited to conduct the research in homes or apartments that are located in neighborhoods that we later learn have been subject to violent crime and excessive policing. We have thus also had to consider the risks, to researchers, students, and participants, involved with our presence in such environments.

The analysis and presentation of our data, once it is collected, has brought with it another collection of challenges, including (1) making sense of video recordings that are time-matched with physiological data; (2) integrating this analysis with material from couples' interviews, individual interviews, self-report questionnaires, daily diaries, and fieldnotes; and (3) pairing our analyses with follow-up interviews and video-recall data. All the while, moreover, we must constantly be thinking of the ways in which we want to present our findings to various audiences. In terms of the everyday pragmatics of data triangulation in our study, the challenges of connecting, building, merging, or embedding our analyses are thus not insignificant.

The process of conducting this study has, finally, prompted us to consider what we might be willing to give up in future research across our disciplines. The mixed-methods, interdisciplinary nature of our approach to data collection thus provides seemingly endless, flexible considerations for future research, even as we navigate the almost constant need to make smaller compromises and adjustments to the present study as it proceeds: things like working with couples to adapt to their schedules, coming up with strategies for staying constantly in touch with our large team, and, most recently, adapting our protocol for remote data collection in the wake of the COVID-19 pandemic. In conclusion, however, it is important to note that even in the process of facing these multiple and complex challenges in the collection, analysis, and publication of data, DeCaro, Pederson, and I are all in agreement that the collaboration has been both personally meaningful and incredibly valuable in terms of the ways in which it forces us to confront our biases, learn from one another, and come up with creative solutions to logistical and disciplinary conflicts. As a case study of mixed methods, interdisciplinary research, our study serves as an example both of the joys and possibilities of conducting such a project as well as the frustrations and challenges of doing so.

11.5 Conclusion

Just as technologies like audio or video recorders can be understood to "afford certain possibilities for action while limiting others" (Black 2017, 48), research methods can be understood as affordances for engaging strategically with our research questions, our fieldsites, and our participants. Speaking from the perspective of linguistic anthropology, however, no method is necessarily incompatible with the traditional methods of participant observation, interviews, and recording interaction. All research methods in the social sciences provide insight and information about what is happening in a situation. No method can "do it all," however. Despite various claims to objectivity, every method requires perspective-taking among both researchers and participants, even those that are quantitative in nature. The notion of what constitutes objectivity in anthropology, or whether anthropologists should consider objectivity a valid goal, has been debated extensively elsewhere (see Ochs et al. 2006; Collins and Gallinat 2010; Schensul and LeCompte 2013; Black 2017). Rather than framing the value of mixed methods research in terms of the ways in which they offer more or less objective strategies for engaging with a research topic, then, I would like to conclude with a return to Weisner's (2012) call to think of different methods as different languages. In this framing, mixed methods studies thus emerge as conversations between and across such differences. Bringing such conversations to bear with regard to a specific research question or topic, as this chapter has demonstrated, involves a number of practical as well as ethical considerations that each researcher or team must navigate anew with each study. The central importance of study design in terms of expertise, ethics, and appropriateness of fit between research question and research method, however, is a vital consideration in making this conversation worthwhile.

11.6 Ethnographic Activities

1   Mix and match among the methods listed in Table 11.1 and formulate a plan for conducting a mixed-methods study that also uses traditional methods in linguistic anthropology. Think about the design of the study in terms of the models presented in Table 11.2 and the analysis and reporting of results in Tables 11.3 and 11.4. Discuss or write about what goals your study might accomplish and what some of the challenges that you would face might be.

2   Discuss or write up an imaginary software program that integrates data collected with linguistic anthropology with one or more other methods. What tools might be included for transforming one type of data into the other? What other features would such a program have?

11.7 Questions to Consider

1 To what extent do you think researchers working on a team need to fully understand one another's methods in order to responsibly and meaningfully carry out a mixed methods study?
2 What is the difference between an integrative and an additive approach to mixed methods research?
3 Do you think mixing methods and/or interdisciplinary work always require some kind of compromise? If so, when might it be worth making such a compromise?
4 This chapter argues that linguistic anthropology is not essentially incompatible with any other method? Do you agree? Why or why not?

11.8 Notes

1 In citing Ronald Fisher here, it is important to acknowledge the violent and racist history within which this researcher dwelled and, indeed, as head of the Department of Eugenics at University College London from 1933 to 1939, participated in vigorously. By reproducing his sentiment dramatizing the need to incorporate diverse experts in the design of a study, I am in no way endorsing either his personal or his professional views regarding the ultimate goals of mixed methods research.
2 Though it took time and a great deal more convincing, it is now standard—even required in many cases—to include a biostatistician on every proposal at the outset of its design, at least in the biomedical sciences.

11.9 References Cited

Alim, H. Samy, John R. Rickford, and Arnetha F. Ball. 2016. *Raciolinguistics: How Language Shapes Our Ideas about Race*. New York and Oxford: Oxford University Press.

Arnold, Randy. 2019. "Cultural Models of Retirement." MA, Anthropology, University of Alabama.

Bacon, Chris K. 2020. "'It's Not Really My Job': A Mixed Methods Framework for Language Ideologies, Monolingualism, and Teaching Emergent Bilingual Learners." *Journal of Teacher Education* 7 (2): 172–87.

Banks, Marcus, and Howard Morphy. 1997. *Rethinking Visual Anthropology*. New Haven: Yale University Press.

Black, Steven P. 2017. "Anthropological Ethics and the Communicative Affordances of Audio-Video Recorders in Ethnographic Fieldwork." *American Anthropologist* 119 (1): 46–57.

Bonilla, Yaromar, and Jonathan Rosa. 2015. "Digital Protest, Hashtag Ethnography, and the Racial Politics of Social Media in the United States." *American Ethnologist* 42 (1): 4–17.

Borgatti, Stephen P., and Daniel S. Halgin. 2013. "Elicitation Techniques for Cultural Domain Analysis." In Jean J. Schensul and Margaret D. LeCompte eds., *Specialized Ethnographic Methods: A Mixed Methods Approach*, 80–116. Lanham: AltaMira Press.

Cacioppo, J. T., B. N. Uchino, and G. G. Berntson. 1994. "Individual Differences in the Autonomic Origins of Heart Rate Reactivity: The Psychometrics of Respiratory Sinus Arrhythmia and Pre-ejection Period I." *Psychophysiology* 31 (4): 412–9.

Calhoun, Kendra. 2019. "Vine Racial Comedy as Anti-Hegemonic Humor: Linguistic Performance and Generic Innovation." *Journal of Linguistic Anthropology* 29 (1): 27–49

Castleden, Heather, Theresa Garvin, and Huu-ay-aht First Nation. 2008. "Modifying Photovoice for Community-Based Participatory Indigenous Research." *Social Science and Medicine* 66: 1393–405.

Clemente, Ignasi. 2013. "Conversation Analysis and Anthropology." In Jack Sidnell and Tanya Stivers eds., *The Handbook of Conversation Analysis*, 688–700. West Sussex: Wiley Blackwell.

Cohen, Sheldon, Tom Kamarck, and Robin Mermelstein. 1983. "A Global Measure of Perceived Stress." *Journal of Health and Social Behavior* 24 (4): 385–96.

Collins, Peter, and Anselm Gallinat. 2010. *The Ethnographic Self as Resource: Writing Memory and Experience into Ethnography*. Oxford and New York: Berghahn Books.

Corwin, Anna I. 2012. "Changing God, Changing Bodies: The Impact of New Prayer Practices on Elderly Catholic Nuns' Embodied Experience." *Ethos* 40 (4): 390–410.

Corwin, Anna I., and Taylor Brown. 2020. "Emotion in the Language of Prayer." In Sonya E. Pritzker, Janina Fenigsen, and James M. Wilce eds., *Routledge Handbook of Language and Emotion*, 325–43. London and New York: Routledge.

Creswell, John W., Ann Carroll Klassen, Vicki L. Plano, and Katherine Clegg Smith. 2011. *Best Practices for Mixed Methods Research in the Health Sciences*. Washington, DC: Office of Behavioral and Social Sciences Research (OBSSR), National Institutes of Health.

Cromley, Ellen K. 2013. "Mapping Spatial Data." In Jean J. Schensul and Margaret D. LeCompte eds., *Specialized Ethnographic Methods: A Mixed Methods Approach*, 117–92. Lanham: AltaMira Press.

Daniels, Julia R. 2018. "'There's No Way This Isn't Racist': White Women Teachers and the Raciolinguistic Ideologies of Teaching Code-Switching." *Journal of Linguistic Anthropology* 28 (2): 156–74.

Das, Sonia Neely. 2013. "La Francophonie and Beyond: Comparative Methods in Studies of Linguistic Minorities." *Journal of Linguistic Anthropology* 22 (3): 220–36.

DeCaro, Jason A. 2016. "Beyond Catecholamines: Measuring Autonomic Responses to Psychosocial Context." *American Journal of Human Biology* 28 (3): 309–17.

DeCaro, Jason A., Sonya E. Pritzker, Joshua Pederson, Mackenzie Manns, and Robert Else. 2019. "Embodying Narrative in Interaction: A Biocultural Linguistic Study of Couples in the Southeastern U.S." Society for Psychological Anthropology Biennial Meeting, Albuquerque, NM.

Desjarlais, Robert. 1992. *Body and Emotion: The Aesthetics of Illness and Healing in the Nepal Himalayas.* Philadelphia: University of Pennsylvania Press

Deumert, Ana. 2014. *Sociolinguistics and Mobile Communication.* Edinburgh: Edinburgh University Press.

Duranti, Alessandro. 1997. *Linguistic Anthropology. Cambridge Textbooks in Linguistics.* New York: Cambridge University Press.

Durrani, Mariam. 2018. #Metoo, Believing Survivors, and Cooperative Digital Communication. *Anthropology News.* https://doi.org/10.1111/AN.1062.

Eisenhauer, Scarlett. 2019. "Youths' Individual Pathways towards Contextual Well-Being: Utilizing Electrodermal Activity as an Ethnographic Tool at a Theater After-School Program." *Ethos* 47 (2): 168–89.

Fetters, Michael D., Leslie A. Curry, and John W. Creswell 2013. "Achieving Integration in Mixed Methods Designs—Principles and Practices." *HSR: Health Services Research* 48 (6): 2134–56.

Fisher, Ronald. 1938. "Presidential Address to the First Indian Statistical Congress." *Sankhya* (4): 14–17.

Flores, Nelson, and Jonathan Rosa. 2015. "Undoing Appropriateness: Raciolinguistic Ideologies and Language Diversity in Education." *Harvard Educational Review* 85: 149–71.

Gershon, Ilana. 2015. "What Do We Talk about When We Talk about Animation." *Social Media + Society* April–June 2015: 1–2.

Goodwin, Charles. 2007. "Participation, Stance and Affect in the Organization of Activities." *Discourse & Society* 18 (1): 53–73.

Goodwin, Marjorie Harness, and Asta Cekaite. 2018. *Embodied Family Choreography: Practices of Control, Care, and Mundane Creativity.* London and New York: Routledge.

Gottman, John M., and Clifford I. Notarius. 2002. "Marital Research in the 20th Century and a Research Agenda for the 21st Century." *Family Process* 41 (2): 159–97.

Haase, Claudia M., Sarah R. Holley, Lian Bloch, Alice Verstaen, and Robert W. Levenson. 2016. "Interpersonal Emotional Behaviors and Physical Health: A 20-Year Longitudinal Study of Long-Term Married Couples." *Emotion* 16 (7): 965–77.

Harper, Krista. 2012. "Visual Interventions and the 'Crises in Representation' in Environmental Anthropology: Researching Environmental Justice in a Hungarian Romani Neighborhood." *Human Organization* 71 (3): 292–305.

Hay, M. Cameron. 2016a. *Methods That Matter: Integrating Mixed Methods for More Effective Social Science Research*. Chicago and London: The University of Chicago Press.

Hay, Cameron. 2016b. "Ethnography in Need of Numbers: Mixing Methods to Build Partnerships and Understand Tigers." In Cameron Hay ed., *Methods That Matter: Integrating Mixed Methods for More Effective Social Science Research*, 41–8. Chicago and London: University of Chicago Press.

Hine, Christine. 2011. *Virtual Ethnography*. London: SAGE.

Hollan, Douglas. 2005. "Setting a New Standard: The Person-Centered Interviewing and Observation of Robert I. Levy." *Ethos* 33 (4): 459–66.

Hosemann, Aimee J. 2019. "Constructing a Decentered Archival Method: Ailla Recordings and Wanano/Kotiria Kaya Basa 'Sad Songs.'" *Journal of Linguistic Anthropology* 29 (2): 188–94.

Hymes, Dell. 1977. "Qualitative/Quantitative Research Methodologies in Education: A Linguistic Perspective." *Anthropology & Education Quarterly* 8 (3): 165–76.

Jones, Graham M., and Bambi B. Schieffelin. 2016. "The Ethnography of Inscriptive Speech." In Roger T. Sanjek and Susan W. Tratner ed., *efieldnotes: Makings of Anthropology in a Digital World*, 210–28. Philadelphia: University of Pennsylvania Press.

Kohn, Tamara. 2010. "The Role of Serendipity and Memory in Experiencing Fields." In Peter Collins and Anselm Gallinat eds., *The Ethnographic Self as Resource: Writing Memory and Experience into Ethnography*, 185–99. Oxford and New York: Berghahn Books.

Kozinets, Robert V. 2015. *Netnography: Redefined*. Los Angeles: SAGE.

Larsen, Denise, Keri Flesaker, and Rachel Stege. 2008. "Qualitative Interviewing Using Interpersonal Process Recall: Investigating Internal Experiences During Professional-Client Conversations." *International Journal of Qualitative Methods* 7 (18–37).

Lassiter, Luke E. 2005. *The Chicago Guide to Collaborative Ethnography. Chicago Guides to Writing, Editing, and Publishing*. Chicago: University of Chicago Press.

LeCompte, Margaret Diane, and Jean J. Schensul. 2013. *Analysis and Interpretation of Ethnographic Data: A Mixed Methods Approach,* 2nd ed. Lanham, MD: AltaMira Press.

Levine, Robert A. 2016. "Repairing the Fractured Social Sciences: An Introduction from a Historical Point of View." In Cameron Hay ed., *Methods That Matter: Integrating Mixed Methods for More Effective Social Science Research*, 3–12. Chicago and London: University of Chicago Press.

Levy, Robert, and Douglas Hollan. 1998. "Person-Centered Interviewing and Observation." In H. R. Bernard ed., *Handbook of Methods in Anthropology*, 333–64. Walnut Creek: AltaMira Press.

Liebenberg, Linda. 2018. "Thinking Critically about Photovoice: Achieving Empowerment and Social Change." *International Journal of Qualitative Methods* 17: 1–9.

Locke, Harvey J., and Karl M. Wallace. 1959. "Short Marital Adjustment and Prediction Tests: Their Reliability and Validity." *Marriage and Family Living*, 21: 251–5.

Manns, Mackenzie. 2020. "'That Ancient People': Exploring an Ideology of Rock Art at Tsul'kalu Rock." MA, Anthropology, University of Alabama.

Mendoza-Denton, Norma, Scarlett Eisenhauer, Wesley Wilson, and Cory Flores. 2017. "Gender, Electrodermal Activity, and Videogames: Adding a Psychophysiological Dimension to Sociolinguistic Methods." *Journal of Sociolinguistics* 21(4): 547–75.

Ochs, Elinor. 2012. "Experiencing Language." *Anthropological Theory* 12 (2): 142–60.

Ochs, Elinor, Anthony P. Graesch, Angela Mittman, Thomas Bradbury, and Rena Repetti. 2006. "Video Ethnography and Ethnoarchaeological Tracking." In Marcie Pitt-Catsouphes and Ellen Ernst Kossek ed., *The Work and Family Handbook: Multidisciplinary Perspectives, Methods, and Approaches*, 387–409.

Petitmengin, Claire. 2006. "Describing One's Subjective Experience in the Second Person: An Interview Method for the Science of Consciousness." *Phenomenology and the Cognitive Sciences* 5: 229–69.

Petitmengin, Claire, Martijn Van Beek, Michel Bitbol, Jean-MIchel Nissou, and Andreas Roepstorff. 2018. "Studying the Experience of Meditation through Micro-Phenomenology." *Current Opinion in Psychology* 28: 54–9.

Phillips, Susan. 2013. "Method in Anthropological Discourse Analysis: The Comparison of Units of Interaction." *Journal of Linguistic Anthropology* 23 (1): 82–95.

Porges, Stephen W. 2011. *The Polyvagal Theory: Neurophysiological Foundations of Emotions, Attachment, Communication, and Self-Regulation*. New York: W. W. Norton & Company.

Postill, John, and Sarah Pink. 2012. "Social Media Ethnography: The Digital Researcher in a Messy Web." *Media International Australia* 145: 123–34.

Pritzker, Sonya, Joshua Pederson, and Jason A. DeCaro. 2020. "Language, Emotion, and the Body: Combining Linguistic and Biological Approaches to Interactions between Romantic Partners." In Sonya Pritzker, Janina Fenigsen and James M. Wilce eds., *Routledge Handbook of Language and Emotion*, 307–24. London and New York: Routledge.

Pritzker, Sonya E. 2014. *Living Translation: Language and the Search for Resonance in U.S. Chinese Medicine*. Oxford and New York: Berghahn Books.

Pritzker, Sonya E. 2016. "New Age with Chinese Characteristics? Translating Inner Child Emotion Pedagogies in Contemporary China." *Ethos* 44 (2): 150–70.

Pritzker, Sonya E. 2019. "Technologies of the Social: Family Constellation Therapy and the Remodeling of Relational Selfhood in China and Mexico." *Culture, Medicine, and Psychiatry* 43 (3), 468–95.

Pritzker, Sonya E., and Sabina Perrino. 2020. "Culture Inside: Scale, Intimacy, and Chronotopic Stance in Situated Narratives." *Language in Society*. Online first: doi:10.1017=S0047404520000342

Romney, A. Kimball, Susan C. Weller, and William H. Batchelder. 1986. "Culture as Consensus: A Theory of Culture and Informant Accuracy." *American Anthropologist* 88 (2): 313–38.

Saxbe, Darby E., and Rena L. Repetti. 2010. "For Better or Worse? Coregulation of Couples' Cortisol Levels and Mood States." *Journal of Personality and Social Psychology* 98 (1): 92–103.

Schensul, Jean J., and Margaret D. LeCompte. 2013a. *Specialized Ethnographic Methods: A Mixed Methods Approach*. Lanham, MD: AltaMira Press.

Schensul, Jean J., and Margaret D. LeCompte. 2013b. *Essential Ethnographic Methods: A Mixed Methods Approach*, 2nd ed. Lanham, MD: AltaMira Press.

Schensul, Stephen L. 2013. "Using Archival and Secondary Data in Ethnographic Research." In Jean J. Schensul and Margaret D. LeCompte eds., *Specialized Ethnographic Methods: A Mixed Methods Approach*, 50–79. Lanham, MD: AltaMira Press.

Seligman, Rebecca. 2014. *Possessing Spirits and Healing Selves: Embodiment and Transformation in an Afro-Brazilian Religion. Culture, Mind, and Society*. New York: Palgrave Macmillan.

Shohet, Merav. 2013. "Everyday Sacrifice and Language Socialization in Vietnam: The Power of a Respect Particle." *American Anthropologist* 115 (2): 203–17.

Skinner, Jonathan. 2010. "Leading Questions and Body Memories: A Case of Phenomenology and Physical Ethnography in the Dance Interview." In Peter Collins and Anselm Gallinat eds., *The Ethnographic Self as Resource: Writing Memory and Experience into Ethnography*, 111–28. Oxford and New York: Berghahn Books.

Smalls Krystal A. 2019. "Languages of Liberation: Digital Discourses of Emphatic Blackness." In Netta Avineri et al. eds., *Language and Social Justice in Practice*, 52–60. London and New York: Routledge.

Stodulka, Thomas, Nasima Selim, and Dominik Mattes. 2018. "Affective Scholarship: Doing Anthropology with Epistemic Affects." *Ethos* 46 (4): 519–36.

Trotter, Robert T., Jean J. Schensul, and Margaret Weeks. 2013. "Conducting Ethnographic Network Studies: Friends, Relatives, and Relevant Others." In Jean J. Schensul and Margaret D. LeCompte eds., *Specialized Ethnographic Methods: A Mixed Methods Approach*, 193–254. Lanham, MD: AltaMira Press.

Wang, Caroline, and Mary Ann Burris. 1997. "Photovoice: Concept, Methodology, and Use for Participatory Needs Assessment." *Health Education & Behavior* 24 (3): 369–87.

Weisner, Thomas S. 2011. "'If You Work in This Country You Should Not Be Poor, and Your Kids Should Be Doing Better': Bringing Mixed Methods and Theory in Psychological Anthropology to Improve Research in Policy and Practice." *Ethos* 39 (4): 455–76.

Weisner, Thomas S. 2012. "Mixed Methods Should Be a Valued Practice in Anthropology." *Anthropology News* 53 (5): 3–4.

Weisner, Thomas S. 2016. "Findings That Matter: A Commentary." In Cameron Hay ed., *Methods That Matter: Integrating Mixed Methods for More Effective Social Science Research*, 393–408. Chicago and London: University of Chicago Press.

Welsh, Deborah P., and Joseph W. Dickson. 2005. "Video-Recall Procedures for Examining Subjective Understanding in Observational Data." *Journal of Family Psychology* 19 (1): 62–71.

Wilce, James M., ed. 2002. *The Social and Cultural Lives of Immune Systems*. London: Routledge.

Wisdom, Jennifer P., Mary A. Cavaleri, Anthony J. Onwuegbuzie, and Carla A. Green. 2012. "Methodological Reporting in Qualitative, Quantitative, and Mixed Methods Health Services Research Articles." *Health Services Research* 47 (2): 721–45.

Worthman, Carol M. 2016. "Ecocultural Theory: Foundations and Applications." In Cameron Hay ed., *Methods That Matter: Integrating Mixed Methods for More Effective Social Science Research*, 13–37. Chicago and London: University of Chicago Press.

11.10 Further Reading

Hay, M. Cameron. 2016. *Methods That Matter: Integrating Mixed Methods for More Effective Social Science Research*. Chicago and London: The University of Chicago Press.

LeCompte, Margaret Diane, and Jean J. Schensul. 2013. *Analysis and Interpretation of Ethnographic Data: A Mixed Methods Approach*, 2nd ed. Lanham, MD: AltaMira Press.

Weisner, Thomas S. 2012. "Mixed Methods Should Be a Valued Practice in Anthropology." *Anthropology News* 53 (5):3–4.

12

Grant Writing for Projects in Linguistic Anthropology

Sonia N. Das

12.1 Introduction

Successful grant writing for projects in linguistic anthropology depends on knowledge of, and expertise in, scientific research design and the humanistic exploration of issues, phenomena, and debates shaping the human experience. The subfield's commitment to rigorous standards of linguistic and ethnographic data collection and analysis, including sociolinguistic methods and discourse, conversation, and narrative analytic techniques used to identify patterns in semiotic processes and communicative practices across discourse events, translates into high ratings for linguistic anthropological projects usually in terms of methodology and data analysis. Linguistic anthropologists are more likely to face difficulties in highlighting the originality of their research question(s), demonstrating their project's intellectual merit in cross- or interdisciplinary terms, and emphasizing the broader significance of the research for advancing general knowledge. For linguistic anthropological research to be funded on par with other anthropological subfields, scholars are often required to carefully translate or gloss specialized terms into recognizable concepts without misrepresenting their technical meanings. Other difficulties not limited to linguistic anthropological projects arise out of improper or inadequate articulations of the logical connection between the research question(s) and hypotheses on the one hand, and the data collection and analytic methods on the other. Also, scholars may neglect to justify why the project should be located in a particular setting or time period and among a certain population or otherwise consider important issues of representability and bias in the sampling methods. In describing potential solutions to these issues, this chapter seeks to communicate the value of situating linguistic anthropological knowledge in dialog with broader social scientific agendas.

Below, I provide an overview of the different grants currently available for funding research projects in linguistic anthropology at both the junior and senior levels, the components of a successful research design, and the differences in priorities between science-focused and humanities-focused funding agencies. This chapter further discusses the implications of securing internal versus external grants, and seed-grants versus large grants, for early-to-mid career advancement. It evaluates the benefits of conducting collaborative research with co-PIs in linguistic anthropology and related fields against independently designed research projects and those reliant on outside consultants. The politics of engaging in social critique of government agencies is addressed with reference to the writing of abstracts and inclusion of ancillary materials, such as human subjects review approvals and letters of invitation from collaborating institutions in the host country or region. Finally, this chapter offers insights into the timeline of the entire grant writing process and some tips about writing organization and style, including how to employ topic and concluding sentences in each paragraph to effectively advance the proposal's argument.

To illustrate these issues and themes in a concrete fashion, I draw on my own grant writing experiences as a graduate student and faculty member. My postdoctoral research focusing on de/escalation in police-civilian interactions in South Carolina was awarded a Senior Research Grant by the National Science Foundation's Programs in Cultural Anthropology and Law and Social Sciences in collaboration with Dr. Sherina Feliciano-Santos, and a Wenner-Gren post-PhD fellowship. My doctoral research on Tamil heritage language education in Quebec was awarded a Doctoral Dissertation Research Improvement Grant by the National Science Foundation Program in Cultural Anthropology and an area studies grant from the Association for Canadian Studies in the United States. Although these projects have different aims and goals, they contribute to the ethnographic study of language ideology and interaction in North America.

12.2 Writing the Grant

12.2.1 Grants for Projects in Linguistic Anthropology

Numerous granting agencies sponsor research projects in linguistic anthropology. At the PhD level there is federal funding available in the form of the National Science Foundation's (NSF's) Doctoral Dissertation Research Improvement Grant (DDRIG), and scholars can apply for this through the Program in Cultural Anthropology[1] or Linguistics[2] or both. A private organization, the Wenner-Gren Foundation,[3] also funds doctoral research projects. Recognizing the specificity of linguistic anthropological research, the program directors of the NSF and Wenner-Gren solicit the feedback of linguistic and cultural anthropologists to evaluate a proposal's competitiveness. Other non-disciplinary-specific yet popular grants for doctoral research outside of the United States include the Social Science Research Council (for US citizens)[4] and Social Science and Humanities Research Council (for Canadian citizens),[5] the Fulbright IIE[6] and Fulbright-Hayes,[7] and area studies grants funded by public and private foundations. Students should note that the NSF awards REG (Research Experience for Graduates) and REU (Research Experience for Undergraduates) supplements[8] for independent research conducted under the mentorship of a senior researcher with existing NSF funding. Rather than supporting dissertation research, these grants provide students with early exposure to methods and practices of research design and data collection. Large R1 universities may also offer limited, competitive internal grants for research.

At the senior researcher level, the National Science Foundation runs a competition for a three-year grant, the Senior Research Award,[9] and a five-year grant, the Faculty Early Career Development Program (CAREER),[10] for pre-tenured faculty who show exceptional leadership and potential in research and teaching. Similarly, scholars can apply for the post-PhD research grant[11] through the Wenner-Gren Foundation. Both funding agencies permit collaborative research with co-PIs.[12] In addition, area studies foundations often partner with other organizations to award research fellowships; for example, the Council of American Overseas Research Centers (CAORC)[13] represents a conglomeration of research centers that funds research across multiple countries. The American Council of Learned

Societies (ACLS),[14] National Endowment for the Humanities (NEH),[15] and American Philosophical Society (APS)[16] award a number of fellowships for research and writing by collaborating with philanthropic foundations such as the Mellon, Luce, and Getty. Senior scholars may also seek out internal grants, considered "seed money," from their research universities to support a preliminary period of data collection. Internal grants often facilitate in securing more substantial external grants.

With doctoral degree-granting institutions increasingly offering five-year or more packages to incoming PhD students to be used in full or partial funding of their doctoral studies, the repercussions and inequities of these changes regarding the compensation structure of graduate education are as of yet unclear. For one, they highlight the ongoing neoliberalization, and corporate management practices, of higher education. Will scholars who do not or are not required to seek external funding be disadvantaged and seen as less competitive when applying for future grants, postdoctoral fellowships, and tenure-track positions? Will research universities and liberal arts colleges evaluate internal funding on par with external funding when reviewing tenure and promotion cases? Will increased funding for doctoral students lead to the contraction of graduate cohorts and impede the replacement of tenure-track faculty lines? As the number of contract faculty positions increases and the demographics of faculty governance shifts, will universities grant the right to contract faculty to apply for grants without requiring a tenure-track or tenured faculty as principal investigator? Despite these changes and regardless of personal career trajectories, since past grant success remains one of the strongest predictors of future grant success, junior and senior scholars are equally advised to cultivate effective grant writing skills.

12.2.2 Components of a Successful Research Design

This section references excerpts from two successful grants awarded in 2018 to discuss the standard components of a linguistic anthropological research proposal. The National Science Foundation's Programs in Cultural Anthropology and Law and Social Sciences awarded a Senior Research Award in the amount of $476,041 to me and my collaborator, Dr. Sherina Feliciano-Santos, for the first submission of our proposal, "Collaborative Research: Socio-linguistic analysis of cross-cultural encounters and their outcomes."

This three-year project included funding for two years of ethnographic fieldwork and three years of data analysis of bodycam and dashcam footage of police-civilian interactions. Later that year I also received a post-PhD grant in the amount of $20,000 from the Wenner-Gren Foundation for the second revision of my proposal, "Fighting Words or Speech Rights? A Linguistic Ethnography of Police Discretion in the U.S. South," providing me with an additional year of funding to conduct ethnographic research on police training and community policing. Together, these grants supported research on the role of language and communication in the US criminal justice system, focusing on data collection and the analysis of (1) verbal and nonverbal (multimodal) de/escalation; (2) ideologies informing the interpretation and use of multisensory evidential forms such as sound, odor, and visuals, in policing[17]; and (3) the production and circulation of this evidence in and through legal discourse. Although the two grant applications adopt different formats, the components are mostly similar.

The first section of a research proposal, called the *introduction* or *overview*, is by far the most important. In the introduction scholars should seek to construct a narrative that richly contextualizes and describes an original sociolinguistic phenomenon that will elicit both general *and* disciplinary interest. This can be achieved by interweaving ethnographic, historical, and linguistic facts to explain "who" or "what" the study is about; "when" or "where" the study will be undertaken; "how" the study will be conducted; and "why" the study is original, significant, and timely. Reviewers, who are usually anonymous, commonly critique proposals that do not start off by deeply engaging with the multiple facets of an issue or phenomenon or by justifying the study's narrow focus on a particular place, group, activity, or ideology. To avoid these critiques, scholars should explicate the representative nature of their object, site, and group and identify if the data points are to be evaluated as exemplary, average, or outliers. Stated otherwise, do the data feed into a comparative corpus or is it a singular phenomenon, that is, the exception to the rule? After reading the introduction, reviewers should be able to answer such questions.

In the second revision and successful submission of my post-PhD research grant proposal to the Wenner-Gren Foundation, in response to one of the reviewer's questions about why I chose to locate the study in Columbia, SC, and focus only on DUI arrests, I gave the following explanation:

> Richland County, which comprises the capital city of Columbia, is ideal for studying how police discretion perpetuates white supremacy through protocols

designed to distinguish between protected and unprotected speech in routine police-subject interactions. First, the county has a distinctly stratified social, geographical, and demographic profile that allows for clear-cut comparisons to be made between towns: (1) Columbia (racially mixed, lower-middle class), (2) Arcadia Lakes (mostly white, upper-middle class), (3) Irmo (mostly white, middle class), (4) Cayce (mostly white, lower-middle class), and (5) Eastover (mostly black, lower class) (U.S. 2010) [...] Second, recent incidents of police shootings or killings of unarmed black people over the last three years frame a particular moment in history and present an opportunity to examine how the discourses and practices of white supremacy are perpetuated in small cities, towns, and rural regions, which have not received the same attention as large cities when discussing conflict and violence in America. Third, we were invited by Douglas Strickler, former public defender of Richland County, to access this video archive. The data is not available under the Freedom of Information Act and police can also use their discretion to withhold video footage from South Carolina courts (Balko 2016).

(Das 2018)

Since fighting words must be uttered face-to-face to be legally valid as expressing the intent to incite imminent violence, we have chosen to focus mostly on DUI stops because only these protocols were conducted face-to-face and legally mandated to be video recorded between 2015 and 2017. Recently, lawyers presiding over traffic stop cases have started to rely on dashcam and bodycam evidence. The RCPD has expressed willingness to allow us to access this data and incorporate it into our study.

(Das 2018)

In the second paragraph I clarified that, even though DUI arrests are not representative of all criminal arrests, they are *exemplary* in the sense that only DUI arrests are legally mandated in South Carolina to be recorded and stored on bodycam and dashcam video. These interactional data are also an *outlier* in that only my collaborator and I have been granted access to the corpus by the Public Defender of Richland County, which is an *average* mid-sized urban area in the South, where there has been little research on police-civilian interactions and violence. By explicating the representability of my study, I made a stronger case for its originality and intellectual merit.

After describing the topic, one goes into greater detail when outlining the overall research design. This overview begins with a *research objective*, which explicitly states the *research question(s)* and *hypothesis/es*. Other terms such as "*research problem(s)*" and "*expectation(s)*" may be substituted here, depending on the author's preference or the funding agency's specific protocol. Scientific protocol requires the research question to generate a testable hypothesis through empirical data collection and analysis, whereas humanistic research depends on the systematicity of evidence to verify conclusions. Regardless of these disciplinary differences, strong research questions meet similar criteria: they are stated in a language understandable to specialists and non-specialists; they are specific and appropriate to the discipline; they engage in conversation with existing literatures (see Richland, this volume); and providing answers is feasible (see Hall, this volume).

To evaluate the originality of the project, reviewers will then assess if the research question is capable of generating new evidence or if the question can be answered with an existing corpus. If the sufficient condition of generating new evidence is not met, the research may be negatively judged as derivative and the proposal deemed to be less competitive. A single, focused research question is ideal. However, sometimes one can divide a research question into two or three subparts. More than three subquestions become unwieldy for the grant writer and distracting for the reviewer. When the coherence of the project is negatively impacted, this is due to an inability to show how each subquestion corresponds to a single hypothesis. As a potential answer to a research question, the hypothesis makes apparent the necessary relationship between the different components of the research design. I illustrate with an example from my NSF grant:

> **Questions.** To investigate the unpredictable legal outcomes through which verbal and nonverbal communication between police officers and subjects is construed as leading to criminal or civil offenses and the forms of technological mediation that enable these outcomes and conclusions, this study asks the following questions: **(1)** What does the escalation or de-escalation of violence look and sound like as an interactional achievement?; **(2)** Why do some verbal or gestural practices count as evidence of the intent to incite harm and not others?; and **(3)** How do audio and video recordings and written documentation files differently constitute what counts as evidence of "unprotected" speech, keeping in mind the onus placed on the police to recognize subjects' constitutional right to disagree with and insult public servants?

> **Hypotheses.** The following hypotheses correspond with the above-mentioned research questions: **(1)** Officers and subjects are differently sensitive to linguistic and gestural signs in predicting aggression against their bodies; **(2)** Linguistic features that index a foreign or minority ethnoracial identity, such as non-standard lexicon and phonology, as well as bodily movements or gestures that are glossed as being abrupt or frenetic in the written case

files, correlate significantly with charges of breach of peace, public disorderly conduct, and resisting arrest in a pragmatically meaningful way; and **(3)** Audio and video recordings and transcripts that set up legal expectations for referentially transparent evidence of the "micro-features" of an act of escalated conflict serve to obscure how written case files and courtroom interactions are key sites for the negotiation of language ideologies pertaining to claims of speech rights.

(Das and Feliciano-Santos 2018)

Although this excerpt does not illustrate the following point, questions suggesting two or more alternative answers are effective in generating testable hypotheses. For example, I could ask, "Do subjects' threatening nonverbal gestures (e.g., clenching fists) lead to an escalation in officers' verbal or nonverbal responses?" A possible hypothesis could state that threatening forms of nonverbal gestures will more often escalate in the form of officers' verbal responses than nonverbal responses. In order for this hypothesis to be interpreted as reasonable, however, preliminary research or secondary literature on interaction in conflict situations should affirm this propensity.

The *literature review* follows the hypotheses and provides a focused discussion of the disciplinary and interdisciplinary scholarship on the chosen topic. This section is sometimes referred to as *theoretical contributions* and is frequently divided into three subsections, each labeled with a subtitle delineating an established area of inquiry. For our NSF grant, the three areas that we highlighted included (1) hate speech and free speech, (2) language and race, and (3) policing and surveillance. Although some reviewers may seek to assess if the sources include both classic and recent works, scholars should be selective, not exhaustive, in their citational practices. Particularly effective is a narrative that constructs the literature review as a dialog structured between past studies and the questions posed by the proposed research study to demonstrate how the latter will advance knowledge in the field. Each paragraph would begin with a topic sentence stating a single theoretical claim. Subsequent sentences would explore key studies and insights pertaining to this claim, whereas the last sentence in the paragraph would assert how the proposed research will contribute to the ongoing discussion, either by correcting prior misconceptions, providing additional perspectives, or addressing a noticeable lacuna. For example, in the following excerpt of the literature review of our NSF grant, my collaborator and I argued that linguistic anthropological discussions of the historical development of liberal ideologies provide additional perspectives to legal positions on the indeterminacy of law:

The dominant conceptualization of free speech in the U.S. draws on liberal concepts originating from 17th and 18th century Western Enlightenment thought to assert the premise that truthful language emerges from the talk of rationally-minded individuals free from government constraints (Bauman and Briggs 2003; Lahav 1987). Although the minority legal position also recognizes the social and emotional costs of free speech caused by racism and other forms of bigotry (Meiklejohn 1948), scholars in Critical Legal Studies (Unger 2000), Critical Race Theory (Matsuda et al. 1993), and Feminist Jurisprudence (MacKinnon 1993) take this critique one step further and unequivocally reject the notion that words can have permanent and universal meanings. These scholars instead point to the indeterminacy of law to suggest that moral beliefs, power relations, and linguistic ideologies and practices hold sway over cases of unprotected speech (Krotoszynski 2006; Streeter 1990). Adopting such pragmatist perspectives, this study highlights the importance of combining ethnographic and linguistic methods to disclose the performative effects of language across contexts and trace interdiscursive processes linking free speech to hate speech.

(Das and Feliciano-Santos 2018)

The organizing principle of the literature review is to advance the rationale for your project one paragraph at a time and give added weight to a hypothesis to which you refer explicitly. For instance, we began a prior paragraph writing, "Constitutional scholars who debate whether or not hate speech should be legally protected have pointed out that this type of speech is notoriously difficult to define legally as a civil or criminal offense due to first amendment protections of the U.S. Constitution (Gelber 2012; Moran 1994; Rosenfeld 2002; Walker 1994)." After providing examples of countries where hate speech laws do exist, we reframed one of the original research questions and its corresponding hypothesis in light of this discussion about constitutional law:

> If a police officer were to interpret a DUI subject's speech as hateful and the gestures as aggressive and frame these as threats in the written case file, the act of labeling a subject's language as "fighting words" or as a "true threat" would justify an escalation in police force and treat language pragmatically as unprotected speech. The researchers hypothesize that this escalating effect is due to practical, if not constitutional, power asymmetries in the protection of free speech rights.
>
> (Das and Feliciano-Santos 2018)

This back and forth between a focused discussion of the literature and reference to the research design drives a narrative that incrementally builds an argument for the study's intellectual merit, which I discuss in greater detail subsequently.

In the next section detailing the methods of *data collection and analysis*, scholars should identify distinct methodologies and justify their utility and capacity to generate new evidence to test a hypothesis or verify expected results corresponding to the previously stated research questions. Regardless of whether or not the reviewers are trained in linguistic anthropology, they will expect to be convinced of the methodology's suitability and the scholar's training in these techniques. Problems arise when scholars list multiple or mixed methods without discussing their potential areas of incompatibility such as, for example, between conversation and discourse analysis and with statistical analyses (see Pritzker, this volume). One common mistake is to incorrectly refer to content analysis, which examines the themes of a text, as discourse analysis. In a similar vein, proposals calling for archival research without also justifying the historical period, archival collection, and coding and analytic techniques to be used with the evidence obtained from the archival materials demonstrate the scholar's lack of experience with historical analysis. I learned this lesson during the peer review process when I submitted a manuscript discussing colonial linguistics and printing in nineteenth-century French India to *Comparative Studies in Society and History*. Although the manuscript was later accepted and published, one reviewer asked why I only examined documents in the Archives Nationales d'Outre-Mer in Aix-en-Provence. I could have avoided this critique by explaining that the extant literature on French India had neglected to analyze documents pertaining to a printing press in Pondicherry, available exclusively in this archive.

Specificity is key when detailing the number of interviews (see Perrino, this volume), recordings of "naturalistic" discourse (see Kohler and Murphy, this volume), collected artifacts, and documents in the methodology section. A large sample size is not always better. Since big data sets would need to be analyzed for statistical significance, this would pose a dilemma for linguistic anthropologists who may lack training in statistics (although consultants can help in this regard). In contrast, projects that employ the comparative method would require a large enough sample size to assess the impact of one or more dependent variables on an independent variable; a control group is also essential. Even though comparative methods are helpful in eliminating sampling biases, most projects in linguistic anthropology disprefer working with large samples (see Pritzker, this volume). Rather, for projects such as my own that seek to identify the role of language ideologies in mediating the existence of sociolinguistic categories through different forms of uptake in interactional contexts (Gal and Irvine 2019; Silverstein 2004), they mostly rely on the discourse analysis of few texts to discern this dialectic relationship (Wortham and Reyes 2015). Whether or not one's project is directly concerned with the study of language ideologies, a brief discussion of the ideologies pertaining to the proposed study helps non-specialist reviewers to understand how language matters deeply to communities in political, economic, and social terms.

In our research on police-civilian interactions, after consulting with outside experts we learned of a potential sampling bias exacerbated by the undefined legal status of bodycam and dashcam videos. Since we were accessing the videos through the public defender's office and receiving footage of DUI and other traffic arrests that only involved criminal defendants, rather than civilians who are stopped but not arrested, our analysis would reproduce a sampling bias skewed toward the experiences of civilians falling under the racialized categories of those who have prior criminal records or who agree to take a field sobriety test. This sampling bias would conceal variation in the incidence and type of traffic stops among those leading to arrests and generating tickets or warnings. Such a bias would also make it difficult to ascertain which dependent variables directly contribute to escalation beyond the mere fact of the arrest. To compensate, we proposed using the methods of discourse analysis to produce richly coded transcripts of video-recorded police-civilian interactions and "examine recurring patterns in the co-occurrence of variables of race, ethnicity, immigration status, language use, and arrest rates or additional charges, looking specifically at the use of: (1) stigmatized accents, (2) non-standard English lexicon, (3) codeswitching, (4) obscenities or 'fighting words,' and (5) interactional stances indicating charged-up emotions and aggression or non-compliance" (Das and Feliciano-Santos 2018, 10). We also stressed the value of supplementing video analysis with the participant observation of policing practices across different jurisdictions and of training protocols at the South Carolina Justice Academy. When identifying "participant observation" as a method as we did in the grant (see Pritzker and Perrino, this volume), scholars should provide specific details about the observed activities, including the collection and recording of the linguistic and non-linguistic evidence (even as fieldnotes) and access scholars have to participate in these activities.

In the section describing *preliminary research and training*, the scholar should demonstrate their knowledge of the proposed topic and their ability to conduct the study in the designated time period. Although this section may be briefer than others, it establishes two crucial parameters. First, it should articulate the expertise required for the completion of the project, such as knowledge of foreign languages, legal or medical codes, botanical systems, computer-generated modeling, statistical programs, and so forth. Second, it should explain why the principal investigator (or PI) is qualified to undertake the study. Although outside consultants such as translators, language tutors, and statistical experts are permitted, the expectation is that PIs will be knowledgeable in most areas. Linguistic anthropologists should have advanced proficiency in at least one field language yet may seek instruction in other field languages, especially when it is widely known that resources for instruction in this language are scarce in US universities. For instance, my NSF grant proposal to conduct dissertation research on Tamil heritage language education in Quebec requested tutoring services to learn regional differences between linguistic varieties of Tamil local to Jaffna and Chennai, versus those more commonly spoken in other cities in South India and Sri Lanka from which Tamils in Montreal emigrated.

Generally, the proposal concludes with an overview of the research project in terms of its *intellectual merit* and *broader significance*. These categories are explicitly labeled as such in the NSF proposal but can be adopted for any application. Whereas a discussion of intellectual merit refers to how the research will directly advance knowledge within the discipline and in the topical fields mentioned in the literature review, the broader significance refers to the project's practical applications for non-academics and general benefits to society. Commonly discussed are the development of pedagogical materials for K-12 schools and universities, the mentorship of underrepresented minorities, the development of crucial infrastructures and technologies, the sharing of information through digital media platforms, the creation of protected databases for the preservation of cultural and linguistic heritage, and so forth. Some public foundations, such as the NSF, prefer US-based consultants, whereas government agencies such as the State Department and the Fulbright IIE imagine scholars as cultural ambassadors to other countries and prefer that the goals of international collaboration be emphasized. Increasingly, funding agencies require *data management plans* that explain how the collected data will be organized, stored, shared, and protected for a certain period of time. Careful reading of the grant's guidelines and the funding agency's mission can provide clues as how to discuss the project's broader significance and devise an appropriate data management plan.

The final components of a grant proposal are a precise timeline for the completion of the project, a detailed *budget* that lists and explains the rationale and estimated costs for all fundable items and activities, the scholar's *curriculum vitae* in either the full or abbreviated form that foregrounds previous grants or awards and publications on related topics, letters of invitation, and a selected *bibliography* or *works cited* page. A spreadsheet detailing a month-by-month plan of fieldwork activities, data coding and analysis, publication preparation, and conference presentations will help reviewers evaluate the project's feasibility and timeline for completion. Close attention will be paid to see if budget items are reasonable and necessary. Generally speaking, costs for travel and transportation, food and accommodation, essential technology (see Kohler and Murphy, this volume), and incentives for research subjects are covered for graduate students. For senior researchers, additional costs such as publication fees, childcare under limited circumstances, conference travel, research assistants, outside consultants, teaching releases, and summary salaries may be covered. An addended letter of invitation from the authorizing organization or contact person stating their endorsement of the project is often crucial. Scholars should heed page limits and, whenever possible, use existing templates to complete these sections. It is strongly recommended to copyedit the entire proposal several times, including ancillary materials, to correct for grammatical errors and improve style (e.g., eliminate redundant statements, vary word choice, use active voice, etc.). Scholars should conservatively plan to set aside at least two months to plan and write an external grant and one month for an internal grant. If the grant is not awarded in the first attempt, incorporating feedback from the reviewers may ensure better success in the future round.

12.2.3 Priorities of Different Funding Agencies

Though the basic principles of research design apply equally across the arts and sciences, the distinct priorities of science, social science, and humanities-focused funding agencies may sometimes influence the structural organization of a grant, and this is relevant for linguistic anthropological projects that bridge disciplinary divisions. A science-focused proposal would seek to foreground the data collection and analysis and the genesis of testable hypotheses. A proposal in the social sciences, or one that is anthropology-specific, might delve more deeply into contemporary debates that animate the field, rather than cite classic studies found in the literature. Additionally, a humanities-focused proposal may also emphasize interdisciplinary connections and open-ended areas of intellectual inquiry through a more narrative-like writing style. Regardless of these differences, a proposal that inspires and impresses non-specialists will fare better than research primarily concerned with disciplinary issues in the grant review process.

12.3 Addressing Ethics

Although predicting all ethical issues that might arise during the course of a research project can be a daunting task (see Black and Conley Riner, this volume), undertaking this exercise is critical to the success of grant writing and the minimizing of risks to human and/or animal subjects involved in the study. Other ethical issues bearing on the research design include working with vulnerable populations, accounting for the likelihood of data requests under the Freedom of Information Act (FOIA)[18] and by legal subpoena, defending academic freedom, and curating open access. Below I share some experiences from my own grant writing experiences.

12.3.1 Human Subjects Review

Vulnerable populations are individuals who cannot easily advocate for themselves. Inclusive of pregnant women, human fetuses, neonates, prisoners, children, individuals with physical disabilities, mental disabilities, or cognitive impairments, economically and socially disadvantaged individuals, the terminally ill or very sick, racial or ethnic minorities, and persons institutionalized in correctional facilities, nursing homes, or mental health facilities (Swarthmore 2020), these groups have been the traditional foci of linguistic anthropological research, although this is in flux due to political, economic, social, and public health factors. Human subjects review is recommended by funding agencies. Some require proof of awarded or pending approvals, and university Institutional Review Boards (IRBs) require a copy and proof of the submitted grant proposal. Although universities are revising IRB protocols to expedite the approval of projects involving minimal risk to human subjects, full review is beneficial to identify and incorporate mechanisms of accountability into the overall research design and address any ethical issues or situations potentially harming human subjects (see Black and Conley Riner, this volume).

In the case of my dissertation research on Tamil heritage language education in Quebec, I encountered several ethical dilemmas when applying for IRB approval to observe, interview, and record the conversations of children of Indian immigrants and Sri Lankan refugees. First, since my research required that I record interactions occurring in the classroom, I planned to seek the permission of all parents of the children attending Tamil heritage language classes. However, given the possibility that I would not receive blanket permission to record classroom interactions, I decided not to transcribe the remarks made by children whose parents did not give me consent. Second, since most Sri Lankans living in Montreal are refugees and many are undocumented, the disclosure of personally identifiable information could jeopardize future asylum hearings and expose family members to deportation. I was also concerned about informants who would speak critically of the World Tamil Association headquartered in Toronto. If I published personal information, they or their kin could face deadly retaliation. To minimize this potential for harm, not only did I use pseudonyms for informants, but I also altered their defining traits and avoided publishing any incriminating information, no matter how significant the data were to the research.

12.3.2 FOIA and Legal Subpoena

Another situation that could arise during the human subjects review process involves the possibility of research documents and recordings being identified as at risk of legal subpoena, including linguistic anthropology data in the form of naturalistic discourse or "grassroots literacy" (Blommaert 2008) deemed valuable for civil or criminal cases (FOIA-accessible documents are exempt from this liability). IRBs rely on legal experts to evaluate whether documents are protected under FOIA and, if not, how to inform vulnerable populations of the risk of subpoena, if inadequate protections can be afforded by the researchers themselves.

My application for IRB approval from New York University to work with a non-publicly disclosed corpus of video recordings of police-civilian interactions illustrates these various legal quandaries. In April 2017, my co-PI and I received a signed Memorandum of Understanding from Douglas Strickler, Esq., the Public Defender of Richland County, granting us exclusive access to view, copy, archive, and transcribe a digital archive of bodycam, dashcam, and precinct footage recorded between 2015 and 2020. The subsequent public defender, Fielding Pringle, Esq., renewed the MOU and expanded our access to encompass traffic, bicycle, and pedestrian stops as well. She also instituted strict protocols to protect her clients from possible coercion. Only an attorney or a legal intern could initiate contact with a former criminal defendant by telephone call from the public defender's office and request permission to release the video or be contacted for an interview. Also, since contact could be made only after a case was closed and no other cases involving the same defendant were pending, this stipulation limited our research to single offenders. Believing these protocols to be sufficient, I was surprised when the IRB at New York University commented that the footage and transcripts could be subpoenaed by prosecutors and government officials pursuing criminal and civil cases. Legally, the videos fall under a gray area; they are neither the intellectual property of the defendants or police officers nor subject to FOIA. After consulting with the IRB, we reached an agreement that an adequate response would be for me to explicitly state the risk of subpoena on the consent form. This extra step to inform of further risks to vulnerable populations, who have been historically discriminated against by the criminal justice system, outweighed the constraints placed on our sample size and representability.

Although legal considerations did not influence how we originally wrote the grant, one should think proactively about how anthropological data, especially that which falls under national security, law enforcement, and personal privacy, and is thus FOIA exempt, could possibly circulate in unexpected ways long after the completion of the project and present unforeseen hazards to informants and other populations. I thus recommend including a brief discussion of FOIA and legal subpoena in the data management or methods section of the grant.

12.3.3 Academic Freedom

Regarded as protection from censorship or retaliation afforded to tenured faculty in the United States, academic freedom can be considered a special case of the First Amendment's free speech protections. Since no laws effectively prohibit hate speech in the United States (Walker 1994), American universities have been generally unwilling to arbitrate controversies involving hate speech for fear that these policies could potentially limit academic freedom and threaten the institution of tenure.[19]

However, scholars employed in American universities often have research relationships in other countries that oblige them to consider non-US-based hate speech, anti-libel, or sedition laws in the grant proposal. These ethical issues manifest themselves when scholars apply for research visas, request letters of invitation from foreign institutions, and write publications. These cases invite reflection on the limits of academic freedom in light of broader societal concerns.

I encountered issues of academic freedom when I was writing grants for both doctoral and postdoctoral research projects. Although I did not require a visa to conduct research in Quebec on account of my dual Canadian and American citizenship, working with a pro-nationalist school board, Commission Scolaire de Montréal (CSDM), nonetheless curtailed my academic freedom when I was perceived as endorsing an anti-nationalist political agenda. In response to a request made by the IRB at my doctoral institution, University of Michigan, that I submit a letter of approval from the CSDM to grant me permission to observe Tamil classes within their school district, the director requested to review my NSF grant proposal. After forwarding the grant to the association of parents, teachers, and school principals, the board rejected my application to observe heritage language classes, stating that the content of my research was "too political." In my grant I had highlighted studies of the negative views expressed by racial and ethnolinguistic minorities in Quebec toward a nationalist law requiring immigrants to enroll their children in French, rather than English public schools. After instead securing permission from the English Montreal School Board (EMSB) to observe Tamil classes in their schools, the director alluded to how politics shaped the different reactions of French and English school boards to my grant (see Das 2016). After this experience I learned more practical ways of avoiding political entanglements. Rather than writing explicitly about police brutality in the NSF abstract, I reframed the project to speak to more generic issues – as the study of cross-cultural exchange in the context of police-civilian interactions – to preclude government censure. Sharing the abstract rather than the entire grant proposal is another strategy to avoid such issues.

12.3.4 Open-Access Data Sharing

With funding agencies increasingly endorsing open-access data sharing plans and platforms, ethical issues concerning the protection of local or traditional knowledge and the recognition of collective rights that do not fall under intellectual property legal regimes may arise in linguistic anthropological research. Cultural and linguistic anthropologists have demonstrated that, despite lack of official recognition, local models of knowledge circulation often challenge contemporary notions of legal property rights (Anderson and Geismar 2017; Debenport 2010). For the purpose of grant writing, scholars can draw on these insights to identify problems arising from data sharing and devise an appropriate management plan. For instance, data sharing may exacerbate the risks disproportionately impacting individuals falling under the legally protected categories of vulnerable populations – such as women, children, racial and ethnic minorities, and so forth. In these cases, additional measures taken to inform the subjects of risks, strip data of personally identifiable information, and temporarily restrict access are considered appropriate.

12.4 Conclusion

Grant writing affords linguistic anthropologists the opportunity to communicate with a broad or interdisciplinary audience and demonstrate the value of their methods, theories, and social engagements. Although their research is unique in combining ethnographic and linguistic methods, a successful research proposal will follow similar principles endorsed across the social sciences, whether submitted for review to a science-focused funding agency such as the NSF or a humanities one such as the ACLS. First and foremost, the proposal should inspire reviewers by demonstrating the study's intellectual merit and originality. Second, it should explicate a logical or necessary connection between the research question, hypothesis or expectations, literature review and preliminary research, methodology and expected results, and data analysis. Writing in a style richly populated with relevant citations and key examples from the literature should advance an argument rationalizing the choice of site, historical period, population, activity, and object of study; explain the representability of the sample; and vet for issues regarding sampling bias, the protection of rights by data management plans, and other ethical dilemmas emerging out of the research. A narrative writing style that includes a topic and concluding sentence in each paragraph, the effective use of subtitles and introductory and concluding paragraphs to structure and organize the proposal, and the appropriate use of specialized terminology elicits reviewers' confidence in the expertise of the scholar, feasibility of the study, and fundability of the project.

12.5 Ethnographic Activities

1. Writing Paragraphs to Advance the Argument through the Literature Review

Write a four-sentence paragraph exploring a particular theoretical claim in the literature that is relevant to your proposed research. Write the first sentence to explain this point and identify the major studies that have contributed to this claim. Write two or three more sentences describing ethnographic cases or linguistic data that illustrate the diverse ways in which this claim has been studied. Write a fourth sentence explaining how your research fills in a missing gap, contributes to a different perspective, or challenges the claim entirely, and advances knowledge in the field.

2. Articulating Logical Connections between Research Question, Hypothesis, and Method

Identify a research question that leads to two or three possible outcomes. Restate one of these outcomes as a testable hypothesis or an answer to the research question. Identify sources in the literature or preliminary research that render this hypothesis a reasonable expectation. Choose the data collection and analytic methods to generate evidence to test the hypothesis. Specify how this evidence will relate to other data points (i.e., independent and dependent variables) and identify the control group and sampling biases potentially impacting the interpretation of results.

12.6 Questions to Consider

1 Will the research question generate new evidence (rendering it competitive for funding), or can it be answered with existing evidence (rendering it less competitive for funding)?

2 Are there sufficient ethnographic, sociological, and historical details in the introductory overview to impress upon a non-specialist the project's originality and intellectual merit?

386 Research Methods in Linguistic Anthropology

3 Are the choices of site, historical period, population, activity, and object of study fully explained and justified to illustrate the representability of the proposed research study?

4 Is there an argument that is being advanced through the proposal's narrative that logically connects together the research question, hypothesis, methodology, and data analysis?

5 Are specialized terms used appropriately and defined clearly when first introduced?

6 Has the research design been modified to address sampling biases and ethical issues?

12.7 Notes

1 See NSF. https://www.nsf.gov/funding/pgm_summ.jsp?pims_id=505057&org=BCS&from=home

2 See NSF. https://www.nsf.gov/funding/pgm_summ.jsp?pims_id=5408&org=BCS&from=home

3 See Wenner Gren. http://www.wennergren.org/programs/dissertation-fieldwork-grants

4 See SSRC. https://www.ssrc.org

5 See SSRC. https://www.sshrc-crsh.gc.ca/funding-financement/programs-programmes/fellowships/doctoral-doctorat-eng.aspx

6 See Fulbright. https://us.fulbrightonline.org

7 See Fulbright-Hayes. https://www2.ed.gov/programs/iegpsddrap/index.html

8 See NSF. https://www.nsf.gov/pubs/2016/nsf16044/nsf16044.jsp

9 See NSF. https://www.nsf.gov/funding/pgm_summ.jsp?pims_id=505513

10 See NSF. https://www.nsf.gov/publications/pub_summ.jsp?ods_key=nsf17537

11 See Wenner-Gren. http://www.wennergren.org/programs/post-phd-research-grants

12 The PI, or principal investigator, is the awardee of the grant and the lead researcher for the project. In some cases (e.g., NSF) the doctoral student's faculty advisor will be the PI on the grant, and the student conducting the research will be the Co-PI.

13 See CAORC. https://www.caorc.org/fellowships

14 See ACLS. https://www.acls.org/Fellowship-and-Grant-Programs/Competitions-and-Deadlines

15 See NEH. https://www.neh.gov/grants/listing

16 See American Philosophical Society. https://www.amphilsoc.org/grants/research

17 For example, we investigate how police refer to the noise of gun shots, the distinct odor of marijuana, and the suspicious facial expressions or body movements of an individual, as evidence to justify probable cause for stopping and arresting a civilian, and how these different sensory forms of evidence fare in the court adjudication process.

18 Since 1967 the Freedom of Information Act has made it possible for citizens to request documents and records from federal agencies. Exception to FOIA requests involves personal privacy, national security, and law enforcement. See https://www.foia.gov

19 An exception is university policy on sexual harassment, which would be covered by state law.

12.8 References Cited

Anderson, Jane, and Haidy Geismar, eds. 2017. *The Routledge Companion to Cultural Property*. New York: Routledge.

Blommaert, Jan. 2008. *Grassroots Literacy: Writing, Identity, and Voice in Central Africa*. New York: Routledge.

Das, Sonia. 2016. *Linguistic Rivalries: Tamil Migrants and Anglo-Franco Conflicts*. New York: Oxford University Press.

Das, Sonia. 2018. "Fighting Words or Speech Rights? A Linguistic Ethnography of Police Discretion in the U.S. South". The Wenner-Gren Foundation.

Das, Sonia, and Sherina Feliciano-Santos. 2018. "Collaborative Research: Policing Free Speech and the Language of DUI Arrests in the U.S South." National Science Foundation.

Debenport, Erin. 2010. "The Potential Complexity of 'Universal Ownership': Cultural Property, Textual Circulation, and Linguistic Fieldwork." *Language & Communication* 30 (3): 204–10.

Gal, Susan, and Judith T. Irvine. 2019. *Signs of Difference: Language and Ideology in Social Life*. New York: Cambridge University Press.

Silverstein, Michael. 2004. "'Cultural' Concepts and the Language-Culture Nexus." *Current Anthropology* 45 (5): 621–45.

Swarthmore. 2020. https://www.swarthmore.edu/institutional-review-board/vulnerable-populations, accessed January 11, 2020.

Walker, Samuel. 1994. *Hate Speech: The History of an American Controversy*. Lincoln: University of Nebraska Press.

Wortham, Stanton, and Angela Reyes. 2015. *Discourse Analysis beyond the Speech Event*. New York: Routledge.

12.9 Further Reading

Lutz, Catherine. 1990. "The Erasure of Women's Writing in Sociocultural Anthropology." *American Ethnologist* 17 (4): 611–27.

This essay highlights issues of inequity entangled with knowledge production in anthropology, discussing the persistent gender gap in citational practices that is enacted through grant writing.

Wortham, Stanton, and Angela Reyes. 2015. *Discourse Analysis beyond the Speech Event*. New York: Routledge.

This overview of discourse analysis, drawing on theories and methods in linguistic anthropology to analyze the development of discourses over time, is a useful resource for research design.

Index

A

academic freedom 380, 382–3

access

adaptability 129

advocacy 60, 106, 352

analysis 3, 8, 11, 14, 16, 19, 21–3, 29,
31–2, 45–6, 52, 61, 63–5, 70,
76, 91, 95, 97, 106, 108–10, 120,
126–7, 130, 140–2, 144–5, 149,
151, 153, 157, 159–60, 163,
167, 187–8, 192–4, 200, 205,
208–9, 212, 220–1, 223, 231–4,
239, 246–7, 251, 254–5, 257–9,
261–77, 279–83, 285–93, 295,
298, 300, 302, 304, 310–19, 321,
326–7, 329, 332–33, 336–8, 341,
343–4, 347–9, 356–7, 359, 362,
365, 367, 370–1, 373, 376–7, 379,
384, 386–8

analytic notes 143, 145–6

analytical 7, 11, 16, 19, 23, 26, 28–9,
32, 38, 52, 212, 221, 264, 298,
304

anonymity 6, 105–6, 110–13, 118, 200,
298, 308, 316

archival research 376

archiving 229, 250

artifacts 129, 275, 297, 376

audiences 56, 109, 111, 148, 206, 262,
266–7, 274, 276, 280, 282, 284,
286–8, 317, 350, 352, 356

audio-recording 202, 217

authority 55, 57, 63, 77, 101, 103, 108,
165, 167–8, 283–4, 289, 293, 317,
320, 344

autoethnography 337

B

backups 216, 237, 250

behavior 46, 100, 102, 107, 117, 128, 130,
132, 136–40, 183–4, 201, 207,
220–1, 249, 291, 297, 316, 341,
359, 361, 364

bias 99, 152, 198, 342, 368, 377, 384

Briggs, Charles 11, 69, 120, 153, 192, 291,
325

budget 84, 216, 227–9, 234, 335, 379

C

camera 110, 116, 141, 145, 149, 197–9,
201, 207–17, 221, 224–38, 240,
242–5, 247–50, 252–58, 318,
337, 353

care 5, 11, 54, 69, 97–105, 107–9,
111–23, 154, 167, 181–2, 258,
292–5, 347, 360

categorization 14–15, 18

Center for the Everyday Lives of Families
(CELF) 130

chain referral 90, 92

children 83, 88, 93, 122–3, 130, 149, 154,
177, 221, 224–5, 227, 230, 234,
242, 244, 246, 249, 252, 255, 258,
269, 272, 284, 291–4, 299, 343,
353, 380–1, 383–4

citation 33–4, 51–2, 55–6, 70, 102, 384

codes 146, 175, 264–5, 272–4, 339, 378

coding 8, 84, 146, 257, 262, 264, 269–74,
311, 318, 376, 379

collaboration 5, 34, 102–3, 120, 267, 287,
289, 305, 327, 356, 368, 378

collaborative annotation 269

communication studies 208, 340, 352, 354

Index

communities of practice 8, 127
community 8, 10, 26, 36, 44, 59, 69, 75,
77, 85, 88, 90, 93, 96, 98, 102–4,
106–7, 110–13, 117–19, 122–3,
125, 127–8, 132, 134, 136, 139,
154, 165, 170, 224, 227, 236, 242,
244–5, 252, 256–7, 267, 282–3,
286, 289, 298–302, 304–5, 307–24,
325, 328, 333, 335–7, 342, 347,
359, 371, 377
compensation 78, 87, 89, 104, 226,
242, 370
compromise 209, 216, 342, 352, 354–6, 358
confidentiality 6, 87, 105–7, 111–13, 115,
118–19, 267, 276, 337, 351
consent 7, 87, 104–5, 110, 112–13,
115–16, 120, 147–8, 169–70, 202,
224, 226–7, 229, 241–5, 246, 249,
251, 254, 287, 298, 314–16, 351,
353, 381–2
conversation analysis 126, 153, 193, 208,
220, 280, 282, 290, 292–3, 295, 359
cost 84, 116, 202, 209, 219, 375, 379
curiosity 132, 310

D

data 1, 3–4, 6–9, 14–16, 19–20, 22–4,
26–30, 32, 35–41, 53–4, 60–2,
64–7, 73–6, 80, 82–5, 87, 89–94,
97–8, 104–7, 109–17, 125–7,
129, 131, 133–8, 140–2, 144–6,
148–52, 159–60, 162–3, 165, 168,
186, 188, 190, 192, 195, 197–200,
202–4, 206–12, 216–19, 221,
223–8, 230, 234, 236–41, 245,
247, 249–52, 254–7, 258, 261–74,
276–9, 287–90, 310–16, 318, 323,
324, 331–41, 343–4, 346–57, 360,
362–5, 367, 369–73, 376, 378–86
data analysis 61, 212, 258, 259, 310,
313, 348, 367, 371, 384, 386
data collection 6–7, 32, 66, 76, 80,
83–4, 87, 93–4, 97, 104–5, 109,

111–14, 126–7, 145–6, 148, 162,
186, 197, 239, 263, 288, 310–11,
318, 336, 346, 356, 367, 369–71,
373, 376, 379, 385
data management plan 378, 384
decontextualization 312
denotational text 6, 163, 167, 172, 177, 181
descriptive notes 144
diaries 144, 356
digital ethnography 206, 309, 328, 334
discrimination 5, 79, 102–3

E

empirical data 19, 22, 24, 26, 29–30, 35,
269, 373
ethics 5, 11, 52, 54–6, 64–5, 74, 86–7,
97–100, 102–5, 111, 118–23, 147,
152, 156, 161, 192, 220, 222, 226,
257, 259, 276, 282, 312, 314–16,
323–4, 325, 327, 340, 351, 357,
359, 380
ethical issues 3, 5, 7–9, 97, 108, 110,
113, 118, 146, 151–2, 161, 169, 189,
314, 323, 340, 351, 380–1, 383, 386
ethical practice 112, 287
ethics of representation 276, 282
ethnoarchaeological tracking 155, 221,
248, 258, 362
ethnographic interviews 108, 137,
159–60, 162–4, 171, 177, 331, 353
evidence 33, 58, 84, 137, 231, 258, 268,
270, 280, 284, 288, 320, 326, 344,
371–4, 376–7, 385, 387
expertise 5, 8, 34, 63, 95, 110, 166, 347,
357, 367, 378, 385

F

features 198–9, 203, 205, 209–10, 212,
227–9, 235, 255–6, 258, 262–3,
268, 271, 273–4, 277–8, 280,
283–4, 289, 313, 357, 373–4
fieldnotes 4, 6, 10, 54, 98, 125–7, 129,
131, 133, 135, 137–53, 155–7,

199–200, 211, 219, 226, 248, 250, 270–2, 289, 309, 356, 377
first-person perspective 229
focus groups 335
form factor 197, 199, 205, 210–12, 219, 228
format 2, 51, 107, 117, 144, 151, 162, 170, 197, 203, 205, 208, 210, 214, 218, 254, 257, 276, 281, 349–51, 354, 371
fractal system 15–16, 18–19, 28–9, 32–3, 36, 40
funding agencies 237, 368–9, 378–80, 383

G
grammatical features 273
grounded theory 270–1, 291

H
harassment 5, 102–3, 120, 387
head notes 143–4
human subjects review 368, 380–1
hypothesis 4–5, 9, 82, 137, 142, 263, 266, 335, 351, 367, 372–6, 379, 384–6

I
identity 14, 20, 23–5, 29–30, 33, 35–40, 44–7, 57, 69, 94, 105, 107, 115–16, 122, 128, 153, 161, 165–6, 171, 189–90, 194, 243, 275, 287, 291, 298, 301, 304, 306–7, 313, 318–19, 324–5, 327, 329, 342, 354, 373, 387
ideology 1, 16, 21–4, 27–8, 33, 38, 45, 47, 59, 93, 110, 122, 126, 194, 299–303, 307, 309, 312, 314, 316, 318–20, 322, 326, 336, 341, 343, 358, 360, 362, 368, 371, 374–7, 387
immersion 128, 148, 232, 343
initiation 98, 345
inscription 198, 271, 274–5, 295
Institutional Review Board (IRB) 87, 169
interaction 1–3, 6, 8, 10–11, 14, 16, 25, 31, 45–6, 74, 76–7, 87, 95, 105, 108–9,

112–13, 117, 122, 125–6, 130–1, 133, 135–7, 139–43, 149–51, 153–4, 163–6, 168, 171–2, 176–7, 181–6, 191–4, 198, 200, 204–5, 208, 211, 214, 217–18, 220–6, 229–31, 234–5, 237–8, 242, 244, 247, 252–3, 257–8, 262–3, 267–9, 272, 279–80, 282, 284–7, 289–90, 292–5, 297–9, 303–5, 309, 312, 323–9, 333–6, 338–9, 341, 343, 345, 347, 349, 351–5, 357, 360, 362–3, 368, 371–2, 374, 377, 381, 383
interactional text 163–4, 172, 177, 181–3, 185
Internet 44, 88, 121–2, 133, 216, 237, 297, 303, 311, 315, 324–6, 328, 334, 345
interview 6–8, 11, 21–2, 29, 44–5, 73–4, 79, 87, 89–93, 98, 100, 105–10, 116–17, 120, 122, 134, 136–7, 143, 147, 154–6, 159–73, 175–9, 181–95, 202–5, 211, 217, 223, 246, 257, 262, 270–1, 277, 289–90, 309, 312, 331, 336–7, 341, 347–9, 351, 353–7, 362, 364, 376, 381–2
intimacy 24, 47, 155–6, 171, 175–6, 182, 193, 291, 308, 327, 354, 363

J
jottings 143–4

K
knowledge production 15–16, 18–19, 23, 26, 28, 31, 33, 39–41, 66, 99, 109, 115, 165, 388

L
Labov, William 121, 154, 193
language gloss 282, 290
legal subpoena
	linguistic analysis 160, 257, 275, 282, 370
	linguistic features 313, 373

392 Index

literature review
logging 8, 262–4, 270, 272–3, 290
logs 144, 264–6

M
making predictions 131
material artifacts 275
metapragmatics 16, 45, 50, 59
methods 1–4, 6, 8–12, 14, 16, 18, 20, 22,
    24, 26, 28, 30–2, 34, 36, 38, 40, 42,
    44, 46–7, 50, 52–4, 56, 58, 60, 62,
    64, 66, 68, 70, 74, 76, 78, 80, 82,
    84, 86, 88–90, 92–6, 98, 100, 102,
    104, 106, 108–10, 112, 114–20,
    122, 125–8, 130, 132, 134, 136, 138,
    140–2, 144–6, 148, 150, 152, 154–7,
    160, 162, 164, 166, 168, 170, 172,
    174, 176, 178, 180, 182, 184, 186,
    188, 190, 192, 194, 197–202, 204,
    206, 208, 210, 212–14, 216, 218–22,
    224, 226, 228, 230, 232, 234, 236,
    238, 240, 242, 244, 246, 248, 250,
    252, 254–6, 258–9, 262, 264, 266,
    268, 270, 272, 274, 276, 278, 280,
    282, 284, 286, 288, 290, 292, 294,
    298, 300, 302, 304, 306, 308–12,
    314, 316, 318, 320, 322, 324, 326–8,
    331–3, 337–8, 340–65, 367–70,
    372, 374–8, 380, 382, 384–6, 388
microphone 199, 203–5, 210, 214–15, 217,
    228–9, 234–5, 237–8, 252, 256
mode of representation 284
morality 99–100, 147, 222, 267, 287

N
narratives 21–3, 29, 45, 47, 137, 159,
    161–2, 165–9, 172, 178, 186–91,
    193–4, 274, 277, 318, 354, 363
    narrative analysis 192–3, 273, 277
new media 8, 79, 83, 91, 93, 95, 105, 111,
    121–3, 292, 297–303, 305–7, 309,
    311, 313, 315, 317, 319, 321–3,
    325–7, 329

Northern Italy 6–7, 143, 155, 162, 164,
    177, 193
NSF 352, 369, 373–4, 378, 383–4, 386

O
objectivity 135–8, 151–2, 219, 357
ongoing awareness of 249
open access 380
originality 367, 372–3, 384–5

P
participant observation 4, 6, 10, 36,
    73, 120, 125–41, 143–7, 149–53,
    155–7, 257, 292, 309–11, 316, 331,
    334, 345, 347, 357, 377
participant observation and fieldnotes 6,
    125, 127, 129, 131, 133, 135, 137,
    139, 141, 143, 145, 147, 149, 151,
    153, 155, 157
participant transposition 171–2, 176–7,
    186, 191, 193
participatory action research 331, 343
person-centered interviews 108, 347, 349
perspective 2, 4, 8–10, 15, 18, 27, 29,
    35, 44–5, 47, 54, 60, 69, 99, 103,
    108–9, 111, 116, 122, 126–7,
    131–2, 138, 141–2, 148, 153–5,
    160, 163, 171, 190, 192, 200, 221,
    229–30, 232, 247, 258–9, 295, 300,
    305, 308, 314, 319–21, 324, 332,
    335, 339–42, 345, 347, 349, 351,
    353–4, 356–7, 361–2, 374–5, 385
phasing 82
phonological representation 282
photovoice 337, 359, 362, 364
positionality 33, 40, 82, 114, 121, 135
power 33, 41, 45–7, 63, 69, 77–8, 97–8,
    101–3, 107, 111, 115, 117, 126,
    137, 147, 165, 205, 207, 217, 234,
    236, 245, 248, 262, 267, 270, 272,
    283, 287–9, 293–4, 325, 336–7,
    363, 375
    power dynamics 147, 267, 288

project planning 80, 82, 89, 216
public anthropology 343

Q
qualitative methods 332, 341, 345, 361–2
    qualitative analysis 270, 273
questionnaire 108, 162, 164, 170, 186,
    188, 290, 353, 356

R
rapport 73, 82–3, 93, 95, 98–9, 115,
    132–6, 147–8, 152, 154–6, 161,
    176–7, 184, 186, 193, 204, 353
reciprocity 87–9, 103, 270, 284, 286–7
recontextualization 305, 312
recruitment 80, 83, 90, 92–3, 242, 315,
    338
recursive process 8, 17, 262, 264, 266
reflexivity 120, 138, 310, 322
relationships 78, 81, 84–5, 87, 92, 98,
    100–3, 105–7, 109, 111, 114–15,
    117, 128, 131, 147, 159, 166, 171,
    177, 185, 271–2, 294, 298, 316,
    334, 338, 355, 383
reliability 344, 362
representability 368, 372, 382, 384, 386
representation
    representational (transcript) choice
    286
    representational choice 287
research design 31, 88, 90, 97, 99, 101,
    103, 332, 345, 367–70, 372–3, 375,
    379–81, 386, 388
research interviews 163, 165, 187, 189,
    194–5
research question 3–5, 9–10, 13–17,
    19–43, 45, 47, 74–6, 80, 86, 127,
    129–30, 134, 137, 139, 144, 146,
    219, 227, 261, 264, 266, 311,
    340–1, 343–5, 351, 354, 356–7,
    367, 372–3, 375–6, 384–6
research trajectory 19, 30
ritual analysis 274

S
sampling 74, 82–3, 89–90, 93, 205, 248,
    290, 338, 348, 368, 376–7, 384–6
    sampling bias 377, 384
scratch notes 143
screen recording
selective representation 262
self-reflection 140, 144, 152
semi-structured interviews 79, 162
semiotic 11, 16, 19, 22–3, 25–7, 29–30,
    46–7, 220, 223, 262, 264, 271, 275,
    279–80, 282, 298, 301, 303–4,
    311–13, 322, 367
    semiotic acts
    semiotic elements 264
    semiotic information 282
    semiotic resources 26, 262, 279–80, 313
    semiotic-material 275
semiotics 70, 96, 293
situated speech event 6, 159
snowball 89–90, 92–3
social network analysis 338
sociolinguistics 1, 6, 25, 44, 70, 109, 122,
    126, 136, 159, 162, 293, 325, 328,
    342, 360, 362
specific methods 89, 136, 332
speech communities 75, 127
speech community 75, 127, 154
storage 127, 203, 216, 236, 312
storytelling events 168, 176, 185
structured interviews 79, 162

T
technology 4, 7–8, 36–9, 46, 83–4,
    100, 129, 139, 141, 156, 169,
    192, 197–9, 201–3, 205, 207–15,
    217–21, 224–5, 227, 241–5, 261,
    267, 276, 298–300, 308, 326, 328,
    356, 363, 378–9
text artifacts 275
theoretical contributions 29, 374
theory 5, 8, 11, 24, 26–7, 29, 35–6,
    38–9, 45, 50–1, 57, 61, 68, 70,

Index

95, 99, 119, 123, 151, 160, 192,
208, 220, 255, 257, 261–4, 266–7,
269–71, 274, 289, 291, 294,
325–6, 341–3, 349, 362–4, 375,
384, 388
theory-building 274
third-person perspective 229
time management 82–3
topical salience 4, 14, 20–6, 28–32, 34–5,
39, 42–3
transcribing 4, 8, 234–5, 247, 250, 262–3,
266, 268–70, 272, 276, 282, 284,
287–9, 295
transcription 3, 8, 87, 110–11, 187, 189,
191, 234, 240–41, 250–1, 254,
255–6, 261–3, 265–9, 271, 273,
275–7, 279–81, 283–91, 293–5,
312

transcription conventions 189, 191,
277, 280
transcripts 3, 8, 106, 120, 149, 166,
188, 190, 256, 262, 267–70, 272–4,
276–7, 282–4, 288–90, 292, 318,
374, 377, 382
translation 21, 41, 45, 52, 104, 110, 156,
178, 188, 191, 267, 282–3, 363

V

veterans 100, 113–17, 207
video recall 339, 351, 354
video-recording 7, 114, 139, 143, 150,
152, 190, 197, 201, 209–11, 228–9,
249, 311

Y

yoga 113–17